# ROBERT BROWNING

## ESSAYS AND THOUGHTS

BY
JOHN T. NETTLESHIP

WITH A PORTRAIT

KENNIKAT PRESS
Port Washington, N. Y./London

ROBERT BROWNING

First published in 1895
Reissued in 1970 by Kennikat Press
Library of Congress Catalog Card No: 79-105815
ISBN 0-8046-1028-2

Manufactured by Taylor Publishing Company    Dallas, Texas

# PREFATORY NOTE

SOMEWHAT less than half of this book was written more than twenty years ago, and the remainder at various dates from 1882 to the present time. The book is not therefore in the ordinary sense a continuous whole, and indeed I might, in respect of some portions of it, claim almost an Editor's immunity. But as each essay or thought when written was a genuine outcome of Browning-study, they are all left without alteration so far as essential idea is concerned.

Although nothing is there which I would rather have left unsaid, many things might have been better expressed ; as for those things which ought to have been said, their name is legion ; still, though the work has no claim to completeness, it should, regarded as sincere study, show an upward tendency.

# CONTENTS

———

# PREFACE

TO THE ESSAYS PUBLISHED IN 1863

---

IN an age when knowledge, for its own sake, is by a large class of men as eagerly sought as gold, some apology seems necessary for a composition which professedly avoids facts, and deals in speculation. More especially would this apology seem to be due from anyone attempting to handle the works of a master, the beneficence of whose genius has led him to range in fields of knowledge so wide, and for their own sake to store harvests of learning so plenteous. Any such apology as may be due on this ground I am willing to make; but I should fail in my duty of respect were I to stop there, and refrain from expressing, though in feeble words, the extent of my debt in another way.

The life and the passion, the sin and exaltation, of men and women—all the beauty which thrills us in everything human because of its humanity—form together a study beyond the mental grasp of all save a few great and loving souls.

If, without fearing the charge of adulation, one may add to the list of these the name of Robert Browning; if we may affirm that wide and ripe as is his learning, his highest glory is the unflinching zeal with which he has mastered and given to the world the results of human strife, toil, and achievement, I do not fear to maintain such a conclusion ; and while acknowledging the profundity of his research, I still venture to pay the dearer tribute, due from my soul to his, of recording here the purpose and the love which have been awakened in one man's life, not by the consciousness that the poet knew so much, but by the overmastering truth of those delineations of human strength and weakness, those strong and tender warnings and encouragements, which have times out of number intensified the desire for truth and right, cheered despondencies, and sweetened triumphs.

# ESSAYS ON BROWNING'S POETRY

—— :o: ——

## INTRODUCTION

IT is not my purpose in the following Essays to enter into any criticism in the usual sense of the word ; that is, in the sense of an examination of the merits or demerits of artistic style. Nor will this be the place to speak of the poet in comparison with other poets present or past. That much is to be said in the way of criticism of style and of comparison with other poets I do not deny; but there is so much important thought of another kind to be worked out in a study of his books, by the process of interpretation, that I could not within reasonable limits handle both criticism and interpretation without sacrificing the latter in an undue degree. Again, considering that no poet of the present day has worked in so wide a field, it would at first sight seem the imperative duty of the essayist to look at the poems in their historical aspect, and enter into a careful treatise on the various sources of knowledge from which Browning has derived his subjects. But to do this worthily one would have to fill volumes; and our more immediate concern is to show results, not seek for causes; to remind the world of the force of the

man's brain who has so laboured, not examine into proofs
which we may well accept on his authority.

Let me therefore, by way of introduction, state merely
such results of (I hope) a careful observation as may
perhaps help those who may choose to become students
of Browning to arrive at definite conclusions as to his
merits, and as may be necessary to explain the mode
in which the main subjects of these Essays will be
treated.

Looking at all his works in the four volumes in which
they are at present published, we find that he has written
no single poem or piece, except 'Christmas-eve' and
'Easter-day,' which does not profess to be more or less
dramatic in its nature; for although we do not overlook
the careful subdivision of his first volume into 'Lyrics,'
'Romances,' 'Men and Women,' we are reminded in a
note at the beginning of that volume that its contents are
'always dramatic in principle, and so many utterances of
so many imaginary persons,' not the poet's.

Now, though this dramatic quality is so observable, it
must be admitted that, vivid as his portraits are, and
great as is his power in delineating all human passion,
there is no poet the fabric of whose works is so invariably
sustained by a master-thread of subjectiveness. I shall
not in this place give examples to prove this; a comparison
of any one of the plays with any of the professedly subjective pieces, will at once disclose the   ʳong individuality
of thought which is common to both.

But it would be culpable to omit from such a discussion
as the present some mention of certain salient characteristics which are plainly discernible in everything the
poet has written.

For instance, no one can fail to be struck by his overwhelming sense of the actual existence of a personal God,
who rules men's souls, not by moral laws applicable to

(what we may for the present purpose call) right and wrong in this life, but by rewards and punishments dealt to such souls, according as they shall develop themselves through all their successive stages of existence.

And when we have completely mastered that idea as displayed in all his deepest thoughts, we are scarcely surprised to find, in connection with or as a result of it, his firm-rooted belief that a man's business on this earth is to learn the actual extent of his own soul's powers, and having learned them to develop them straightforward, not necessarily in accordance with human or social laws prevailing in this life, but absolutely for the soul's perfectibility hereafter.

The form which these ideas take in the poet's mind is very plainly the result of his almost super-human love for every form of life, animate or inanimate, in this earth; a love so intense that one is tempted to believe the man has actually in his nature the sympathies and attributes of every form of life he sings about ; a love which is blended with and relies upon a very noble sensuousness, displaying itself in two forms : the one being a special physical sensuousness evidenced by the peculiar sympathy which his writings express for bodily strength, love or passion, and all forms of physical beauty, and the other being a spiritual or intellectual sensuousness evidenced by his peculiar sympathy for art of all kinds, more particularly music and painting.

His love for the display of strength, whether of body or mind (a love which is after all the necessary consequence of the rest of his qualities) ; his hearty goodwill towards all persistence of endeavour, are naturally accompanied by a generous allowance for weakness and evil as much as delight in strength and goodness, provided only the attribute be human ; a divine sympathy, mixed with a beautiful kindly humour, which perhaps in English literature is nowhere else so strongly developed as in George Eliot's writings.

Such are the main features, more or less plainly displayed, which characterise all of Browning's writings. I have mentioned them thus particularly in this place, because it is necessary to remember them in considering the working of the poet's mind, and particularly in any attempt to arrive at a conclusion on the value of the thoughts worked out in the poems we are to discuss.

Having thus marked out in broad outlines the nature of the mind with which we have to deal, it is expedient to lay down the plan on which we are to proceed, to describe plainly the range of subjects which will be treated, and to indicate the nature of the thoughts on which we are to be occupied.

Since we have laid aside all criticism as such, whether artistic or comparative, and have freely trusted our author on the ground of history ; since we are to examine the conclusions to be fairly drawn from the work placed before us as the result of the author's research, and not the form into which he has thrown it, the method of our examination will be throughout more or less analytical in its character, and will deal with the working of the impulses of the men and women portrayed in a few of his more powerful productions.

The subjects treated will be a few poems from the volume called ' Lyrics,' ' Romances,' ' Men and Women,' and the poem ' Sordello.'

In looking through the volume called ' Lyrics,' ' Romances,' ' Men and Women,' the student is at first bewildered, not only by the number of subjects handled, but also by the wide range of learning from which the poet has drawn his ideas.

It becomes absolutely necessary, in order to obtain a complete view of the whole, to marshal the poems on some plan of division under which they can be looked at with reference to each other. Their arrangement in the book is at present one of a purely artistic kind : but whether the reader desires to master them all for his own behoof, or proposes to write upon them a series of essays like the present, he must for the time disregard that arrangement, and mass the subjects of them under their different heads.

By far the larger portion numerically of the poems contained in this volume have for their subject the passion of men for women, and of women for men.

Several longer poems of great value deal with art in all its branches; and these are specially interesting because they deal, not with the great names which have become household words, but with earlier and obscurer representatives of the different arts—men whose work was the foundation of the masterpieces which are now world-renowned—men who, desiring no fame, were content to begin the building which is praised by the world as the work of their successors. And whether we travel back to listen to the early music of Italy and Germany; whether we stand reverently before the forgotten frescoes of Florence and the old Catholic churches; whether we mourn with ' Pictor Ignotus,' yearn with ' Andrea del Sarto,' enjoy with ' Fra Lippo Lippi,' or ponder on the aspiring philosophy of ' Cleon,' we feel after each study that all these art-workers are worthy to be learned by heart, as bygone builders of a grand temple, and have been nobly and worthily remembered by their brother of the nineteenth century.

Religion, too, in its most bigoted as well as its most liberal forms is ably handled; from the old Testament of the Jews, from the effect of the after development of the Christian religion, down to the modern scepticism of Bishop Blougram, a fund of powerful thought is evolved

which is of incalculable use for estimating religion in its
historical bearings.

The subjects of patriotism and party and the early
dawn of learning, give scope to some of the poet's noblest
utterances.

In all these special subjects that peculiarly subjective
mode of treatment which has before been alluded to gives
to each of the portraits a sort of mannerism, which
appears not only in the mode of treating the accessories,
but even in the cast of expression. The thoughts in
'Saul' (a poem dealing with the early times of the Jewish
monarchy) are strongly tinged with the wide liberality of
the poet's own spiritual thought; so are those in
'Karshish,' 'Master Hugues of Saxe-Gotha,' and 'Cleon.'

This is perhaps more especially the case where the
subject is one in which religion forms a part; whatever
the date of the story may be, the impulse seems irresistible
to add to the probable thoughts of the *dramatis persona*
the possible thoughts which, were he as far seeing as the
poet himself, at this day, would have arisen out of his
actual knowledge and been prompted by his hypothetical
aspirations.

But whatever loss may be thus sustained in the absolute
truth of the portraiture is more than counterbalanced by
the many new views which are presented, and by the
lessons, always valuable, which one may learn from the
artist's expression of the characteristics of his subject.

Now, besides the subjects which have been already
indicated, this volume contains several poems which do
not come under any one head, and which, as might be
expected, are professedly of a more subjective and abstract
nature.

Of this class there are some few which perhaps possess
higher importance than all the rest. For while the
poems to which we have alluded concern themselves with

special classes of men, special modes of thought or worship, these so-called subjective poems deal with hopes, fears and struggles, common to all men as human beings. And the depth and the width of the thought contained in these, and their practical value as setting forth views of life which may be actually worked out by any man, give them in the eyes of any one who professes to be in earnest an inestimable value.

Passing over several small pieces which seem almost purely subjective, such as 'Earth's Immortalities,' 'De Gustibus,' 'My Star,' we notice a few which may be classed as treating of social life. These are 'Up at a Villa,' 'A Pretty Woman,' 'Before and After,' 'A Light Woman'; two or three which, without coming under the head of art as a subject, have an artistic tendency, namely, 'Women and Roses,' 'Englishman in Italy,' 'Artemis Prologises'; two of historical interest, 'My Last Duchess' and 'Protus'; and three stories, 'The Glove,' 'The Pied Piper of Hamelin,' and 'The Flight of the Duchess.' Lastly there are three which unite with their subjective character an analytical spirit, namely, 'Instans Tyrannus,' 'Waring,' and Childe Roland,' and it is to the two latter of these that the remarks just made apply in particular.

In choosing from among this mass of subjects those pieces which seem to present the widest surface for examination, one naturally selects such as are best adapted for the proposed method of treatment ; that is to say, those whose artistic or historical aspect, being their least important part, can best dispense both with technical criticism and with any examination into the grounds of knowledge on which the poet based them.

In the artistic point of view the poems generally may be and have been handled by abler men than myself; in the historical or scientific view, it is competent to anyone to examine them for himself with far more minuteness than would be compatible with the size of a work like the present.

But when we consider that of all living poets we are dealing with the profoundest thinker; when we see what a wide and life-giving philosophy he promulgates; we shall agree that for actual use of all men, whatever their mode of life, it is more important to evolve thoughts than to trace beauties or faults of construction—more useful to discover lessons for actual life than to examine historical evidences.

The following essays then will deal entirely with such poems and such poems only as present in connection with their subject some view which, apart from the accessories of time and place, is of value either for abstract thought or for moulding our own lives upon.

Taking the subjects under which the poems in this volume have been arranged in the foregoing pages, a selection will be made first from those whose subject is the passion of love, either in man or woman, and, secondly, from a few of the subjective or analytical poems.

## POEMS ON LOVE

THESE are remarkable for their perfectly simple, natural tone, and for their freedom from that quality, strongly displayed in recent publications, which by many able critics has been condemned as morbid sensuality.

Now, although it is far from my purpose to enter into any critical comparison of the poems just now under discussion with similar poems of other writers either of the present or of former times, it is only fair to remark in passing that whatever merits may be possessed by other amatory effusions, not only on the score of beauty of colouring and expression, but of their courageous liberation of the art of poetry from trammels of prudery, the subjects of this essay are marked by a singular clearness and force of drawing, a distinct form, as well as a beauty of colour, which contrasts very favourably with past and contemporary writings, and, while always steering clear of uncleanness, is perfectly open and unashamed.

It is a strong male spirit which has dictated these utterances. A spirit always the master and never the slave of passions which may be made either gracious or bestial ; a spirit which, having true courage, is never afraid to speak out those things which, in his healthy and unwarped judgment, ought in the interests of humanity and art to be spoken freely.

Of the poems whose subject is the passion of love, about two-thirds represent the feeling of the man and one-third the feeling of the woman. We notice that the feeling of the man may be classed broadly under two heads.

The first comprises the more ordinary cases, where the man's thought does not go beyond this life, in respect of love, and where even in this life the love takes up his whole brain, seeming absolutely the best and only thing he can possess, without reference to anyone except himself; where, in fact, love in its consuming selfishness exalts itself over all other phenomena for no reason assigned; and this sort is divided into successful and unsuccessful love.

The effect of successful love in different men under different circumstances is shown in 'Meeting at Night,' 'Love among the Ruins,' 'Another Way of Love,' 'In Three Days,' 'Mesmerism,' 'In a Gondola,' 'Porphyria's Lover.'

The effect on different men of failure in love, whether from the indifference, pique, or misunderstanding of their mistress, is shown in 'The Lost Mistress,' 'A Lover's Quarrel,' 'Misconceptions,' 'A Serenade at the Villa,' 'One Way of Love,' 'Love in a Life,' and 'Life in a Love,' 'Time's Revenges,' 'Rudel to the Lady of Tripoli.'

Under the second head we see how men of high intellect, whether they fail or succeed in love, find in their power of loving more use than actual present enjoyment, and are compelled by their aspiring nature to search for causes and effects, for the good their love may do, for its use here or hereafter.

Of those who succeed, three instances are given; those namely, which are described in 'By the Fireside,' 'Respectability,' and 'One Word More.'

Of those who fail, the utterances are to be found in

'Cristina,' 'Evelyn Hope,' 'The Last Ride Together,' and 'Two in the Campagna.'

It should be noticed that male jealousy is not treated at all.

The feeling of the woman as represented in those poems which depict the passion of women, has a less wide range, and though not so clearly marked out in divisions, may also be classed under the heads of failure and success.

The effect on the woman of her love being reciprocated is instanced in 'The Confessional,' 'Parting at Morning,' 'A Woman's Last Word,' 'Any Wife to Any Husband,' 'Count Gismond.'

The effect on the woman of that love being despised or thwarted is only twice delineated, namely, in 'The Laboratory,' and 'In a Year.'

There remain two love poems which either as stories or dialogues, or in their mode of treatment, deal with the mutual love of a man and a woman. These are 'In a Gondola, and 'The Statue and the Bust.'

In none which relate to the woman do we observe the width of view and intellectual power which are attributed to the male lover; and the only poem in which anything beyond the actual love of this life is even imagined is 'Any Wife to Any Husband;' but even here the range of thought is not so wide as it is in 'Evelyn Hope,' for instance; though there is some sort of kindred in the thoughts of each.

In all the poems which relate to the feelings of the man under the first head, we observe that however beautiful the ideas expressed, the mind is influenced wholly by a selfishness which shows itself in utter want of appreciation of any state of circumstances other than that in which the speaker finds himself.

But in those which relate to the man's feelings under the second head there is a width of view, a power of grasp,

which has probably never before been so forcibly portrayed.

In the poems which relate to the woman's feelings we
notice principally (where her love is returned) an absorption of her spirit into that of the man, a blind clinging to
some idea of God as formed through education and
association merely, and an absolute want of originality
and of power to look at the passion of love in an abstract
sense, outside the woman herself and her lover.

These distinctions are worth noticing because of the
importance of the subject in present social life.

One may fairly presume that in giving us portraits of
selfish love the poet intended us to see not only how
beautiful, how eloquent, is the passion, but also that the
selfishness of it is in general a fatal drawback to its
influence as a useful thing: that unless there is the
elevating power of some hope beyond the actual personal
gratification, the love, however consuming, however ideal,
is more or less of a pernicious influence, paralysing or
imprisoning all the other powers.

But the few poems in which men are swayed by love in
its widest and most far-reaching sense, deal with the
passion as something outside the speaker, whose existence
as a force in the world to be used for good or for evil he
recognises just as clearly as he recognises any other force
or power of brain.

And although by the majority of artists, whether of
past or present times, love is usually treated as a praise-
worthy thing, to which all other feelings may lawfully be
sacrificed; although even the most self-sacrificing lovers
are rarely practically unselfish, either in fiction or real
life; and although few men are capable of looking as
calmly at the subject of their own love as the speaker in
'Evelyn Hope,' or in 'By the Fireside'—simply because
these are men of exceptional power—still the teaching

contained in the poems before us is valuable to us all, as setting up an ideal to which any man may at least strive to approach.

Let us now select some few poems whose profundity, obscurity, or wideness of range, afford the best materials for our speculation.

We shall confine our attention to those poems which treat of the man's feelings under the second head already mentioned. Of these 'Cristina,' 'Evelyn Hope,' 'The Last Ride Together,' may well be considered in conjunction; while 'By the Fireside,' 'Respectability,' and 'One Word More,' form a second trio which also presents a continued train of thought. One poem already mentioned, dealing with the woman's feelings, 'Any Wife to Any Husband,' also deserves special notice.

'Cristina,' 'Evelyn Hope,' and 'The Last Ride Together,' present three pictures of three different men who have accepted their fate as failing to achieve the gratification of their passion. In the first and last the lovers fail by reason of their mistresses' misappreciation; in 'Evelyn Hope' the speaker mourns over the death of a girl whom he loved, but who died before she was old enough to understand his love.

As all three will bear explanation, it will be well to consider the actual subject of each in turn, and then to look at them together as a group of studies not only very interesting in themselves, but also possessing a further purpose of actual teaching.

'Cristina' comes first in the book, and is a lyric of considerable beauty in its wording and rhythm.

At first reading it seems a slight fugitive piece to be passed by with a comment on its grace and beauty, or its idle dreaminess. But on looking closer into the nature of the man who speaks in it we shall find thought fit for a lifetime.

The image of the man rises before us, as one who not only fails here, there, and everywhere in things of this life, but who perhaps boasts of not one true friend. In his huddled ungraceful pose, and odd but not unkindly face, one sees bytimes a strange dumb yearning, showing the need for sympathy from without. Men and girls pass unheedful, or perhaps noticing him only with a gentle scornful pity. But one girl he sees—Ah, that moment! not counted in the years; not remembered as on such a day of such a year; but standing by itself, a white gleaming flame in the darkness of a lonely life.

The man, hitherto used to groping in darkness, will hereafter, in his weariest moments, turn to that flame to keep in use his faculty of sight. The thought which the girl's face kindled in him thus finds utterance in speech :

I.

She should never have looked at me
    If she meant I should not love her !
There are plenty . . . men, you call such,
    I suppose . . . she may discover
All her soul to, if she pleases,
    And yet leave much as she found them :
But I'm not so, and she knew it
    When she fixed me, glancing round them.

'At last,' he cries, 'in this jostle of brutal men and women, I feel one gentle healing touch, which will soothe my remembrance for ever. Not the touch of one of those scornfully compassionate who say, " How good to bestow oneself on this undeveloped barren man, and adorn his dreary life with a pearl of love ; " or (still worse), " I with my strange yearning of sympathy, will lavish myself on this poor block of humanity, and in my wealth of nature give myself to be swallowed up in his all receptive slough of stupidity." No ! I am stupid enough, but do I not

know at least, if only by moments, what my true endowments are? Surely, too often, as I journey, a shock
reminds me of the false step, the blind guide, blindly
followed; too often a spark shows me all my failure, all
my desire. Nay, more; in lonely midnight watches, in
raging noonday battles, a feeling tells me often that had I
but followed an impulse here, a conscience there, all my
waste would have been fertility. But, alas! such impulses, such consciences, instead of a guiding light, are
ever a blazing fire which burns to ashes the toil or the
aspirations of years.'

### III.

Oh, we're sunk enough here, God knows!
  But not quite so sunk that moments,
Sure tho' seldom are denied us,
  When the spirit's true endowments
Stand out plainly from its false ones,
  And apprise it if pursuing,
Or the right way or the wrong way,
  To its triumph or undoing.

### IV.

There are flashes struck from midnights,
  There are fire-flames noondays kindle,
Whereby piled-up honours perish,
  Whereby swol'n ambitions dwindle,
While just this or that poor impulse,
  Which for once had played unstifled,
Seems the sole work of a lifetime,
  That away the rest have trifled.

And now, not my impulse, not my conscience, but (far
more precious) another soul, comes out like a star from
twilight to draw me towards its brightness. It is the star
of love. With her eyes, she says to me, 'We are here in
this world for the sake of love; we came here through
untold ages for that; we shall go hence for untold ages

having gained or lost that. But if, being here for the chance of love, we do not use it, we have lost it for ever ; never in the times to come will a woman come to you, or a man come to me, to seek and find it. Mayhap we shall have deeper blisses, higher ends; but not that bliss, not that end !

'The light of her eyes which tells me this is God's secret; but neither God nor devil shall wrench it from me.

'And now, whose is the gain ? It is mine; she knew this thing, but would not follow it to accomplishment. She has lost, I have gained, what we both lived for. Her soul, her secret, are mine; in the glory of her eyes I will walk secure, even to the close—'

> Life will just hold out the proving
>   Both our powers, alone and blended ;
> And then, come the next life quickly !
>   This world's use will have been ended.

The words of 'Evelyn Hope,' like those of 'Cristina,' are the words of a dreamer; but the utterance is wrung out of the sorrow of death; and its keynote is a hope for the fulfilment of love in other lives, not the knowledge of love in this life. Cristina's lover was undeveloped, warped, and unsuccessful ; the mind of the speaker in 'Evelyn Hope' is already large and developed, with aspirations beyond flesh and mortality, beyond the utmost hope of a fervent Christianity. He, too, walks ever with the touch of God upon his brow, under the brooding wings of God, who keeps him safe from wounding; but while the other seems morose and blockish, this man is kindly, humorous, gay, sensuous. There is glowing faith in his yearning :

### III.

Is it too late, then, Evelyn Hope?
  What, your soul was pure and true,
The good stars met in your horoscope,
  Made you of spirit, fire and dew—
And, just because I was thrice as old,
  And our paths in the world diverged so wide,
Each was nought to each, must I be told?
  We were fellow mortals, nought beside?

### IV.

No, indeed! for God above
  Is great to grant, as mighty to make,
And creates the love to reward the love:
  I claim you still, for my own love's sake!
Delayed it may be for more lives yet,
  Through worlds I shall traverse, not a few:
Much is to learn and much to forget
  Ere the time be come for taking you.

For that which God made good shall in the end have its purpose in being good; and no least earthly beauty, no little flower, no white sunray, no gold hair, red mouth, pure brow, shall go unhonoured to darkness and the grave:—

### V.

But the time will come—at last it will,
  When Evelyn Hope, what meant, I shall say,
In the lower earth, in the years long still,
  That body and soul so pure and gay?
Why your hair was amber, I shall divine,
  And your mouth of your own geranium's red—
And what you would do with me, in fine,
  In the new life come in the old one's stead.

### VI.

I have lived, I shall say, so much since then,
  Given up myself so many times,
Gained me the gains of various men,
  Ransacked the ages, spoiled the climes;

Yet one thing, one, in my soul's full scope,
    Either I missed or itself missed me :
And I want and find you, Evelyn Hope !
    What is the issue ? let us see !

What is the issue? Millions of years hence the imperial intellect, the boundless knowledge of that man
grown pure, shall rise, twinned with the full crowned
beauty of his love grown perfect, and draw into themselves those earthly beauties which sank to dust here,
only to awake to immortal beauty beyond the stars.

VII.

I loved you, Evelyn, all the while !
    My heart seemed full as it could hold—
There was place and to spare for the frank young smile
    And the red young mouth and the hair's young gold.
So, hush,—I will give you this leaf to keep—
    See, I shut it inside the sweet cold hand.
There, that is our secret ! go to sleep ;
    You will wake, and remember, and understand.

---

'The Last Ride Together,' though a comparatively
simple poem, is mentioned here because it seems to be in
some sort a development of the ideas contained in the
two former.

A man who has spent years in a passion for a girl, is at
last told he must hope no more. Possessed of that
strength which eventuates under failure in a strong
cheerful fatalism, he has the courage to crush down the
rising despair, and ask for a last ride with his mistress.
A little favour to grant; but one which, with the grand
imagination of love, he makes the foundation of a boundless ideal :

II.

My mistress bent that brow of hers ;
Those deep dark eyes where pride demurs

When pity would be softening through,
Fixed me a breathing-while or two
   With life or death in the balance : right !
The blood replenished me again ;
My last thought was at least not vain :
I and my mistress, side by side,
Shall be together, breathe and ride,
So one day more am I deified—
   Who knows but the world may end to-night.

### III.

Hush ! if you saw some western cloud
All billowy-bosomed, over-bowed
By many benedictions—sun s
And moon's and evening star's at once,
   And so, you, looking and loving best,
Conscious grew, your passion drew
Cloud, sunset, moonrise, star-shine too,
Down on you, near and yet more near,
Till flesh must fade for heaven was here !—
Thus leant she and lingered—joy and fear !
   Thus lay she a moment on my breast.

In the bright air, with the blessed presence at his side,
he turned resolutely, yet by no effort of will, to make the
best of what he had done, what he lost :

### IV.

Then we began to ride.   My soul
Smoothed itself out—a long-cramped scroll
Freshening and fluttering in the wind.
Past hopes already lay behind.
   What need to strive with a life awry ?
Had I said that, had I done this,
So might I gain, so might I miss.
Might she have loved me ? just as well
She might have hated—who can tell ?
Where had I been now, if the worst befell ?
   And here we are riding, she and I

'I have given my life for love,' says he ; 'I see statesmen, soldiers, poets, painters, musicians, who give their lives for patriotism and art. The statesman and soldier are rewarded by an epitaph which they never read ; the artists fail, are poor, grow grey with striving, and in the end are no nearer their goal than those who have never started in the race. I, who gave my youth, at least have one desire fulfilled ; for am I not riding with her ? I at least have one last chance of drawing back from the gulf of despair into which I was fast rushing. And then—

### IX.

Who knows what's fit for us ?   Had fate
Proposed bliss here should sublimate
My being ; had I signed the bond—
Still one must lead some life beyond,—
    Have a bliss to die with, dim-descried.
This foot once planted on the goal,
This glory garland round my soul,
Could I descry such ?   Try and test !
I sink back shuddering from the quest—
Earth being so good, would heaven seem best ?
    Now, heaven and she are beyond this ride.

If I had gained my ideal, should I have looked for heaven ? Could I have died, as I shall die now, with a hope beyond ? Would heaven seem best, if earth were so good ? At least I retain that hope, of heaven, and perhaps of her, in another life.

But, at the last the old earth hope comes stealing back, as he looks again at her. How if that hope of heaven, which a moment ago was formless and vague, be an actual fulfilment ; how if that which is his highest pleasure now, be destined to become, from temporal, eternal—from weakness, strength—from dimness, clearest vision ? How if this yearning of his be the germ of a yearning ever fulfilled, the same in kind, but infinitely magnified in degree—

> And Heaven just prove that I and she
> Ride, ride together, for ever ride?

Now these poems present us with three distinct notions or ideals of love. The first is that the *main* purpose for which each man and woman is born on this earth is to love some other woman or man, and that if that purpose is not carried out it will never be allowed gratification in any succeeding life. The second, assuming the existence of love in a man or woman, concludes that that love if honest will, though it fails of achievement here, be surely fulfilled in some future life. The third speaker creates a further ideal which is a development of the others. He has lost his hope here; but while making the best of his loss, and contrasting himself favourably with other failing strivers, inasmuch as he gets something while they get nothing, he buoys himself with the hope that the highest bliss *may* be the change from the minute's joy to an eternal fulfilment of joy.

A close examination of these three views (whose seeming inconsistency we accept at first sight on the ground that three different men, three different sets of circumstances, are depicted) show us that there is a kind of unity between them.

The speaker in 'Cristina' lays down as an abstract proposition with regard to the purpose of our life here, that we must, or ought to at some time or other, call into action a faculty which until so awakened lies dormant within us, the faculty of loving. The speakers in 'Evelyn Hope' and 'The Last Ride,' taking love as a thing existent which is swaying them at the moment, and not being called on by necessity of circumstances to seek for causes why it should be there, simply create for themselves out of their hopelessness here, and their desire of fruition hereafter, two very high ideals. These ideals, while harmonising with each other, do not violate but rather carry out the principle of the aspirations which moved Cristina's lover, in that they fulfil the condition of the actual existence of love in this life.

But while we observe this consistency of view in utterances professedly dramatic; while we are glad to find that the aspiration of each speaker perfects and supplements the others; we must not forget an important element common to all three which stamps them yet more decidedly with a unity of purpose.

As has been observed before, in almost all the poems on love, the simple gratification of the personal desire, however idealised, is the mainspring of the thought. But the ideas in these three poems are applied by each speaker (unconsciously perhaps) not only to himself and his love, but to the loves of all humanity. At first sight it may seem that their high hopes are the result of overweening egoism. But if it be so, the egoism is but the necessary consequence of genius, and while seeking rewards for itself, seeks only from a deep sense of justice, a feeling that what is meant to be fulfilled in the particular case must in the end be fulfilled under similar conditions in the case of every other human being.

These are no selfish lovers, who can see no further than their own individual entity, they each and all, even while claiming the highest possible boon, do in fact separate themselves from themselves, and without knowing it stand apart and judge of their own passion as an actual existing attribute common to all other men. Should we in this sense consider their conclusions as one whole, what use can we make of them, when thus blended ?

If we believe with Cristina's lover that we are here in this life, as distinguished from all other lives before and after, for the purpose of loving somebody; with Evelyn Hope's lover, that, having fulfilled that condition here, we shall surely enjoy it to the full in some future state ; and with the lover in ' The Last Ride,' that it is possible that love enjoyed may be, not only one fulfilment of a future state, but that fruition which is more glorious and all-satisfying than any other, we do but intensify powers of which we are assuredly possessed, and by the very nature of our hopes for their exercise, elevate and purify our desires.

Finding ourselves possessed of certain instincts, whose development is the passion of love, and which claim exercise in one way or another ; finding, as a physical fact, that such instincts repressed have almost universally a harmful effect, and therefore that within proper limits the exercise of them is physically speaking an actual necessity ; finding that not only as reproductive agents are these instincts in themselves of incalculable importance, but moreover, that in their exercise for that purpose they expand our sympathetic powers, and nourish and extend the power of action of our other attributes ; we do but take another step, to learn first that perhaps the passion is but a symbol of the infinite yearning of a first cause, a type of that boundless love which, wedded to boundless power, has been imagined as the all-ruling Deity; and then that this very passion, infinitely extended, may be the means of our helping untold millions as God's vicegerents in other existences.

And again, if we believe that, since the attribute or power of loving exists in us, it exists for a purpose which, in the nature of things, must be satisfied by an object to work on ; if we believe that no love which has honestly sprung up in any man's breast can go unrewarded altogether, lest thereby so much power be lost in the machine of the universe ; and if, following up this thought, we see the possibility that that love which must be re-warded somewhere because of its necessary use as a working force, may be the very actual force which shall sway planets and stars in boundless eternities, where sin and suffering are not ; if we thus dare to weld together the thoughts expressed in these three poems, what a glorious picture is unfolded to our view!

Who shall say whether the little germ of one man's love truly begun, for one woman, may not in some far away life arise an infinite passion, by whose glowing impulse the two shall mount upwards, fashioning to themselves out of the unperfected instincts and lessons of former lives a knowledge always growing?   And if for many lives he and she toil on, failing, learning, and accumulating force for efforts always redoubled in strength —surely at last, when learning is as the sea dried up, and knowledge the mysteries of its depths laid bare, the two will stand blended by their now boundless passion into one transcendent being, in the sky of perfect power. When labour and pain are over, and division and duality are things of forgotten ages, the perfect human entity, taking throne at the foot of God, will wield the sceptre of power, instinct with the spirit of love, over the millions who are still toiling and climbing, and in the end the whole world will blend in the inconceivable splendour of a star that blazes through an ever present eternity !

---

'By the Fireside,' 'Respectability,' and 'One Word More,' show us three men who have been successful in their passion, and present to us views of the use of love which, while less transcendental than those put forward in the three poems we have just been considering, are perhaps of more practical value for the working life of the present world.

'By the Fireside,' one of the most valuable poems in this volume, contains the history of two lives fused into one by the flame of love reciprocated; and while possessing high merits as an analytical study, is marked by a more obviously subjective character than most of the poet's works.

The speaker is a man who has been a citizen in many realms of knowledge, and has already passed the stormy spring-time of his youth. In one of those golden hours which, as they pass, drop a blessing on our prime of summer, he sits down by the wayside ; and casting his thoughts forward into the future, prophesies what will employ his reposing spirit when he has reached old age.

### II.

I shall be found by the fire, suppose,
   O'er a great wise book as beseemeth age,
While the shutters flap as the cross-wind blows,
   And I turn the page, and I turn the page,
Not verse now, only prose !

### III.

Till the young ones whisper, finger on lip,
   'There he is at it, deep in Greek :
Now, then, or never, out we slip
   To cut from the hazels by the creek
A mainmast for our ship ! '

### IV.

I shall be at it indeed, my friends !
   Greek puts already on either side
Such a branch-work forth as soon extends
   To a vista opening far and wide,
And I pass out where it ends.

### V.

The outside-frame, like your hazel-trees—
   But the inside archway narrows fast,
And a rarer sort succeeds to these,
   And we slope to Italy at last
And youth, by green degrees.

When he is old, he will, in thought, retrace the paths of knowledge he has trod, and he compares himself, in reference to the knowledge he will have acquired, to a traveller through a many-columned vista of a wood, who explores every path in it. The outside paths, which he will explore first, will show him the common English growths (hazel trees), namely the knowledge acquired in and from England. Each inner path will have rarer kinds of trees ; the innermost of all, the rarest. When he shall have explored all the other paths, he will come at last to the innermost sanctuary of the wood's vista, and pursue that inner path alone, knowing the rest by heart. This innermost path is his own inner life ; and pursuing it in retrospect, he will come to Italy, where his youth was spent, and at last reach the first beginning of his life, the moment when his own and his wife's spirits became first blended into one.

With a loving word in passing to that Italy, which seems in some sort to symbolise his own beloved, he pursues his train of thought. He will find himself once more on that very mountain path where his troth was plighted ; and will tenderly con over all the things he saw there, seeing in each double meanings by the light of experience, and love enjoyed. He will see once more the ruined chapel far up in the pass ; a thing which had, like himself, a pathetic past of its own, to which he and his love, with an unknown future before them, were proceeding.

Another step, and they two stood in the midst of the great maker, nature; the power which dumbly influences the little lives, the everlasting loves, of men and women. The thread of water joyously leaping over the ravages of the bygone storm-torrent, typified those little lives lightly threading their way through the destruction of past ages. As that thread of water crept down to feed the lake below, so *her* life moved onwards to feed and blend with his; while above them earth's greatest things (the mountains), meeting the eternal heaven in purity, pointed whither small humanity might aspire, and reach.

These two lives, separate as yet, went on by a narrow path side by side. Close to them the tender growths and reproductions of nature's earth-life clung to the ruins of past times, even as the present of man is joined with the past of God, even as the gracious deeds which may be done by man will beautify a wilderness of sin.

At that point of his life he seemed to be entering an early autumn; his life's fruits, though—like the chestnuts falling that day—they seemed to fall almost too soon, might yet, like the creepers' crimson and gold leaf, beautifying the fairy needled moss, be of use thereafter for grace and tenderness. And as autumn had its sudden good growths of one night—the mushrooms, shining pure amidst the evil growths of the same night, the toadstools —so that early autumn of his life might bear sudden unlooked-for good fruits among the equally sudden evil fruits of bad impulses.

He and his love came at last to the chapel, with its pathetic past, standing in the midst of stagnation, which was to be the womb of two new births.

As the chapel stood in the midst of stagnation, so his heart seemed to stand in the world, dead, and longing to be revived. As the smallest midges were not ashamed to grace with their dancing the stagnation and lifelessness which surrounded the chapel; as the smallest growths of lichen and ivy were not ashamed to beautify the chapel and its surrounding rocks; so no heart, however seemingly lonely and sterile, is too useless for God; He will ever take care that in some way, hidden or revealed, it shall bear fruit, even though it be only the fruit of being a joy perhaps to small unknown beings, the fruit of being a stronghold on which small creatures clinging may live and suck nourishment.

The chapel too, whose old age was helpful to the few low people who came to worship and get comfort within it, symbolised the speaker's future old age, and its hopeful use in experience and sympathy.

And as the chapel with its product of art, so the speaker in the glow of his youth, had each stood as a monument of the beginning of man's aspirations after beauty, and both still bore the marks of their former glory. Now, all alone, the chapel was left to the love of a single bird, was left to watch over the stray sheep who came to drink at its pond, and the poor men who came to drink their religious life at its altar. Thus the chapel left alone with the bird and its song symbolised the retirement of age, and the reminiscent chord of youth which would thrill through it.

And here he breaks off the thread of his thought and takes up a new one.

### XXI.

My perfect wife, my Leonor,
  Oh, heart my own, oh, eyes, mine too,
Whom else could I dare look backward for,
  With whom beside should I dare pursue
The path grey heads abhor ?

### XXII.

For it leads to a crag's sheer edge with them ;
  Youth, flowery all the way, there stops—
Not they ; age threatens and they contemn,
  Till they reach the gulf wherein youth drops,
One inch from our life's safe hem.

Why, says he, do I dare go so minutely, step by step, over the path of my youth ? Only because it led to you, my love ! In this my thought, I am looking forward to a time of age when I shall have to look back, and shall look back with joy, along the path of my youth. To that path the majority of those who are growing old, as I must do one day, shun looking back at all. For they have gone on blindly, they have never looked before them into the future as I am doing now, so that when they come to the end of youth, it is like coming to the edge of a precipice at unawares. On they go, heedless of or despising age, who threatens them momently, till, for want of foresight, they and their youth drop over into the gulf, when if they had stopped an inch before, they and it would have been kept safe through life.

### XXIII.

With me, youth led—I will speak now,
  No longer watch you as you sit
Reading by firelight, that great brow
  And the spirit-small hand propping it,
Mutely, my heart knows how.

### XXIV.

When, if I think but deep enough,
  You are wont to answer, prompt as rhyme;
And you, too, find without a rebuff
  The response your soul seeks many a time,
Piercing its fine flesh-stuff.

### XXV.

My own, confirm me! If I tread
  This path back, is it not in pride
To think how little I dreamed it led
  To an age so blest that by its side
Youth seems the waste instead?

Now our two lives are one: no obstructing rocks can stop the stream.

### XXVII.

Think, when our one soul understands
　　The great Word which makes all things new—
When earth breaks up and heaven expands—
　　How will the change strike me and you
In the house not made with hands?

And when our two souls, drawn into one stream, come to the ocean of heaven, how will the change strike us?

Still as we wander through that ocean, you will be first to see in it, you will make me see, new depths, new wonders. Could we have expected this at first? But since it must and will be, nay, is so, let me for very love come back to the beginning and see how it has come about.

### XXX.

Come back with me to the first of all,
　　Let us lean and love it over again—
Let us now forget and now recall,
　　Break the rosary in a pearly rain,
And gather what we let fall!

I had lived my life much as that small singing bird by the chapel lived, unheeding trouble save when (like the hawks) it came in sight. But in that early afternoon of my life (as it seemed), I, like the bird, began to feel my heart convulsed with the yearning to speak itself out. In that afternoon, I found you. The rest of the world around me was still, and you could hear my voice. We took the mountain path, talking indifferently; we gave tender regard to the old chapel with its past (in half prophetic mood), and gave wonder to the moss, whose deeper meaning is now so clear. We saw that the chapel's precious things, like the precious things of a man's life, and of my life, were locked out of sight of the crowd of gazers and plagiarists; and then we came back to our present moment.

XXXVII.

Oh moment, one and infinite !
  The water slips o'er stock and stone ;
The west is tender, hardly bright ;
  How grey at once is the evening grown—
One star, the chrysolite !

At that moment, and just as the brightness seemed
fading out of my life, just as it seemed to be growing grey
like the evening, one star arose to bless it.   I stood there
alone, looking at my new risen star momently brightening my heaven, whose lights and shades throbbed around
that star in agony of yearning to blend with it.   It was a
moment when a sound, a breath, more or less, made all
the difference between the blackness of despair and the
blinding glory of hope fulfilled.

XLI.

For my heart had a touch of the wood-land time,
  Wanting to sleep now over its best.
Shake the whole tree in the summer prime,
  But bring to the last leaf no such test :
' Hold the last fast ! ' runs the rhyme.

XLII.

For a chance to make your little much,
  To gain a lover and lose a friend,
Venture the tree and a myriad such,
  When nothing you mar but the year can mend !
But a last leaf—fear to touch !

XLIII.

Yet should it unfasten itself and fall
  Eddying down till it find your face
At some slight wind—(best chance of all)
  Be your heart henceforth its dwelling-place
You trembled to forestal !

I, in that early autumn time of my brain, stood there

like an old wood-god worshipping a nymph changed to a tree, which tree had now shed all its summer glory, and held but one last autumn leaf. I knew that there was no chance for me to gain any token of love from that tree, with its one precious leaf, by any act of my own. The tree must give me its leaf or I must go lacking; I was not in that summer prime when I could take by force of brain what gifts I would. But the tree was good to me. At the slight wind of my unexpressed mad longing, it unfastened its leaf and let it flutter into my bosom, where it rests now. In that moment, you fulfilled my hope, and the heaven was complete with its blended star. What though the night seemed to hide the heaven? The heaven knew that it held its star, and that was enough. The great maker nature had in her forests dumbly influenced our two little lives, and made them one. Day by day since that time we have seen how through that moment's product, through that thing done by you and me, all that we see and know has its full worth, all the world is in harmony with our lives. What we have done since is to love; thus have we forwarded the general work of mankind; and while recruiting the race by our efforts in accordance with the great order, have lived our own lives as well.

### XLIX.

How the world is made for each of us !
  How all we perceive and know in it
Tends to some moment's product thus,
  When a soul declares itself—to wit,
By its fruit—the thing it does !

### L.

Be Hate that fruit, or Love that fruit,
  It forwards the General Deed of man,
And each of the many helps to recruit
  The life of the race by a general plan ;
Each living his own, to boot.

LI.

I am named and known by that hour's feat;
    There took my station and degree:
So grew my own small life complete
    As nature obtained her best of me—
One born to love you, sweet!


LII.

And to watch you sink by the fireside now
    Back again, as you mutely sit
Musing by firelight, that great brow
    And the spirit-small hand propping it
Yonder, my heart knows how!


LIII.

So the earth has gained by one man more,
    And the gain of earth must be heaven's gain too,
And the whole is well worth thinking o'er
    When the autumn comes: which I mean to do
One day, as I said before.

---

The piece called 'Respectability,' though very short, is
very significant:

I.

Dear, had the world in its caprice
    Deigned to proclaim, 'I know you both,
    Have recognised your plighted troth,
Am sponsor for you: live in peace!'
How many precious months and years
    Of youth had passed, that speed so fast.
    Before we found it out at last—
The world, and what it fears?

The idea expressed is that the independence of thought
and action which forms the necessary groundwork for the
making of a character, is incomplete unless it is itself
founded upon the love of a woman for the man, of a man

for the woman, begun and carried through in perfect indifference to, and if need be defiance of, the laws of society.

II.

> How much of priceless life were spent
>   With men that every virtue decks,
>   And women models of their sex—
> Society's true ornament—
> Ere we dared wander, nights like this,
>   Through wind and rain, and watch the Seine,
>   And feel the Boulevart break again
> To warmth and light and bliss ?

Had their love been first recognised by the world, they, becoming by that recognition the world's debtors, would have been compelled to conform to its rules, all the while wearing their strength by chafing under the restraint. But now that the two have dared to do without that recognition, instead of passing many years of fruitless striving against those fetters of conventionality which, through their obligation to society and their ignorance of its weak points, they could not have broken save at the expense of years of toil, which would have wasted their powers, the two have had all the priceless years of their youth to spend in developing their true instincts, their pure and unchecked sympathies.

---

The beautiful lines called 'One Word More,' are addressed by the poet to his wife, and one feels almost afraid to touch them with the rude hand of the critic. If we speak of them reverently in a few words, it is because the thought of them, in its depth and sweetness, is a standing lesson to every artist. How graceful how touching is their opening music !

II.

Rafael made a century of sonnets,
Made and wrote them in a certain volume
Dinted with the silver-pointed pencil
Else he only used to draw Madonnas:
These the world might view—but one, the volume.
Who that one, you ask? Your heart instructs you.
Did she live and love it all her life-time?
Did she drop, his lady of the sonnets,
Die, and let it drop beside her pillow,
Where it lay in place of Rafael's glory,
Rafael's cheek so duteous and so loving—
Cheek, the world was wont to hail a painter's—
Rafael's cheek, her love had turned a poet's?

III.

You and I would rather read that volume
(Taken to his beating bosom by it),
Lean and list the bosom-beats of Rafael,
Would we not! than wonder at Madonnas—
Her, San Sisto names, and her, Foligno,
Her, that visits Florence in a vision,
Her, that's left with lilies in the Louvre—
Seen by us and all the world in circle.

And then he tells us of Dante's attempt to draw an
angel for Beatrice ; and then—

What of Rafael's sonnets, Dante's picture?
This : no artist lives and loves, that longs not
Once, and only once, and for one only
(Ah, the prize !), to find his love a language
Fit and fair and simple and sufficient—
Using nature that's an art to others,
Not, this one time, art that's turned his nature.
Ay, of all the artists living, loving,
None but would forego his proper dowry :
Does he paint? he fain would write a poem—
Does he write? he fain would paint a picture,
Put to proof art alien to the artist's,
Once, and only once, and for one only,
So to be the man and leave the artist,
Gain the man's joy, miss the artist's sorrow.

Every artist who lives and loves a woman, desires to honour her by employing some highest attribute of his nature (kept in the innermost holy of holies of the temple, sacred from the world) in order to produce a work which shall give her delight.

In so doing he gets for himself the delight of an exercise of faculty irresponsible to any critic save his own loving heart, unchallenged by any opinion save the fondest praise of his woman love.

And why does this exercise of such faculty yield him such pleasure, and why is such pleasure never realised by him in the exercise of his proper art? Because Heaven's gift, which impels his spirit in its art career, has ever an earthly alloy in it, the alloy of harsh criticism, of ungrateful carping, of brutish infidelity. It is this harshness, ingratitude, infidelity, which is so fatal to the honesty and truth of the artist's work, and cripples his best efforts. And it is the unreserved sympathy of a woman who loves him, which is the strongest talisman to keep him pure, and reinvigorate his brain, nerveless with much striving. Take an instance, not of an artist, but of a patriot.

### IX.

> He who smites the rock and spreads the water,
> Bidding drink and live a crowd beneath him,
> Even he, the minute makes immortal,
> Proves, perchance, his mortal in the minute,
> Desecrates, belike, the deed in doing.
> While he smites, how can he but remember,
> So he smote before in such a peril,
> When they stood and mocked—'Shall smiting help us!'
> When they drank and sneered—'A stroke is easy!'
> When they wiped their mouths and went their journey,
> Throwing him for thanks—'But drought was pleasant.'
> Thus old memories mar the actual triumph;
> Thus the doing savours of disrelish;
> Thus achievement lacks a gracious somewhat;

O'er importuned brows becloud the mandate,
Carelessness or consciousness, the gesture.
For he bears an ancient wrong about him,
Sees and knows again those phalanxed faces,
Hears, yet one time more, the 'customed prelude—
' How shouldst thou, of all men, smite and save us ? '—
Guesses what is like to prove the sequel—
' Egypt's flesh-pots—nay, the drought was better.'

When Moses first gave water to the thirsty Israelites, they were ungrateful first, and unbelieving in God's power shown through Moses. When he did that miracle again, how could *he* do it in pure faith, when he remembered *their* infidelity? How could *he* do it in honest purity of desire to help them, when he remembered *their* ingratitude? And again, he can never make the unfeeling crowd love him for his human sympathy; he can only make them obey him through fear, by his mysterious power as a prophet. Then, how refreshing, how purifying, how strengthening for his work in the world, to have one woman's face to love.

For her sake, he would give up all his power and prophethood, only to have the right to minister to her wants as a man. Nay, he would even envy the camel which kneels patiently down to be killed for her sake, in order that its little hoard of bitter water may be used to quench her thirst.

Reverting to the examples of Dante and Rafael, the poet says :—

XII.

I shall never, in the years remaining,
Paint you pictures, no, nor carve you statues,
Make you music that should all express me ;
So it seems : I stand on my attainment.
This of verse alone, one life allows me ;
Verse and nothing else have I to give you.
Other heights in other lives, God willing—
All the gifts from all the heights, your own, love !

And yet I may do something here, if not in Rafael's way, at any rate in my own way, for my love.

For as a fresco painter will for his love's sake curb his hand and become illuminator to adorn her missal, so I who have soared as dramatist, epoist, analyst, and lyrist, may write you these tender verses untouched, unaltered, because they are prompted by my great love.

Let then my labour as an artist be for all men, my untouched words, straight from the brain and the heart, are for you.

Let my manner of speech be worked out and polished for all my common works; for you the very poverty of my speech will endear it to you, because love prompted it.

And then, to return to my old conceit : see the moon yonder ! Suppose she loved a mortal; would she show him the side she showed the world? No ! she would show him a new side—

> Side unseen of herdsman, huntsman, steersman,
> Blank to Zoroaster on his terrace,
> Blind to Galileo on his turret,
> Dumb to Homer, dumb to Keats—him, even !
> Think, the wonder of the moonstruck mortal
> When she turns round, comes again in heaven,
> Opens out anew for worse or better !
> Proves she like some portent of an iceberg
> Swimming full upon the ship it founders,
> Hungry with huge teeth of splintered crystals ?
> Proves she as the paved-work of a sapphire
> Seen by Moses when he climbed the mountain ?
> Moses, Aaron, Nadab, and Abihu
> Climbed and saw the very God, the Highest,
> Stand upon the paved-work of a sapphire.
> Like the bodied heaven in his clearness
> Shone the stone, the sapphire of that paved-work,
> When they ate and drank and saw God also !

XVII.

What were seen ?   None knows, none ever shall know.
Only this is sure—the sight were other,
Not the moon's same side, born late in Florence,
Dying now impoverished here in London.
God be thanked, the meanest of his creatures
Boasts two soul-sides, one to face the world with,
One to show a woman when he loves her.


Even so do I by you, even so does every artist by his
love.

Even so, too, do you, my moon, for me.

You, who, having the praise of the world too, can yet
show me new beauties which the world never can know;

Thus they see you, praise you, think they know you !
There, in turn I stand with them and praise you,
Out of my own self, I dare to phrase it.
But the best is when I glide from out them,
Cross a step or two of dubious twilight,
Come out on the other side, the novel
Silent silver lights and darks undreamed of,
When I hush and bless myself with silence.


XIX.

Oh, their Rafael of the dear Madonnas,
Oh, their Dante of the dread Inferno,
Wrote one song—and in my brain I sing it,
Drew one angel—borne, see, on my bosom !

---

The lovers in 'Cristina,' 'Evelyn Hope,' and 'The
Last Ride Together,' spoke of love as an aspiration which
was not to be realised here at all, but must have its
completion in some other life.   Failure created in them
their ideals; and what the possible development, and
how splendid the consummation of such ideals, we have
seen.

Dreams, alas ! are too often the result of some thwarting of an object; but how ravishing in its unreality is the fantastic beauty of a dream !

The lovers who speak in 'By the Fireside,' ' Respectability,' and 'One Word More,' have succeeded, and are wedded to their loves; and their dreams, though beautiful, are less unreal and less fanciful. There is too, at first sight, less inconsistency between the ideas of each, than in those of the other three; for each is turning to actual use the same possession, the same fulfilment. But though the selfishness of success is a stronger trial to purity than the selfishness of failure, these large-hearted men do not fail to see the true use of their love, both for themselves and for others.

The speakers in 'By the Fireside,' and in 'Respectability,' have each the same end in view, namely, how to use his own and his mistress's attributes for the widest good.

The speaker in ' One Word More,' adds to those of the others, in its full beauty, the ideal of the artist. All of them acknowledge that the love which has been blessed by enjoyment, is not to be used for selfish ends, but for widening of sympathy: and that just as we cannot complete our nature here without exercising the faculty of love, so if we do exercise it at all, and successfully, it must be used to help us towards the far away height to which the faith of the failing spirits has lifted them; that whether their ideal is to come to pass or not, at least the fortunate ones on this earth should do their little human work to help on the great harmony of God's work above, and while blending love with power for the purpose of helping all who need it here, may hope that when death comes, they too may be translated to the seat where power and love are unchecked and unblinded by sins and shortcomings.

We have now discussed all the most important love

poems whose subject is the feeling of the man.  Those which speak of the feeling of the woman are of unquestionable importance too, as dramatic efforts; but in treating them analytically, and selecting such only as go beyond the province of dramatic portraiture, we are as before hinted reduced to one poem which, expressing a woman's feelings, at the same time shows any sort of ideality as connected with other lives of other women, or with other existences after death.

This poem is ' Any Wife to Any Husband,' and general as is its title, it displays far deeper insight into the usual character of the passion of even high-minded men than is, we fear, possessed by most women of the present day.

As in the other cases, we will take the poem and describe it shortly.

A wife lies dying in her bed; her husband's hand is in hers, and her eyes are dim with the shadow of the wing of death.   Their love has been whole and perfect in body and soul for years; but not so blind, not so unreasoning on her part, as to prevent her from seeing clearly, more clearly perhaps from out of the grave's darkness than in the daylight of life, what is her husband's weakness, what his strength.

I.

My love, this is the bitterest, that thou
Who art all truth, and who dost love me now
    As thine eyes say, as thy voice breaks to say—
Shouldst love so truly, and couldst love me still
A whole long life through, had but love its will,
    Would death that leads me from thee brook delay !

II.

I have but to be by thee, and thy hand
Would never let mine go, nor heart withstand
    The beating of my heart to reach its place.
When should I look for thee and feel thee gone ?
When cry for the old comfort and find none ?
    Never, I know : Thy soul is in thy face.

Though I faded, our two souls would see clearly their own beauty, and renew their power in the failing of the flesh. For we should both remember whence our souls sprang; we should fear to dishonour God by mistrust in the darkness, having safe our soul's spark, given from his immortal fire. Then indeed you would be perfect and pure through life, and then what plaudits would ring from the next world, when, new winged and cleaned from earthly stain, you sprang to the sky and to the angels for new fellowship in perfect truth !

But now, with my earthly love gone from you, how bitter is it that you, who are so true and grateful that you treasure even the flowers of one holiday, must sink into impurity; you, who can let strange things remain strange, but having found love once, can keep it through years, though it was only awakened by one slight tune, one passing glance; you who, if we had only once met and parted, would, having loved me, do all gracious things to keep my image in your memory.

### IX.

But now, because the hour through years was fixed,
Because our inmost beings met and mixed,
　　Because thou once hast loved me—wilt thou dare
Say to thy soul, and Who may list beside,
' Therefore she is immortally my bride,
　　Chance cannot change my love, nor time impair.

### X.

' So, what if in the dusk of life that's left,
I, a tired traveller, of my sun bereft,
　　Look from my path when, mimicking the same,
The fire-fly glimpses past me, come and gone.
Where was it till the sunset ? where anon
　　It will be at the sunrise ! what's to blame ? '

### XI.

Is it so helpful to thee ? canst thou take
The mimic up, nor, for the true thing's sake,

> Put gently by such efforts at a beam?
> Is the remainder of the way so long
> Thou need'st the little solace, thou the strong?
> Watch out thy watch, let weak ones dose and dream!

Can you say, again, 'Because there is other beauty, I can still enjoy it without failing from any allegiance to that great beauty who is dead ; this is no more than preferring to see pictures instead of the bare wall ; still the new beauty admired detracts nothing from the old beauty worshipped?' Ah me! So it must be ; I must myself see from my heaven above how you so fail ; must myself allow you, nay authorise you, to steal from me all the love and truth you gave me, and bestow it on others. Love, then, again if you will ; say you were in a trance of grief and have awoke ; speak the words and give the looks to new women, which are stamped with the image of the love wherewith I glorified them. Still you are mine ; false however long, you must come back to me at last.

### XVII.

> Only, why should it be with stain at all?
> Why must I, 'twixt the leaves of coronal,
> Put any kiss of pardon on thy brow?
> Why need the other women know so much,
> And talk together, 'such the look and such
> The smile he used to love with, then as now!'

If I could live longest, should I be so false? Would ɪ not glory to go into your very tomb and sit there, seeing your face on its walls, the better that they are so blank and bare? Did I not even want more time to get you by heart, that when I too came to die, I might be fitter to join you beyond the grave? And you, who are the nobler of us two, can you not take this truth to me as a trial, and for very pride, keep it unsullied?

### XXI.

Pride?—when those eyes forestal the life behind
The death I have to go through!—when I find,
　　Now that I want thy help most, all of thee!
What did I fear?　Thy love shall hold me fast
Until the little minute's sleep is past
　　And I wake saved.—And yet it will not be!

———————

There is a terrible and bitter truth in all this dying reproach. Few men have such a sustaining power of love as to keep them firm in resisting the fleshly desires, when she who has idealised those desires is dead. So long as there is a hope of regaining a mistress or a wife who is still loved, many a man will remain faithful; but it is only one in a million who has faith enough to keep the image in his heart after the body is gone, and by the tender beauty of that image to charm away the rising lusts which will claim gratification. 'The desire of the man is for the woman, the desire of the woman is for the desire of the man;' and every true woman finds more than enough to fill her imagination and her life in the passion which she has inspired in, and the passion which has been roused in her by, one man who has loved her, and whom she has loved, truly and wholly.

Looking at this poem as a powerful epitome of the highest hopes and joys of womankind generally in connection with the passion of love, let us ponder upon the manifestations so put forth of the highest form of woman's passion for man.

We see that although less aspiring, it is purer; though not so strong, it is longer lived; that as a fitting complement to and support of the male love which in its highest development is always struggling upwards, it stands, in its mute humility, a type of that perfection which looks to one superior; and it teaches the man that his purity and constancy should be firmly established before he dares to assert supremacy over all nature.

This woman-love, into which doubt enters not, is a realisation here of that perfect faith which man strives after and fails to find; it is a love which has done already what the man aspires to do; for it ever works to do good to his nature as worthily representing the whole of humanity; is now as unselfish as he can ever hope to be even in his wildest dreams; and always strives to help him to become more pure and more perfect.

The real love of the man is never born until the love of the woman supplements it; for the first feeling, refine it as he will, is but lust made clean for a little; it is merely the desire for instant fruition.

But when the full abandonment and absorption into himself, the full faith and constancy of the woman's love is made plain to him, then he begins to see that there may be wider uses for his desires; that the highest ideal of the object of love is already manifested in the purity and sympathy of his mistress; and that as he strives more and more to reproduce that ideal in himself, he and his mistress may at last, not in the flesh but in the spirit, when her tender unaspiring love is absorbed into his winged passion, blend into one perfect creature which exercises its double yet united powers for the unspeakable gladness of all that has life.

# THE FLIGHT OF THE DUCHESS

This poems tells a simple story, which all men to whom I have talked about it have professed themselves at a loss to unravel. And they are not content with merely saying that it is unintelligible : they lift up their hands at its rugged-ness and want of melody, and exclaim, Is this poetry? Did anyone ever see such barbarous rhymes? Is there anything in it after all? Or is it merely a freak of this uncouth mind, so cramped and cooped by the exigencies, which must be respected sometimes, of rhythm and rhyme, that it must needs let out all its most fantastic moods in one stream, and once for all relieve itself of an oppressive burden? To answer such critics in speech has been impossible, perhaps because the only answer is an indirect one. But while writing about other and more musical utterances of the Poet's, I feel the necessity, according to the plan of these Essays, of giving a word or two in explanation of, and assigning a motive to, this much-abused poem.

The story is laid in a northern principality (whose duke was a vassal of a Kaiser of Germany), which kept its rough simple traditions in its own wilds, long after the court had got a flavour of luxury and pageantry.

The speaker is an obscure retainer of the Duke, and is the son of an old huntsman of that Duke's father. The

Duke of the story had taken for his Duchess a girl brought up in a convent; and the poem concerns the flight of that Duchess, or rather her abduction by an old gipsy woman.

The speaker opens his story with a description of his lord's principality :—

> Ours is a great wild country :
> If you climb to our castle's top,
> I don't see where your eye can stop ;
> For when you've passed the cornfield country,
> Where vineyards leave off, flocks are packed,
> And sheep-range leads to cattle tract,
> And cattle-tract to open chase,
> And open chase to the very base
> Of the mountain, where at a funeral pace,
> Round about, solemn and slow,
> One by one, row after row,
> Up and up the pine trees go,
> So, like black priests up, and so
> Down the other side again
> To another greater, wilder country,
> That's one vast red drear burnt-up plain,
> Branched through and through with many a vein
> Whence iron's dug, and copper's dealt ;
> Look right, look left, look straight before—
> Beneath they mine, above they smelt,
> Copper-ore and iron ore,
> And forge and furnace mould and melt.
> And so on, more and ever more,
> Till, at the last, for a bounding belt,
> Comes the salt sand hoar of the great sea shore,
> —And the whole is our Duke's country !

The speaker goes on to tell how, when the old Duke had an heir, he was summoned by the Kaiser to present himself at court; how he obeyed the summons, and how at the end of a year, sinking beneath the tedium of pomp and etiquette, the old rough Norseman sickened and died.

When he died, his Duchess left the principality (where

she had managed her husband's affairs during his lifetime) and took the infant Duke with her to Paris.

At last, back she came, bringing with her the young
Duke, now grown to manhood.  But his life at Paris had
transformed him into a pert little elf, with all sorts of
strange notions about the glory of his northland home,
the virtues and heroic mould of his ancestors and subjects.
He set to work to dig up and exhibit to a wandering
world a quantity of fossil observances of venery and
middle age manners.  He perpetually worried his re-
tainers' souls out of patience by his horrible usages and
costumes :—

> And chief in the chase his neck he perilled,
> On a lathy horse, all legs and length,
> With blood for bone, all speed, no strength;
> —They should have set him on red Berold,
> With the red eye slow consuming in fire,
> And the thin stiff ear like an abbey spire !

At last the time came that he must marry; and a lady
was chosen for him, who had lived her life in a convent,
but who was young, loving, and beautiful.

She was a woman, says the speaker, with a great loving
heart, born to be the wife of a man to whom she could be
helpful and cheering; but here, alas ! she had nothing to
do but sit and look stately; for had not this ape of a
Duke, in his rage for mediæval romancing, got an officer
here, there and everywhere ?    Was not everything done
by rule and precedent ?    What on earth could the poor
little warm girl do but pine in her ghastly splendour and
die of it at last ?

This gradual pining of hers, though it sorely irritated
the Duke and his mother, was treated by them with the
patronising superiority with which grown-up people
sometimes treat the humours of a fractious child, for
whom a fit punishment will be found in due time.

Well, one autumn, the Duke having looked into his
books found that the proper thing to do was to have a
hunting party. He vexed his household's life with
getting up the proper costumes; and when he had settled
everyone's part, his own included, it occurred to him to
search for some rule ordaining the Duchess's duty. He
found one at once :—

> When horns wind a mort and the deer is at siege,
> Let the dame of the castle prick forth on her jennet,
> And with water to wash the hands of her leige
> In a clear ewer with a fair towelling,
> Let her preside at the disembowelling.

This settled, the Duke signified to the poor little Duchess
his wish that she should play her part in the masquerade.
But she, weighed down, poor thing, beneath ceremony
and pomp, and with little spirit left for anything but
moping, begged to be excused. And what wonder ?
Quoth the speaker (a sportsman himself)—

> Now, my friend, if you had so little religion
> As to catch a hawk, some falcon-lanner,
> And thrust her broad wings like a banner
> Into a coop for a vulgar pigeon;
> And if day by day, and week by week,
> You cut her claws, and sealed her eyes,
> And clipped her wings, and tied her beak,
> Would it cause you any great surprise
> If, when you decided to give her an airing,
> You found she needed a little preparing?
> —I say, should you be such a curmudgeon,
> If she clung to the perch, as to take it in dudgeon
> Yet when the Duke to his lady signified,
> Just a day before, as he judged most dignified,
> In what a pleasure she was to participate,—
> And, instead of leaping wide in flashes,
> Her eyes just lifted their long lashes,
> As if pressed by fatigue even he could not dissipate,

And duly acknowledged the Duke's forethought,
But spoke of her health, if her health were worth aught,
Of the weight by day and the watch by night,
And much wrong now that used to be right,
So, thanking him, declined the hunting,—
Was conduct ever more affronting?
With all the ceremony settled—
With the towel ready and the sewer
Polishing up his oldest ewer,
And the jennet pitched upon, a piebald,
Black-barred, cream-coated, and pink eye-ball'd,—
No wonder if the Duke was nettled !

So he handed her over to his hell-cat of a mother to be scolded. And a scolding she got with a vengeance; which perhaps made her more obstinate, for she must have had ·a little pride left. So the Duke, not to be baulked, sallied forth on his hunting party, to do without the towel and ewer as best he might.

Just as he and his train issued from the court-yard, a troop of gipsies met them. These gipsies were a queer uncanny folk, whom the speaker describes in rough, vigorous words :—

Now, in your land, gipsies reach you, only
After reaching all lands beside ;
North they go, south they go, trooping or lonely,
And still, as they travel far and wide,
Catch they and keep now a trace here, a trace there,
That puts you in mind of a place here, a place there.
But with us I believe they rise out of the ground,
And nowhere else, I take it, are found,
With the earth-tint yet so freshly embrowned ;
Born, no doubt, like insects which breed on
The very fruit they are meant to feed on.
For the earth—not a use to which they don't turn it,
The ore that grows in the mountain's womb,
Or the sand in the pits like a honey-comb,
They sift and soften it, bake it and burn it—
Whether they weld you, for instance, a snaffle,

With side-bars never a brute can baffle;
Or a lock that's a puzzle of wards within wards;
Or, if your colt's forefoot inclines to curve inwards,
Horseshoes they'll hammer which turn on a swivel
And won't allow the hoof to shrivel.
Then they cast bells like the shell of the winkle,
That keep a stout heart in the ram with their tinkle;
But the sand—they pinch and pound it like otters,
Commend me to gipsy glass-makers and potters!
Glasses they'll blow you, crystal clear,
Where just a faint cloud of rose shall appear,
As if in pure water you dropped and let die
A bruised black-blooded mulberry;
And that other sort, their crowning pride,
With long white threads distinct inside,
Like the lake flower's fibrous roots which dangle
Loose such a length and never tangle,
Where the bold sword-lily cuts the clear waters,
And the cup-lily couches with all the white daughters;
Such are the works they put their hand to,
And the uses they turn and twist iron and sand to.

The oldest of the gipsies, a hideous woman, bent double, dressed in ragged wolfskin, and with no eyes at all to speak of, came up to the Duke and offered a present; for the gipsies come yearly to this Northland, and regularly give their presents to the dukes, always getting a money equivalent.

But this Duke, being of a stingy turn, or having no precedents for gipsies in his books, was not ready for the emergency, and declined to give the old crone anything. So she, to quicken his wits, said she was come to pay her duty to the new young Duchess. This woke the Duke up in another way. He thought what a capital school-mistress this horrible hairy old woman would make for his smooth, delicate girl-wife.

So, briefly telling the old gipsy the story of his wife's wickedness, and commanding her to frighten the lady thoroughly, he ordered the man who tells the story to take the gipsy, and present her to the Duchess.

The man took the gipsy, and bade her follow; and no sooner had the Duke and his train left, than a marvellous transformation took place in her. She grew taller by a head, and more dignified, and all her aged look vanished; her old tattered wolfskin changed to a robe fringed with gold coins, and her eyes came out unmistakably.

When the pair arrived at the presence-chamber door, the crone was admitted by the Duchess's tirewoman, Jacynth, who happened also to be the speaker's sweet-heart. Jacynth and the gipsy went in, and left the man alone in the balcony. Suddenly he heard a strange melodious sound in the presence chamber; and pushing the window open, he looked in and saw Jacynth lying asleep before the door, and a shape, a queen, that had been the gipsy woman, sitting on a state throne, with the Duchess at her feet. She was speaking or singing to the Duchess in a strange inexpressible melody, which as the man listened, shaped itself into burning words, telling how life is made for us that we may exercise love on all men and all things throughout the whole world: how that is what the gipsies live to do; and how the Duchess herself may live to do it too, if she will fly from this intolerable splendour and display, become one of the gipsies, and be ever cherished and watched over by them :—

> Only be sure thy daily life,
> In its peace or in its strife,
> Never shall be unobserved;
> We pursue thy whole career,
> And hope for it, or doubt, or fear,—
> Lo, hast thou kept thy path or swerved,
> We are beside thee, in all thy ways,
> With our blame, with our praise,
> Our shame to feel, our pride to show,

Glad, angry—but indifferent, no !
Whether it is thy lot to go,
For the good of us all where the haters meet,
In the crowded city's horrible street ;
Or thou step alone through the morass
Where never sound yet was,
Save the dry quick clap of the stork's bill,
For the air is still, and the water still,
When the blue breast of the dipping coot
Dives under, and all is mute.
So at the last shall come old age,
Decrepit as befits that stage,
How else wouldst thou retire apart
With the hoarded memories of thy heart.
And gather all to the very least
Of the fragments of life's earlier feast
Let fall through eagerness to find
The crowning dainties yet behind ?
Ponder on the entire past
Laid together thus at last.
When the twilight helps to fuse
The first fresh, with the faded hues,
And the outline of the whole,
As round eve's shades their framework roll,
Grandly fronts for once thy soul.
And then as, 'mid the dark, a gleam
Of yet another morning breaks,
And like the hand which ends a dream,
Death, with the might of his sunbeam
Touches the flesh and the soul awakes,
Then——

The words stopped. The poor huntsman became suddenly aware that the Duchess was being bewitched. He sprang from the balcony to the ground, and was just going to burst open the door to save her, as he thought, when the Duchess met him, with a face so changed to the beauty of a new-tasted happiness, that he felt all was for the best. So he saddled for her the very palfrey which brought her to the castle to be married, lifted her on it, stammering a few words of clumsy faithfulness, and

Then, do you know, her face looked down on me
With a look that placed a crown on me,
And she felt in her bosom—mark, her bosom—
And as a flower-tree drops its blossom,
Dropped me—ah, had it been a purse
Of silver, my friend, or gold that's worse,
Why, you see, so soon as I found myself
So understood,—that a true heart so may gain
Such a reward,—I should have gone home again,
Kissed Jacynth,—and soberly drowned myself!
It was a little plait of hair
Such as friends in a convent make
To wear, each for the other's sake,—
This, see, which at my breast I wear,
Ever did (rather to Jacynth's grudgment),
And ever shall, till the Day of Judgment.
And then,—and then,—to cut short,—this is idle,
These are feelings it is not good to foster,—
I pushed the gate wide, she shook the bridle,
And the palfrey bounded,—and so we lost her.

Such is the story ;—a story so simple, now it is told, that I must crave the indulgence of the philosophic reader who may perchance hope to find some attempt at profound thought in every line of these Essays. And what is the moral of the story? This, too, is so simple that it may seem almost a platitude. But if I may venture to ask that these Essays shall be read to the end, it will be seen that the moral or thought of this poem, simple though it be, has its place in a scheme, and is but a guide to deeper speculations to come, as the transparent brook is our guide to the sea.

Let me be forgiven, then, if I proceed, in homely phrase, to set forth what seems to be the use and purpose of this poem, as one in its place in a series.

In this age when, notwithstanding our professions, we are so apt to think that all the higher attributes of our common humanity are not common after all, but are confined to the men and women who lead lives of grace and culture, one feels thankful to a true poet who is not ashamed to show us, in uncouth language, the love that can spring straight from the heart-fountain of rough servants and immoral vagrants, who through long un-lovely lives have ever striven, without knowing it, after kindliness and honesty.

What a pathos, fit to draw tears, is there in this rude, simple tale of the poor huntsman ! I protest there are passages in it—which speak of the dumb striving of a humanity prisoned in too earthy a chamber, of a yearning which ever and anon, at the real moments of life, breaks forth in spite of hindrances—passages, I say, which, while they move my heart and make my throat swell time after time, seem always fresh and new as the spring buds are. The strange, awkward attempts at giving a connected artistic finish to the story; the light-hearted way in which the man puts down sentimental fancies (as he would call them) that will spring up; and the genuine outspoken contempt for display and nonsense of all kinds—these things, so truly written down, give to the poem a flavour which is lacking in smoother compositions, perhaps more melodious according to the rules of art.

Melody, in its widest sense, is the expression in any manner howsoever of the love and sympathy of man for men; and that is the melody which thrilled the heart of the great man who told this story, and found an answer-ing chord in the great heart of the poet who, hearing this story in some far-away village, or reading it in some book of forgotten folk-lore, knew a loving nature when he found it, in whatever station, in whatever age.

What of this Duchess and her stupid Duke in their bygone half-barbaric splendour ?    What of that old worn-out gipsy in her poverty-striken dotage ?

As surely as there is a law (which in spoken words and great men's hearts is centuries old), that commands us all to give out our hearts in genuine love and sympathy for all fellow-creatures with whom our lot is cast.—so surely have the Duke and his mother to answer for their persistent crushing of the hidden love which throbbed beneath the bosom of the poor little convent girl.

Every man who will not open his heart to the unspoken desires of a brother for reciprocating love is sinning not only against himself but against his whole race, past, present, and to come. No man can say how tremendous may be the effect of damming up one such love-stream : the swelling volume of the water will surely at last grow to a muddy turbulent river, overleap its banks, and bring devastation and ruin on the fair fields which bloomed on either side. How often does continual misunderstanding, caused by coldness which the smallest effort of will might have dispelled, freeze into hatred not only of one man or class, but even of a nation ? The terrible consequences tell their own tale.

But let us turn from the dark side of the picture to the light thrown on the gipsy crone. Throughout the world, God, who is above human laws and reverences them not, works with means which men would despise. What to Him are the virtues which we call morality and respectability ? Nothing. But love, helpfulness, honesty, are precious as fine gold.

That old gipsy, so decrepit and doting, was but the earthen vessel in which, hidden from sight, a queen soul shone, instinct with power and sympathy. A soul which having grown and drawn nourishment out of the long experience of a hardly-won life, had learned, straight from God's mouth, lessons which kings and priests strive and fail to find. She had gone straight to her great mother, the wife of God, whom we call Nature; and from her breast had drawn the yearning which Nature draws from the divine embrace and sends out in renewed love

for her children and her Husband.  From Nature's touch
the old gipsy drew her passion to reclaim one soul fast
slipping into the abyss of indifferentism and despair.
From Nature's touch, she who seemed to the world,
perhaps to her own tribe, despicable and useless, could
perpetually renew her life when any struggle to save one
human creature demanded her energy.  Holding Nature's
hand she would go right on until her body, worn into
shadow and nothingness, slipped from the arms of her
weeping tribe, and her soul flew straight upwards—
whither?

This is an old burden; the poem does but tell us that
it is for love we are here; not for the love of a man for a
woman, not for the love of a woman for a man—not for
these only—but for the love of all men and women who
seem unlovely, and careworn, and prosaic, whose eyes and
mouths are depressed with low cares, who have never
spoken, and perhaps scarcely know if they ever thought,
what the finely-balanced so-called sympathetic man calls
'beautiful ideas.'  The poem is one more voice in the
multitude of voices which are always crying to us, these
men and women have in them, though they know it not,
all the capability, in greater or less degree, of expressing
love if there be need for it, perhaps not here, perhaps not
even in the next life to this, but at any rate in God's good
time.  Is it for us to slight them or speak harshly of
them?  For aught we know, any poor man or woman
may hold a fund of power and sympathy as large, as
life-giving as the gipsy mother held; at least they are
all God's as we are, and shall be, as we hope to be, purified
and made clean.

Why has this gospel been preached more or less
earnestly in all religions, up to the highest of all which
the Nazarene burned himself out in proclaiming?  Why
do we all feel that religion still working within us?  Why

has the religion of Positivism based itself on the same sure foundation ?

Because, whether in personal or subjective immortality; whether as kings and melodists in a world where there is no night, or scattered among the tribes in inconceivable atoms, our power is never lost; because even as we strive to make perfect our faculty of love here, even to that degree shall we have the boundless delight of its eternal exercise, for healing and helping all who suffer in this earth or in other worlds, when the dress of our flesh has dropped into ashes, and we wake up naked and not ashamed in the unblinding splendour of the life everlasting.

# WARING

It may seem a paradoxical thing to say, but it is never-theless true, that all the greatest works of a poet, in the sense of those which have the greatest influence over the thoughts and acts of men, are the works which are most incomplete. Such poems as contain in themselves the complete story or thought which was their life spring (and which are in themselves useful as direct teachings from the master mind in either love, beauty, or know-ledge), have the merit according to their excellence of lessons to the reader, but they are nothing more. The reader sits in the attitude simply of a listener, a pupil, who takes the thing presented and admires it, and sees it in its completeness, but finds no imperative occasion for use of his own thinking powers further than is necessary to the understanding of the actual poem. He is not com-pelled to pursue any train of thought of his own. But the incomplete works, those which show that the poet's mind worked silently up to the point when he could hold his peace no longer, give a far more serious impetus to the thinking powers of the reader. He feels that a substratum of thought lies beneath, supporting the rough pregnant utterances ; that a long train of reflection must have been pursued before the actual words were written down—a train of reflection which he is piqued into finding out for himself by the very incompleteness of the work before him. He feels that the poem is the birth of the poet's long travail, the very topmost keystone of the arch which he had been building, as it were in secret; nay, that he himself may, by successful interpretation, become in some sense a discoverer. So much for the use of incomplete poems to each individual reader. But in their collective influence, that is, their influence over minds as a whole, they have a higher use still. All words actually spoken will bear different senses to different minds; the premises to be assigned to or the conclusions to be drawn from words which, as is the case with these incomplete poems, are only a context, so to speak, of the whole passage or subject which occupied the poet, admit of and will actually meet with far wider differences of interpretation from different minds than completed works do, simply because there is wider range for the exercise of the individuality of each interpreter.

And any true poet would surely rather that his work, whether complete or incomplete in actual words, should furnish a field for the labour of many minds and for much speculation, than that all minds should come to exactly the same conclusion with regard to it. Anything in the world which can exercise men's thinking power, and thereby make them act, must be of use; and so long as the speculations pursued with regard to these incomplete poems are truthfully pursued, their absolute correctness with regard to the actual thoughts in the poet's mind when he wrote the poem, is a matter of comparatively small importance. If one may venture to carry out these thoughts in a simile, these incomplete poems, already compared to the keystone of an arch, have as a support, not only the first wing of that arch, springing from its first stone, from the first beginnings of the thought thus traced in the poet's brain to fulfilment, but also the other wing of the arch, which, really leading up to the key-

stone, seems thrown out downwards from it. From the
actual spoken words of the poem, the eyes of the earnest
thinker are led downward through the far future, stone by
stone, of the thought which thus stands as the thing
shown; his eyes see new stones, new reflections, new
aspirations, all of which will go on adding strength to the
fabric, all tending backwards and upwards to the keystone,
till he comes to the last stone of the arch, the last foundation block which makes the arch a complete rainbow
thing, the final evolution of the thought or idea at its
farthest bound. But if there be any truth in this simile
of the arch, may we not pursue it a step farther? In the
beginning and ending of the idea which prompted and is
prompted by the poem, there is a likeness, an equal level,
without which the spoken word, the keystone, cannot be
sustained. Whether it be a life, a death, or a nation's
career, of which the poet tells us, or of which he has been
dreaming, all his thought, all our speculations thereon,
spring from that great whole, the world or universe which
is the flooring of the arch. From the world of men and
women, the world of beauty and warmth, the idea sprang;
it ascended hidden in mists, hidden in the secret places of
the poet's brain; it broke forth in a flame at the highest
point; and once more hidden, when its work of showing
is done, back to the world it returns, for love of that
foundation from which it sprang, to base itself firm
through eternal ages. As the rainbow's colours are hid
in clouds and mist, its beauties are hid in the brain of the
maker; but as the sun shining on the clouds draws out
the colour of the rainbow, so the warm loving thought of
other minds draws from the hidden place of the maker's
brain the beauties of the thought which is enclosed there.
And suppose that a man sees a glorious flower hanging
high in a forest of verdure, but can see no path by which
he may reach it, is he not likely to be bettered in craft, in

strength, in the sights he may see, the lessons he may learn, if he is obliged to find out a path to it, and perchance to climb on hands and knees, and suffer much hardship to gain it? Does not that man, having found the flower, gain not only the experience of his journey, but also all the beauties and fruits which hung around him? Does he not, having reached the summit where the flower hangs, find a pleasure, a new knowledge, in going down by a different path with the flower in his hand, keeping its savour and beauty to cheer him, and still gaining new growths, new fruits, new knowledge, until he reaches the kind earth whence sprang both the upward and the downward path? Even so, a man trying to trace a path up to the spoken thought, gains fruits of knowledge, thought, and love, perhaps his own and the poet's, perhaps only his own, until he arrives at the point when the thought burst into flower of speech; even so, when he has reached the spoken thought, he will be bettered by using his gained experience in treading the path which still has to be trodden by him; he will be able to trace new developments in the future of the thought, by reason of and born of the ideas which led up to it; he will gain a prophetic power, a foresight, a use for his own life for the years to come. Again, we all know how dear both to the painter and to ourselves are those sudden sketches in which one piece of colour or form is predominant, and the rest mere points and lines leading up to it as to a centre. That sketch is the seizing of one beauty which mother Nature shows only to her beloved ones the artists; and it is they only who, as the priests of nature, can teach us what is good and what is not good to be seen in her. The incomplete lines in that sketch show us what in the scene depicted is, as compared with the completed colour or form, of minor importance; the painter, who alone knew their relative value, shows

us that we, the learners, must use his mere rude indications in order that we may gain to ourselves much force
of imagination by trying to find out what were the
colours, what were the completed forms which in the
original scene filled up those rudimentary lines. Thus
we, the learners, gain a far more vivid idea of the picture
as it was given by nature, than if we had blindly trusted
to a complete picture, satisfying us in all details.

Thus, then, the very reason that the poem of ' Waring '
is an incomplete rude sketch, dashed off by a master who
never works carelessly or without a purpose, would make
it worth earnest study. That it has been chosen as one of
the most important of the Romances, is due, however,
not only to this incompleteness, but also to its subject,
which establishes a yet stronger claim to consideration
and thought. For it deals with the modern life which is
growing up in our midst, underneath our respectability;
the life which, as one often hears said, has in it far more
tragic force of intellect, fiercer lights and gloomier shades,
than the older times which have become historical.

We are strongly reminded, on reading ' Waring,' of
the obvious truth that the world is very full just now;
that the struggle for life, the perpetual battle of brain
with brain, as it rages at present, is fiercer and more
deadly from day to day. The actors in this romance
enlist our sympathy, because we feel that its passion
belongs so especially to our own time; because we feel
that its incidents in any other age, when there was less
jostling and crowding, could not have taken place at all.
And since every one of the crowd of men perpetually
coming into the world, adds his strength to swell the
strife which roars all round us; since the added numbers
are daily producing new growths of brain, new thoughts,
new actions; the value of the romance is increased by the
grandeur of the portrait it draws of one great life, which,

though nameless in history, has in its component parts, whether it be a fiction or a reality, many representatives as obscure as Waring; the life of every one of whom is inexpressibly important in the aggregate life of to-day and to-morrow down to future years.

Thus, then, reasons are obvious why it has seemed good to deal with this poem elaborately, not only in the direct thoughts contained in the words of it, but in all the collateral and indirect ideas which a man may by earnest thought create or evolve out of it.

The tale is a simple one. A man, young in years, and whose manners had the reserve of intense pride, used to live in London, unknown save to a score of friends. Even by these, his mighty aspirations occasionally spoken, his astounding claims, rarely put forth, were generally treated as mere wind and vapour. They thought him a dreamer, who was likely to produce no good seed or useful work. But his good-nature seemed so imperturbable that these friends did not hesitate to speak or hint to him their low opinion of his powers, or at any rate of his achievements. This sort of thing had gone on for some time, when one night he disappeared. When they had lost him, his friends, or at any rate one of them, found out how much indeed they had loved him; found out how much there was in him to love, cherish, revere. Various guesses were hazarded as to his whereabouts, his possible future career; and those who before had so consistently underrated him, now prophesied for him all manner of splendid success. Will he suddenly appear with European fame at Moscow, a general in the army of the Czar ? Will he be known as a fiery regenerator of India, or of forgotten slothful Spain ? Best of all, perhaps, he is hidden somewhere in London,

> And now works on without a wink
> Of sleep, and we are on the brink

Of something great in fresco paint.
Some garret's ceiling, walls, and floor,
Up and down, and o'er and o'er,
He splashes, as none splashed before
Since great Caldara Polidore.
Or Music means this land of ours
Some favour yet, to pity won
By Purcell from his rosy bowers—
Give me my so long promised son ;
Let Waring end what I begun ! '
Then down he creeps and out he steals
Only when the night conceals
His face : in Kent 'tis cherry time,
Or hops are picking : or at prime.
Of March he wanders, as, too happy,
Years ago when he was young,
Some mild eve, when woods grew sappy
And the early moths had sprung
To life from many a trembling sheath,
Woven the warm boughs beneath ;
While small birds said to themselves
What would soon be actual song,
And young gnats, by tens and twelves,
Made as if they were the throng
That crowd around and carry aloft
The sound they have nursed, so sweet and pure,
Out of a myriad noises soft,
Into a tone that can endure
Amid the noise of a July noon,
When all God's creatures crave their boon,
All at once and all in tune,
And get it, happy as Waring then,
Having first within his ken
What a man might do with men ;
And far too glad, in the evenglow,
To mix with the world he meant to take
Into his hand, he told you, so,
And out of it his world to make,
To contract or to expand
As he shut or oped his hand.

Will he astonish the world as an actor, a satirist, a poet,

or a dramatist? How will this strange forgotten star rise again in the heavens that are yearning for him?

When all conjectures had proved fruitless and his friends despaired of ever seeing or hearing of Waring again, suddenly a man arrived from a cruise in the Mediterranean, who had seen him—seen him, not as statesman, artist, or soldier; not in wealth, luxury, and power; but as a poor sailor, the captain of a smuggling vessel in Trieste bay.

Such is the story, worked out with much simplicity and grace of diction. Of Waring's character some especially vivid passages give us a speaking portrait. With an almost feminine softness of character, he blended a sternness which was forgotten in presence of his ever ready sympathy and good nature. His love, offered willingly to but rejected by his friends, is compared to the gracious love of some lady with a tender but unbeautiful face, who in years gone by had with untiring patience made gentle but unsuccessful attempts to gain a nestling-place in the flinty bosoms of intellectual male youths, imperially arrogant. She, ever patient, ever tender, would not reproach, but, like Waring, when, all too late, they thrust from them her full bounty of nature, retired without a murmur, looking back with sad wistful eyes on the blind fools who knew not that they were slighting and despising an angel.

> E'en so, swimmingly appears,
> Through one's after-supper musings,
> Some lost lady of old years
> With her beauteous vain endeavour
> And goodness unrepaid as ever;
> The face, accustomed to refusings,
> We, puppies that we were . . . Oh never,
> Surely, nice of conscience, scrupled
> Being aught like false, forsooth, to?
> Telling ought but honest truth to?

What a sin, had we centupled
Its possessor's grace and sweetness!
No! she heard in its completeness
Truth, for truth's a weighty matter,
And, truth at issue, we can't flatter!
Well, 'tis done with; she's exempt
From damning us through such a sally;
And so she glides, as down a valley,
Taking up with her contempt,
Past our reach; and in, the flowers
Shut her unregarded hours.

The closing scene, showing the sternness of Waring's nature, as indicated by the pitiless contempt with which he had left his friends without a word of leavetaking, is worth study. 'When I last saw Waring,' says his friend

'We were sailing by Triest,
Where a day or two we harboured;
A sunset was in the west,
When, looking over the vessel's side,
One of our company espied
A sudden speck to larboard;
And as a sea-duck flies and swims
At once, so came the light craft up,
With its sole lateen sail, that trims
And turns (the water round its rims
Dancing, as round a sinking cup,)
And by us like a fish it curled,
And drew itself up close beside,
Its great sail on the instant furled,
And o'er its planks a shrill voice cried
(A neck as bronzed as a Lascar's)
"Buy wine of us, you English brig?
Or fruit, tobacco and cigars?
A pilot for you to Triest?
Without one, look you ne'er so big,
They'll never let you up the bay!
We natives should know best."
I turned, and "Just those fellows' way,"
Our captain said. "The 'long-shore thieves
Are laughing at us in their sleeves."

> In truth, the boy leaned laughing back ;
> And one, half-hidden by his side
> Under the furled sail, soon I spied,
> With great grass hat and kerchief black,
> Who looked up with his kingly throat,
> Said somewhat, while the other shook
> His hair back from his eyes, to look
> Their longest at us.'

This closing scene contains analogies which cannot be passed over in silence. At sunset of the day—sunset of Waring's life in England—he, like the sun about to disappear, shone forth once more before he sank beneath the intellectual horizon of his friends. At the moment when it seemed there was no hope in England of hearing more of him, his little frail smuggling craft came dancing up by the big formidable English vessel in which his friend was sailing, and offered to bargain with them and help them. These confident British youths were just becoming aware that it was possible their sun might set and leave them dark, when he shone out once more ; but not to give them light : the time was past for that. They in their former arrogance, symbolised by the English brig, had disdained Waring, in his shyness, reserve, and incapacity, symbolised by the seemingly incapable smuggling smack, just as the brig, with its captain and its crew, disdained the help of the smuggler. Waring left his friends when they refused to acknowledge him : the smuggler left the brig when she disdained his offers. The Englishmen were left to look big and try and shoulder through the world : the brig was left to try and get up Triest bay ; both without Waring for a pilot. Even as the smuggling craft went off into the rosy and golden sunset to begin a new day, leaving the brig in a hopeless night behind it, pilotless, so did Waring to begin his new day, leave his ungrateful friends in the night of their stupidity and ignorance.

> ' Then the boat,
> I know not how, turned sharply round,
> Laying her whole side on the sea
> As a leaping fish does; from the lee
> Into the weather, cut somehow
> Her sparkling path beneath our bow;
> And then went off, as with a bound,
> Into the rosy and golden half
> O' the sky, to overtake the sun
> And reach the shore, like the sea-calf
> Its singing cave; yet I caught one
> Glance ere away the boat quite passed—
> And neither time nor toil could mar
> Those features: so I saw the last
> Of Waring!' You? Oh, never star
> Was lost here, but it rose afar!
> Look east, where whole new thousands are!
> In Vishnu-land what Avatar?

Such are the main features which strike us in the spoken words of the poem. It is but a sketch, and no more; a few powerful lines giving a vivid portrait; a bit of central drawing, with the accessories of past and future only hinted. These hints, and the incompleteness of the sketch, tempt us to indulge in a world of speculation on the past of Waring's life, before and up to the period of his disappearance; and on the future of his life, after his reappearance, to the end.

How had this wondrous nature first sprung up from the great level plain of humanity, to culminate in the crisis which gives occasion for the poem? How did his soul rise to the topmost keystone of the arch, that highest act of intellectual daring, the knowledge when to separate himself from his friends, break off ruthlessly all old and dear ties, and begin a new life? To learn this, let us trace his life from its beginning to that point when he so dared and achieved.

Nursed in luxury, brought up as a gentleman in the

conventional sense, did he not weary of a round of colour-less days, chafe at perpetual petty observances ?   In his youth, he had wandered up and down—a solitary *gauche* youth, mingling with his mother Nature, and dreaming of what he would do with the world.   He was not a man who had been soured and warped by poverty; he must have been well to do, for we find his friends blaming him for not writing and speaking earlier—blaming him for laziness and pride, for voluntarily choosing not to mix with the world.

Slighted from his earliest boyhood, he very early cast aside what he called the trammels of conventionality; wandering whither he would, he soon overcame or silenced the remonstrances of a fond mother—of aunts or sisters who found him incorrigible, nay, most likely saw nothing in him except a very awkward creature, perpetu-ally in everybody's way.   Awkward enough, possibly; but tall and straight, with large eyes, often dull in ex-pression, only lighting up by fits; a colourless, almost lifeless face, with no feature to recommend it, save a brow preternaturally broad and full, a mouth wide, firm set, and tender, given rarely to twitching, of kinship with the eyes, but trenched on either side by early pronounced lines from the far-stretching nostril—lines that gave a settled look of scorn to the face behind which so much love lay hid.   A face which looked at you with-out any consciousness of expression in it, without trying to see what effect he was producing, only seeming to know that you were a human being who must be loved if possible, and whose aspirations, if you would but give them, should meet with a full response and a warm embrace !

Early in his life he thought he saw all that was wrong in the world; with the confidence of youth, day by day he would strike out, in his woodland walks, utopian

plans, whereby perhaps artists should be made rich and
appreciated (for he must have had an artist's nature),
armies should be reorganised, monarchies overthrown,
the poor made well off, republics raised into being, education enforced, game laws, excise laws, monopolies, sunk in
an ocean of freedom. For this young fighter, unworn as
yet by actual struggle with men and women, was superb
in his self-created supremacy.

But at last a time came when he must leave his loneli-
ness and mix with the crowd of London. How would he
behave there ? He feels too certain of his own originality
of conception to desire a large circle of friends; he is too
proud and impatient of falseness to gain himself a place
and a name by flattery and acknowledgment of famous
charlatans, almost too proud to give praise even to famous
true men.

With a spirit truly regal, for it trusted in its own
power above all else, he was content to let friends come
to him, without caring to seek them. But in his intercourse with men of his own age he contracted a few
friendships which he maintained with strict loyalty. To
these he gave all his inmost soul; to them he told all his
plans, all his aspirations. But alas, his confidence only
met with good-natured rebuffs; for his friends were still
tied and bound, as Waring would have said, with the
chain of precedent and public opinion, and dared not call
those men obscure whom the world called famous, dared
not recognise one whom the world had not yet recognised:
and what was he, who, save scribbling a few rough notes,
had done nothing to reveal his inner nature, that he
should claim for himself a place above all the great men
of the day ? But the blows so good-naturedly dealt him
by his friends only seemed to make him tougher : day by
day his strong will and ever youthful individuality
sprang up fresher from renewed rebuffs, and his intellect

grew until a fixed purpose had formed itself. Hitherto he had done nothing but dream and talk; try as he would, he could not make men acknowledge his self-known worth, and still less as it seemed could he by mere talk and jottings of ideas make his plans known to the world. How was he to do this? If he went on dreaming, he must at last sink into a discontented railer; he must indeed acknowledge that these well-meaning friends were right and the world better as it was. Gradually he came to see that he must do some *actual* thing before he could hope to assert his place in the world.

At the very time when the blows seemed to rain thickest, when his spirit seemed most beaten, his inner nature was arming him for a last struggle.

In silence he laid his plans for intellectual escape, but it was to be an escape from bondage to freedom, from the kingship of dreams to the empire of fact. How was he to begin? Seeing how useless his dreaming life had been, his thoughts naturally turned in the opposite direction, towards a life which would admit of no dreaming.

To bid farewell for a time to all imperial visions, to quench his love of abstractions and deal with hard actual facts, was no light thing; but to go away from the intellectual life which had been so dear, so barren of fruit, and learn new lessons from the physical life, was very hard. And yet the thing must be done; he had laid down the principle that no man can prove himself unless he has the energy to develop his body; and now was the time to try how that principle worked. In what way would he arrange his plans for the first step towards physical development? To enlist in the army in London or enter the navy, would be to ensure himself a brute's life for years, and the eventual discovery some day that his intellect was dead indeed. No; whatever the service, it must at least fulfil the condition of giving not only freedom from brutality in its associations, but, if possible, brainwork, though of the lowest sort; it must also chime in with his pre-established sympathies, which rather rebelled against established forms of government.

But in laying his plans for this new life, in which he was to be born again as a babe just awaking in a new world, one important detail did not escape his attention. Hitherto his greatest dreams had been of power; power was the god of his worship, or rather was the hidden jewel which he strove to find and keep. In that placid brow and undemonstrative mouth were lines which indicated a terrible force lurking within, hitherto kept under by perpetual reverses, but nourishing its strength all the same; hitherto kept quiet by the caressing sympathy of his nature, but ready, when occasion should call for it, to leap forth and assert its existence unmistakably.

Thus, while considering how to train his body, he did not forget the importance of that desire to dominate. Some time he meant to use it with a purpose; to take the world 'into his hand, he told you, so!' and in order to fit himself for that consummation he must now choose some bodily employment which would gave him captainship.

Dismissing the idea of serving as a soldier or sailor for England, he glanced for a moment at continental armies. But then, service in them would involve too much attention to drill, too much martinet discipline, to suit Waring's hitherto loose and ungoverned notions; besides which he could scarcely become a soldier at all in Europe (unless he went to the Polish patriots) without serving the cause of one who, in his eyes, was a despot. Spain was too sunk in sloth and immorality; he was not ready yet to regenerate Turkey, whatever dreams he might have; in Sweden and Norway the men were too content: so that soldiership in Europe seemed a useless career, unless he could work for some cause of freedom. Was it the

word 'freedom' that suggested to him Italy? Italy!
Was not hers a cause of freedom? But when he came to
consider it fairly, his mind, hitherto undisciplined, grew
impatient at the thought of the useless embroilment of a
political warfare, such as the cause of Italy would, in his
own judgment, involve; besides which, the first step of
heading a band of Patriots seemed distasteful to him when
he recollected all that he had heard of Italian soldiery;
and he shrank from the name of banditti. Perhaps, too,
he felt himself too untutored at present, and mistrusted
his capability to undertake a cause, which, as he believed,
must, unless thoroughly ably handled, involve much sin
and little good. He was going to begin a new life in an
elementary state of being; what he wanted then was
some simple elemental physical life, some simple elemental
physical command; a life and a post which, while leaving
large room for contemplation, would afford not only
opportunities for stern action, exercise of courage, nerve,
and generalship, but also continual contact with and
influence over a few simple men, unknowing of much*evil,
unscathed by the strong hand of despotism.

Thwarted in every direction on land, his thoughts
turned to the sea; and since no field for his labour was at
present discernible out of Europe, the Mediterranean
must be his training-ground.

He remembered how in former cruises he had seen
smuggling craft, with wine, fruit, tobacco—all kinds of
contraband goods—going up and down like sea-fowl,
rarely harmed, because apparently so inoffensive.

Musing on these, he began to draw a parallel between
their physical and his own intellectual life. They had
found the physical laws of society too hard and binding;
he had found the intellectual laws the same. They had
been always treated as low despicable folk, with no good
in them; so had he. They had rebelled against men's

contempt or repulsion and sought a life for themselves, as he was going to do. They were free, as he hoped to be. Waring, the self-constituted intellectual king of the world, dethroned by those subjects who would never acknowledge his sway, takes the crown from his brow and goes forth;—not to seek fellowship with the prosperous and wealthy, not to commune with other intellects in other lands, but to find brotherhood with the lowest, simplest men, among whom at least he could learn how to love unchecked, and who at least would return his love.

In their company he could learn what the winds and waters sang; why the sunset yearned, the sunrise aspired. They would teach him how to bear and be strong; and while they helped him in hospitable offices, he could show them new paths, new hopes, new aims.

Thus, joining sympathy with the lowest to aims after the highest life, and both these to direct bodily culture, he embarked in the opportunity thus afforded for developing old dreams all his capital of energy, and deserved to succeed.

His sun has set in England, the ship of his life has sailed beyond the extreme sea-line; the star of Waring will be seen no more in English skies. But there are other heavens;—

In Vishnu land what Avatar?

Look at him gradually stealing his way into the hearts of his sailors, until they changed from wild simple loving men, to instructed cultivated thrifty seamen, with hopes beyond plunder, fears beyond priesthood, and desires for better things than a wild sea life and occasional debauches. Is this Waring the dreamer? This man who, firm-sinewed and healthy of brain, is brother and captain to these poor contrabandists? He and they have done for each other the utmost they could do in this poor earth; but he has bade them a passionate farewell for a new work, and a new life. Like lovers he and they have been. Have they not sung songs and prayed prayers beneath the yearning sky, in front of the unknown sunsets? Have they not given healing and help to all who needed it, man, woman, and child? Waring, in his sailors' eyes, is god-like: they think he holds in his bosom secrets of heaven and earth. The fame of his craft, courage, and strength will ring down the shores of the Mediterranean for many years, when he has passed away. Is this Waring the dreamer?

But there is work to be done yet; and his strong individual nature and a kind of selfishness in him demand work which gives fruition. Seeing as he does, that any attempt at regeneration in Europe must eventuate in failure at first, in a mad striving after impossible ends, and certainly in much bloodshed, remembering that he himself could expect, even if he attempted any such regeneration, no sight of that for which he has toiled, he falls back on that idea of working simple elemental natures which has proved such a success, and determines to apply the same principle in a wider field.

Europe sickens his peculiarly fastidious intellect: there is too much civilisation, too much intrigue, too much hurry, and, as he thinks, too much selfishness. Where in the world are there men who, while more advanced in intellect than the sailors, have their grand simplicity, their love and hospitality, their pure reverence? Not in Europe, nor in Africa, nor probably in America. But are there no Eastern races with creeds, philosophers, poets of their own, scarcely a word of whose wisdom or beauty has reached these cold regions; What of India? There England, which has discarded Waring, exercises what he considers the most gigantic despotism of the earth; there the European, tyrannising, not over other Europeans, but over the inferior brain of the Asiatic, forces him to yield up his rich land to aggrandise the greatest merchant race in the world. What war can be holier than a crusade against invaders not only of hearths and homes, but of morals, religion, intellectual life, and all the inner feelings of a great but enervated nation ?

Here in the East may Waring's star rise, to lead a new company of wise men to their redemption; he perchance will be the man who shall bring to triumphant fulfilment that idea of emancipation of India from European thraldom which, since Waring was seen in Triest bay, has already made itself felt through the fervid words of a few earnest thinkers.

Now what lessons does the poet intend that we should learn by this life of Waring, such as it has been, such as it will be ? These lessons seem to be two: one which concerns Waring's character, the other which concerns the responsibilities of his friends towards him.

In the manner of Waring's development of his own nature, we observe throughout a carelessness of other people's opinion and an apparent selfishness in pursuing his own ends. But when a man has, as Waring seems to have had, certain fixed ideas, no matter what, of whose truth he feels certain, is it not better for him to work them out by himself, to make mistakes it may be, and have to tread over again the old ground, thus losing much time; is it not better, so soon as he has discovered any one idea which is indubitably his own, that he should carry it out to its furthest consequences, always judging for himself as much, and consulting others as little, as possible ? Is it not better, in short, to keep each man's individuality pure and unsullied, so far as possible ? This world of men, though it be a great whole, is yet made up of men each of whom is a world in himself; each has doubtless the same groundwork of nature, but in the common attributes of each one there are such wide differences in degree as to constitute almost differences in kind. It is by the proper use of these differences of degree that the work of the world is carried on; and wherever any one natural attribute is so peculiarly developed in a man as to amount almost to an individual quality, it is surely the man's duty to make that attribute do its fullest work by employing it to the utmost, so far as he honestly can. That attribute is a thing with an innate force of its own; it grows with daily exercise; if it receives assistance from other minds it rapidly degenerates in strength, just like a child for ever walking in leading strings; losing its self-supporting power, it does not perform half the work in the world which it would perform if self-nurtured. Let it then be subjected to the rigorous exercise which it will be sure to give itself, if left alone to the man's own self-esteem and the help of his other faculties.

On such grounds as these it was thoroughly right for Waring to dream out his dreams, so long as he kept clearly before him what he was doing; his dreams perpetually led him into mistakes, but those mistakes made him patient, roused his ingenuity, kept his faith in exercise by the perpetual whipping of doubt; and at last drove his soul onward to that step whose wisdom was proved by its issue.

Waring, who was not ashamed to blot out all his past life almost as if it had not been, who did not flinch from learning all his lesson of life afresh like a little child, was a stronger man at the end of the mental struggle through which he passed to gain that step than he was at its beginning, just as a man is stronger at the end than he was at the beginning of a course of physical training; and the consequences showed themselves in any influence for good which he had with the sailors; may show themselves in future influences for good in India. Whatever good has been done or shall be done hereafter will have been accomplished by means of that stern development of self, as distinguished from absorption into other minds, which Waring strove to work out.

But what shall we say of the responsibilities of his friends? Here were men who by ordinary insight, might have seen that they had a prince among them; a rare nature, which, instead of being crushed and thwarted, should have been gently encouraged and soothed; a nature which these common men ought to have been well content only to have kept alive. But instead of this, they perpetually baffled him by senseless laughter and more senseless exhortations: and had not the power of his individuality sustained him, had not his strong kindly insight into all human nature kept his temper true, his intellect must have died beneath their hands. As it was their punishment was adequate; for by their blundering they lost, not only for themselves but for England and for Europe too, a soul which would have shone like a beacon to light all nations.

Every man of us is responsible to himself and to the world for the manner in which he treats the intellect of every companion, be that intellect great or small: how much more then is he responsible, not only to himself and to the world but to that companion, if he fails to do all he can to foster any exceptional powers which may lie hid under an uncongenial surface?

The murder of a man's soul is just as culpable as the murder of his body. The men who would not acknowledge Waring till it was too late were indeed to all intents killers of his soul, although they did not succeed in crushing him; and every man who sins as they sinned will have a bitter reckoning to pay some day, either to himself or the world, when the divinity which might have saved us soars away in sad disgust from an unappreciative humanity.

## 'BEFORE' AND 'AFTER'

THESE two poems, in a few lines, place before us a series of arguments on the duty of men to avenge wrong. The motive of the poems is a quarrel which has taken place between two men; and the arguments used both for and against the prosecution of the quarrel are vivified, first in the mind of a bystander, roused by a sense of wrong done somewhere, second in the mind of the wronged man, when he has glutted his vengeance.

Few of the author's works, even including his dramas, display so fully as does the poem called 'Before,' the universal existence in mankind, not only of a natural striving after the truth, but also of that hatred of tyranny and wrong, high faith, and stern sense of justice above forgiveness, which prompt the feeling, very seldom expressed, that we are here as champions for the right, and cannot afford to carry out to the utmost Christian principles; while in the few lines called 'After,' we have an equally masterly delineation of the remorse which attacks a brave kindly man, whose blood, roused a moment ago to madness, has now, after he has wrought his vengeance, sunk to an ebb in solemn repentance.

The scene in 'Before,' shows us two men who have on a sudden determined to refer a deadly quarrel to the ordeal of battle.

The usual peacemaker is there, the usual bellicose second.

But there is also present a man who, perhaps, seeing clearer than either of these what must be the consequences of letting such a quarrel right itself, and in order if possible to get at the truth, puts before the peacemaker a number of arguments, clear, forcible and complete in themselves, though not unanswerable.

> Let them fight it out, friend, things have gone too far ;
> God must judge the couple ! leave them as they are,
> Whichever one's the guiltless, to his glory,
> And whichever one the guilt's with, to my story.

> Why, you would not bid men, sunk in such a slough,
> Strike no arm out further, stick and stink as now,
> Leaving right and wrong to settle the embroilment,
> Heaven with snaky hell, in torture and entoilment ?

The thought which we may fairly express in prose as that which is the key to the meaning of this poem is as follows :

Here have two men quarrelled, and we do not know which is the wrongdoer, which the wronged man : all we do know is that a wrong has been done.

Both men are eager to fight, urged either by hate, fear of suspense, or desire for vengeance.

This being so, no human judgment can avail to settle the dispute; for the wrongdoer will not confess, and if he did, the wronged man's blood is so hot, that confession and human penalty will not suffice him. So he must leave them to the impulses which God gave them, impulses whose springs we cannot see, but which God alone can work, and will work to the displaying of the truth. For if the wronged man gets the victory, as he ought to do, his remorse (he being human) will too surely force him into speech which will show clearly that it was the dead (or conquered) man who did the wrong. If the wrongdoer gets the victory, *his* remorse, doubly severe for his first wrong, and the second shame of killing an innocent man, will force the truth from *his* lips.

Thus, in any event, the truth must appear; and when a wrong has been done, it is better that it should come to the world's sight, even through the death of one man, than that the mystery should remain untold, making a festering sore of lies in the wrongdoer, a festering sore of injury unavenged in the wronged man ; and leaving the world at large in suspense and puzzlement, to deal its random blows of judgment and criticism against both alike, and through them against all mankind, who are bound alike in the chain of fellowship, and no one of whom can suffer without affecting the rest.

If we are to leave every entanglement to be unravelled by abstract laws of right and wrong, with no agency of man, we shall find ourselves in a slough of calamity indeed; the age of miracles is past; God is silent, and has retreated behind a veil of centuries; He leaves men now to work out the world by themselves, and having so left them, He will never be too hard in judging a little wrong, done to secure a great right, the right of truth.

Thus we have dealt with the wrong done, as it must exist in one of these two men.

Now let us deal with each of the two in turn, and see how they will be better or worse for fighting the quarrel out.

> Who's the culprit of them ?   How must he conceive
> God—the queen he caps to, laughing in his sleeve,
> ' 'Tis but decent to profess oneself beneath her ;
> Still, one must not be too much in earnest, either !'
>
> Better sin the whole sin, sure that God observes,
> Than go live his life out !   Life will try his nerves,
> When the sky, which noticed all, makes no disclosure,
> And the earth keeps up her terrible composure.

Let him pace at pleasure, past the walls of rose,
Plucks their fruits when grape trees graze him as he goes.
For he 'gins to guess the purpose of the garden.
With the sly mute thing beside there for a warden.

What's the leopard dog thing, constant at his side,
A leer and lie in every eye of its obsequious hide?
When will come an end of all the mock obeisance,
And the price appear which pays for the misfeasance

First, says the speaker, take the wrongdoer. It is
obvious, that having dared to do this wrong, he must be
in the habit of thinking of God as he thinks of the queen,
whose courtier he is; he must say to himself about God,
as he says to himself about his queen—'For the world's
sake, for general opinion, I must seem to reverence God
outwardly as I do the queen; but I must preserve a shred
of independence in my inner self; I must not let my
conscience be too much fettered by moral restraints, for if
I do, I shall lose what I care for most, the right I claim to
do what I like to secure my own ends, always taking care
not to render myself amenable to the penalties of social
laws in what I do.' So *he* must look on that secret God.

Which, then, is the better for him? To go on in a
craven lying life, never asserting, never denying (in words
at least) that he has done the wrong; or to dare all consequences, human and divine, and carry his wrong to its
furthest bound?

Surely, God will judge him with a less harsh judgment
*if* he at least shows desperate courage, and faces his lie
out to the end, than he would if the man shrank from
that test, and fearing at once God's judgment and men's
censure, feared death as well.

Then, for his own development, which is the better?
Here, again, conscience, his second god, shows which is
the better. If he dares not fight, life and his conscience
will gradually sap his strength, gradually eat out his vital

force; and he will shrink to a crawling reptile. Let him lap himself in pleasure, take the flowers and the fruits of this life; for all that, his sin will ever accompany him like a leopard at his side, ready to spring and throttle him at any moment. He will see too clearly what this garden of his life is; what its enjoyments might be, what its fruit for himself; he will see all this, and for very fear of that leopard, sin, he will not dare to take his eyes off it, he will be obliged to turn from enjoying all the sweets of the garden, lest ceasing to watch he be taken at unawares. 'When,' he will madly exclaim, 'When shall this horrible suspense come to an end? When will this fearful sin spring and kill me, to put an end to this life, which is a torture?'

And then, for the world, which is the better? Is it not better, first, that the truth be driven out of this man, as we have pointed out, and, secondly, that the world be rid, if possible, if necessary, of the canker of a being who is false?

> So much for the culprit. Who's the martyred man?
> Let him bear one stroke more, for be sure he can!
> He that strove thus evil's lump with good to leaven,
> Let him give his blood at last, and get his heaven!
>
> All or nothing, stake it! Trusts he God or no?
> Thus far and no farther? farther? Be it so!
> Now, enough of your chicane of prudent pauses,
> Sage provisos, sub-intents, and saving clauses!
>
> Ah 'forgive, you bid him? While God's champion lives,
> Wrong shall be resisted; dead, why he forgives.
> But you must not end my friend ere you begin him;
> Evil stands not crowned on earth, while breath is in him!

Second, take the wronged man. He has endured one wrong. Suppose the worst, suppose he is killed. If he has borne one wrong, can he not bear another? Will he not, in dying for an innocent cause, atone for his sins, and

win Heaven by his atonement ?   Does he not, in fighting,
show that his desire is for the good, that he considers
himself God's champion for right against wrong ?   May
he not well afford to stake his truth against the chance of
death ? may he not well trust that the veiled God will
surely arbitrate aright, either here or hereafter ?   Yes !
he trusts God, he shall not fail.

Suppose, on the other hand, the possibility of his killing
the wrongdoer.   Will you on that possibility bid him
forgive, in order that he may spare life ?

I say to you that since God has veiled Himself, and
does not now declare right and wrong by unmistakable
signs as of yore, the man who knows of a wrong is bound
as God's champion to avenge that wrong.   And, as before
said, God, whose world this is, will forgive and mend the
slight fault for the sake of the great gain.   If indeed the
man dies, his death, in itself a sacrifice, is forgiveness of
the wrong.

Again :  if it is a man's duty, knowing wrong, to avenge
it for God's sake, when the moment of vengeance arrives,
he begins a new life, becomes a new man, as God's
champion to avenge that wrong.   If he, knowing the
wrong, and his duty as a champion, were to abstain from
doing vengeance, and were to forgive, he would be taking
on himself the office of judge instead, and would indeed
be ending his new life, given him by God for the purpose of fighting that battle, before he had well begun it.

No ! the only thing that can save the fight is that
the wrongdoer should confess his wrong, and thus in
the cause of truth rise in spirit on his own trampled
morality.

> Once more—will the wronger, at this last of all,
> Dare to say ' I did wrong,' rising in his fall ?
> No !   Let go, then !  both the fighters to their places !
> While I count three, step you back as many paces !

### AFTER

Take the cloak from his face, and at first
Let the corpse do its worst.

How he lies in his rights of a man !
Death has done all death can.
And absorbed in the new life he leads,
    He recks not, he heeds
Nor his wrong nor my vengeance—both strike
    On his senses alike,
    And are lost in the solemn and strange
        Surprise of the change.

Ha ! what avails death to erase
    His offence, my disgrace ?
I would we were boys as of old
    In the field, by the fold ;
His outrage, God's patience, man's scorn
    Were so easily borne.

I stand here now, he lies in his place ;
    Cover the face.

After the fight, all the impulses which God gave to
man to blind his tenderness when right must be done,
ebb and still ; and in the great mercy of that God, the
memory of the tendernesses of a loving past, of the
innocence and youth of their past companionship, comes
surging up to choke and overwhelm the champion who a
moment ago was so terrible.

For God keeps himself veiled for a purpose ; He will
not let it be known by clear manifestation what He thinks
right, what He thinks wrong, lest thereby men lose all
sense of responsibility, and become mere vegetables.
Still He keeps a veil of doubt hanging over them, and will
not let the clear light be seen, lest men be blinded and
lose their sight, lest they die in the swooning splendour
of a perfect day.  Thus it is that what seemed right on

the other side of a deed, seems wrong on this ; thus it is that before the mystic uncertain face of death the proudest courage quails.

Shall we say that this man's death was of no use ? Had he lived, where would have been the yearning backward thoughts of the time when indeed he was innocent and pure ?   Where would have been that very tenderness of life, that rising of an inexpressible sympathy ?   But now, the lesson God has taught is this : you shall find out what is right and what is wrong for yourselves ; you shall strive blindly for the right, and shall in striving to get it buffet many men, and suffer much yourself.   But do not despair.   Every unworthy buffet given to others shall remind you in its consequences that you are not infallible ; that you might perhaps have looked deeper, and seen clearer.   Thus you will have learned one lesson : thus you will gain in courage, in sympathy, in experience, in all that makes a man.

# CHILDE ROLAND

'THE words of genius,' says George Eliot, 'bear a wider meaning than the thought which prompted them.' After long and careful study of and reflection on this poem of Childe Roland, after several fruitless attempts to decipher the exact meaning which the poet desired to put before the world, the passage above quoted seemed to sound in my ears like a possible help to interpretation. I know that it is no light thing to attribute meanings to a poem which the maker of it would disclaim ; but the present romance is so full of suggestiveness and possibility of second meaning that I should not feel justified in passing it by in silence or with no more than a slight comment. For when I see, as I am obliged to see, that in power of words, in graphic drawing, and even in dramatic force, it stands among the foremost of Browning's works ; when looking through all he has done I observe how very thrifty he is of his words, how seldom he writes down a phrase or a line unless he has some aim beyond mere abstract force or beauty of expression, I cannot but think that in his mind there was some second meaning, some hidden lesson intended to be conveyed.

Whether or no I have hit the right meaning I feel by no means confident ; but at least I have I hope given a consistent plan to the thought which the poem awoke in me, and I even venture to believe that that thought may find here and there a response in other men's minds.

The subject of the poem may be described as follows :—
At the end of a long day, the last of a series of years of
travail and search, a man who has been enrolled among a
band of knights organised for the purpose of finding out
a certain mysterious stronghold called the Dark Tower,
and who is the last of the band, finds himself at a place
where from the highway an uncertain path strikes out
towards the sunset. All his companions dead, many of
them proved false, he is weary at heart. He does not
know whether to take this path towards the sunset or
not ; and in despair asks an old cripple who sits at its
entrance, which is the way to the Dark Tower. The old
man says nothing ; but with a seemingly malicious leer
points with his crutch along that westward path, and
makes no sign other than the scarcely suppressed glee
with which he observes the knight's mistrust.

Weary of his quest, utterly lost to hope, the knight,
firmly convinced the while that the cripple is lying to
him, turns down the path, with no feeling in his paralysed
heart save a longing that at least he may fail like his
peers, if only to bring the bitterness of life to a close.

### v.

As when a sick man very near to death
  Seems dead indeed, and feels begin and end
  The tears, and takes the farewell of each friend,
And hears one bid the other go, draw breath
Freelier outside ('since all is o'er,' he saith,
  'And the blow fallen no grieving can amend ;')

### vi.

While some discuss if near the other graves
  Be room enough for this, and when a day
  Suits best for carrying the corpse away,
With care about the banners, scarves and staves,—
And still the man hears all, and only craves
  He may not shame such tender love and stay.

### VII.

Thus, I had so long suffered in this quest,
  Heard failure prophesied so oft, been writ
  So many times among ' The Band '—to wit,
The knights who to the Dark Tower's search addressed
Their steps—that just to fail as they, seemed best,
  And all the doubt was now—should I be fit.

### VIII.

So, quiet as despair, I turned from him,
  That hateful cripple, out of his highway
  Into the path he pointed.  All the day
Had been a dreary one at best, and dim
Was settling to its close, yet shot one grim
  Red leer to see the plain catch its estray.

No sooner had he turned down the path, than he looked back again in mistrust.  But it is too late ; cripple and high road are gone ; there is nothing in front but the evening ; nothing but grey plain all round :—

Nothing but plain to the horizon's bound ;
I might go on ; nought else remained to do.

The plain is a very waste of sterility ; he comes upon traces of past life, but it is life which seems to have grudged all other life, for the dock-leaves are trampled and bruised :—

——'tis a brute must walk,
Pashing their life out, with a brute's intents.

He has seen but one live thing besides himself since he entered the plain, and that is a half-dead half-asleep blind horse.  Utterly maddened by this hideous travesty of past labour, the knight tries to rouse his own ebbing life by memory of past faith in his companions.  He is rewarded by mocking recollections of their faithlessness.  He is roused from that retrospect to find himself suddenly come upon a little black river, wrathfully foaming along:

> So petty yet so spiteful ! all along,
>   Low scrubby alders kneeled down over it,
>   Drenched willows flung them headlong in a fit
> Of mute despair, a suicidal throng ;
> The river which had done them all the wrong,
>   Whate'er that was, rolled on, deterred no whit.

In his morbid condition of brain he imagines dead men lying at the bottom of the river as he crosses it, and fancies he hears a baby cry from beneath its waves as he plunges his spear to seek for hollows.   When he reaches the other side he finds traces, which almost bear out his nameless terrors, of a desperate battle.   But there is no footprint to or from the battle ground.

Next he comes on evidence of what seems archaic cruelty ; a strange engine of a wheel, looking like a monstrous torture machine, but now ruined and useless,

> ——with all the air
> Of Tophet's tool, on earth left unaware,
>   Or brought to sharpen its rusty teeth of steel.

#### XXV.

> Then came a bit of stubbed ground, once a wood,
>   Next a marsh, it would seem, and now mere earth
>   Desperate and done with ; (so a fool finds mirth,
> Makes a thing and then mars it, till his mood
> Changes, and off he goes !) within a rood—
>   Bog, clay, and rubble, sand and stark black dearth.

#### XXVI.

> Now blotches rankling, coloured gay and grim,
>   Now patches where some leanness of the soil's
>   Broke into moss or substances like boils ;
> Then came some palsied oak, a cleft in him
> Like a distorted mouth that splits its rim
>   Gaping at death, and dies while it recoils.

Still no help, no path.

When suddenly, silently, a great black bird sails past, and with its wings brushes his cap. And, as if this strange omen had awakened his sense of sight, he becomes aware that the plain has given place to mountains all round, and finds that he can get no further. But just as he was going to give up the search altogether,

> ———came a click
> As when a trap shuts—you're inside the den !

### XXX.

> Burningly it came on me all at once,
>   This was the place ! those two hills on the right,
>   Crouched like two bulls locked horn in horn in fight;
> While to the left, a tall scalped mountain. . . . Dunce,
> Fool, to be dozing at the very nonce,
>   After a life spent training for the sight !

### XXXI.

> What in the midst lay but the tower itself ?
>   The round squat turret, blind as the fool's heart,
>   Built of brown stone, without a counterpart
> In the whole world.  The tempest's mocking elf
> Points to the shipman thus the unseen shelf
>   He strikes on, only when the timbers start.

The dying sunset kindles ; the solemn pealing of inexpressible sound tolls increasing, and shapes itself into articulate words:

> Names in my ears,
> Of all the lost adventurers my peers,—
> How such a one was strong, and such was bold,
> And such was fortunate, yet each of old
>   Lost ! lost ! one moment knelled the woe of years.

### XXXIV.

> There they stood, ranged along the hillsides, met
>   To view the last of me, a living frame
>   For one more picture ! in a sheet of flame

> I saw them and I knew them all. And yet
> Dauntless the slug-horn to my lips I set,
> And blew. ' Childe Roland to the Dark Tower came.'

Such is the story told by this terrible poem, every word of which seems to speak of one of those deep hid unspoken tragedies which convulse the intellectual and moral life of man here and there.

In this connection the remarks with which the Essay on ' Waring ' is prefaced are in some degree applicable to ' Childe Roland ' ; for, like that romance, ' Childe Roland ' is eminently incomplete, eminently suggestive. There are, however, differences in the two poems, quite apart from their subject-matter. The impression left on the mind of the reader by ' Childe Roland ' is stronger than that left by ' Waring,' although such impression is of a vaguer, stranger, grimmer sort. In ' Waring' we felt ourselves at least on human ground ; but here the imagery and fancies are weird and unearthly, and sometimes rise into grandeur. We scarcely dare to think whither the poet is leading us so boldly. Does he summon us to the Gate of Death ?—is it the very God Himself whose wings seem to almost fan us as we walk along that awful plain with the lonely wanderer at set of day? Both God and devil seem to be there, though unseen ; and the terrible evidence of effects without visible causes, chills our hearts with nameless horror. And yet let us reassure ourselves, and remember that we are dealing with nothing but human attributes ; that it is humanity which soars the highest and plunges the lowest in joy or sorrow ; that humanity is capable of the most tremendous convulsions and changes ; and that the highest force in the terror of even the most awful and so-called supernatural phenomena is the result of human thought or imagination, the work of human brains.

Now it is obvious that if we are to treat this poem as a

mere legend, graphically written, to speak of it would not come properly within the scope of these Essays ; but if, as I believe and have already hinted, we are justified in assigning to it some second meaning, then we can scarcely go too far in the importance we attach to every line, nay, almost to every word of it.

The purpose with which that band of knights set out may have been any purpose you please which had the truth and purity for its object.

That 'round squat turret . . . without a counterpart in the whole world '—may it not be some strange, seemingly fantastic end, which men have proposed to themselves ere now, as the one end which had in it the truth, and was of power to set the world free and make it happy ? Does it not often happen that such ends, pursued with varying energy and sometimes flagging interest, are only kept in the minds of their promoters by a dim mystery of doubt which hangs over them ? And when, as will sometimes happen, the end comes in sight very unexpectedly, does it not often strangely fall short of preconceived ideas, and stand up in hideous prosaicness amid the tragic signs around it of the toil, warfare and struggle through which it was won ? Surely all this is sometimes only too true. But let the man's end be what it would, all had failed save himself, and he desired nothing but failure. Whatever the purpose was, it had no visible, tangible landmarks ; it had been known only in the hearts of its adherents, and in their speech one with another. Happy years ago they had been cheered by the great hope because it was far off ; here and there a failure or a stumble did not affect them, for were there not years of futurity to retrieve losses ? In their youth and strength they counted stumbles and bruises as nothing, little thinking that the time would come when all these were so many steps lost. One after one had dropped into the night ; and each one, as he dropped away, dragged down with him some shred wrenched from the garment of hope which kept the survivors warm.   When at last all were gone except this lonely man, he felt himself naked to the chill blast of despair, and only desired to numb his senses by death, in order to escape the bitterness of remorse.

Who has not felt this allegory in his own life ?   For a man begins—every man begins—with some purpose in which he is buoyed up by the knowledge that other men are striving as he is, or have striven as he strives.   In the long happy years of youth he goes on collecting evidences of success, and noting evidences of failure ; but they are the evidences of success which he keeps, with which he warms himself, from which he makes for himself the garment of hope ; the evidences of failure he throws aside as worthless, rejoicing in his strength, and forgetting that those failures, if woven in with the successes, would make him a garment in which fear made many strands ; a garment which, perpetually pricking his flesh, kept hardening it and inuring it to that future when he must cast it aside and bear to go alone and unshielded.   Because he has not kept these sterner threads, we find him abject and purposeless ; this is why his faith is gone ; for faith is not only the belief that what has been will be, but it is the conviction that what has not been, what has failed to be, will be, somewhere, somewhen, if only the purpose be kept clear before the eyes, if only no effort be left unmade, no failure or bruise left to cure or heal itself.   Every failure turned to account on the spot, every bruise utilised at the time by extracting from it pain for the present, will surely eventuate in additional hardness for the future.

And now let us bring these floating thoughts into some sort of connected whole, and trace the man's life from its beginning, to see how and why he came in this strait ; let us try and trace also what may be the end to this man, even after the terrible catastrophe is past in which we leave him.

Now, as in this Essay, and here and there in those which succeed it, I shall venture on ground which is, and always will be, dangerous in a controversial point of view, let me at once discharge my duty as an essayist by declaring, on the one hand, my personal conviction as to a certain vital point in the subject, and by acknowledging, on the other hand, the convictions or conclusions of other men. Let me, in short, while freely acknowledging for my own part my personal conviction of the existence of a God, inscrutable, passionate, ever-labouring, acknowledge as freely the fact that such a conviction is possessed with by no means equal intensity by other men. So that, as it is my purpose to bring the thought of this and other poems within the mental appreciation of as wide a circle of thinkers as possible, I may be the better able to take a ground on which all may stand with me, and draw conclusions, watch, blame, or praise for reasons which must sway our common humanity.

Whether there be a God or no God ; whether God is the all-pervading nature, or is only millions of forces, each acting on its atom in the world, or is again a person and a shape somewhere in the sky; every man has at least certain feelings, inseparable from his emotional part, however kept under or stifled by his reasoning part, which stand him oftener or seldomer in the place of a God; no man can have gone through his life without the dim sense of a darkness which his eye cannot pierce, of a presence behind or within that darkness which his flesh creeps at the possible touch of.

And so, in the words which follow, if I here and there speak of God as an assumed existence, let each reader bring to his perusal of them his own deepest convictions on the subject; or if he has conquered all such, let him try to allow that in himself too the feelings I have spoken of sometimes assert themselves.

When a child comes into the world, he comes to live a life, and possesses certain attributes which shall enable him to live that life well or ill, as the consent of men calls well or ill. During his childhood, he is blessed with eyes which see things in a rosy light, a sense of hearing which makes him listen as to the strains of a heavenly choir. He is fenced round with precious sights and sounds, which are precious because of that rose light, because of that divine harmony. The sight and the hearing of the child seem to us like God's spirit which moves brooding over him in every step of his path, and will not let disease or ill thoughts touch him. That is how the child is made naturally; youth is strong in its earlier years to resist the evil influences which afterwards too surely mar and maim him, and which men have called the work of the devil. Nay, for some time after those evil influences begin to hurt him their effect is transient; for however immoral he may eventually become, he is blessed oftener or seldomer with the power of wondering, which is the spring of reverence : and reverence, when once he has it, oftener or seldomer acts as a shield against the arrows of sin, acts as a light to illumine his path. So, step by step, every day a step, the child goes on in his life journey, until he comes to youth. Then as his brain becomes stronger, his imagination becomes more brilliant; imagination increases his power to wonder, wonder strengthens his reverence, and for a time at least he is more pure than in the early child days. He gets a far off look in his eyes, and everything in the world has a fresh significance for him as his soul's horizon daily widens, as each thing comes within the range of it. His path, too, which before was indistinct, soft, with tempting bypaths on all hands, becomes more clearly marked out, and flowers border it, making every step he takes a pleasure. Before, he strayed aimless in a balmy plain, heavy with flower scents; gradually, he knows not how, the clear-defined path appears more beautiful than all the rest of the world. For the feeling of self-consciousness is beginning; it is in its concentrating power like the clearly marked path to the aimless wanderer. Then comes the knowledge, whence he knows not, that he possesses what seem to him fearful and wonderful faculties; and then comes the feeling, whence he knows not, that he must possess all these for some purpose. His eyes, which have gazed all round him, look upwards now. Turning them upward to where the clouds are, and the sky, he seems to see moving above him a spirit, nameless, awful in power. The Spirit of God ! he whispers with hushed breath. And his reverence takes a concrete form, for the wonder is at its height. God becomes all in all to him; he knows not how it is, but he feels within him that it is God who gave him these attributes, and knowing no more he strains in agony for a further knowledge. Not getting it, he turns to think of the attributes themselves, and what they can do; and having plainly the concrete idea of God, he comes to the conclusion, more or less distinctly, that at least He who gave them must have given them for a purpose, though he knows not what the purpose is. This is a step further; before he only knew in himself that he had the attributes, but knew not whence they came. Now he sees, or thinks he sees, that the purpose is in God's breast. But failing to see what God's purpose is, he begins to turn about and examine the various attributes and see which of them is likeliest to prove a motive power. He finds that he has judgment, a distinct consciousness that this is right and that is wrong; fear, hope, desire. He sees that it is his judgment which is the motive power, and he turns to improve and strengthen that; and having decided so far, and being still convinced that he has his judgment for a purpose (unknown) of God, he begins to feel another sensation, that of responsibility to God. He uses his judgment naturally in the first instance to find out, if possible, what is God's purpose in giving him the other attributes; and decides probably at length that God has given him these qualities to use as one piece of a vast machinery, which is the world. He tries more or less to do nothing without consulting his judgment; and in the exercise of his judgment he falls to observing the ways of the world around him. Very quickly follows, as the first result of this observation, a new feeling, which comes like the rest as an effect without visible cause; and which compels him into the observance of some rule of life by which he shall exercise his attributes in accordance with some standard, either set up by the world, or formed by his own mind on deductions from what the world does. This feeling, or this setting up of a standard, is the feeling, the laying down of a law, of right and wrong. The moral sense is born in him. Of this moral sense he knows not the reason, but he is always more or less compelled by his judgment to follow it, and to appeal to it in every emergency.

Hitherto he has used his reason hardly at all; his processes of thought have been 'instincts, blind, unreasoned out'; but a time comes when he meets with fellow-travellers, and exchanges ideas with them. Then his reason comes into play; and he gradually begins to formulate some actual plan of life, to lay down some actual rule by which he may turn his faculties to a definite use, which shall identify and give a name to the mere abstract use of pleasing God by fulfilling his part as an item in the machinery of the world. Thus gradually between himself and his companions, or in contemplation of past men, a plan is formed which he will mature, either with companions or without, as best he may. The plan developes itself and grows; new members are perhaps added to the number of fellow-travellers, new ideas spring up. But hitherto, while each depends on the others, and would be nothing without them, there is no plan common to all. Each has his own standard, his own aim. While union is their strength (for none have individuality enough to walk alone) their union is merely useful at present to keep each on his legs, and is of no use in developing any one plan which shall gain enormous force by the concentration of many minds on one purpose. But affection begins to work on one and all of them, and they are soon bound in a strong chain of fellowship, pure and simple. This affection and fellowship tends to additional and more frequent interchange of ideas; and before long — out of sympathies which all find they possess in common—some one plan, dear to all, is fused and welded into a whole, into an end which all may pursue together and help each other to pursue. Then come rebuffs and failures to one and another; but these are easily borne and lightly thought of because of the fellowship and affection. Their failures are thrown aside; it is their successes which they remember. Then, perhaps, one after another leaves the band, to work out the idea in some branch of it, or in its main point, in some other journey. Then, perhaps, some fail, some turn traitors, some are disgraced this way or that.

At last the child grown man is left alone, he alone to pursue that path which the rest have pursued; all of them have failed.

Now a point comes in the man's life, when the idea of God gradually fades, and at last withdraws itself altogether, the spirit ceases to visibly accompany him in his path, and the scales fall from his eyes. Now he sees, not with the glorified vision of youth; now he hears, not with the tingling sense of youth; but with actual commonplace eyes and ears.    It seems as if a voice has said to him: I have brought you thus far on your journey; you have gained judgment, moral sense, reason; you have taken from your companions all that they could give you of love and esteem, and you know wherein they are false or true.    You have had the benefit of fellowship in your failures or successes; I have been near you too.    You have had the chance of estimating the value of both failure and success, and have lessons enough to last your lifetime.    Now I show you that I have given you these attributes to use for your own absolute development as part of a whole; but the attribute of wonder, the attribute of reverence must stop here, except so far as you choose to make use of them for your own absolute development. I will not help you by visible signs along the road; I will no longer give you pleasures without any labour of your own; I will give you neither new companions nor a new past to work on; you must now use those old companionships and the past which I showed you, and trace each to its farthest limit.    Everything must be done by yourself: you must make of everything you see, whether it be beautiful or ungracious, the best use that is possible.

Thus in his journey the man comes to this point, when he sees clearly how much his energy has been nourished by adventitious aid; how much of his truth-seeking has been due to flattery of friends, their affection, his own transcendentalism, his obstinate refusal to see the possibility of mistake; how much his courage has been due to his blindness to danger, his seeming triumphant success to the ignorance of failure.

And now, when all these aids are gone, and he is really left to rely on himself, comes the time when his mettle is tried indeed.

He finds himself alone: the last day of his youth is settling to its close, and he feels more and more lonely. For he sees that failure is more than success, he sees that one man and another has dropped out of the ranks of the battle dead or disabled: he is no longer able to comfort himself with other men's success, to plume himself on other men's failure. On the contrary, the failures which he ignored before, now arise in appalling phantom shapes to mock him; God has retreated behind the cloud, and he is left alone to do battle, with failing limbs and an aching heart, against the terrible enemies who rouse themselves out of the twilight of his life. He begins to feel what it is to be left without God in the world—the God who has, he thinks, voluntarily left him, but who perhaps really watches afar off with that inexpressible yearning to help which is the greatest prototype of all human love.

And now comes the time when it behoves the man, out of the tangled mass of contradictions he sees in the world, to judge what is to be done and what is to be left undone. For not only must he separate true from false, but he must also use the false as well as the true, and extract from the false all that is true in it. He must leave nothing untried; he must not reject counsel offered by a lying tongue, or help offered by a false hand; he must take both counsel and help, making sure that he himself sees and uses only what will be of service to his purpose. If at that crucial test, at that supreme moment —(such are of daily occurrence in the world, and happen once at least to every man); if then his mistrust rises and nearly overwhelms him; if he fails to use his own judgment and reason; if, when it becomes necessary to ask the way, he asks with a spirit weary with striving, weary with much failure, and without that faith which is the higher knowledge veiled—that faith without which no work is done—then begins his time of trial; then,

too, begins his time of regeneration.    Trite as the saying
may be, it is worth while to repeat it here, that no man
achieves an end without failure first, the more disastrous
the better.    Failure is the baptism of fire, the new birth
which shall rise and become the truth.    Having lost his
faith, poor Childe Roland still asks of the cripple who
sits there, which is his road.    Because the cripple looks
like a liar, he will not trust him; that is to say, that at
this point of unbelief in a man's career he uses his reason
too much, forgets that he must use bad instruments as
well as good, and that a lie may often be the road to truth,
if only a man will refuse to remember that it is a lie, or
rather will strive his utmost to extract from it all the
truth he can.    But instead of this, he only thinks of it
as a lie, and starting with this thought, he becomes
desperate, and takes the road pointed out in sheer sickness of heart and desire to end his life one way or another.
From that moment his purpose is dead, unless some
exceptional convulsion shakes it into life again; and
from that moment it is worth while to follow him down
the darkened road, if only we may learn by his stumbles
to avoid the pitfalls.    Now, then, he comes on a new
phase of life.    His failure to use his faith, his failure to
see the germ of truth in the lie, is punished at once; his
safe road is gone: he stands blank and purposeless in a
grey plain of chaotic doubt.    His faith gone, his power of
buoyancy is gone, and his power of reason too.    He is
left at the end of his day, with that grey plain all round
him, an evening of dull middle age and old age stretching
far into the distance before him, and nothing to light
him save a mocking gleam from the sun of truth, which
he has despised.    That sun of truth, just setting, would,
if he had looked to it, have taught him that he ought to
follow whither it has gone.    Now, it only adds its lurid
glare to the ghastly nothingness of an immeasurable

horizon. And yet in this seemingly cruel entrapment, there is a purpose of God; even this may turn to good yet. For the man is brought to that direst strait of all, that hopeless abyss, only in order that he may see that he must now drop all his past associations, all his early reverences, all his old loves; that he must begin a new life on his own responsibility. He must indeed keep fast hold of the weapons he has made for himself in the journey—judgment, moral sense, reason; but love and beauty are left out of the account, and he must do without them for awhile. Well would it have been for him then, if he could have kept the dying sunset before his eyes, and remembered past pleasures with pure thought; well would it have been for him then, if all the barren-ness round him could have been turned to account,—not to beat his spirit down, but as an evidence of the loving spirit of a God who, out of a desire to make his child worthy, had brought him into this weary plain of difficulty.

Love and pleasure being gone, he is left to make the best of what is round him. All the world around him seems purposeless and dead, and there seems no hope that anything short of the Judgment-day can bring graciousness and love and beauty into life again. The man is amid the wreck of past time; he is to learn all that cruelty and wrong—that is, the failure to do right— have caused of woe and desolation; he is to extract their lesson for his own behoof. He sees too plainly all the results of sin and suffering, without being permitted to see their causes; then let him learn from this fact that as it is in the order of things that he shall never be permitted to see with absolute certainty both cause and effect, he must be content to use his attributes according to his past experience of judgment, reason, and moral sense, as so many causes of which the effect is at present purposely

hidden from his eyes.   Let him, in short, use his imagination, and wed it to his reasoning and sympathetic power;
and, not shrinking from the severest test, let him learn to
work his nature out absolutely for itself, without any
present hope of a result.   But let us take these traces of
sin and suffering as they are presented to us; the bruises
on the dock-leaves—have they not another meaning?
Surely, yes.   They show the man how numberless little
nameless things done by his companions before him, and
which seemed so harmless then, are really full of harm;
they show him how it is ever wrong to do even the
slightest seeming injury for wantonness or pleasure,
lest some day he come to find that the lowest creatures so
wronged would have had their use to him or his companions if only that wanton freak had been spared; he is
taught that not the meanest thing can be injured now
without some terrible result, such as this total desolation
round him in some far off future age.   The blind horse
he sees: what does that teach?   Alas, it reminds him, not
of past labour, and rest duly earned, but of sin, and
suffering earned by sin, because the man has lost his
faith.   Is not this, too, a fellow-creature; does it not
symbolise the existence, under the most repulsive outward
forms, of aspirations and hopes, long since past, but once
as high as his own?   That stiff blind horse: is it not also
an image to him, if he will know it, of what he may yet
come to if he lets his aspirations sink, and allows failure
to weigh him down into a mere daily drudge?   Does it
not symbolise yet again, that terrible image which sometimes flits across a man's fancy (always caused by some
sight of another man), of what *he* may come to if the
energy which consumes him now should die out amid
half-burned embers?   An image of this sort always arouses
hate of the keenest sort in the kindest breast; there is no
hate so rancorous as the self-hate which wakes at the

thought of a future lost, or of an idea spurned. Blessed
is this hate ; for it seems in some sort to choke self-love,
and spur a flagging spirit to new efforts at escaping from
an ugly nightmare ; and this of itself often lifts us by its
struggles out of a present slough of ease or sloth.

But now Childe Roland tries to look into the past, and
cheer himself with thoughts of his past companions.
Alas, once more he has lost faith ; he only remembers
their sins, and not all the helpful fellowship, and he *will*
not remember that that fellowship had its use apart from
the sin which was its inevitable companion. He forgets,
too, what he ought to remember, that it is not by the
past he must govern himself now : he must no longer
trust to the history of dead men who have won, the
warning of dead men who have lost ; he must no longer
lean on what his friends have said or done ; he is a child
again ; he has learned the lessons of the young life, and
he is beginning a new and older life, of which the essence
is that he must work as if he were the only man in the
world. Such work is only for a time ; but its hardening
effect is just as necessary as it is necessary to keep a new-
born babe shielded from rude touches of common men, as
it is necessary to keep a new-moulded impression safe
from touch, lest the design become blurred and indistinct.

So when he comes, unexpectedly, because he has lost
hope and forethought, on a further evidence of sin and
misery, what will it teach him ? That 'sudden little
river' symbolises, perhaps, the stream of a great calamity,
which has pitilessly gone its course, unheeding the cries
and entreaties of the poor human beings who were ruined
by it, and who still cry and lean over it to catch some
wreck of their past happiness from its rapid onward
torrent. Faith is again lacking to him ; he fails to see
that his business is not with the horror of this, but that
he must ignore it, and cross it as if it were a harmless

stream : what is it to him whether there were dead men in it, when his business is to go right on and let the dead bury their dead ? This river is again a symbol showing that a man must not stop to speculate in the abstract on misfortunes or sins of which he knows not the cause: it teaches him again, in large, what the bruised dock-leaves taught him in small, that no misfortune or sin is without its use for unnumbered ages ; the utmost that concerns him is its effect ; and he is taught that, while its immediate effect is bad enough, it may probably come to be a stumbling-block, a thing of offence even to himself, the obscure one ; that it increases men's difficulties in unlooked-for ways, and that any least sin of his own may, beginning as a thread of water, swell to a stream as terrible and deathdoing as this.

Hitherto, all the signs given him have been signs of abstract things or events, having no special reference to his own career. But now, as he journeys along the path which his companions took, he comes upon unmistakable proofs of their work, of their failure—proofs which must be used by him now, when he has forgotten how to use failure. These footprints and traces of that terrible struggle baffle him ; he is utterly at a loss to know how they came there, who were the fighters, and what they fought for. Those marks are nothing more nor less than the marks of the struggles which his companions had gone through before him when they came near to the consummation of their and his desires, and they were meant to draw his mind to the necessity for girding his loins and waking up his perceptions for the struggle he himself must go through. And as all these signs had a double meaning, the traces of that struggle, with no footprint to or from them, are a symbol, too, of the effects on a man's self of his past sins, which effects, in his life's journey, he is perpetually coming across and feeling the horror of, but

his memory being dulled by long stifling of conscience, he
cannot trace whence the horror arises; he has lost all
recollection of the struggle he had to win the victory; he
knows not that he was defeated; all that he sees is a
trampled mash of mud and blood long since dried up and
hardened, which might have been a fertile and blooming
garden. These traces also symbolise the marks on
another man's face of mental struggles *he* has gone through,
marks which to the unheeding man give only a dim
feeling of terror or dislike, but which to the observant
man will give cause and effect in a direct sequence, to be
used by him as a warning against failures of a like sort in
his own person; for at some point of every man's life,
some intellectual or moral tragedy enacts itself which
leaves its traces in his face, or, if he be gone, in his history;
traces that should be a warning to those who come after;
and every man who comes across them is bound to find
out by his own past experience, and by the evidences left
of the struggle, how he may escape where the other has
been captured.

But Childe Roland has not yet had warning enough of
what agonies his companions suffered. The bad engine
which had been an instrument of torture next blasts his
sight. This symbolises, perhaps, some great distress
which happens to every man in turn, and which had
happened to each and all of his companions—the distress
of love, or ruin, or death of friends. And when he saw
the evidence of such distress, was it not his duty to beware
lest he should also fall into the same trap, and do his best
to look forward for other evidence, lest the change which
such distress would bring upon him should be even now
drawing nigh, and should find him unprepared? For
distresses of this kind always betoken some great change
to come after. Every man comes from them more or less
mangled, just as he was less or more ready and braced to

meet them, and stop the tearing of the wheel by stratagem or device. And as the bruised dock-leaves showed the man how wrong might affect the meanest things, perhaps this horrible brake and the trampled ground before it have yet another lesson. Perhaps they are meant to show in all its bald ugliness, at once the cause and effect of some monstrous scheme of tyranny, or even of some end proposed as good, and of which the movers were so convinced of the purity, that they hesitated not at the rankest cruelty : say the Inquisition terrors, or the burning of heretics in Mary's time. In this connection they would be meant to warn the man to look into himself, and make use of his own purity of intent, before (in seeming high-mindedness) he ruthlessly trampled on old laws and old loves. In any event they were meant not to weigh his spirit down as they did, but to show him the full and awful significance of failure in its widest sense of mistaking the truth of an end; in any event they were meant as warnings of the possibility of there being somewhere a brake which was not rusted and useless, ground untrampled yet, to be the scene of a second struggle, distress, or sin, which may happen yet, be as pure and prepared as we may. Never take your armour off, these grisly things seemed to cry; there is not yet an end of sorrow; and sensation is quick to feel pain even now.

Then come further signs of the results of distress—the utter waste and demoralisation which follow on a man or nation caught too suddenly in that distress, and unable to till and cultivate the rest of life (symbolised by the ' waste ground, once a wood,' once a fruitful soil of a man's or nation's nature).

Then come strange hideous travesties of colour and beauty, symbolising the attempts by which a man or nation, having gone through such a distress, will try to make life bearable, say by debauchery or the like.

'And just as far as ever from the end.' For Childe Roland having lost faith, is not able to see the significance of these things, and does not know that when he meets with all these signs of past woe, their only use to him is to remind him that some like woe may any moment surprise himself, if he does not look out for his own safety.

And last of all—a clearer, more significant sign, than all—the forerunner raven sails past, telling him that will listen that calamity is close at hand. The raven is no myth : he is the embodiment of those unmistakable inner indications which are given to all—but which only one in a thousand heeds—that time is slipping, many failures are to be retrieved, and much desperate fighting is to be done.

And then, when all these signs have been unheeded, the great woe itself dawns upon the benighted wretch. He has had all the signs and has not heeded them, and now he begins to see that he is indeed trapped. Now comes the lesson, now we the bystanders look fearfully to know how he will win through his fight. He has seen the bruised plants, the blind horse, the false friends of the past, the wrathful river, the battle-ground, the torture-engine; are all these to go for nothing? Will the man remember none of all these things? Has he merely seen them to wonder and be frightened at, like a child in a twilight room? What is the past if he cannot use it? What are his own sins if he cannot learn by them to avoid evil? Is he even now to be caught in a snare more terrible than all, as if he were just at the beginning of his journey and knew nothing? He has gone through all his life not consulting the right dictates of his nature, only consulting the wrong ones; and the very purpose with which he set out, though kept always before him, has been so kept by a light which was a false light, and which goes out just when it is most wanted.

Then indeed it flashes upon him how he has been wrong all along; then hope dies out utterly, and despair really begins. The light of truth (the sunset) shines out once more to show him all his folly and blindness; then memories come flocking in of all the men who have failed, and of all those traces of conflict and desolation which rightly used would have secured to Childe Roland full success.

Then indeed is the time to try the man's whole strength. But God, or what stands to him in God's stead, does not desert him even yet; and it depends on the courage which is implanted in him whether he will yet, even in this darkest hour, be able to hurl defiance against all these forces.

Forgotten pledges and devilish traps are as nothing; so long as life remains, the glory of conquering the consequences of defeat is greater than the glory of a bloodless victory. A man may go on failing until all the world's judgment says he is lost; God has not lost him until the moment of death; and if even in the moment of seeming death he brings his courage to the breach, keeps himself ready and hurls down the climbing despair and thoughts of failure, God will come to him, the battle will be his own, 'the fiend voices,' the giants, the horrors, will sink into nothingness; the great purpose will be won; and as in his golden childhood, God will be all in all.

In this life of ours, every manifestation is put before us as an effect, and with no visible cause; once we are started in that life-journey of which I have spoken, when we are to depend on ourselves, we have to search out every cause by ourselves, and from the springs of our own nature. Every man is a problem to himself, to be worked out first; when he has done that, he may perhaps be able to make use of the lessons around him. But let no man say that the cause of evil is impossible to be known;

it *can* be known, and it is the very essence of the scheme of the world that the grim consequences of past defeat should stand nakedly up, frozen to stone perhaps, but more eloquent in their deadness than the living struggles of a vast humanity, in order that men may see for themselves that, without a series of efforts, each man for himself and against his own evil nature, he too will be swallowed up by the flood of evil, to be left bare and dead, another monument of defeat, when the flood has rolled by ; in order that men may see for themselves how every effort left undone is one more support wrenched away, gives one more help to the sapping water which, with the irresistible power of a pouring ocean, will come hurling through the inland, to deal destruction to the coming ages, and leave behind it monuments of hideous wreck more appalling in their petrified writhings than the primeval forms, shaping out the consequences of past evil, which already lie strewn in a deathly immortality about the grey plain of this our world.

# SORDELLO

HAVING already called attention to the professedly dramatic character of almost all Browning's works, to the actual subjectiveness therein, and to the special manner in which that subjectiveness is displayed, it will not be premature to say in this place that 'Sordello' purports to be a poem not dramatic but analytical: that the main drift of it is to show step by step the development of a soul from infancy upwards. One would remark of such a poem, that, to treat it properly, the identity of the writer ought to be completely sunk in his subject, more completely even than would be the case in a drama: for in a drama, while it is necessary only to represent truly the characteristics of the *dramatis personæ* as they are called forth by the action of the story, it would be beside the purpose to seek into the causes of those characteristics; whereas in a poem which is, like 'Sordello,' analytical, it is necessary to seize the first rudiments of the mind which is to be developed, trace them in their upgrowth, and not only show the workings of the mind as affected by external circumstances from its birth to its death, but even to show the causes of those workings so far as that can be done by a reference to the data given by the first glimpses caught of the mind in its rudimentary state. While it is plain, therefore, that if ever Browning had a chance of sinking his own individuality in his subject, it was in such a poem as this, I am bound to remark that, whether it be for good or for evil, all or nearly all the characteristics I have mentioned are to be found in full bloom in the poem of Sordello : and it is on this account, as well as for the reasons hereafter set forth, that the poem will be treated in the exceptional manner I am now going to mention.

We all know that Robert Browning is rugged and obscure : but we are rather apt to assume this knowledge without seeking causes for such ruggedness and obscurity. It seems to me that we may find good reasons for the existence of these defects, so-called. He evidently considers that his first duty as a poet is to give us direct from the fountainhead, either his perceptions, so far as they can be expressed in language, or his thoughts ; that his toil should be spent in digging out straight from its hiding-place the pure unalloyed perception or thought for men to see. Thus his argument would be, either that so long as the true worth of the metal is seen, any labour spent in approving or making smooth its actual visible shape is a waste of power, or that such labour if bestowed has only the effect of lessening the bulk and tarnishing the brilliancy of the untouched conception. Hence much, if not all, of his ruggedness and obscurity will be found amply compensated, after a little trouble, by the wonderful purity and directness of the idea when once that is grasped ; just as one would be better satisfied at the possession of an unshapely nugget of pure gold than at the possession of that same nugget trimmed into a globe, or of the same weight of beautiful-coined sovereigns. As for 'Sordello,' one must remember that that poem, being more elaborate, is for that very reason (upon the grounds already stated) more rugged and obscure, at first perusal, than anything else the poet has written. For as there is more thought, and thought deeper laid, in this than in any other of his works, so it becomes more necessary for him on *his* principle to bring that *thought* to his readers before attempting to please their *senses*. The pleasure thus lost by reason of ruggedness is repaid with interest in directness and brilliancy ; and to take up the former simile, his reader and he both feel more sure that they have got the genuine gold which they have dug with their own hands, than they would feel if they held stamped money which they had spent no sweat to obtain. Therefore, bearing in mind the poet's individuality, and his notion of his duty to the world, let us strive to deal with his creation in the manner in which he would have us deal with it ; that is, work straight to the bottom of it ; and extract the thought from it, trusting to him for the facts on which the thought is based. For this reason, then, I have thought it better to pursue the main purpose of the poem, rather than turn aside to examine into contemporary history, or into the sources from which these facts are derived. The head miner has, after long travel and inquiry, found a gold mine ; he has sunk the shaft, he has set up his engines, he has gone down alone to wring from mother earth her precious metal. It is no business of ours to pursue all the weary ways he trod before he found his mine : the mine is found, and there is gold in it ; our business is to go thither by the straightest way, take his instructions at the mouth of the pit, go down by the ways he has gone down, work out what he has begun, and take and keep the gold he has toiled to get for us. If it turns out spurious metal, that is *his* responsibility, for which we may surely call him to account. When a poet presents to us a series of pure thoughts, the result of his labour, it is better surely to give our whole mind to developing these thoughts ; for in reality any divergence or inquiry into the ways by which those thoughts are produced, the accessories by which they are supported, would be a waste of force. It is the real gold we come to seek; we care nothing for the nature of the stratum in which it is imbedded.

'It is now time to take up the story of Sordello, and the construction of the poem, and to give an account, as concise as possible, of the *action* of the poem, treating, so far as it may serve this object, of the history of the principal characters. It is scarcely necessary to say that the whole of this part of the subject is extracted from the poem itself.

Between 600 and 700 years ago Lombardy was split into two factions, called Guelf and Ghibellin. The former, Lombards by birth, were firm allies and subjects of the Pope. The latter, immigrants from Saxon Germany, were feudatories of the Kaiser.

These two great parties were naturally always at feud.

In Mantua they were represented by two families : the Guelf by the Adelardi, the Ghibellin by the Salinguerra family, who had also large possessions in Ferrara. The heir of the Adelardi family at that time was a girl named Linguetta. The head of the Salinguerra family had just died, and his heir, Taurello, was under age. A marriage had been arranged by old Salinguerra between his son Taurello and Linguetta, which would have united in his house the wealth and power of the two factions, and established the supremacy of the Ghibellins in Mantua. At his death, however, the Guelfs of Mantua, jealous for their faction, repudiated this arrangement, carried off Linguetta, and married her to Azzo d'Este, Lord of the Guelfs. Young Taurello, in natural wrath at this treachery, withdrew from Mantua, nursing in his breast a deep-rooted hatred of the d'Este family. He made alliance with Heinrich the Kaiser, whose daughter

Retrude he married. He then returned with tokens from Heinrich to Mantua, dislodged Azzo from the Salinguerra palace in Ferrara, and completely overbore the Guelf faction in the two cities. The chief of the Ghibellins, Ecelin Romano, seeing Taurello's energy of character, invited him to Vicenza, holding out as an inducement the promise of his aid to secure Taurello's complete restoration in Mantua and Ferrara. This plot, however, being detected by Azzo, and by Richard Boniface, Count of Verona, who were both then in the city, Ecelin and Taurello were expelled. But in their flight they burned Vicenza, and Salinguerra's wife Retrude and his boy were both reported as killed. Ecelin had had many wives: his present wife was Adelaide the Tuscan, a woman whose indomitable energy and consummate craft kept him in his place as head of the Ghibellins. At the burning of Vicenza the panic-stricken Ecelin basely left Adelaide and her child to be saved by a common archer, while her own and Ecelin's escape from the city was entirely due to Taurello's daring. Adelaide, seeing at the juncture that Taurello, not Ecelin, was the real chieftain, was moved by admiration of the one and scorn of the other to snatch from the carnage Taurello's wife and child, who thus escaped the burning. The mother, Retrude, died in the journey. The child was Sordello.

Adelaide's motive in saving him appears to have been to make him in due time head of the Ghibellins. He was taken by her to Goito Castle, near Mantua, where she gave it out that he was the child of the archer who had saved her. Her reason for her present concealment of Sordello's real birth was, as I think, that she did not choose to let Ecelin know the truth until Sordello was old enough to take the station she intended for him; and it has been suggested to me that her reason for keeping Taurello in ignorance was that she saw he would have no care to assert his real place if he thought he had no son to succeed him, and that he could thus be kept more securely in the service of Ecelin.   I think this suggestion is valuable; but that her real motive was a desire that Taurello's aggrandisement should be wrought by her hands alone. Before, however, she could carry out her project for Sordello, she died.

During the infancy and boyhood of Sordello, Adelaide also brought up at Goito Castle a girl named Palma, daughter of Ecelin by a former wife.   She was betrothed in early life to young Richard, Count Boniface.   At Goito Castle Sordello lived in seclusion till he reached the age of eighteen or twenty, when he visited Mantua, where by a fortunate chance he was enabled to display his gift of song, to the discomfiture of Eglamor, the chief Troubadour of Richard Boniface, at a Love Court which Richard and Palma were holding there previous to their espousal. This was almost the first time Palma had seen Sordello, and she fell in deep love with him.   Eglamor died of grief at his defeat, and Sordello was appointed Palma's minstrel.   As such he lived at Mantua for about ten or twelve years, getting various meeds of applause and censure.

After the death of Retrude and the supposed death of his child, Taurello seemed to lose all care for chieftainship in Mantua or elsewhere; he therefore of his own will put himself second to Ecelin, and became his Prime Minister. In this capacity he ruled at Ferrara a number of turbulent years (signalised by perpetual broils between Ghibellin and Guelf), until, about a year before Sordello's death, Adelaide died; and Ecelin, left a prey to his own weak impulses, retired to a convent, gave up his place as head of Romano, and dismissed Taurello.   Taurello thus deserted, went to his native town Mantua for a time. Meanwhile the negotiation for Richard's and Palma's marriage proceeded, and, after a short stay at Mantua, Taurello returned to Ferrara, where the Guelfs since Ecelin's defection had gained ground. Taurello, seeing that Romano's fortunes were tottering, and being desirous at all hazards to prevent the total absorption of that house into the Guelf faction, which would ensue if Palma married Richard, left Ferrara for Padua, and visited Palma at Goito, gained her consent to postpone the marriage, and her authority to act as Romano's Vice-gerent, rightly judging that the Ferrarese Guelfs would give him an occasion to break off the match, by committing some outrage on the Ghibellins there. His judgment was right. The Guelfs took advantage of his absence to burn and plunder everything Ghibellin. Then came Taurello and restored order, crushing the Guelfs. On this Azzo and Richard Boniface besieged Ferrara; and at last Taurello, calling a parley, induced Richard to enter Ferrara, and kept him there a prisoner.

Palma this while was in Verona waiting, an unwilling bride, to be espoused to Richard, who had by Taurello's adroitness been trapped into breaking his engagement, and made a prisoner in Ferrara. Palma, who loved Sordello only, and who knew the secret of his birth, summoned him from Goito (whither he had retired after his first failure as a poet in Mantua) to visit her in Verona. She told him how near to destruction Ecelin's defection had brought Romano's house, and how as the chief of her house she had authorised Taurello to take extreme measures for maintaining Romano's ascendancy; and being determined to advance Sordello's fortunes and wed him herself, persuaded him to come with her to Ferrara in disguise, before the arbitrators could arrive who were to treat for Count Richard's ransom. They arrived at Ferrara, and had audience of Taurello. The result of the interview was that Taurello (who had acted on Palma's licence, entertained proposals of the Kaiser, and obtained from him authority to name the head of Romano) invested Sordello with the badge of the house. Within twenty-four hours after he had been invested with this dignity, Sordello died.

As to the construction of the poem, it is in form a narrative; and the poet apologises at the outset for taking the historic mode, instead of making Sordello speak for himself in his own manner. But as the analysis of a soul is his great object, it is surely of the highest importance to give the development of that soul a stamp of portraiture as clear and direct as possible ; to reproduce not only modes of thought, but even as far as possible turns of expression. And while on the one hand it is imperatively necessary for the workman to absorb himself into the subject-matter of his work in such a poem as this, on the other hand the narrative form is by far the most tempting to any display of the author's individuality. Still, although we must lament that all established rules were not thrown away, for the sake of presenting the clear picture with which it is undoubtedly the poet's earnest desire to furnish us, we must not forget that what we lose in the way I have indicated we gain not only in sympathy with the mind which produces the work, but also in the good result of such toil as the added obscurity entails upon us.

As to historical framework, the dedication gives us to understand that it has no further prominence than a back-ground requires; but is it good (I ask as one unversed in technical construction) that the history should be told as it is, backwards ?

The opening scene occurs just before Sordello's death; and when we are already somewhat exhausted with the effort of understanding that opening scene, we are ruthlessly hurried back to the beginning of the real action of the story, and find ourselves at a loss to account for dates. Then again, after bringing us through Sordello's development to the close of his life, that is to the date at which the opening scene took place, is it fair to plunge us in a vast sea of digression into Browning's own inner life, occupying nearly four hundred lines, which comprise perhaps the hardest part of the book, and utterly throw us out of the unity of the story?

But it is time to say something of the character of Sordello.

Roughly, his life may be divided, according to a hint in the poem, into two portions or circles, by no means equal in extent of time, but quite equal in respect of importance. The first three books are taken up with his development as a great egoist. The last three books are taken up with his development as a great altruist; and in both circles he ended at the point, and with the same hopes, from which he started.

> For he—for he,
> Gate-vein of this heart's-blood of Lombardy,
> (If I should falter now)—for he is Thine !
> Sordello, thy forerunner, Florentine !
> A herald-star I know thou didst absorb
> Relentless into the consummate orb
> That scared it from its right to roll along
> A sempiternal path with dance and song
> Fulfilling its allotted period,
> Serenest of the progeny of God,
> Who yet resigns it not ! His darling stoops
> With no quenched lights, desponds with no blank troops
> Of disenfranchised brilliancies, for, blent
> Utterly with thee, its shy element,
> Like thine upburneth prosperous and clear.
> Still, what if I approach the august sphere
> Named now with only one name, disentwine
> That under-current, soft and argentine,

From its fierce mate in the majestic mass,
Leavened as the sea whose fire was mixt with glass
In John's transcendent vision—launch once more
That lustre? Dante, pacer of the shore
Where glutted hell disgorgeth filthiest gloom,
Unbitten by its whirring sulphur-spume—
Or whence the grieved and obscure waters slope
Into a darkness quieted by hope;
Plucker of amaranths grown beneath God's eye
In gracious twilights where his chosen lie,
I would do this! if I should falter now!


## BOOK I.


In dealing with the first circle of his life, we must consider Sordello's development as *man*, and the creation of his poetic soul, by the influence of his commerce with inanimate nature.

He lived in his boyhood at Goito Castle in the enjoyment of childish and boyish pleasures; in the warm weather watching outdoor nature; in the winter peering through the picture galleries and dim chambers. His face, with its wide delicate nostril, sharp cut, restless lips, and calm brow, indicated a soul fit to receive delight at every sense. Framed for pleasure, his was the finer sense for which the skies are bluer, the sun more dazzling, than for other men. Such was Sordello *in his boyhood*.

Now the souls of poets may be divided into two broad classes. The first is one which, loving every disclosure of Nature in turn for the sake of its beauty, and investing each idol of an hour with life from itself, strives to blend itself with, and absorb itself irrevocably into, every external fresh discovered beauty. The second is frequently a development of, but is always stronger in this life than, the first, and always overthrows it here when they come into collision. Such a soul looks on external

beauty not as a thing to be worshipped, glorified, and
blended with, but as a revealment of a like quality pre-
existent in himself, hitherto hidden or only dormant; he
asserts his power at any instant by force of his will to
rouse into being within himself the prototype of any form
of nature, from earth's simplest shape to heaven's most
complex essence.  But it is sad to find these souls sinking
into indolence, since, as they say, this life, and time, are
too narrow an arena to display their full power of mastery;
and it is still sadder, if a desire seizes them to force this
life, and time, to display their full power of mastery here,
instead of waiting for the opportunity which only another
life, or perhaps eternity, can afford.   Now, whether
Sordello's soul was one of the first or second class
described, or a modification of either or both, it will be
the task of an honest translator of this poem to determine.
His boyhood glided calmly away at Goito Castle, his only
human associates being some old women-servants.  In
full health and youth, his imagination wreathed about
each new discovery in the nature round him some infantile
conceit, imparting in fancy to each in turn so much of
his own thought and sense as he hoped would enable it to
stand alone and serve him as a companion, toiling that he
and it might be blended into one being.  The world did
not yet destroy this cobweb-work of fancy; care and pain,
which would have destroyed it, were absent.  Selfish he
was, having no check, and no object of equal sympathy;
selfish, and with no moral sense whatever; for how could
he know that others desired to share his joy, when he
saw nobody?  His poetic genius, born in no fiery throes,
gradually woke to life in the quiet interchange of summer
and winter.  But time brought growth of brain and
thinking power, and these soon put a stop to his cobweb-
spinning.  He found himself living alone among his
woodland sights.  He began to see the true relationship

between himself and them. Indiscriminate enjoyment of everything he saw began to be insufficient; he desired to direct his energy of pleasure in some one or limited numbers of channels. How can I, thinks he, achieve this employment of my energy by using the outer world of men, and having chosen my pleasure, enjoy it in imagination by proxy, and by sympathy, and so save myself the trouble of actual working to get it? His will had awoke; it drew him away from simple love; his judgment claimed the enjoyment *in imagination only*, and by force of his will, of attributes of men. His will claimed men's acknowledgment of such his power. So for him it was now an absolute necessity to live before a crowd. In the host of men his fancy summons to personate the crowd, he discovers many attributes, some which he knew already, more of which he had had no conception. He sees that in this crowd of men each has his own separate ideal, lives his own separate life. And in all these attributes, and in himself, no sign tells him which is good and which is bad. His own pleasure then shall decide which of these he shall use and make men acknowledge his power to use; and at length he concentrates such as his judgment decides are worthiest, being fain to hope that he himself will by his own real parentage and fortune prove to be equal to the ideal he has thus created. This ideal man is greatest of poets, greatest of kings, Apollo himself. An Apollo whom woods and trees, winds and skies, join together in worshipping; who triumphs over right and wrong, and draws the hearts of all the girls of the earth out of their old loves into adoration of his transcendent Divinity. And when Apollo has satiated his soul with the fancy loves of those who yield, he turns to the only real girl, who scorning all other men, and having no old loves to wrench away, has not yet paid to him her tribute of worship. This girl is Palma. He waits, growing

grave and lean and pale with expectation and desire, for
a real crowd, a real stage, a real love.

## BOOK II.

In this book we trace Sordello's development as poet,
and further development as man, by influence of his
commerce with living men in their joys only ; and the
temporary demoralisation of the man-part, and temporary
extinction of the poet-part, by this influence.

At last a day comes when Sordello's impatience drives
him wandering out, half fancying that he would see and
secure Palma at once.   His ramble brought him to
Mantua walls, where were assembled a *real* crowd, gay
and laughing, round a pavilion.

While he stood abashed and faltering at this first sight
of real men and women, who ought to have yielded *him*
homage, Eglamor, Boniface's Chief Troubadour, came
out and sang to them.   Sordello, recognising in the
story a fancy of his own, sprang to Eglamor's side, and
took up his theme.   When the maddening applause was
over, his eye suddenly lighted on Palma,

> the very maid
> Of the north chamber, her red lips as rich,
> The same pure fleecy hair ; one weft of which,
> Golden and great, quite touched his cheek as o'er
> She leant, speaking some six words and no more.
> He answered something, anything ; and she
> Unbound a scarf and laid it heavily
> Upon him, her neck's warmth and all.

The magic of fancy, which had been arrested by his
first glance at the real crowd, moved again under the
touch of love, and he became unconscious of the outer

world till he found himself back at Goito with a prize at his feet, learned that Eglamor was dead of grief, and that Palma chose *him* for her minstrel. He passed a week in delicious reverie, from which he awoke a new man. For hitherto his life had been passed in unexpressed perception, with no event which showed either directly or indirectly the effect of *actual* as distinguished from *fancied* contact with man and woman. Thus his thinking power had not been exercised at all, there being no occasion calling forth the *expression* of thoughts. He had only *perceived*, not *thought*. But here had been the first instance in which his mind had been called upon to influence other minds by the *expression verbally* of thought; and his mind being once set in that channel, its streams were henceforth divided; the pure stream of perception flowing still, side by side with the new and sometimes turbid stream of thought. He began to consider why he had beaten Eglamor. He proceeded to analyse the motives which impelled him to the first triumphant exercise of the poet-part of his Apolloship, and concluded that since his fancy made him actually love the subject of the song, as well as and above the act of singing, men who *applauded* his rhymes would surely *adore* his power of fancy. And as he arrived at this conclusion, Eglamor's corpse was borne towards him through the woods, to be buried far from the scene of his defeat. The trouveres were chanting at the head of the bier a song of praise of Eglamor. That song told Sordello how the art of verse was to Eglamor the worship of nature as a Divine power, the lifting of a veil, the performance of rites whereby some sound or sight of beauty, thus created, were fixed in rhyme, and made his own, to mix with his life and unloose at pleasure for easing pain and trouble. He was the priest of the temple, apart from all other men, freed from care for the world's coldness. Sordello, shaken by strong pity at the sound of the verses, took his own crown and laid it on Eglamor's breast.

Thus, then, had the two souls—Eglamor's the first class mentioned in Book I, Sordello's fast developing into the second class—come into collision; Eglamor's being the weaker, had been overcome. But Eglamor's death taught Sordello's awakening sympathies to embrace not only strength, but also the tender beauty of weakness. For here was Eglamor, needy, obscure in birth, yet nursed in the hearts of his own people. Can Sordello win such love, supposing (horrid thought) that he may after all be no real prince? He sternly determines before doing anything else to learn who and what he is. He finds that he is the reputed son of a common soldier who had saved Adelaide and her child when Taurello and Ecelin burned Vicenza.

His hope of kingship overthrown, he takes the next step in his development. Thrown back on himself and his qualities as simple man, irresponsible because unshackled by any grace or power added by the world, why need he follow any known example? He who does *not* act, is already greater by virtue of *fancy* than those who *do* act, who have a distinct purpose, which as a star guides all their life; he can and will gain by his fancy all the results which they by their action have striven or will strive to get. 'My soul shall express the essence of all beauty by its self-consciousness thereof; and if the world can wonder at men who (like Eglamor) themselves wonder, and can idolise men who (like Eglamor) themselves bow to an idol, how shall it worship me, who neither wonder nor idolise, but express, by the self-consciousness of my soul, all that *is* wondered at or idolised? I will express by song all joys that are, without tasting one; I will win from men the love which must be given to him who leads each man's soul to see the thing he most longs for.'

His plan thus made, he visits Mantua. There he is received with rapture, and begins to try and work out this new ideal by actual song.

He conquers his first repugnance to work, and achieves success sooner than he expected. Dazzled by its brilliancy he for a moment shamefully longs for the very joys which it is his plan to abjure; but again bends to his work; and as influence over men by song is his first object, resolves to adopt the dramatic form.

Having re-wrought his Language,* in his perception he creates a drama, and presents it in its *new* panoply of *new* language. But, alas ! he finds that language, how ever modelled, is purely a work of thought; that thought is a thing made of successive pieces, while perception is a thing whole and simultaneous—that by consequence, if on the one hand (in his desire to present the perception whole) he clothes it with thought, he hampers it as much as one would hamper a man bred up to go naked by clothing him with an armour of many pieces. Or, if on the other hand (in his desire to show men the perception at any cost), he presents it in successive pieces of thought he is really only trying to show men what an entire thing is like, by first tearing it in pieces, and then pre- senting the parts successively for *them* to put together according to their knowledge. So, remembering that even if he could present the perception *entire*, this would be an impertinence, seeing that by virtue of his will he could *be* the perception—and seeing, moreover, that his audience was not likely to imagine anything higher than the highest idea he presented, which they praised already —he falls back on his old mode, and contents himself with men's old praise, thinking ' go further, fare worse.'

* ' . . . . slow re-wrought
That Language,—welding words into the crude
Mass from the new speech round him.'

But here he is met by a new difficulty. Whatever mode he chooses, his audience decline to recognise in his portraiture his power by will to *be* the men he portrays; and seeing in him only an ugly, stunted, weakly minstrel, insist on giving him praise for his *rhymes*, and his heroes praise for their *deeds*, keeping each carefully distinct. This angers him. Why, he hotly asks, should he care about the recognition of the Mantuans? His hope of self-display by force of will (his poet part) thus thwarted, a division arose in Sordello. His man-part which insisted on immediate and adequate reward for every piece of work, calmly tied up the wings of the poet-part and took its own way, simply snatching any chance to secure *some* prize which should by its brilliancy acquit the poet-part of contempt. The poet-part being thus crippled, its twin sister, the art of verse, by which Sordello was to assert his Kingship, became virtually palsied too. While the poet-part, ever struggling against its bonds, perpetually called on him to stick to his ideal, abjure actual joys, and compel the age to know him, by force of his will producing self-revealment, the man-part fiercely urged him to shake off lethargy and timidity, and enjoy, while there was time, mixing with men. But before he could decide, the Mantuans, who cared nothing for his doubts, threw him out of thought by their intrusions; and he had no choice (having no time to work out his thoughts) but to take a neutral ground, and go in for a humdrum minstrel's life, performing the every-day duties which fell to the lot of Palma's troubadour. In this deep abasement he met a new trouble; for he had to converse : and could not at first do other than think carefully out any topic proposed to him. Now the Mantuans had all *their* opinions duly sorted, and ready for immediate delivery; but Sordello, untrained as yet to speak half-truths sounding well, could not give any immediate opinion otherwise than by guess, which was as likely to be wrong as not. So that on any topic started he was in this dilemma: In the present turmoil of his double self, he was compelled first to guess what effect his speech would have on others; and then, to try and represent in his speech what was passing in his brain; and his conscience not being yet deadened, disgust at the part he played outwardly made him somewhat tardy in expressing any idea at all. Thus the total failure which ensued, unless he could give birth to his idea at the moment, demoralised him, and the end was that he disgraced his intelligence by giving out any common opinion or saw as his own thought, without really troubling himself to think at all. How, then, in this abasement, could he care to take interest in men, for love or hate of them? Here, too, he saved his mind the trouble of thought by praising and blaming as others did.

To such a depth had he sunk as man; how then did he fare as versemaker? As such he had to keep his place against rivals, and succeeded to some degree. His poet-part, however, still struggling with its bonds, insisted that it was not enough for him merely to show the external view of any subject; that he must give his strength full play, root up the thought of the subject, and show root and all. This the Mantuans object to. 'You are a bard,' say they, 'not a philosopher, and where is the use of over-refining your thoughts? This is of no use in poetry; stick to common sense. Not that we should restrict the poet, but the knowledge that he is one should be his sufficient reward.' Such arguments, repeated *ad nauseam*, maddened him like fleabites; he succumbed only to get rid of the torture. But even in his complaisance, he was sometimes foiled, not divining exactly what drift of his thoughts the Mantuans were pursuing; whence ensued blunders, which he was forced to rectify by lies.

At last he sunk so low, that his will became powerless, his fancy imbecile, and at the announcement of an intended visit of Taurello's to Mantua, he fled back to Goito.

## BOOK III.

The third Book treats of Sordello's further development as man, by the influence of renewed commerce with inanimate nature ; and by the influence of retrospection on the experiences of the two first developments ; and his completion of the first circle, that of egoism, by attainment of his first desire for self-aggrandisement.

Goito, having got Sordello back again, speedily worked out of him all Mantuan thoughts and reminiscences. Men, whom he would have used as a machine to compass self-perception, by forcing his godlike half into clay which could only be convulsed, never transmuted, thereby, were all gone ; and his will, finding that if it flowed at all, it must flow between bounds, retired back to its fountainhead, his soul.

Better, surely, he thinks, in his despair, to be un-revealed, than only part revealed ; since men, who should have acted as the machine for displaying the power of his will, would not act as that machine, where was the good of trying to use his will at all?

> To need become all natures, yet retain
> The law of my own nature—to remain
> Myself, yet yearn . . . as if that chestnut, think,
> Should yearn for this first larch-bloom, crisp and pink,
> Or those pale fragrant tears where zephyrs stanch
> March wounds along the fretted pine-tree branch !
> Will, and the means to show will, great and small,
> Material, spiritual—abjure them all
> Save any so distinct, they may be left
> To amuse, not tempt become ! and, thus bereft,
> Just as I first was fashioned would I be !

Nor, moon, is it Apollo now, but me
Thou visitest to comfort and befriend !
Swim thou into my heart, and there an end,
Since I possess thee !—nay, thus shut mine eyes
And know, quite know, by this heart's fall and rise,
When thou dost bury thee in clouds, and when
Out-standest : wherefore practise upon men
To make that plainer to myself ?

So he passed a year alone, in torpid delight ; but
conscious, at odd times, that he was torpid. His trick
of verse was gone ;

One declining autumn day
Few birds about the heaven chill and grey,
No wind that cared trouble the tacit woods—
He sauntered home complacently, their moods
According, his and Nature's. Every spark
Of Mantua life was trodden out ; so dark
The embers, that the troubadour, who sung
Hundreds of songs, forgot, its trick his tongue,
Its craft his brain, how either brought to pass
Singing at all ; that faculty might class
With any of Apollo's now.

The year
Began to find its early promise sere
As well. Thus beauty vanishes : thus stone
Outlingers flesh : Nature's and his youth gone,
They left the world to you, and wished you joy.

One day, the marsh was buried by an earthquake, and
Mincio became a lake in its place. This incident roused
him from his torpor, to think, Is nature then subject to
the same fate as I ?

No ! youth once gone is gone :
Deeds let escape are never to be done.
Leaf-fall and grass-spring for the year ; for us—
Oh forfeit I unalterably thus
My chance ? nor two lives wait me, this to spend
Learning save that ? Nature has time to mend
Mistake, she knows occasion will recur—

Landslip or seabreach, how affects it her
With her magnificent resources?    I
Must perish once and perish utterly!
Not any strollings now at even-close
Down the field-path, Sordello! by thorn rows
Alive with lamp-flies, swimming spots of fire
And dew, outlining the black cypresses' spire
She waits you at, Elys, who heard you first
Woo her, the snow month through, but ere she durst
Answer 'twas April!   Linden-flower-time long
Her eyes were on the ground; 'tis July, strong
Now; and because white dust-clouds overwhelm
The woodside, here or by the village elm
That holds the moon, she meets you, somewhat pale,
But letting you lift up her coarse flax veil
And whisper (the damp little hand in yours)
Of love, heart's love, your heart's love that endures
Till death.   Tush!   No mad mixing with the rout
Of haggard ribalds wandering about
The hot torchlit wine scented island-house,
Where Friedrich holds his wickedest carouse,
Parading—to the gay Palermitans,
Soft Messinese, dusk Saracenic clans
Nuocera holds—those tall, grave, dazzling Norse,
High-cheeked, lank-haired, toothed whiter than the morse,
Queen of the caves of jet Stalactites,
He sent his bark to fetch through icy seas,
The blind night seas without a saving star,
And here in snowy birdskin robes they are,
Sordello! here, mollitious alcoves gilt
Superb as Byzant domes that devils built!
Ah, Byzant, there again! no chance to go
Ever like august pleasant Dandolo,
Worshipping hearts about him for a wall,
Conducted, blind eyes, hundred years and all,
Through vanquished Byzant where friends note for him,
What pillar, marble massive, sardius slim,
'Twere fittest he transport to Venice Square—
Flattered and promised life to touch them there
Soon, by his fervid sons of senators!
No more lives, deaths, loves, hatreds, peaces, wars—
Ah, fragments of a whole ordained to be!

In a strong agony, his spirit wrestles with that bitterest of all despair, more terrible than the remorse of a ruined gambler, which is reserved for those who, renouncing all pleasure for the sake of a higher prize, find, when they have lost it, that the joys they spurned have slipped from their reach for ever.

How much better, he raves, is the use of common men! for they blend what little they see with their limited being, and make it their own; they strive to blend with their body and soul what is alien to each, *so far only as they can*, but no further. And they therefore succeed. But what have *I* required for *my* soul? Nothing less than the blending of the world. Ah, bitter truth! My will, which does comprehend the whole world, is chained to a body so feeble that my ideal depended on my body's renouncing the joys of the world, in order that my soul and will might reveal them in full power of imagination. Therefore I have failed. Shall my ideal be worked out hereafter? Shame! I myself might, perhaps, have worked it out, had I watched still closer my human sympathies, and traced them to their source. Why did I flee from Mantua? Why did I complain that my will was fettered, when all the time I myself allowed it to remain inactive? All the time, with the full knowledge that I *could* have unravelled the human mystery, I merely elaborated the surface humanity casually brought before me, either in actual life or by books, by the dim light given by my predecessors, when if I had struck one honest blow myself, I should have brought the real flame forth which would have given me clear light. My minstrel trade gave me men to see; my business was to gain for myself all their *real* attributes, freed from the clouds gathered on them by custom, chance, or the blindness of myself or my books. Thus was I hidden from the pageant which was passing, which has passed, will not return, and which I might have seen by exercise of a little more will. Let me get at least some impress of the world through my will upon my consciousness, even though I get it by tearing up and destroying the whole of my past life, which is now like a ruined and blasted flower-bud; better this than leaving that past life dormant, like (as it were) a bulb lying dormant in the grasp of a mummy.

At this point, Naddo the trouvere, breaks in upon Sordello's meditation, and gives him a summons from Palma to come to Verona. This summons Sordello obeys (in emptiness of heart and desire to see his love). On his arrival, Palma tells him in minute detail her past life, and winds up with proposing a scheme whereby Sordello may be made head of the Ghibellins, and espouse her.

Here, then, is the chance of actual kingship which Sordello had dreamed of in his early Goito days, and despaired of achieving. He sees now that no soul without external help from station or riches is sufficient either in means or in *skill* to work such means, first, for his own delight, and displaying its will; and, second, for making men recognise that will by display of power. He finds also that his will, which, thus proved insufficient, he had commanded to abdicate its throne, may still sit on that throne, and suffer his soul to enjoy mankind, but in a way different from his first desire; that is, his soul may enjoy them, *not* by taking their attributes, and in the exercise thereof compelling them as subjects to render homage to the display of power, but by taking them as independent beings and making them as a body act out their faculties by the influence of his soul, which he can bring to bear by the external help of actual power. He therefore resolves to assume his kingship and wield the mass of souls and bodies entrusted to his care, even though in so doing, he should have to live solitary, as the core of the fruit is shut in by the rind. Thus is Sordello brought round to the fulfilment of the first desire with which he started in life.

## BOOK IV.

The second circle of Sordello's life is occupied with his development as an altruist; and in this Book we shall trace his further growth as a man, by the influence of renewed commerce with men in their sorrows, and the elevation of his nature caused by that influence.

In the interval between Sordello's departure from Goito to Verona, Azzo and Richard had stormed Ferrara, and Richard had been entrapped by Taurello. Ferrara was torn in pieces by Guelf and Ghibellin, and the mass of the people were in great misery.

Sordello, on his arrival with Palma from Verona, had visited Este's camp near Ferrara, had inspected the crowd of great ones there, and his meditation on the sight is pursued in Taurello's garden in Ferrara. This crowd of great men and small which he meant to task to its utmost by making it act out as a body its various attributes by the influence of his soul—What were they, after all? He saw the great men in luxury, he saw the small men in misery; and he found that, as the shrubs in Taurello's garden, which were passed over in looking, drew his attention to the large trees, which seemed made more prominent by the mediocrity of the others, so the effect of his thoughts of the multitude of undistinguished people who were only looked at by his mind's eye in the mass, was to make the very few *real* chiefs great only by the insignificance and massing of that multitude which, like the smaller shrubs, seemed passive and uncared for. What pitiable herd of men was this, which seemed to put a good face on its unimportant misery : certainly never thought of interfering with Sordello's desired enjoyment of life ; and by its manner of taking any enjoyments it *had*, at once betrayed its good or bad estate ?  A great yearning of pity, working in his heart, brought up with new effect old Mantuan memories of all his early dreams of great men, all his after dreams of making men work as a body to his soul ; and, out of the old memory and the pity, was forged, before he knew it, a bond which fastened him to this poor mankind.  He found that without any effort of his, and in a totally unforeseen way, mankind and he were really blended.  For the misery he had seen called up in his imagination the misery of all poor men ; a misery that bound its victims in a thrall more severe than the thrall of the weakness of his flesh.  Here, then, was a body for his soul ; not a body to do what his soul commanded, but a body chained by misery, and to be made free.  So he turned from the joys of the few great, to observe the sorrows of the many little.  This body of poor mankind should be made of equal privilege with those rich.  He had erred greatly ; he ought all this while to have thought of and tried to satisfy men's *wants*, not to claim their possessions, as his own.  So he sighed deeper now, because of the fleetness of joy ; for there was the people to care for besides himself.  But seeing his past fault, he decided to try first the minor task of making these people happy, and to that end to confront Taurello ; for there was surely an instant way to it, viz., by espousing whichever cause would bring the people most good.

Wandering through the city scarcely an hour after his interview with Taurello, he saw that through misery men and women were brought below love or self-respect, and that he himself was not safe from murder.  He heard what seemed to show that men would slay their own kindred for their cause ; and then the very (supposed) fratricide turned and asked him to 'drive bad thoughts away' by a song ! Fain as he was to refuse, and hope that some real great one (Apollo) had the charge of this poor people, and thus get off the self-imposed responsibility to reclaim so lost a race, he retained still the power to build songs on the broad human nature ; and so sang to them.

At midnight of that day, by a watchfire, Sordello learned of Palma that both Guelf and Ghibellin subsisted by the same injustice ; and found to his dismay that whoso ranked with either must be a foe to man. Then I am absolved ! says he. If *I* have done nothing, these have done worse than nothing. Nay, *I* had the notion of a service ; what indeed else brought me here ? Stay ! what if there be a cause distinct from these, left for *me* to discover ? (Here a watcher came to them, and told Sordello, as the subject for a ballad, the story of Crescentius Nomentanus ; who in the absence of Pope John and King Otho, tried to restore Consular Rome. But the Pope and King returning in the nick, crucified him). Rome, then, thought Sordello, shall be *my* groundwork ; the two factions of Lombardy try after their manner to make a Guelf or Ghibellin Rome. I will make a new Rome, keeping the old in mind. And in the morning twilight he went forth to work out his plan among the people.

## BOOK V.

Here we find the revival of his poet-part by the renewed commerce with men in their sorrows ; and his further development as man by the same influence, as evidenced by a fresh step in altruism, viz., the taking upon himself the stern practical task of an endeavour to make poor men happy.

In the evening of that day, having fully learned the hopelessness of trying to make this miserable rabble fit for his imperial city, and mourning over the fading of this last beautiful dream, a low voice arrested his ear. It said, 'Sordello, awake and listen ! A man sees two sights : the first, the whole work ; the second, the first step to that whole work. Why take the end instead of the beginning ? You were God in conceiving the whole work ; be man now and take the first step. Remember that collective outstrips individual man ; and apply this principle to this dream of yours. Who first sought to work the people's good by welding them as a body to one soul ? Charlemagne, the incarnation of joy, thence unfeeling and therefore strong, did it by simple strength, and men were happy so far as unity and irresistible force could make them. Go forward along the road of time, and you find the peoples, already whole in strength, gradually getting experience of sorrow by the contests caused by that strength. Out of the accumulating mass of that sorrow a soul arises which shall heal the wounds of the body of strength, by its new attribute of knowledge. Hildebrand, the incarnation of sorrow and *knowledge*, thence feeling, therefore stronger than Charlemagne, by his knowledge, as the soul of the peoples, wielded their strength, and made it work to help knowledge, and so made men happier than Charlemagne could do by simple strength. Hildebrand's work having conquered and blended with Charlemagne's, both works proceed by instruments of whom indeed a few only can be discerned now, but who still have furthered the work of the people's happiness, each doing his own life's portion and no more. The next step, of overthrowing strength entirely and working *knowledge* by knowledge to make the people

happiest of all, cannot be taken yet ; for we cannot yet
do without strength ; when we can, perhaps Sordello's
dreams may be realised.  Thus, then, are you shown how
useless is the mad striving to overleap your life's work in
order to achieve a result only to be got after ages of successive labour.  If you *will*, spurn the notion of being
only one of a series of workmen ; fall back, forego all
strife, and dose your life away in imagination.  Only
remember that you have given yourself to men to work
for them.  You have welded yourself and mankind into
one being, they the body, you the soul.  How then can
yourself, the soul half, please yourself and men, your
body half, by fancy only ?  Look at all the misery around
you, and think ; it is possible you are chosen by fate as
her instrument to take the chances she has wafted to you
for helping the work one step.  Will you yet spurn these
chances and advance upon the end ?  Go persuade
Taurello.  If you fail, then—

But this was enough.  He sprang up, determined on
the side of mankind, and taking the Guelf cause as the
National, and therefore the most just one, proceeded to
the chamber where Taurello sat with Palma, in order to
plead that cause before him.  When he first began his
oration, he succeeded little, not expressing in his speech
the feeling which was in his heart.  Finding no visible
effect from his speech on Palma and Taurello, he became
desperate, fearing that he had lost all power to work or
express the need of it, thinking there was no alternative
but to mope his life out in poet dreams.  But this his
awakened conscience could not brook ; he began again.
Taurello heard him patiently, repeated his arguments for
*Guelf*-domination to Palma the Ghibellin, and asked her
how they would suit her, with a sneer at a poet taking
up soldier's or statesman's business.  This contempt for
a moment paralysed Sordello, but only for a moment ;

the next instant he was stung by it into action and
resistance ; out of his perceptions he answered Taurello.
For he felt that the people whose cause he espoused were
his judges, and would not let him sink into carelessness ;
that if he succeeded now, they would indeed make him
king.  What, thinks he, have I forgotten my kingship,
which I have by virtue of my poetship ?

> ‘ Thus I lay
> On thine my spirit and compel obey
> His lord—my liegeman—impotent to build
> Another Rome, but hardly so unskilled
> In what such builder should have been, as brook
> One shame beyond the charge that I forsook
> His function ! Free me from that shame, I bend
> A brow before, suppose new years to spend—
> Allow each chance, nor fruitlessly, recur—
> Measure thee with the Minstrel, then, demur
> At any crown* he claims !   That I must cede
> Shamed now, my right to my especial meed—
> Confess thee fitter help the world than I,
> Ordained its champion from eternity,
> Is much : but to behold thee scorn the post
> I quit in thy behalf—to hear thee boast
> What makes my own despair ! '   And while he rung
> The changes on this theme, the roof upsprung—
> The sad walls of the presence chamber died
> Into the distance, or embowering vied
> With far-away Goito's vine frontier ;
> And crowds of faces (only keeping clear
> The rose-light in the midst, his vantage ground
> To fight their battle from), deep clustered round
> Sordello, with good wishes no mere breath,
> Kind prayers for him no vapour, since, come death,
> Come life, he was fresh-sinewed every joint,
> Each bone new-marrowed as whom gods anoint
> Though mortal to their rescue : now let sprawl
> The snaky volumes hither !

‘I have always been royal ; if I fail now it is because

* In the edition of 1868 ‘crown’ is misprinted ‘crowd.’

by trifling at first and never putting forth the worth which being original makes me king, I have been unworthy to hold my throne. My power to profess all forms of life at pleasure was, I thought, in its novelty, my proof of kingship. But too late, I see this was not so, for I was but the copier of nature. Truly this power, as means to an end, does constitute that original worth which gives me kingship. What, then, is the end? It is that I might use this power to embody myself in men, that I might further use it to impress men with my soul, and that at last they may embody themselves in me. To achieve this object, would give me kingship. Thus should I live and move and have my being in mankind; thus should I secure for myself a crown which (when the world had taken my full essence) I would transmit to a successor more potent. Of such a race of kings I am one! Does pride of this elate me too much? No! for as my kingship consists in embodying myself in men and men in myself, by this process men are made equal to me; I am their brother, since by my words they have been brought to knowledge, and they and I have a better thing to satisfy us than mere deeds. For as in the beginning there was chaos, and to still the noise thereof Saturn emerged, so from the chaos of deeds has song emerged and was embodied in a poet, who like Saturn stilled the tumult and took throne supreme. And why is the poet supreme? Because his power of song is the fullest effluence of the finest mind; because his mind, different in degree only from the other minds, has (instead of keeping on level ground and taking one single object to be gained, or to impress itself on as these do) left behind all single objects, in order to attain them collectively in the end. Do you ask how has this attainment been achieved? I answer, by thought; by the power of taking all acts by fancy and representing them in words, and thus by the influence of words, making men produce acts. Thought is then to acts what the soul is to the body. The poet disengages thought (the soul) from acts (the body) and by exercise of his will, *not* by acts of his own, makes men work, as his body. How, then, shall I do the work of thought by song? First, I will take simply evil and good, and by strong contrasts of light and shade, show you the chief of men in good and bad ; I the while, not standing above men but blending with them and sympathising with them in their estimate of such my work. Then I will take such men in good and bad and affect them by the circumstances of the world, showing how thus their nature works. Then I will take as my audience, not the whole world, but a few, and show *them* the inmost life, the very beginnings of all human attributes in good and bad ; till a time will come when those few can do for all these stages what I did ; and we shall talk as brothers talk, discontinuing old aids. For now we shall have a past to work on ; and we who are the judges, without appeal, can by a touch of ours alter to great or little, and decide the relative importance of the structures of that past. Then will the poet take a new step; he will use what has been accomplished to create a new structure; till the seal is razed from all the greatest works, and poetry takes and shows the world all their results as one result. But whoever achieves this last grand work, labours like me for mankind ; he too like me, must be content to express not a tithe of what there is to say.

'Thus having established my royalty, I cast away fancies; I turn to the work of this moment ; I bow Taurello to the Guelf cause ; content to die, now first I estimate the boon of life, with the people for my support ! '

Taurello, overcome by the flood of eloquence of which the substance has been here feebly indicated, takes a sudden resolve, and throws over Sordello's neck Friedrich's badge, making him head of Romano; and proceeds to declare his plan, beginning with Palma's and Sordello's espousals, but breaking off there. For without words the conviction came on them that Sordello was Taurello's son; which conviction Palma confirms by telling Adelaide's dying confession, which there was now no need to conceal.

Taurello having at length somewhat recovered from his first astonishment, proceeds to unfold his plan for subjugating the Guelfs, throwing Friedrich over, taking Lombardy and keeping it for Sordello. Then, at that point, Palma took Taurello away, to give Sordello a chance of collecting himself and of thinking over the astounding fortune thus thrown in his path.

## BOOK VI.

We are now come to the last agony of the great fight, the last scene of this soul's tragedy. Sordello stands alone, face to face with a strong temptation. He has made his firm resolve to spend his life and will in getting joy for the people; he has roused his soul to superhuman eloquence in pleading that people's cause before Taurello; and Taurello, smitten with his fervour, has determined to draw this mighty power from the cause of freedom to the cause of tyranny, and by a sudden and commanding gesture, has thrust into his hands, will he, nill he, a great engine of power. The moment that act is performed, Palma discloses the secret of Sordello's birth, and adds tenfold to the force of the temptation by showing that he is what he first desired to be, noble by parentage, born to rule. At this critical moment, they leave him alone. And in the solemn twilight, and in the bare presence chamber, his soul stands up, fettered by his body, as a bull is tied to the stake, to fight with the last grim enemy.

At his imperative summons, his past life came before him, holding in its hand, for his light in the combat, the lamp of truth. And now the fight began. He hurled aside the lures presented to him by the enemy, and looked steadfastly back. So looking, he saw each effort was right, save where it checked another; that his whole career showed the existence in him of an all-embracing sense which yet demanded some power above him, as the moon is above the sea. But finding no such power, and, consequently, no love, his all-embracing sense had wandered irresponsibly and he had remained functionless. Thus he was inferior to others who (with but half his strength) bowing to a superior power, were able to fulfil their course. Now Sordello had found no such power sufficient to yearn to; should he doubt, then, that he would find such? Or suppose there were no such power for him, and he were reserved to be a law and a love to himself? Suppose *his* law, *his* love, should be the necessity to remove all the incompleteness which prevented him from securing the rest? Suppose, indeed, all such laws prescribed for others were in fact such a necessity, but in mercy to weakness were embodied in some shape or power for a lure? Perhaps his vision was clearer, and he could endure to see the law, unclothed in any such shape or power. To test his strength of vision he asked himself, was he then less impelled to help the Guelfs in virtue of their *humanity* than he would have been impelled to help them because they were *Guelfs?* And if any how he did help the Guelfs, would he thereby be proudly forsaking the whole of humanity (that is himself)? No! serving a part does not immolate the rest. He must serve each part in its due time. A great scorn of his weakness in the purpose of helping the

*present* need of the Guelfs came upon him; this present
need he had hitherto kept in view, as easier than the long
task of wholly regenerating all humanity. But now,
seeing that present need, he finds how little his service
will do. Facing this truth, the Guelf woe, he is aghast to
find that the small possible service he can do them will
last a lifetime. But even while he sees the necessity for
fixing this one truth, and that to fix it merits crowning,
he cannot help mourning that such effort is only the
striking out one stray spark of the entire flame of truth
which always lies buried somewhere, and would, if loosed,
right the world. ' But, at least,' he cries, ' I will produce
that spark; throw over Taurello's proposals, and thus
attest my own belief.'

At this opportune moment, the enemy thrusts before
his eyes the badge, and bids him, before he does this,
think once more. Quoth the enemy, ' Is doing this *really*
service ? Yes, in the end; but is it *now ?* One sees the
ultimate effect; but the intervening causes are not so
plain. If, indeed, to-day's work were as clear in evidence
of good as the life's work ! To maintain the Guelfs in
rule (your life's work) is, past doubt, right; but one's
day's work must be tempered to the natures one has to
deal with; and those natures must be moved according to
the end in view; *i.e.*, as they impede or not the Guelf
rule. If, indeed, each man proclaimed by outward mark
his tendency, 'twere well enough, but alas ! the future of
a cause duly determined has never been held to be
superior in claims to the undetermined wants of the present.
Shall you then smite or spare on a warrant so slight as
your future end gives you ? Break your present sympathies, bear your present aversions, merely for such a
feeble end ? This were work indeed, but at cost of
other work; shall you spoil a half-completed orb to
get a new quarter of an orb ? Rise one step with

the people, and sink one yourself, or not one step
only, but utterly? Are old faith and courage wrong
because they were born from a wrong cause? Surely we
see on all hands evil beautified. Shall we then, to banish
evil destroy beauty? Is evil a less natural result than
good? For, if you overlook animal life and *its* evil (and
whoso tries to pry into that finds nought but a grinning
taunt for solution) and care for men only, you can but
see that good and evil claim you alike. Does not the
Guelfs' claim rest upon evil? If they had no sorrow,
how could they claim your help? What happiness could
you distinguish in the miseries you saw this morning?
None but a fool's who passed a jest upon you for a Ghibellin; and much hold he took on you by his happiness!
Nay, on men's own account evil must stay; else can there
be no joy, which consists in removal of evil, and is itself
a partial death, being the freeing of the soul's essence
from some small sphere, merely to enter a larger sphere
and crave new enlargement. Who among men had the
world perfect, and free from obstruction? Sordello himself at Goito, who was disgusted with the perfection and
smoothness. There is salvation in every hindrance.
Men *must* climb; they are not caught up to the height,
without wings, to see the view at once; that view is laid
lower; and the higher men climb the more they see,
heartened by each discovery; they seek the whole in
parts; if they found it at once, where would be the enjoyment of retrospect, of past gains? Nothing would be
gained but leave to *see*; there would be nought to *do*;
for looking beneath soon sates the looker; looking above
tempts only to die. Then, Sordello, live first, and die
soon enough; feed on the shame that you are not vilely
lodged with Lombards, but can force joy out of sorrow,
and while you seem to barter your attributes for filth, get
gold from that filth. For, though you get gold, it is only

from what the world discarded; what would remain filth did you not touch it; and if you were to share the gold thus got with the world, you would simply be ruined, and the world not saved. Why then should sympathy make you give up joy, when the world's woe would not thereby be removed? For would *all* get joy? No. Then do not try to force all into joy, before they are ready for it: and thus thwart your own soul, which is ripe for joy. All will achieve joy at last; and let their time come as soon as possible— but think how you could achieve joy at once by this badge !'

The tempter had fought warily; Sordello was yielding. He felt that his time of action with reference to the world had in it a power of joy gigantic compared with the pigmy impotence of the world to profit even at the expense of that joy. He turned his back on the light of truth, and cried in his darkness, 'Shall I, because my time is short, make nothing of it? I will rather use grief, taste vice (that I may be eaten through with life). Time indeed may reason out these as mischiefs hereafter, but I shall be gone. The few who stir are a match for the many who rest. Let me be employed then, and even though men suffer by my employment, 'tis but one pang for each. Who, with Rome in prospect to govern, *can* sit still? Let me have life first. What, shall I wait for some transcendent life to follow this? No! I trust my soul for the after-life to fate. For if it was so easy for her to make for me so gorgeous a thing as this present life, what wonder if, when that is shrouded by death, she can throw before my soul a second and superber spectacle? What future joys can recompense me for giving up present joys? Does fate bid me drink at the rivulet by my side, or say nought is worth drinking save the fount at the mountain's top? I will serve the crowd, if thereby I do good; if not, why require it of me? If men must

set life aside (and give it to me) why should I refuse the
gift? I engage never to repent of having used it.
Suppose the world *is* a mere ante-room to a palace, why
should I become courtier before the due time? Why
should I forego the luscious pleasure of that ante-room?
Why, when I am admitted to the presence and the new
joys, should I have cause to grieve that I have not tasted
the old joys? Should I be blest now if heaven came
before earth? No! Let me have stronger limbs; but I
want no wings: Let heaven be peopled with Titans, not
men!—Yet stay a moment;' (he turns towards the light
again) 'how is it that the full cup of life, whose extreme
dregs I so long for, has been dashed aside so oft? Show
me what it was the martyrs renounced, what it was which
they found to master life, and I will do as they did. As
it is, I feel; am what I feel, know what I feel; why must
only one side of life (the gloomy one) be right? What
is abstract right for me? It is' (and he turns away from
the light again) 'that my youth is endowed with power to
exist in every mode of being, whether as king or slave.'

But here his past life gently stole again upon this
world-worn fighter, and soothed his eyes once more with
that gentle light. He cast himself out of the enemy's
arms into the deep yearnings of his soul's essence; the
chain of the flesh grew weaker, the truth-light burned
clear, the enemy waxed fainter. His soul said within
itself: May it not be that good and evil, great and small,
are only modes of time, not of force to bind eternity as
they bind time, not of force to bind mind as they bind
matter? The fleshly chain was gradually weakening;
the soul began to feel the earthly surroundings fading
from beneath it, leaving it quite alone; the enemy had
sunk into the gloom.

Sordello, out of time and the world, turned in the
last moments to ask, 'What made the secret of my past

despair ? Despair which was keenest, which seemed most imminent, when my soul was maddened with struggles to expand and use its power, *not* by craving more power ?' And one voice answered: ' This was the secret: If the soul, which is thrust as a prisoner into the body, tries that body beyond its straining point, sorrow comes. Do you ask, how avoid sorrow ? You are thus answered. The sphere of this life, whether great or small, was nevertheless, being a thing with bounds, a prison to the absoluteness of the soul; the only way to have avoided sorrow in the life which you have lost was to match the infinite soul's efforts to the body's finite powers, and whenever the soul's powers strove to transcend the bounds of the body, to lull the impatient Titan to sleep.'

Thus, then, was the dreamer's despair accounted for, and put away with the past. Thus did Sordello's soul, which transcended eternity, the whole series of spheres, learn in the bitterness of death, its incompleteness for time, the one sphere.

But does knowledge extend no further in the present life than this ? No, the battle is over; the chain is broken; the winged soul has shot up beyond the clouds, and is free. The earthly Sordello is dead, with the badge beneath his foot. He knows now, but he is gone; the hermit bee, which has fashioned his house this eventide by God's counsel, and will wake to-morrow to do God's counsel, knows here the secrets of this life sooner than Sordello, who will wake no more.

Such is the history of the life and death of Sordello; thus we have seen how in the second circle of his life (as in the first), he came back, before he died, to the aspiration with which he started, that of helping, even by self-sacrifice.

But it would not be right to dismiss the poem without

entering on an enquiry into the nature of such a soul as Sordello's, its use for the Italians, and its use in the world.

This enquiry would, perhaps, be hardly necessary, if idealists only were likely to study the poem; for they would all be ranged on the side of Sordello, and would almost by intuition, at any rate by sympathy, be only too ready to exalt his worth. But to realists, one feels that some apology is necessary for the earnestness with which we lay stress on the royalty of this poet soul, whom they may call a poor dreamer, but whose life and whose dreams were, perhaps, not so utterly useless after all.

A realist would probably say something of this sort : You have shown me a man, who, till he was near twenty, never saw a responsible human being, whose boyhood was passed in luxurious ease, free from all moral restraint, and doing, to all appearance, no more brainwork than a butterfly. This man, when he first came into contact with men, saw no better end than to magnify himself in their eyes : and, on being baffled in this object, turned away like a craven child, and cried himself to sleep in his mother Nature's lap. He was only dragged out of this shameful retreat by the weakest of all passions for a gold-haired girl; and her intoxicating words, and nothing else, roused him to do something which yet was to be only a repetition of his former attempt to aggrandise himself. His first sight of misery and suffering was sufficient to turn his weak stomach sick, to unnerve his boastful purpose, and change him to a dreamer more pernicious in his influence than before, since now his dreams went to make other men mad besides himself. He did, indeed, make one strong effort in the direction of helping the world; but his self-introspection had so enervated the power of his brain for practical working, that he was entirely unable to make his hearers comprehend his meaning, and the only effect of his oratory was to raise a wonder and bewilderment in Taurello, which resulted in that statesman seeing that here was an instrument fit for his purposes, an engine powerful indeed when set in motion, but utterly irresponsible, and which could be made work in any direction if only managed aright. Acting on this estimate of Sordello's character, Taurello, scorning the remonstrances of the helpless enthusiast, and ignoring the possibility of his having any groundwork for his ideas for the people, actually invested him, with no resistance on his part, with the headship of the very party which he was seeking to overthrow; such investing having for its object the gaining of Sordello as a powerful engine to work *on the side* of that party, break faith with its supporter the Kaiser, and domineer in conquered Lombardy. Sordello, it is true, went through a final struggle with his temptation, but all his nature roused itself to force him to yield to it, and only death saved him from the unutterable disgrace of passing his days as Taurello's tool and Palma's plaything. Such is the man, to dissect whose nature we are called upon to grope through an obscure labyrinth of verse, the very grammatical construction of which it tasks our utmost energies to master!

Now the realist looks to see every day of a man's life turned to some account; to see every act of his produce some result of good, actual tangible good, either for himself or the world; he will have no dreaming; his cry is perpetually Do, Do, Do! And yet one may perchance show how every day of Sordello's life *was* turned to account; how every act of his *did* produce some good, actual tangible good, either for himself or the world; how although it must be admitted he did dream, his dreams were productive of quite as much result as, nay, of far more result than, if he had been occupied his whole life in doing, doing, doing. It is true that till he was near twenty, Sordello never saw a responsible human being; that his boyhood was passed in luxurious ease, free from all moral restraint, and doing to all appearance no more brainwork than a butterfly; but one must remark at the outset that if this is stated as an objection, the statement assumes one of two things; either it assumes a man's right to protest against the existence of such a nature at all, or else it leads to the inevitable conclusion that Sordello's boyhood was passed uselessly. As to any right to protest, we must take the world and the men in it as we find them; it is worse than folly to object to the existence of any particular form of nature, seeing it is but a part, as we ourselves are, of a great whole; and it is as absurd for one part of a scheme to object to the existence of another part of that scheme as it would be for the wheels of an engine to object to being moved by the piston of the engine; so that any such protest can only lead to the conclusion that the uprooting of the offensive nature is desired, which is probably a step too far. As to the other alternative, that Sordello's youth was passed fruitlessly, we will deal with that more at length, and will seek some reasons to show that the objection is groundless.

Now Sordello was plainly a poet in two senses; first, an Italian poet for the Italians; second, a poet for the world; and he was besides, in the course of his life, both egoist and altruist. Let us consider him first as an Italian poet for the Italians.

We know from the poem somewhat of the life of the Italians; how under their hot sun their brain ripened, so to say, into a double fruit; the one half being composed of hatred, vindictiveness, intrigue, ambition of the aggrandising sort, a cool and devilish power in diplomacy; the other half being warmed with a passion for art, love, and all forms of material beauty, which made it a necessity of their very being to have their unexpressed ideas embodied for them in song or pictures. We have also seen from the poem how the artistic half of the Italian always influenced his truculent half for a good end, if only circumstances gave it a chance of infusing its gracious sweetness into the other's gall; how without the mysterious influences of poetry, painting, and music, to act as gracious excitements in their daily life, that hot blood of theirs would boil up so fiercely in the quarrels and intrigues to which they were already too prone, that nothing short of extermination seemed capable of stopping the demon's course; how, to use a more homely simile, poetry, music, painting, were to them what icebags are to the throbbing head of a fever patient. They needed soothing by the music of verse, softening by its inexpressible tenderness, training to thought and gentleness by its imagery. All the poets who should produce these happy effects were of the same Italian blood, and none was more conspicuous during his short life for the power he displayed, in this direction, over his countrymen, than Sordello. Imagine thrusting Sordello, the Italian poet, *in his boyhood*, into that turmoil of human life ! Remember how his fancy power, absolutely destitute of knowledge of good and evil, seized only too eagerly on any object even of inanimate nature to tire itself upon. How would it have run riot had fate thrown it thus early into the maddening human life, so infinitely more bewitching to a young and ignorant mind than any flower or tree, however lovely ! The river of human passions, violent, turbid, foul as southern blood could make it, would inevitably have drawn to it that broad limpid stream, and, mixing with and discolouring its pure water, would have overflowed on all sides to spread ruin on every hand. Sordello, if bred among men from a child, would have prevailed over the Italians by his

magic fancy, like some tremendous fiend-king, rousing all
their worst passions, crushing all their noblest sympathies.
But put such a soul under the gentle nursing of nature,
and his soul would quietly wake into being amid companions who knew no intrigue, flowers who never went
mad for love, birds who knew no voice but that of
singing, trees and hills, skies and clouds, who looked on
as calm judges, not to try sin and strife, but to tell poor
humanity that silent and passionless as they stood, they
hid a mystery which all the plotting of the world could
not unravel.   Amid such teachers, and such teachers alone,
could Sordello, a young poet who was to work among a
people like the Italians, learn that reverence which is the
beginning of knowledge; here only could he be led to
yearn undefiledly, unchecked, unblinded, after truths too
deep for the greatest masters; here only could he learn
that calm strength of hand which could soothe the feverish
Italian into rest from intrigue, and exalt him from rapine
and lust into graciousness and love; and here only could
he thus have developed in him that force and straining
power which should drive him to seek things too high to
attain, here alone could the spirit of prayer develop itself,
which above all powers, can lead any man to influence
over his fellows.   Thus, then, was it well for Sordello, as
an Italian poet, that he remained untouched by the world
until his soul had attained vigour enough to meet its
rebuffs, until his fancy's wings were strong enough to
bear him in transcendent flights above the worshipping
eyes of his countrymen.

Looking at Sordello as egoist and poet, and afterwards
altruist, in his influence on the world at large, and starting with the acknowledged fact that his poetic faculty was
of original growth and of a supreme order, it appears to
be the fact that the nature of a great and *original* poet
involves in its earlier stages of development a strange

paradox. It is during its youth, on the one hand too intrinsically powerful to depend for sustenance upon any other mind; and on the other it is in its very essence sympathetic to the utmost, and in commerce with men is far more apt to draw into itself and embody in itself all the natures with which it comes into contact, than to lean on them, or sink its individuality in theirs. Now the consequence of this is obvious ; such a soul generally starts with a gigantic power of enjoyment, a power which is far too strong for tender motherly dogmas to restrain, and which therefore, impels it in the direction of securing present happiness, first actually and directly for itself, and then indirectly by bestowing favours and smiles on others ; the object always being to supply food for that rapacious monster, its own individuality. Such a tendency, coupled as it always is with vast powers of attracting, and winning to itself the hearts of others, may, nay must be of pernicious influence (in view of the absence of a morality above hinted at) both to the poet's self and the world. Such a nature being then strong enough to support itself, is much more strengthened, in its earlier development, if thrown upon itself for resources, and untempted save by distractions independent of notions of right and wrong, and untainted by the suggestions (which a day's intercourse with men would produce) teaching the knowledge of good and evil, than it would be if thrown upon men for resources, taught by them what is evil and what is good in this world, and not only continually diverted from its own originality by the sight of and contrast with the qualities of other men, but also perpetually shaken and undermined by the ever-recurring torment of questions whether this or that thing is *right*, or worse still, whether the universal voice of men is just in calling this thing good and that thing evil. For such a soul, which in its earlier stages is so easily affected by the working of the imagination; for such a soul, which takes and absorbs all things with which it comes in collision, as an opal drinks in colours, what fate can there be in store, if all humanity is drawn into its essence, save a terrible chaos of discords and harmonies which in their never-ceasing battle must inevitably tear to pieces the goodly temple they have so profaned? What, in short, can be the effect of too early contact with men, if not either to destroy the soul utterly in its originality, to warp its powers in any direction in which associations may lead it, or unduly to cramp those powers by the effect of the necessary crowding which must ensue where a number of minds jostle on all hands one which is not so fixed and set, and therefore not so strong, as they? Just as one having a rare tree or shrub, would not in its saplinghood set it, on the one hand in a close plantation of other *common* shrubs or young trees of its own age, nor on the other in a forest of full-grown giant trees; but would plant it carefully apart, surrounded with all gentle influences to foster its growth, in a green garden spot of spices and trickling fountains, in a bountiful and prolific soil, where skies were gracious, showers soft, and breezes amorous—where no storm could ravage, no thunder terrify, and no lightning scathe it; so should the young and royal poet be fostered. His soul is a thing too precious to run any risk of the pollution or deformation which too early contact with the world of men and women, old and young, virtuous and godless, is sure to produce; too precious to allow the chance of its total ruin or destruction by the thunder and lightning, the wind and storm, of passion, war, or calamity. Let it be gently dandled to rest night after night by the strong soft hands of the great inarticulate mother whom we call Nature; let it find mystic speech in winds, in the song of birds, in the brooding of the sky; let it learn first kindliness—next positive delight

—next reverence—next perception. And when, thus nurtured, it has attained full growth, then, just as you would delight to set your rare tree, now full grown, among a crowd of other full-grown trees, that so its beauty might be more effulgent by reason of the commonness and dulness of the rest, so with the full-grown soul; you shall, if you will, lead it forth to do battle with the forces of the world of men, to use the strength thus nursed in solitude, to be self-reliant in its strength, and to extract from all sights and sounds about it, fresh food for self-development. And, at last, the development of self will be complete, and the full-armed full-muscled god will be ready to do battle not for himself but for others, and do his endeavour, successful or not, to help them to the happiness which he can see clearly. And whether his career be successful or unsuccessful, his purpose will be honest, his forces rightly applied; if he triumphs, the world will gain a great champion and much prosperity; if he fails, the story of his hard-fought battles will go down through the centuries; and whether they who read that story be few or many, a life spent to its last blood-drop in such honourable striving will have set its seal side by side with the impress of other such strifes on the tablets whereon are sealed all the battles and discords, all the peaces and harmonies, which go to make up the sphere of the great order, and in the mystic records lying hid in the secret places of that unknown God who is the master spirit of universal humanity, those few who are His chosen will read the story, so sad, so joyous, of a life which has been staked and lost.

Thus was it well for Sordello, as poet and altruist, that his nature did not too early contract the stain, the warpings, the crookedness of the world : thus was it well for the world that though his life was an unsuccessful one, it was pure in purpose, true to the end. And had it not been such, should we now enjoy the privilege of examining the precious treasure which the great English Master has dug out for us.

But is it true that Sordello, when first he came into contact with men, saw no better end than to magnify himself in their eyes, and that on being baffled in this object, he turned away like a craven child, and cried himself to sleep in his mother Nature's lap ?

Now if it was well for Sordello in childhood both as Italian poet, as world poet, and as man, to be nurtured apart from the whirl of human life ; if the Italian nature needed the soothing and elevating power of poetry ; Sordello, nurtured as he was (his power of fancy being an acknowledged fact), was a poet well able to govern the intellectual and sensuous qualities of the Italian nature. But as, in this part of the subject, we have only as yet considered Sordello's early youth, it will be well to examine his further development, not only as a great Italian poet for his influence on Italians as such, but also as a great poet and as a *man* for the benefit of the world. And it will probably appear that for all these further developments it was good for Sordello that the first half of his soul's earthly life was passed as an egoist. In short, while admitting that Sordello saw no better end, in this beginning of his life, than to magnify himself in men's eyes (which is another way of saying, what has been said already, that he was at first a great egoist) it now becomes necessary to show that it was this quality of his, this monstrous egoism, which really made him eventually so supreme. Let us then look into the reason of this egoism. The man knew so soon as he came into the society of human beings, as all such men must know, that his imagination and fancy were regal in comparison with those of other men ; the natural consequence was that until he was measured against other men in actual con-

tact, he must assume supremacy over them, and desire to
make them acknowledge him. When he saw then the
royalty of his imagination, and desired to assert it in
actual supremacy, what would he first seek for as most
likely to bring about the accomplishment of his desire?
Surely he would seek for an opportunity to display his
power in order to the assertion of such actual supremacy.
And on his obtaining such an opportunity, whether he
succeeded or failed in it, what would be the next result to
him? His purposes being as yet, by reason of his pure
nature, quite guileless, he would naturally use his power
(whether he had succeeded or failed in his first attempt)
in the direction of making himself stronger still. For if
he had succeeded, his lively imagination, unslaked, would
desire more power; if he had failed, his courage, yet
undimmed by perpetual reverse, would even more hotly
urge him to new efforts in the direction of self-development—self-development which had for its object at first
merely the rightful assertion of superiority.

Thus, then, it seems extremely probable that the
nature of a supreme mind such as Sordello's was, nurtured
as Sordello's is shown to have been, is first to claim and
assert supremacy, and then to strive after self-development to that end. Having seen how the first step, the
assertion of supremacy, is either achieved or at least
attempted, let us see how the second step, the strife
after self-development to that end is carried out. It
appears that the nature of the supremely imaginative mind
of a great poet is such that it is governed in its exercise
of imagination, *mainly* by the things itself sees, only in a
minor degree by the things heard or read; and again, yet
another quality in the nature of such a supremely imaginative mind is a yearning out of itself for sympathy and
love, a magnetic influence which draws other natures into
it; which yearning and tendency, egoistic as they are,

have in them something divinely altruistic, since they
show the necessity for a blending with other natures and
making them happy.  With these qualities then to work
on, how is the strife after self-development carried on by
such a soul as Sordello's, when first transported into the
full glow and fragrance of all human beauty; when transported, as Sordello was, into the midst of luxury, wealth,
and happiness?   Such a soul surely must turn the whole
force of its powers towards self-development in the delineation and enjoyment of these glorious things, beauty
of sight, and sound, and smell, and touch, all blazing and
breathing upon its fine perceptions.   How should it remember sorrow and suffering, the portals to altruism,
terrible phantoms shrouded from sight, and therefore left
out of the question as things unknown or only heard of,
and therefore half believed?

Such a soul as Sordello's lapped in human pleasure,
yet still kept pure not only by its own innate nobility
but by that very desire after supremacy which we have
seen to predominate, is impelled, the imagination being
still supreme, to make gigantic strides towards the highest
in whatever of the things seen it attempts to master.
These things seen are, as shown, the things of joy only,
because of that supremacy of the imagination; and all the
soul's attempts in the direction of joy must, from the
nature of its present egoism, be attempts in the direction
of its own pleasure and aggrandisement.   But are such
attempts enervating in their effect, as being egoistic, as
having luxury for their end?   No; the purpose is still
pure; self-development is still the goal, its efforts urge the
soul not to rest and ease, but to new toil, which toil, from
its very nature, must result in the absolute strengthening
of fibre.   The soul proceeds, daily gaining power, daily
nourished by joy; and still redoubling its efforts for itself,
it increases fourfold its power.

Since then it is the necessity of the soul to strive; since rest even for its own ease is out of the question, the power must go on increasing. And how is that power eventually to be exercised? Not on itself, for that would be self-destruction, which would be as much out of the question as rest. No; the power must eventually be exercised, for an engine to influence men. But until this stage is reached, the egoist must go on developing step by step, until he meets, as he must do, some tremendous rebuff. And now the first real test of his strength begins. His muscles are now mighty, and he opposes force with force. But he finds that the joyful world is, through excess of that joy which he is striving to learn, hard and unfeeling, and is stronger in its buffets than he is who is only working his way up to joy, and who is not unfeeling but sympathetic, though as yet unknowing how to use his sympathy. He gradually gets exhausted, but he does not get really weaker, because all through the battle that sympathy which perhaps weakened the force of his strokes at the time, was a power in him reserving his strength for other and greater combats, a power which would permeate his being like the breath of God. But now, what wonder if, utterly blown and strengthless, he at length sinks beaten in a hopeless combat? Has he shown want of courage? Are his forces ebbed away? No! He is merely faint from loss of blood; when he goes away to recruit himself, the sympathetic spirit will unknown to him, begin to nourish his being, and to nerve his courage for new attempts; give him time, and he will be stronger than ever he was before. All that training which he has undergone, and which is directed only on himself, has developed him to such a degree that, helped by his powers of sympathy, his force must turn into some other channel, if as is Sordello's case, the purity of purpose is unstainable, and since, as is also

Sordello's case, rest or self-destruction is also impossible. Thus then is this egoism a blessed engine for future use, a fitting of the man for strifes greater than this was, when it shall be not himself he fights for, but a cause of which as yet he knows not the existence—the cause of all mankind. Thus the true supreme imaginative soul must by necessity be an egoist, until he is strong enough and responsible enough to take his post as an altruist; and if Sordello was baffled at first, he came back and fought like a man till he saw that victory was hopeless at present.

As to the objection that Sordello was only dragged out of his shameful retreat by the weakest of passions for a gold-haired girl; and that her intoxicating words, and nothing else, roused him to do something which yet was to be only a repetition of his former attempt to aggrandise himself; let us take up the thread where it has just been dropped.

Sordello—who was no craven when he sunk beneath the buffets of the world, but was only a tired fighter acknowledging nobly a real defeat and retreating to recruit his shattered strength—when he awoke refreshed in Nature's lap, justified our estimate of the necessity of his nature to be always striving. For as a true fighter, having recovered from the blows of his battle, begins again to train himself, so did Sordello, awaking, take up the struggle with his own mind, and win the victory over his temptation to yield and be lazy; so did he train his muscles anew for another fight. And since it was the necessity of his supremely imaginative mind to yearn out of itself for sympathy and love, Sordello, egoist still, when he went out at Palma's bidding to cope again with the world, to try another fall, was too true to check his nature in any worthy attribute; and while keeping his thoughts on the coming battle, did not think it shame

to give the rein to the first efforts of his soul towards
sympathy and altruism, even though displayed in the
love for a woman.

We have seen how egoism is good, and how it must be
existent up to a certain point when a man sees only joy,
and no sorrow in other men; and indeed the time for
real altruism was not come yet. The great egoist must
go on increasing in strength and skill, all his efforts now
being guided and nourished by his power of sympathy,
and tending towards the development of his sympathy
with mankind, at present represented only by Palma.
The power of sympathy led him towards Palma. The
scheme she proposed to him showed him a chance of self-
development (for the egoist was not yet complete), but it
also showed his new awakening altruist power a chance
of influencing men, in an egoistic way certainly, but still
in a way far more compounded of sympathy with men
than his former efforts had been. It is clear, then, that
hitherto all his efforts were really in a right direction, that
at least it is not unreasonable to say that Palma's scheme
only showed him a way which he could not know before,
to achieve certain victory over the world in his next
battle with it. We may, therefore, conclude that he was
absolutely and entirely right in listening to her words,
and preparing to embrace her scheme, since though it
did seem in one view to tend towards his own aggrandisement, he did not forget that men were to gain benefits
by the achievement of that very end.

Sordello's first sight of misery and suffering was indeed
sufficient to turn his weak stomach sick, to unnerve his
boastful purpose, and change him into a dreamer; but
whether this dream were more pernicious than before,
since it went to make other men mad besides himself, is
open to doubt. Let us again take up the train of thought
traced down to this point. Sordello, as an egoist, has

attained the highest possible position. The nature of his soul, as already seen, could never have been satisfied in any circumstances with supremacy in the direction it had followed hitherto, because such supremacy would imply rest, which was alien from his nature. We have also seen the existence, as a fundamental attribute of Sordello's character, of the yearning for sympathy and love. Even supposing, then, that as an egoist he had met perfect success, such success would have palled upon his soul, and it would have cast aside its crown, descended from its throne, and turned for new food to use men for themselves, instead of for itself, in pure honesty of purpose; while the very nature of that new employment would develop to its highest his sympathy and altruism. Had he met with ill success, his honest undaunted struggles with repeated failures and rebuffs had now so strengthened the fibres of his soul, that it would have been able to maintain the fight, and see where its force was ill applied; and its power being now redoubled by the alliance of the full-grown angel of sympathy, it would now take stand as so far above the crowd, and yet so intuitively alive to their nature, that hostility, so often the sign of weakness, would be unnecessary; he would be strong enough to turn the fight into an embrace by a single gesture; and in due season (not when it was too late) he would have changed his tactics, and converted the enemy into a worshipping friend by offers of love and even of help. As it was, however, the full-grown egoist had no such slow process to go through in order to reach altruism; for without requiring him to engage in any further struggle, fate graciously wafted him full materials on which to work his now renewed and redoubled strength; in his self-part, heart and brain were fully developed; and behold, that ever-youthful Titan, dewy-eyed, fronted like the morning, called altruism or sympathy with mankind, was awakening rosily in his chamber, and the two-fold Sordello was ripe to cast his whole gigantic force into the cause of curing sorrow and weakness. Because his soul wept at the first sight of calamity, was he therefore weakened by such weeping? Because he was a poet, and as such, a dreamer, must his dreams be therefore pernicious? Have we not acknowledged his power as a poet? Have we not seen how useful and how necessary he was to the Italians as such? how, then, otherwise than as Poet, could his power be exercised? Were his dreams pernicious because they turned in the direction of freedom for slaves? If it were pernicious to dream how to rouse the Guelfs, the real lords of the soil, into a strife for freedom from the Saxons, if it were pernicious to dream how to drive famine and plunder away, and bring home plenteousness and peace—the absurdity answers itself.

But if it is still objected that, although Sordello did indeed make one strong effort in the direction of helping the world, his self-introspection had so enervated the power of his brain for practical working, that he was utterly unable to make his hearers comprehend his meaning, and that the only effect of his oratory was to raise a wonder and bewilderment in Taurello, which resulted in the latter's seeing that here was an instrument fitted for his purposes, an engine powerful indeed when set in motion, but utterly irresponsible, and which could be made work in any direction if only managed aright— let us once more recur to the acknowledged necessity for Sordello and his people that his development should be accomplished in the way which actually happened; and if we have seen how nobly at the right moment Sordello forced his egoism into alliance with his altruism, and espoused the cause of humanity, surely it is plain that he was no irresponsible enthusiast. But it may be worth while to consider shortly the reasons for the obvious fact that Sordello was obscure in his speech and mode of expressing his thoughts.

His nature, then, was, as has been shown throughout, one in which perception was predominant. Instances abound through the poem to show that if in his inmost mind he grasped a truth, he never let it go. But, as must always be the case where the will is greater than the power, the very vigour with which his strong soul clutched the truth in his bosom, made it the more difficult for his weak bodily powers to free it from its imprisonment and display it to men. And since simple truth, simple supremacy, will always seem complex and obscure to low and double-dealing minds, it was not the enervating influence of self-introspection, but the inborn vigour and earnestness of a pure and supreme mind, which made Sordello's utterances, straight from the fountain-head of truth, seem incomprehensible to the dull ears of a man whose life had been spent in double-dealing, in striving after low ideals.

Although irresponsibility and fickleness of purpose in reality formed no part of Sordello's nature, it may be well to deal finally with the last possible objection, which implies the existence in him of these defects, by saying that when he was offered the leadership of the Ghibellins, whom he was vowed to oppose, all his nature roused itself to force him to yield to this temptation, and only death saved him from the unutterable disgrace of passing his days as Taurello's tool and Palma's plaything.

But is it not true that Sordello's soul saw all things in the world by a clear light hidden from common men; and working steadily on by that light, refused to turn to the right hand or to the left from any clear shown truth? When once he was shown the claims of men as superior to the claims of himself, he never rested until he had spent himself in asserting these claims; when tempted

by the kingdoms of the world and their glory, he yet
steadily weighed in the balance the right against the
wrong, the world against self, time against eternity.   Is
this man irresponsible because he is fervent, because he
is unused to tricks of diplomacy, because he sees men's
rights, once plainly put before him, with eyes undimmed
by self-interest ?   Let us judge him rather by that very
agony which seemed to be his timely salvation from
lasting disgrace.   The nobility of his nature was to be
keenly sensuous; the pride of his nature based itself in
the royalty of his imagination; the strength of his nature
pierced through the veil of morality to estimate truly
the reason for the laws of right and wrong in this world.
And when against these strong forces of his nature he
brings to battle a force still mightier, the force of that
stern sense of truth which will compel the bounties of
his being into subjection to the round of duties which
the world gives, when he binds these mighty forces
together in harness like primeval monsters, to plough,
and draw, and toil for the pigmies among whom they
might have roamed spreading destruction, surely the
divinity of his nature in the last fierce struggle asserts
itself, and lets the broad-winged angel free to soar with
plumes unworn, unstained, unshackled, towards the
heaven which is its home !

# SAUL

THIS Lyric, besides possessing as a work of art many excellences which it would be beside my purpose to speak of here, has also beauties in its dramatic element which have arrested my attention. These beauties appeal strongly to the sympathies of any earnest thinker, and find a fit exponent and a full realisation in the collective mind of the strivers of to-day.

The poem details an intellectual battle of the highest order; the working of the imagination up to its highest pitch by means of the will, in order to produce a direct and visible effect upon another man. It is not, however, only because the actual motive of the poem is an interesting one, but because a certain quality of mind is displayed in one of the characters delineated—a quality of mind on which I shall at the end of this essay dwell with some minuteness—that the poem seems to me so important.

But before we enter into any examination of the thoughts arising out of the poem, let us first trace the poem itself in a short explanation, and see what are the effects, direct or indirect, of the struggle of a man's intellect, as those effects are drawn by the poet; that struggle being, one must assume for the present, an historical fact.

The dramatis personæ are, Saul, King of Israel, and David.

As Saul lay in one of those trances of melancholy which so often seized him, they sent for David to come and sing with his harp, that by the charm of his music he might 'cause the evil spirit to depart from Saul.'

David came, and entered the tent where the king hung, supported by his arms, on the cross beam which upheld its drapery.

How does David begin this terrible task, this setting of brain to brain, in a battle more momentous and more awful than the Goliath fight?

Let us picture to ourselves the attitude of the two men's minds.

Here are two human creatures; the one, sunk far down out of the empyrean, where life, the chorægus, leads the chorus of humanity, to the rhythm of a noiseless melody in a perpetual dance of dazzling light; and another who has stooped, bidden by God, down from that empyrean, to plunge into the black slough in which, too inert and dead for any effort at escape, the lost man wallows silently. From the utmost verge of that black slough, from the far-away gate of hell at which he lies, obstinately marrow-less, so stupidly negative that even hell's king scorns to open and welcome him, who can bring him back? Can David, so white and joyous, so glowing with the life dance? Let us see.

He takes his harp, and begins to play a tune by which he calls his sheep, when they must come up to the folding at eventide.

Thus he calls to the wretch's mind that as the sheep must follow their shepherd at the end of a day, so must a man follow his shepherd Nature at the end of a long sin. For a long sin ended in lethargy is the end of a day in a man's intellectual life; he has sucked out of that sin all the good which is necessary to give him the lesson of life which that sin is intended to teach; he has filled himself

full with the poison of it, which will soon rack him with
unutterable pain; the great fatalist work is done for that
time, and he must now come quietly back, bearing within
him the pasturing of guilt, to the fold from whence he
started; he must come back to chew the cud of that
terrible meal, and let Nature do her work, and give him
her nourishment therefrom.

That tune seems to say, Anything is better than deadness and inertia; come, sting yourself with remorse, be
awake, alive; see the sin you have sinned and acknowledge
it, and wrestle and bruise, and beat yourself; you in your
responsibility and your pride are just as liable to Nature's
laws as the sheep are; they, though white and untorn by
bushes of error, meekly obey their shepherd; how much
more then should you, so scarred and wounded by the
stresses of your long wanderings, come home to be folded,
and healed, and made clean !

And then, even as the sheep, the simplest creatures,
come quietly home, even so high above us, at the end of
*their* day, the stars, the creatures of highest mystery,
come back quietly to their home, the sky.   All day long
they have pastured and done their holy unspeakable office
to millions, each a greater than you are; all day long they
have been away, and their great pure fold has been empty
and still; but now one by one from the distance they come
gently in, faintly seen at first, slowly brightening out into
splendour, until the whole mighty fold broods itself into
an intense purple blue, and its countless denizens lie
sparkling and singing in its bosom, penned round by the
dark colourless night.

But Saul hangs motionless still; his spirit will not
come home at the call of the sheep's tune.

Then David breaks into a new melody; that which
draws the quails after him who plays, and makes them
leave each his mate to follow the player.   The sound of

it seems to say to the lawless monarch in grave rebuke:
Will you not acknowledge subjection to the law and the
fold of the shepherd? will you madly insist that you, a
wild untutored creature, are above all laws? Be it so!
Yet even wild creatures are creatures still; Nature keeps
secret spells in hidden places which shall draw even the
wildest when she wills it; above and beyond all acknowledged law is that thing which we call the power of God,
of which the utmost, terriblest force is never shown until
a man is too far gone to acknowledge human laws.

Let Saul then beware; let him leave his mates of
melancholy and black despair, and follow the strange
sound and eerie light of which he knows not the cause,
but which some inner impulse of his nature, also unreasoned out, bids him to follow. That hidden impulse,
that secret law, are sternly existent, will you or no; and
the two between them must draw and drive the sinning
man; but let him once break from the one and avoid the
other, and he must drop into the abyss from which
comes no sound.

But still the spirit of the king is tranced and
deaf.

And again David plays. He plays the tune which
makes the crickets dance and fight; again he reiterates
in it the burden, God's law is above man's law; all
human desires, all human or living sympathies, must
bow in mute obedience to the great supremacy.

Then, for Saul still hangs stark and dumb, a gentler,
stranger, tune comes stealing round him—a tune which
speaks of pleading mercy; a tune which lulls the angry
fiends who rage over the rapt and eyeless soul of the man,
and yearns to make him hear (all in vain) how God, who
can ruin and annihilate mountains and kingdoms, can also
stoop and quietly stroke and sooth his tenderest, wist-
fullest small creatures.

Beyond the reach of the voice which moves dumb creatures, Saul is mad indeed.

By the hopes and joys of human kind, by the whole of grace and majesty, let another effort be made for his deliverance.

The tune of the reapers. Shall it not picture to the king his own lonely subjects, never ashamed to show sympathy and good fellowship? Shall not the warm exultant chords tell him of men who yearn for him, and are ready, nay eager, to stretch out hands and drag him from his quagmire? The tune of the dead man praised on his journey; shall not its solemn cadence, its passionate wail that rises to triumphant jubilance, call up the image of the love men bear to him who is gone, and the gentleness that forgets faults and shortcomings?

The marriage chant: the song that speaks of creation; shall not this thrill him with the thought of new men to be born, and endless blisses of wedded life? The battle song; shall not this rouse the king to stern fight with his inner enemies, and shake him once more into the old warrior's ardour?

No: the pageant of music wings its stately way past the spirit corpse: no motion shows returning life: silence falls.

But hark! In far recesses of his brain Saul hears a little, terrible sound, that swells and swells; upon his nerveless sense comes the throbbing rhythm of a solemn intoned chant; it is the chant of priests who go in set array into the presence of the very God.

Within his shut eyes, he seems to see the cloud, the splendour, which veil the face of the Judge whom he has contemned: the memory of the criminal awakes; and 'in the darkness, Saul groaned.'

David, wrestling in blind darkness with an unknown power, agonising for the mastery, catches a gleam of light to direct his effort. He finds that the deep subtle lessons taught through the dumb animals, have had no effect; that the more obvious lessons taught through human sympathy and suffering, have had no effect; but when that chord is touched, which in its vibration shakes the heart with the mystery and the dreadness of the hidden power, which ruled the Jews before Saul ruled them, and itself created and anointed him king; when the terror of these memories is like to thrust the poor struggler yet further back into the quaking slough, then David adroitly seizes the slight indication of returning life and thought which that groan of remorse showed, and strives to throw to the choking man who has just recovered consciousness in his struggle, a rope of joy. He sings of the mad joy of simple vigorous life under the sky, in the full health of a man; he sings of Saul's boyhood and early days of soldiership; of his piety and love for his parents; of his fellowship with his brothers; of his early friendships, his early aspirations, realised beyond all hope; of his kingship at last; of all the glorious things that his kingship had wrought.

As the inner throes of the rock let free the gold within it, so all the throes, the joys, and sorrows, battles, rages, strengths, beauties, of his life, had combined to one effort, to bring forth in Saul the golden spectacle of a God-nurtured king who should conquer and be loved by the world.

And now, at last, the icy barrier which all the storms and winds of subtle thought had failed to move, tumbled, and fell headlong beneath the force of this direct appeal to his own life and its fruits hitherto in joy and strength, and his new opened eyes saw an image of future bliss and power. The icy barrier fell, even as the snow on the mountain's breast, having withstood all the storms and blasts of winter, falls down before the first warm breath of spring, and leaves its bosom naked to the touch of Nature and a loving sun, to bring forth under that touch new fruits of gracious kindness to all lowly and tender things.

There Saul stood, black, rent, and scarred by past storms; shall David's spirit have power, like the breath of spring upon the naked stone-breast of the mountain, to draw from Saul's stony breast many tender growths of returning life?

As the new spring, which has freed the mountain from its prisoning breastplate of snow, is not ashamed to use its old wiles of many centuries, its old experiences gathered from lowly lands, from little humble bare patches made fruitful, so David is not ashamed to use all the thoughts and fancies whereby in his mind, his own lowly patch of ground, he had raised little seedling herbs, which he meant should grow and flourish into great trees of knowledge and experience and love. As the spring uses the same grand secrets of nature on her greatest and lowliest forms, so David uses all the secrets which he had hitherto garnered, all the soft warm breaths of sympathy and knowledge in which his humble self had grown and rejoiced, to influence this lofty world-renowned man, the king of God.

Having seen from Saul's gesture, that though awakened by his glowing picture of the joy of physical living he yet tacitly put aside such enjoyment as useless, David takes the path which leads him to the higher uses for which the physical life is the schoolmaster and nurse. He shows how Saul's life from its infancy was guarded through all its gracious plenitude of joy, by God's loving spirit, from harm and sin; how like a palm-tree his physical life had grown, broke into leaf, broke into bloom of strength, beauty and manhood. You have done well, says he, to see that all this living, good though it has been hitherto to bring you to beauty and perfection, is yet of no use in itself, if before it bears any fruit, storms of sin and misfortune come over you, strip the leaves and flowers, and leave you nothing but a majestic ruin. But have you not also, besides leaves and flowers, borne fruit? Has not your life been full of fruit in your kingship? True, this fruit seems to have been crushed and trodden by your calamity and this terrible madness: but what of that? Do not men crush the palm-fruit, and out of its juice make a wine which comforts and cures sorrow? Had it not been for nature's tending hand which gently dandled the baby sprout and gently brought up the young sapling until it grew to a mighty tree, where would have been the fruit which we must crush before it will yield us the wine? Had it not been for your long life which grew and bloomed unconsciously to yourself into the full physical life of the man, where would have been those fruits of kingship which have been of some use even hitherto, and must be of more use yet? Even as the wine comes of crushing the fruit, so the good to be extracted from the fruits of a man's life can only be extracted by the crushing hand of suffering and sin. But, while the fruit of the palm-tree would not have come without the growth and beauty of the palm itself, still sooner or later the palm itself must die, while the store of wine from successive seasons of date-harvest will last, to cheer and revive men for many years. Even so, the life of the flesh which produced your fruit, must fade one day; but the wine which suffering has produced from that fruit lasts, and keeps its strength and virtue. Again, each deed which you have done, like the palm-fruit, is gathered in its ripeness; God the Husbandman takes it, crushes it, seems to destroy it, but really uses it to produce the wine of its good effect for the use and comfort of men. Again, as the winter destroys the fruits of the summer, to make fresh forms for the fresh year, so God destroys the effects of your deeds, only to make out of their decay and ruin, new forms for new fruits. And again, as the sun does the good things, though sometimes tempests and clouds will not let him see his work, nay destroy that work; even so, you have done the good things, and though the clouds and tempests of suffering and sin sometimes blind your eyes, these will pass, and you will again behold your deeds breaking out into new flowers of beauty and use. Then use all that you have done, all that you will do, and shine over it with benignant rays of sympathy, to make each little action bear fruit a hundred-fold.

But if unlike the sun, throned high for countless years, your graciousness and strength and beauty fade and fall, you can yet take a new use for age, and look forward. You can foresee that your deeds which were only seeds and shrubs when you looked on them as past things, will in a far-off future become stately trees; you can foresee all the glory and praise which men will heap upon your good actions, till they culminate in the indestructible monument of your trust, your grey tomb of marble heaped four square, on whose face is cut in great characters the story of all your fame.

Thus did David, in the strife of prayer, lift Saul's soul out of the darkness into the light of life. Thus did he at last draw the huge bulk up from the paralysing grasp of the slough snake which had encircled him. Saul, a man once more, was come back to the world, with a new light of wonderful love in his face.

Then out of the unconscious yearning which had prompted that mighty effort of David's, out of that prayer spirit which had sustained him hitherto, there arose to help David, in yet another prophetic flight, a passion too divine to be borne.

Music and harp were useless now; he must use the great irrepressible man-love which welled up in him for music, and say all his say out with the full heart which is greater than all beauty of sight and sound. Scarcely knowing how to use the pile of knowledge he has gathered, he turns to review all that he has said, in order that if possible by his past experience he may learn how to use his love.

'I have spoken and judged of all God's creation: and on every hand, beneath the stress of my agony of prayer, untold depths have opened themselves, all tending to one deeper abyss of knowledge withheld. In the glow of the goodness of Creation, I stand aware of my own nothingness, confounded, shrivelled, by God's perfection. Yet, though I cower so low, I fail not to see, in every one of God's creatures, some special attribute. I tremble, but ask, shall not I, God's creature too, find in myself some such attribute? Looking fearfully into myself, I find that attribute in the motive which impelled me to this task of prayer and prophecy. It was love of God, love of man, love of the king whom I desire to rescue. But finding this attribute, I shrink back appalled from it. In the whole mass of creation, in this very ruin of a king, I see the work of Power. Shall I, the creature, dare to show this my love against God's power, triumph over God and his other creatures because they have it not? Dare I do this? Surely I dare and will! For in thus boasting of my power of love, do I not boast of a thing God has created in me, greater than all the rest? If all the other creatures are only feeble types of their Creator in his different parts, shall not this love of mine, great and overwhelming as it seems, be a feeble type only of God's overwhelming love? Look again! I who would make Saul great, wise, and famous, cannot do it. It is but a desire, it is too only a creation in me by God. Had it been my own creation, my power would have equalled my will. I should surely have given all good things, and then, having given them, crown the gifts with the redeeming of Saul from ruin. But now, I can only imagine, and fall back powerless to achieve. Why then do I not despair for Saul? Because I feel and know that my desire to do, shows the germ of the power to do, at present weak and clogged by the mortal flesh. But since there *is* the germ, I know also that, like everything else which God has made, it is only the feeble finite type of an infinite attribute of God; that my weak unable desire and love are types of God's all-powerful, all-consummating love. And again, as my love is a type of and has its origin in God's love, is not my weakness a type of, has it not origin in, God's weakness too? Surely, as God has infinite power to love, so has he infinite weakness, and power therefore to be beloved. As surely as He, infinitely the strongest, shall bear the heaviest burden, so surely shall he, infinitely the weakest, sink beneath that burden below all human weakness, and from its depths rise up to pity and redeem mankind.

> 'O Saul, it shall be
> A Face like my face that receives thee; a Man like to me
> Thou shalt love and be loved by, for ever; a Hand like this hand
> Shall throw open the gates of new life to thee; See the Christ stand!'

So ends the superb prophecy which David's agony produces from his lips.

And now let us examine into the springs, the forces, which the poet seems to imagine prompted this wondrous rhapsody, and see what mood of mind it dramatically shadows forth.

It has plainly then its foundation in transcendentalism developed from the simple type of worship of bygone ages, and is just as much a human attribute as any other form of intellect developed.

What the attribute of mind is, which produced these wonderful effects, what use that attribute has had, still has, and will have, as a power in working the world, it will be our business to enquire.

It appears then that the attribute of mind which was the moving force in the struggle of David's intellect with Saul's madness as described in the poem, is one which must be called the spirit of prayer.

Now at present I shall do no more towards explanation of this phrase, 'spirit of prayer,' than call attention to the fact that it impliedly relates to what is usually called the religious element in man's nature, and that it would appear to have been handed down from man to man of a particular race. I say this much in order to draw attention to the quarter whence the train of thought will be pursued. This quarter is Palestine, Canaan, the early ground of that religion of the Jews which David held, which was the father of Christianity, and as such author of the highest civilisation. Having indicated the nature of the proposed examination so far, I should observe (just to remove all doubt as to the tendency of the enquiry), that in dealing with the subject of this spirit of prayer it would be plainly useless and beside the purpose to speak of prayer either from the point of view of any religion which has existed or does exist; or, of any special system of prayer, as such, created by any religionists; or even of the question of the efficacy or inefficacy of práying to God; because any one of these subjects would lead only to endless branch-work of theological discussion; because what we have to do is to examine into a particular attribute of a particular Jew, but an attribute shared in different degrees by Jew and Greek, bondsman and freeman, white and black.

Having thus hitherto only stated nakedly what seems to have been the force which impelled David in the foregoing poem to this work of resuscitating Saul; having called that force the spirit of prayer; and having also implied that David was only one of a series in a great chain of people, whose influence (through this spirit of prayer, as will hereafter appear), has been by far the most important influence of any which has worked in civilising the world from the earliest times to the present; it is obviously necessary to go back as far as history will carry us, and trace the stream of that people from its source. And since the spirit of prayer had its development in what we may call the primitive religion of that people; in order to trace its cause, and see clearly its ultimate effect on the civilised world, we must examine into the beginning of that religion. How far back must we go to look for the beginning of this religion? We must go back to the first man who founded the Jews, the author of that religion; and trace upwards from him through his descendants.

The plan of the examination will, therefore, resolve itself into something like this form. We shall be dealing with the history of a religion which has produced the type (shown forth in the Jewish and Christian, Old and New, Testaments), which is admitted to be the highest existing type of God. It is from the Old and New Testaments that we naturally select five chief men, in whose history may fairly be traced the birth and growth of the spirit of prayer. We shall consider the nature of that quality, and note how, in greater or less degree, it would seem to exist still, and to be very often called into exercise, in every earnest man's life; we shall see what it has done, in and through those five Jews, as exemplified in the main points of their history; and from these conclusions we shall deduce its importance as a ruling force in every work.

Taking, therefore, the historical facts of the Old and

New Testaments as a groundwork, Abraham, Jacob, Moses, David, and Jesus, seem to be the five chief men who were the strongholds of this important attribute. Because the prayer spirit dominating these five characters was, through its overpowering force the primal engine in making all the highest religions of the world; and because those religions have been the ruling influence which has made the civilisation of the world what it is, there seems small apology needed for treating of this dominant characteristic with some minuteness, in tracing it up to the point of David's struggles as described in the poem, and downward from that point to the present time.

Of Abraham, whose life is niggardly doled to us in twelve short pages, one feels almost awe in speaking, at this far away time, when the simple men of past ages loom giant-like through a mist of centuries.

He is the first worshipper; a man who stands up before us for a moment, in the sudden blaze out of the darkness of those early times, as one to whom ' God had said.'

The very first historical fact recorded of him shows us the existence in him of some innate yearning which moved him where other men were quiet, and lights up his image around the undistinguishable grey ghosts of the past. It grew and burned in him as he lived an uneventful life among placid pastoral tribes, until at last, consumed by the resistless force of it, he left his native country to work out a life for himself. He became rich in flocks and herds, a king among shepherds; he developed and forged by the heat of that fire, qualities unknown among his peaceful compatriots; and was soldierly, unscrupulous, and yet honourable; superstitious, and yet coolheaded; stern, yet kind and hospitable. But what distinguished him above all his contemporaries was, not any one of these qualities, which doubtless had representatives in obscurer men, but the fire by which he forged his manhood and his sovereignty, the yearning in him which was the spirit of prayer. It was his religion (call it superstition if you will), which was the real force to make him great. A religion which displayed itself in the building of altars, in the seeing of visions, in curious self-thwartings; a religion which was the visible effect of the prayer spirit's domination. Paradoxical man as Abraham surely was, his contradictions did not thwart his purpose, for they were welded into intensified force by the ruling fire.

Perhaps in spite of, and perhaps because of his para-doxes, at any rate by virtue of his radiant vitality, he ruled his fellows, and took his own way. But above and beyond his qualities, great as they were, the quivering wings of the prayer spirit lifted him; wife and nephew, sovereignty and riches, spoils and concubines, were to him only as means to an end; every day was an agonis-ing step towards the prize on which he had staked his life; and every act, kind or cruel, was a result of his own aspiration; to the world he was the mighty shepherd, and the kindly friend; to himself he was none of these.

What was he, then, to himself? what was his object? what seemed his failure? To be the father of many nations; to be the man in whom all families of the earth should be blessed; for these things he lived and died; of these things in his life and till his death } ⌐ realised nothing, save that in the dreary evening of ' life, when pleasure was gone from him, he had one who was to be the vessel in which the sacred fire should be kept safe.

That son, Isaac, does not appear in any way to have exhibited in himself the qualities which show the existence of the spirit of prayer. It is Jacob, the younger of his twins, whose actions show that he was the next recipient of the fire which had slept since Abraham's death. It is curious that this spirit of their great ancestor was so unequally divided between Esau, the hairy fool, and Jacob, his magnificent brother ; but we are compelled by the issue to believe that the world would not have been what it is had they showed that spirit equally ; and the consequence, at any rate, is that while Esau is represented by obscure tribes, who are no further in the world than he was, when he fooled away his birthright, any man in this nineteenth century may be proud if he be, in his greatest mental attributes, a representative of Jacob.

The singular union in Jacob of a perfidy and hardness which had no place in Abraham, with a religious fervour which exceeded Abraham's, and with a fixity of purpose in satisfying his passion for Rachel, which has become a model for all lovers of women to this day ; these characteristics are here noticeable only for showing that all his acts and thoughts, notably perfidious, calculating, passionate, or devotional, were prompted by the spirit of prayer, which made him the man he was. Witness his dealings with Esau, Isaac, and Laban. For what did he trick the great hunter, hoodwink his father, and overreach his uncle ? He bought the birthright for a mess of pottage, because of his firm conviction that he was, or his determination to become, the prince of nations ; he laid secret and violent hands on his father's blessing, because his superstition told him this was a necessary means to that end ; he baffled the cheating of Laban with greater cunning, that he might still keep his supremacy, and be thereafter great; and all these, because his eyes were ever fixed on the same shining goal. His purpose, seething in his brain, troubled his sleep beneath the stars, made him a poet for the nonce, and created the ravishing dream of the Angels' ladder : his purpose, still triumphant in his egoism, wrestled with him as Jehovah in his distorted fancy, and named him Israel, a Prince with God; his purpose, lighting up the dying embers of his brain drove him, by a singular foresight, to bless Ephraim above Manasseh; and yet of its fulfilment we can record only this; that though his life, like Abraham's was one bitter struggle for the fruition of Abraham's dream, he died far away from the land he was to people and to rule; and though he saw children and children's children, could only spend his last breath in a wild prophecy of what, in times as far away as evening clouds, should yet be the triumphant end of all.

The historical steps which lead us from Jacob to the next standpoint on which the spirit of prayer displayed itself, are easy and plainly marked. Through many years of adversity his descendants grew to be a great but oppressed people; and when the time was come for the concentration of the fire in one man, that man arose with a new purpose, as plainly a sequence and development of that which Abraham lived for, as if he had actually spoken it in words to his far-away descendant. The well-known character of Moses shows for itself, without explanation, that to him we must look for evidence of the existence of the spirit of prayer in one man above all others for the time being. See how his generalship, statesmanship, and energy combined themselves with the prayer spirit, and lifted him far above either of his predecessors in its enjoyment; and while it gave his life a greater importance, embittered his death with a more cruel pang. Alone, and by virtue of the prayer spirit he roused the sleeping passions of the great slave nation;—alone, and by dexterous management of Pharaoh's brutality, cowardice, and cupidity, he so intrigued that the very elements seemed weapons of a personal God wielded in defence of a (so-called) chosen people against the godless Egyptians. Alone, by force of that prayer spirit, he

dragged the fierce thousands through deserts, fiery
serpents, scorpions, plagues, and death, to Abraham's
land, crowded with terrible peoples who had been
Abraham's friends; alone, through the prayer spirit,
among awful mountains, in fasting and privations, he
lived out, and declared as the words of God, the law
which has been the moral code of all time, and which he
made the Hebrews believe was the very utterance, the
very handgraving, on God-created tables, of the invisible
Jehovah; and alone, by force of the prayer spirit, he
towered above the people as the Vicegerent of that
Jehovah, through communion with whom he seemed
to rule the waters and the plagues. And now, what
an end was his! The prayer spirit, which gave him his
wondrous personal influence on his people, was hourly
consuming him; he never forgot his power to the last;
he seemed in full sight, and almost touch, of his purpose.
But when the fire had burnt him through and through;
and when at last, his rage for once overcoming him, the
wearied flesh gradually sank beneath its wasting embrace;
out of the emotion kindled by the superstition still
inwoven with his worship, he cursed himself for disobedience to his self-created Deity, and the bitter end of
his dream was, with the last ebb of strength to crawl to
the top of Pisgah, and to die in very sight of the
cruel happy country, which had slipped from his touch—
for ever. Oh, bitter last minutes of the man's life! To
have toiled and thought, intrigued, prayed, and believed;
to have used the thunder as his own, and drawn the
people like one man with the fiction of the God-graven
tables; to have lain tranced in catalepsy before the
sapphire pavement, and come down with glorified face to
the grovelling Hebrews; to have brought the people
home to fulfil Abraham's dream, with power and laws of
which Abraham never dreamed; and at the end—to die

a worn-out old man, at the very threshold of a paradise which the sheep he had folded, leaving his clay behind, would taste to the full! If this is not failure, where is failure? But again, if this is not mightiest success, where has success ever been proved?

After Moses' death, the prayer spirit seems not exactly to have slept, but to have become diffused among the whole people whom Moses left so sorrowfully. Until it narrowed again, to burn through the blue eyes and in the golden hair of that gracious boy whose prophetic force was the subject of the poem that has suggested this train of thought, and whom it is fit that we should consider not only in connection with the actual incidents of the poem, but in those acts of his life which led up to those incidents, and were afterwards such a result of them as gave him the name in his own nation, nay, among many thousands since, of the earthly father of the Creator of the purest of all religions.

But at this point let us pause, and assure ourselves that in going so far back, and dwelling so minutely on the lives of David's forefathers, we have not wandered from our subject. What have these details of the lives of Abraham, Jacob, and Moses, to do with the one struggle of David's spirit which is the avowed theme of the poem? The connection is not far to seek. Abraham's dream, at Jacob's death, was far nearer fulfilment than it was at his own death, and far nearer fulfilment at Moses' death than it was at Jacob's. Jacob saw a small tribe; Moses saw a mighty nation. But even Moses saw only a mighty nation just entering a strange land, to do inevitable battle with mightier men, the dwellers in that land. It was many years, and there were many reverses and successes, before the Jews were great enough to set up for themselves a king; but not until they had done so, did David begin to breathe, or, at any rate, to think.

Abraham's dream, which began in his own bosom, was, in David's time, a household word in the mouth of every Jew; Abraham's spirit of prayer, by force of nationality, circumstances, and social contact, had grown into a sacred flame, kept as patriotically and earnestly as any nation ever kept its visible symbols of nationality. David, a poet from his birth, nursed in closest touch with Nature, had created for the Jews, and for himself, out of the traditions handed down from Abraham, a glorious future far greater than Abraham could ever imagine; in him the yearning which began in Abraham's breast was fanned to a glow by the wings of many hundred years. If, then, it was his desire, as it had been that of Abraham, Jacob, and Moses, to help the great people on their march through Time, have we not abundant reason why he should thus strive to rouse Saul, the head of that people, into burning life, lest the body should fall lifeless and become a prey to the birds and beasts who were thronging around it? And looking at his whole life, before and after he strove for Saul, is not the prayer spirit manifest in him? That he was and is the great poet of religion; that the influence of his acts which it impelled, the wild words it made him write, nay the very failures and crimes in which it involved him, added to the acts of Abraham, Jacob, and Moses, were the groundwork of many of the rhapsodies called prophecy, and were and are the force which helped on the great Jewish and Christian religions, all these consequences resulted from the working in his mind, during his shepherd life, of the supreme spirit of prayer.

That spirit, which roused Saul as we have seen, burned brightly during the bandit life into which David was forced by Saul's gloomy suspicion; he thought always and supremely of the Jews as a people; and when Saul at last fell, he hesitated not for a moment to step into the throne whence his brain could help his people on their great journey.

Fusing into a glowing mass all the heaped up traditions of his life from Abraham downwards, the prayer spirit gradually melted out in his brain an image which was to be the idol of his life. For his *hope* was that he should be the instrument through whom Abraham's ideal should be realised; that he should become, as he did become, the King of the Hebrews, and lead them up to and set them upon a pinnacle of glory high over other nations.

But, again, his *ideal* was, that he should do more than these things; the very highest pinnacle of his dream palace was, having lifted the people thus, to show the world what homage the greatest people could pay to their greatest God in a temple made with hands.

Of this dream he never lost sight. It was with him as the robber chief, among mountains, fastnesses, and shaking perils; it enfolded him when he took Saul's life in his hand, and dropped it back safe in the sleeping owner's breast; it lifted him when he charmed away the giant king's madness with his simple harp songs; it fired him when he killed the messenger who told him of Saul's death; and when he took his throne, and with sure strong feet crushed out the last sparks of rebellion, still his eyes were lit up with its glory. Nay, when his place was safe, and all men bowed to the warrior and the king, even then he never forgot. The people waxed greater and greater beneath him : he was the terror of his world; he had concubines, wives, children; but his ideal never came. He had been a man of blood; and his stained hands might not do for his God the work for which he had spent his life. When he learned in his arrogance that he numbered near a million of fighting men, the pestilence withered his pride; his darling child drove him from his throne; while his mightiest son was to surpass him in splendour, the crowning sin that produced that son thrust David beneath the feet of his own servant; and he died worn out, with shouts of rebellion ringing in his ears.

The traditions of Abraham, Jacob, Moses, and David were, many hundred years after David's death, the life of every Hebrew, man, woman, and child; they had gathered enormous power under the wild times of the captivity, from the fervid prophetic odes, under the rod of the oppressor: but the times were dark; the glory was departed; the real lord of the world had set his foot upon them; there seemed nothing left but to wait, hope, and prophesy.

The prayer spirit which had burned in David's Hebrews, paling as they rose, and brightening with their fall, towered into a star, and descended with the added heat of centuries of passion, among solemn-eyed oxen, into a poor struggling baby, lying in a manger. That night is still wrapped in a weird solemnity of Godhead; for the greatest of all men who held the prayer spirit, had begun to live.

Greater than Abraham; simpler than Jacob; humbler and stronger than Moses; purer than David; his ideal was clearer and higher than theirs, his failure more complete.

Not more than a dozen people knew or cared that he was born; he was scoffed at when he first rose to preach; his very miracles (so called) brought him into great peril; and only the lowest of his people loved him. But when other boys were children, he was a man; he set himself to redeem his people from the Romans; to be pure himself; to make them pure; to make them the greatest people.

And, oh! maddest and sweetest of dreams, he dreamed that he was God's son, and very God; and he set himself to make the world believe it. This was the deep well-spring of his actions, this carried him through his cruel life; this supported him in the pangs of death.

Always gentle and uncomplaining; always tired, but never wearied, he knew and could do such things as the light of superstition and love in those simple times brightened into miracles. He was never giddy at the height to which homage raised him, and his life is undimmed by a single cloud of anger, impurity, or excess.

But the naked torture in whose gripe he sank, would have been a cruel vengeance on the vilest robber; and thus let us seal the last page in the history of the King of Worshippers, lest we blot it with our tears.

Now in the exercise of the spirit of prayer in these five men, which was the moving power in the things they did, which is in greater or less degree existent in every man, and is called into exercise in most days of every man's life, there was, we see, one necessity or fate; every one of them failed in the thing he had to do. Failure was all their dower, failure which was to become success in some future age.

What, then, is it which makes this spirit of prayer so important, if failure is a necessity of its exercise? To ascertain this, we must now examine into the nature of the attribute, and gather from our story what it has done.

We are to consider that particular quality of mind, or, perhaps, it would be more correct to say that particular point in their upward struggle, to which all men's minds do at some time attain, (a point which with reference to the particular mind is the same, but in minds with reference to each other is higher or lower according to relative strength or weakness), which results in, or actually is, Prayer.

The spirit of prayer then is a quality which, when it possesses a man, gives to him as an attribute the necessity of looking and hoping beyond his sight; makes him

create for himself at once, more or less distinctly and
personally, and in the teeth of his reason, a God to whom
he can cry; makes, and has made, all existing ideas of
God. Further, the spirit of prayer imperiously drives its
possessor to spend his whole force in doing or getting
something far beyond his reach; it so drives him, till he
falls nerveless on the ground, crying for very weakness,
'my muscles are flesh, not iron'; having so driven and
thrown him, it works through and through every fibre in
his nature, and while he grovels and screams for help,
tells him—as a triumphant climax, and in the topmost
ecstasy of his agony—that in the darkness stands a formless thing, a shrouded power, his God in fact, who will
now or hereafter do or get for him the thing he desires;
and that what now seems the awfullest failure shall shine
as the mightiest success.

It is not hard to exemplify this definition in the five
men whom we have been considering, and to show what
has been achieved through their possession by the spirit
of prayer.

Of Abraham, it seems scarcely too much to say, that
in virtue of the ideal which he set up, and which was
created in him by the prayer spirit, he is what he
dreamed to be—the man in whom all families of the earth
are blessed. Why? First, because that spirit, which bore
him through life resistless, though it threw him fainting
in darkness at the end, where no ray showed the glory
which was to be, and which he had conceived, has, joined
with the acts of Abraham's life, been a living influence in
every Jew since his time, and has thus swayed the
fortunes of the civilised world from his time to our own.
And, again, it is not only in the realisation of his hopes
that the spirit of prayer has had its fruit. For the very
reason that Abraham *could* propose to himself an object
so far beyond him, so impossible for him to realise; for

the very reason that for a seeming hopeless end, which was to result beyond and above his hopes, in the making of the civilised world, he spent his force, and so far as he could see, failed and fell—for this very reason, and *not* because his dream has come truer than his maddest hopes could conceive, but out of the very cause of his agony, and in virtue of his failure—he is throned above in our thoughts as a chief among worshippers.

So, with Jacob and Moses, in whom glowed, with sustained, but greater intensity, the prayer spirit of Abraham with all its consequences. Both men kept in view Abraham's ideal, glorified by images made out of their own individuality; but, while both seemed to see more of their triumph, their failure was to themselves as bitter as that of the others.

Their superstition was dominant, and as intimately woven in with the prayer spirit as that of Abraham; but this last was intensified in them, both by the fact of their being eaten through with the tradition of their forefathers, that the race of Abraham should rule the world, and by the acquired vigour of growth and circumstances.

And in Jacob and Moses was not their failure a success! Was it not because of that failure, and the necessity for ultimate fulfilment, that the prayer spirit which burned in them was kept alive in their children, till it drove them back to Canaan ? Did it not make them a great people, dictate the great moral law, and to say it once more, help to make us what we are?

And tracing the immediate effects of the spirit of prayer as shown in the immediate successors of Moses, it is fair to say, that David would not have been what he was, done what he did, had it not been for the spirit of Moses descended to him. David, shepherd, warrior, and King; David, the concentration of Abraham's fire; what have we seen was the issue of *his* life? Not once did the prayer spirit forsake him; through his cruelty and crime, his losses and successes, it upheld him. In him far more than in his predecessors the spirit of prayer asserted its power; for it was through the use he made of it in his remorse for his blackest crime that he was able to train up a son who should fulfil his ancestor's desires, be cherished by his subjects, and known in worlds of which David had never heard. It was because of the use that he made of the spirit of prayer that his songs have lived till now, that he was for centuries the pattern for great kings. Last and highest of all, he was, though he never knew it, the direct ancestor of the man who for nearly 2000 years has been worshipped as the Son of God himself. Yet I have shown how he too, like the rest, failed utterly in comparison with his desires ; how pleasure went from him, and he died a wreck.

Jesus of Nazareth has created a firm belief in his Godship, not only in his immediate followers, but in a large part of the world. Through the force of the prayer spirit, he ruled all who approached him ; founded and has maintained a moral code which vivifies that of Moses, and will be remembered when Moses is forgotten.—Through the worship of Jesus men have been humanised ; the worship of Jesus has been throughout the world's history the strongest engine of power.—Yet in his life, more than in all the others put together, is exemplified the truth laid down, that although what seemed the awfullest failure then should shine hereafter as the mightiest success, failure at the time of strife is a necessity of the spirit of prayer.

To sum up all that has been said, let us remember that the prayer spirit has never been independently in any one of those five men, but has derived its added force from the knowledge of what some one else has done ; that, be this as it may, the prayer spirit is still an attribute which each

of those five men, haa they consented to be guided by
their reason, would have made it their life's business to
crush ; but that, since the prayer spirit (which you may
call, if you will, credulity, superstition, or fanaticism)
triumphed over reason, the victory has made its subjects
both princes and saviours.

And, again, let us notice that only when these men
were so wrought with fire that they were carried thereby
to the school of their weakness, to a confession of the
possible veiled power, only then and at that point did
they pray ; only as they possessed and cherished in themselves the God-begotten necessity of striving thus madly,
and could believe that in failing thus utterly they did in
truth triumph, has their work lived till now, and will it
live hereafter.

Having seen, then, how the prayer spirit dominated all
the five men described, how its force created each ideal ;
how that ideal first failed, then succeeded : how triumphant has been Abraham's ideal in the worship of Jesus
—let us see in a few words what the prayer spirit, handed
down through generations from those five men, has
done.

The concentration of purpose, the absolute pitilessness,
with which all of them worked to their end ; these strong
weapons, used perpetually on the men around them,
hewed out some part of the fabric which was to be built,
and cowed and destroyed all opposers, sooner or later.

Always, the fact of any man's having had one burning
idea throughout his life will communicate some of his
fire to some successors ; this contagion spreads, the idea
gains countless forces on its side, and nations make a
pride of some thought or scheme, which single great men
were scoffed at or killed for entertaining.

Although, at this day, no man does what the old Jews
did for a religion or an idea like Abraham's, the principle

which moves a man now in any research or purpose, scientific, political, artistic—what you will—is nothing more or less than the spirit of prayer.

Had it not been for the Jews, Christianity would not have been: had it not been for Christianity, civilisation as it now exists would not have been. Civilisation would have been as nothing had not the same spirit, which made Abraham and his successors erect a God for our worship, urged the great men of Europe in the cause of the world and the men in it.

Surely, then, it is not hard to see how the spirit of prayer has influenced every great modern work, how every great man's life is yet instinct with the fire of it ; not hard to see how the conception of which a man can achieve only the millionth part, is reverently taken up by man after man, until the toil of ages triumphantly completes it amid the silent prostration of the world.

And now, even now, the prayer spirit is neither dead nor dumb ; it struggles and burns in you and me ; it dominates Nature.

And it is in the sound of the wind ; it wakes in the buds of spring ; it leans from the yearning of an evening sky ; it vibrates in the magical promise of the morning.

The cry of a dog is eloquent of prayer ; the horse's nostril quivers with it ; every line in a man's worn face, every knot in a man's rugged hand, is the trace of a bygone prayer.

By it, man is most human, for he only feels beyond his sight, he only desires what he cannot see : by it, man is most godlike, for he only is lifted, through his sense, by his desires, to the kingdom where the veil is rent in twain.

When we want, though we use no words, we pray the more passionately in dumb entreaty, and set our muscles anew to get our desire ; and though we do not get it, the world, and we, are better for the strife.

Through the spirit of prayer, Abraham, Jacob, Moses, and David, still live ; and when the religion of Jesus has passed away, men will remember the dream-life of the Hebrew carpenter, and the blessed consequences of following out the maddest and noblest of ideals.

Such are some of the thoughts which the poem of 'Saul' has awakened ; such are some of the conclusions to which a loving consideration of the thoughts in that poem have led me irresistibly.

We have dwelt at some length on the attribute which seems to have been in the poet's mind when he wrote the poem, and we have traced the course of that attribute from the beginning of David's people to David himself, and thence down to the present time.

Having thus dwelt, as fully as is possible in an essay like this, on the history of the spirit of prayer, let us turn once more to the subject of the poem itself, and see not only how that is an example of the exercise of the attribute, but also what direct thoughts, what actual lessons for ourselves, the poet desired to place before us.

It is plain that David, as drawn in the poem, fulfilled, in the intensity of his mental struggle, all the conditions of the spirit of prayer : that he was striving after an end which was not within the grasp of humanity ; that he was drawn by it far beyond his first desire into regions of prophecy, and into the splendour of an idea which has ruled thousands for so many years — the idea of Christianity.

We see, too, that at the time when he crawled out of the tent, utterly exhausted, none of these splendours blest his eyes in their accomplishment ; for it was not in his life, but hundreds of years after, that this idea was fulfilled.

But we see also that here the spirit of prayer had a

particular field to work in, very different from the wide fields in which it ranged when David's forefathers and successors held it.

Here was no founding of a nation, or establishing a religion ; nothing to win applause of a whole world. It was merely the work of one man upon another, a work prompted by the welling up of human love which, thank God, exists to-day as it did then.

For us of to-day, then, what is the lesson which the poet would teach ?

He surely says to us something like this : In this strife of David's, is there no warning for modern men ? Does not our work lie among each other ? Are there not Sauls enough among us, whose temptations and madnesses, if they lack the gloom or glow of historical majesty, are only too plainly seen in their hideous reality ? Surely every one of us may one day be a Saul, and let none triumph because he is hitherto spotless ; and in the thought of this terrible possibility, let us each try and gather strength to become Davids upon fit occasion.

Let us, in plain words, admit that the duty of every man towards his fellows is, first to keep that sympathetic power at its fullest pitch, which enables him at any moment to bring a kind of mesmeric force to bear on any man who may need the aid of another's mind to expel some of the devils of the world or the flesh. The poem seems to teach us that it is this principle of direct influence over men which produces all the great works : that no man can attain perfection in that influence until he has first made his own life true at least, if not pure also. And when that is done, it matters little, surely, whether his influence be exercised over six men or six millions, so long as the best is done that can be done. The force is existent, and redoubles itself in every new mind which sucks it in ; the force lives, and has more than ample material, during one short life, in the changes and chances which six most uneventful lives may bring about, to work its possessor to the full agony of the spirit of prayer ; once the force is born, it is a living thing whereby the world is moved ; and while it should be enough for any one man to die feeling that his best is done, it is scarcely unreasonable to say that, although the fruit may never be seen beyond the six men during its owner's life, any effort truly directed, may, like the efforts of Abraham, David, and Jesus, directly or indirectly be the very instrument which makes a nation, founds a kingdom, or establishes a religion.

# THE DIGRESSION IN 'SORDELLO'

AT the end of the Third Book of 'Sordello,' the poet breaks off the thread of his story to enter into a long digression, which while singularly obscure in expression, is a remarkable, and of its kind unique effort, in the direction of showing what are the poet's views of the duties of his own class towards mankind. This digression I have not thought it well to speak of in its place in the poem, lest the continuity in the interpretation of the actual story should be disturbed. But the ideas put forward by the poet on behalf of himself and his fellows are so valuable, that it seems right, after having dwelt with some care on the various trains of thought whereby the poet was prompted in writing the poems on which the foregoing essays were written, to give as clearly as possible an explanation of the views expressed in this digression.

It will be remembered that the Third Book completes the first circle of Sordello's life, and brings him within reach of his first ideal of making men act out their faculties, by his influence. The poet at this point of the story lets fall the curtain for awhile, and—in order to account to the world for his motive in writing the poem, —pursues a thread of his own inner life.

He begins by laying it down as a principle, that in all true works (such as he hopes this is) some proofs escape to show that the singer is not giving us the whole of his inner life and hope. Underlying such works, some thought like this seems to be in the singer's mind : ' My life began before and will continue after this work ; although you may think this subject engrosses my whole mind, it is not so; I shall go my way, and leave that subject behind me, perhaps never to take it up again. But do not imagine that when my work on that subject is finished I have ceased to live in thought. You may indeed mourn because I continue silent, you may perhaps complain of me for not giving you the result of the deeper thoughts which did underlie that work, and which I pursue and shall pursue when that work is finished. You may accuse me of inconstancy, in not remaining with you (as the tone of my work seemed to promise I would), to dwell with you for ever upon the subject; you may perhaps complain that I, though professing deep contemplation, do not give you nearly all the result of it; that I never lay before you the scheme, the aspirations, of my whole life. But what then ? My business first is to live my life out, not to speak of it; I must gather experience before I can impart it. If indeed an idea chains me down for a time, and works within me until the fire is kindled and I am obliged to speak, then you have the benefit of my speech; but as soon as I have spoken it I must go away from you to gather fresh thoughts. I cannot stay and brood over this one thought for ever with you. To use a simile :

> 'Tis but a sailor's promise, weatherbound :
> 'Strike sail, slip cable, here the bark be moored
> For once, the awning stretched, the poles assured !
> Noontide above : except the wave's crisp dash,
> Or buzz of colibri, or tortoise' splash,
> The margin's silent : out with every spoil
> Made in our tracking, coil by mighty coil,

This serpent of a river to his head
I' the midst!   Admire each treasure, as we spread
The bank, to help us tell our history
Aright : give ear, endeavour to descry
The groves of giant rushes, how they grew
Like demon's endlong tresses we sailed through :
What mountains yawned, forests to give us vent
Opened, each doleful side, yet on we went
Till . . . may that beetle (shake your cap) attest
The springing of a land-wind from the west !'
—Wherefore ?   Ah yes, you frolic it to-day !
To-morrow, and the pageant moved away
Down to the poorest tent-pole, we and you
Part company : no other may pursue
Eastward your voyage, be informed what fate
Intends, if triumph or decline await
The tempter of the everlasting steppe.'

'I,' says the poet, 'am like a sailor or traveller, whose business is to go perpetually from place to place, and at his stoppages to sell and buy, and communicate his knowledge to those into whose company he is thrown : so long as he is weatherbound, or any use is to be got from the narration, he will sit and tell you all his travels, just as so long as I am bound by an idea, or there is use in communicating it, I give you the full benefit of the idea. But as soon as the landwind springs up, the sailor is off ; and as soon as my idea is exhausted and told out, so soon as its immediate influence is gone from me, I must go on my way too, and gather new fruits.

Now what has the enunciation of this principle to do with the work of the poem of Sordello ?   In the first place, the very fact of the poet's breaking off the thread of his story to enunciate it, is a proof that that work is, so far as he can make it, true; that is, he desires to get at the truth in writing it.   In the second place, he proposes to do what he does not admit that he can be called upon to do, but means to do out of pure love, that is, he proposes to give to the world his deepest thoughts which have made up his life hitherto, his speculations as to what he will do, or ought to do, hereafter; in the third place, feeling that he has an experience which he ought to impart, he proceeds to give it, and to show how the work of the poem 'Sordello' was prompted by that experience, and in what way Sordello's ideal resembled or differed from his own.

Now the musings which have thus been displayed took place as the poet sat upon a ruined palace-step at Venice: and as he came to this point his eyes fell upon some beautiful Italian peasant girls, poor and half-naked, but in the full bloom of beauty, health, and strength. The sight of them, and the blue sky and the bounteous weather, all tending to make him feel happy and contented, roused in his breast, as such influences will in any noble breast, thoughts of other women and men, not so happy and healthy; other skies not so warm and blue, in his own England. These thoughts gradually assume shape, and he seems to see before him a sad dishevelled ghost of a poor woman, who symbolises the poor suffering humanity in England and other countries less favoured than this Italy. This poor ghost symbolises, too, an old ideal of his, which he proceeds to dilate upon. He proceeds in fact to do what he has promised, and give the world the deepest thoughts which have made up his life hitherto, his speculations as to what he will do, or ought to do hereafter, and to show how the work of the poem 'Sordello' was prompted by past thoughts of his life, and in what way Sordello's ideal resembled or differed from his own.

'Long ago,' he says, 'when I was young, I desired that all men should be happy, should have power and riches and health. Gradually I came to see how impossible this was; and when I left England, and came to Italy, the magic weather and the glorious sights and sounds dulled my sense of sympathy, and dazzled my eyes, and I seemed to forget what I had once desired for mankind. But to-day as I looked, the very beauty and health of the women I looked at, the glories of Venice round me, re-called to my mind that old dream of mine, and caused me to feel a pang as if I had been unfaithful. But on looking deeper, I discover that perhaps I have not been so faith-less after all. It may be that the beauty of the life around me has changed my views ; but at any rate I will now take up this old ideal and speak of it, and try to trace how we may adapt it to actual circumstances and make the best of what is ; for though this ideal, so long neglected, has become worn and faded, it is still an old love, and in its weariness and squalor is dearer to me than ever. That is, human beings, which I once loved for what they might be, are dearer far to me now than ever, not for what they might be, but for what they are, sinners all, wretched, starving.

'Alas ! I see now (what Sordello has yet to see), that there is so little happiness to be got out of the world, that do what we will we cannot share it amongst all. Then what can we do ? What shall we do ? Shall we try to give happiness to a score, and leave the rest, thus estab-lishing a claim to the same happiness for all men ? Here, under the influence of the Italian weather, I will do this ; I will say that I have grown wiser ; that it is useless my asking for all men to be made kings and poets ; all that I ask is that each may have strength and health. I see strength and health round me, and nothing more ; and I come to the conclusion that all we can do is to say, since these have health and strength, all who are ill and weak have a right to it. But at this point I feel a pang of un-faithfulness again ; is not this rather a summary, comfort-able way of disposing of the question ? As I think of this, I see again the miserable thousands, I see again the hope I had which would make them all happy. That hope seems to come to me reproachfully again like that worn-out neglected mistress. Can I not do something then to still this awkward conscience of mine? Can I not finish some work towards spreading happiness? or at any rate towards making people see that they cannot alter the first order, and that even by mere kindly allowance to their fellow-men they can do great good?

'Alas! my poor worn-out mistress,' cries the poet, addressing his old ideal in that shape, 'you find me baulked even of this small hope of making people at least healthy and strong; what wonder then if you mistrust my perseverance? You are worn and faded; but I have not lost my faith in you. And truth to say I love you more now, than when I hoped you would be a queen, and all that I could desire.

'For poor humanity will urge its claims, and is never ashamed of pressing them too often; my ideal, if it be a true one, sticks to its master indefatigably, and though bruised and beaten and half naked, is too much a part of him to deny him.' That is, let a man go through ever so many changes, if he has once held any idea which has a spark of honesty in it, that idea, however ridiculous it may come to look, is always dear to him as the worn-out mistress of his early love. He, if he be really true, is ever too ready to remember his debt. Nay the very distress and sadness of that past ruined life, increases his passion for it. And as a man who has once loved a woman truly, who perhaps in their early days has loaded her with jewels and presents, and claimed for her the highest place in the land, when they are both older, if she through no fault of his has become poor and neglected, will then out of his gathered experience try to make her at least comfortable and happy, though his early dreams of queenship are gone and dead

—so does the poet deal with this ideal of his, which he has utterly failed to realise in its majesty, but which perhaps he may bring to some use and comfort even now.—Seeing that he cannot make a heaven of earth and make all men chiefs and bards, what will he do now? He says, Let us at any rate see what we can make of life as it stands; what answer we can make to the sanctified ones who are always proclaiming the hopelessness of evil; can we not say this? Evil exists; but do not men continue to live in spite of evil? Nay, do not even the worst of men keep their own standard of truth? To this they stick, though they lie to the world; so long as they are true to their own standard they don't care for the standard of the men around them. This is better than having no standard of truth at all. So much for their sense of duty. Then how about their happiness? We see that they are denied a multitude of pleasures simply because, since they will not conform to the rules of the society in which they live, they are denied a multitude of rights; yet they get some one pleasure out of some right which they insist on, and succeed in getting, because the world, which suffers wrong by them, and their perverse views, is not wholly unjust. This is better than if there were no pleasure for bad men at all. But perhaps it will be urged, It may be very well to say that bad men have their conceit of truth, but this does not excuse their badness. Nay, have they any conceit of truth at all? Surely not; for do they not tacitly acknowledge that they are bad and deceitful, in trusting, (as they do) the very world which they make a practice of wronging? To this I reply, they have their conceit of truth, and I will prove them to have it out of the very argument you have used. You say, if these men have their conceit of truth, and believe all the rest of the world to be false therefore, why do they trust the world

to which they work evil and wrong? Don't they do so
because they think the rest of the world better than they,
and therefore more honourable? I say, no; they do it for
the very reason that they have their conceit of truth; they
do it for the very reason that they think all other men
stupider than they are, that is, they believe that they
themselves alone know the secrets of the scheme of evil.
They argue, in short, that they have the secret of truth,
and all others·are wrong; that they are obliged to act in
defiance of the world's laws, because these laws are wrong;
that they carry out the scheme of evil (that is of acting
in defiance of the world's laws) in order that they may
achieve their end, and at last make their own idea of
truth and good triumphant; and that since their object
is only to be had by working that scheme of evil, the
good which they labour to produce can only be produced
laboriously by working on the ignorance of the rest of the
world. This view at any rate accounts for the mode of
life of most men, and disposes of all evil save the sickness
which is the cause of death; and that evil is not an evil
of life at all. If then, men do really live in this way, if
this is how the world really works; and if we can't
repudiate our common humanity—our portion in the
common lot—what is one to do? At least one can try
to make ignorance as small as possible; one can try by
honest means to show what really is the truth, the true
life; at any rate this is better than standing idle and proclaiming impossible remedies as some people do, who
vaguely talk of the 'water of life,' and each of whom
arrogates to himself the conceit that he knows where to
find at least a dewdrop of that water.

'These dullards are intolerable; they are as bad and
pernicious to the actual moving, working world as a man
would have been to the Israelites in their desert journey,
if while the whole nation was baked with heat and thirst,

he had stood still with folded hands and proclaimed his wonder that anyone need be thirsty when there were plenty of fountains somewhere. At least the man who attempts to make the best of the suffering which exists is better than such idle rascals, even though his efforts are not always directed in the prescribed course of social laws ; just as Moses was better than the hypothetical proclaimer of fountains, when he disobeyed a mandate by awkwardly smiting the rock instead of speaking to it. But at this point one of these frothy wiseacres interferes ; who is this presumptuous setter up of new creeds ; how does he dare to tell us what the office of our life is, and magnify it to absurdity in his optimism ? Nay, I rejoin, it is not I who set up new creeds, it is you who would do so ; it is not I who can tell you what the office of our life is, nor do I magnify that office unduly; it is you who are always telling us what office that is, and are always jumping to errone- ous conclusions from very insufficient premises indeed. Office, forsooth ! How can we tell, here on this earth, what our office is ? With wrong and failure on every side, with rogues and fools in power and wealth, and honest men and true in obscurity and want, can anyone say that the end and object of life is obtained here? Surely not. We are all of us here on the earth, with varied powers, in perpetual social contact ; we are per- petually altering, developing, we never come to a stop till death. What then can we do here ? If we cannot each finish our lives to a perfect round, we can surely make use of our daily growth to gain experience, we can surely make use of others' daily growth and glean experience from them. We can in short, since we find ourselves in a crowd of fellow-beings, test each other's power and watch each other's developments, and consider how far we can mutually benefit each other by exchange of the good which our respective faculties are readiest at producing :

since on this earth we are only growing, since all we can really do is as it were to watch the construction of an engine out of the various attributes which make up the entire man, let us apply ourselves to do this task as well as possible. When the end comes and we die, then the engine is complete for use ; but it is not complete till then ; and only then is it complete in so far as the workman who made it (that is the man himself) has been earnest and skilful. But is this engine, the complete man, who has been in process of erection all his life, to be absolutely destroyed at the end of it like a child's card-house ? Is the glorious machine, all new and ready for action, to be let stand and become rusty and useless ? Surely not. Our finished being is to be used in another life, where the work of watching construction will be done, for the machine is complete, and no more construction is necessary.

'But to revert to this life, and the men in this world ; I have shown what is plainly a man's urgent duty here. Now although the general principle laid down is applicable to all, that each should get by heart and be master of the attributes of all his fellows, there must necessarily be a large majority whose daily stress of labour occupies them far too closely to allow of their looking aside at their fellows, and a still larger number who have not the power to perform the function of observing. There are again a few who possess this power of observing in a prominent degree ; and these are poets, such as I who speak. We poets then are divided into three classes ; one who sees and says he sees (without describing the *nature* of the thing seen) ; a second who describes the *nature* of what he sees ; a third who imparts the gift of seeing the thing, and its nature, to other men. Now I who preach to men the before-stated ideal, will further assert that each of these classes of poets or makers is bound to exercise his own functions to the utmost. And as I preach this gospel to poets, I will proceed to put it in practice myself; here are three instances of the power which I claim as one of the third and highest of the three classes I have described.

> 'So that I glance,' says such an one, 'around
> And there's no face but I can read profound
> Disclosures in : this stands for hope, that—fear,
> While for a speech, a deed in proof, look here !'
> 'Stoop, else the strings of blossom where the nuts
> O'erarch will blind thee ;  Said I not? she shuts
> Both eyes this time, so close the hazels meet !
> Thus, prisoned in the Piombi, I repeat
> Events one rove occasioned, o'er and o'er,
> Putting 'twixt me and madness evermore
> Thy sweet shape, Zanze ! therefore stoop !'
>                         'That's truth !'
> (Adjudge you) 'The incarcerated youth
> Would say that !'
>           'Youth?  Plara the bard?  Set down
> That Plara spent his youth in a grim town,
> Whose cramped ill-featured streets huddled about
> The minster for protection, never out
> Of its black belfry's shade and its bells' roar.
> The brighter shone the suburb—all the more
> Ugly and absolute that shade's reproof
> Of any chance escape of joy—some roof
> Taller than they, allowed the rest detect
> Before the sole permitted laugh (suspect
> Who could, 'twas meant for laughter, that ploughed cheek's
> Repulsive gleam !) when the sun stopped both peaks
> Of the cleft belfry like a fiery wedge,
> Then sunk, a huge flame on its socket edge,
> With leavings on the grey glass oriel-pane
> Ghastly some minutes more.  No fear of rain—
> The minster minded that !  In heaps the dust
> Lay everywhere.  This town, the minster's trust,
> Held Plara : who, its denizen, bade hail
> In twice twelve sonnets, Tempe's dewy vale.
> Exact the town, the minster, and the street !'

> ' As all mirth triumphs, sadness means defeat :
> Lust triumphs and is gay, Love's triumphed o'er
> And sad : but Lucio's sad.  I said before
> Love's sad, not Lucio : one who loves may be
> As gay his love has leave to hope, as he
> Downcast that lust's desire escapes the springe :
> 'Tis of the mood itself I speak, what tinge
> Determines it, else colourless—or mirth
> Or melancholy, as from heaven or earth.'

' Do you agree to my instances ?  Yes !  Good.  Then
I have vindicated my right, as a poet, to preach to you,
another poet, and have imparted to you the gift of seeing.
Now, let me beg you to take another step, and *believe* the
sights I see.  If you decline to believe in what I say I see,
because you cannot see it, you are sinning against the
law I have laid down, which compels you to strive to the
utmost to master all human attributes.  For what I, a
man, have seen, you, a man, may see too, more or less.  I
may have better opportunities for examination of the
subject; but you are not excused from examining what I
put in your way, merely because you have not the means
of testing my truth by reference to the fountain-head.  If,
on the other hand, you object that the looking at such a
sight as I am obliged to ask you to take on trust is useless,
because you cannot turn it to actual tangible result, I
admit frankly that its use is not here.  Nay I fully admit
that for the purposes of this life the men of action are
better, who see indeed little, but use that little.  But
there is another life; and when the greatest poets not only
see and tell what they see, but turn their sight to use for
themselves and the world, we shall be in heaven indeed.
Still you can hardly object to the greatest poets while
they are here, using their faculty of seeing what others cannot see; even you will admit that they are only doing
what they are bound to do, viz., carrying out the law I
have laid down for them.    And if they are bound to do

this, surely the world's duty is to keep them up to that work, by round abuse if need be.

'So that I bring you round to the subject of my poem, and show you that at least *I* cannot be abused for neglecting this work which I say we poets have to do ; seeing that I drag to the surface Sordello's inmost soul which I *have* deciphered, leaving it to be deciphered by you as best you can.   Not that if you turn and rend me for my work I shall be vengeful, like Hercules in Egypt: indeed the true suffrage of one friend is enough for me—

> Yours, my patron friend,
> Whose great verse blares unintermittent on
> Like your own trumpeter at Marathon—
> You who, Platœas and Salamis being scant,
> Put up with Ætna for a stimulant,
> And did well, I acknowledged, as he loomed
> Over the midland sea last month, presumed
> Long, lay demolished in the blazing West
> At eve, while towards him tilting cloudlets prest,
> Like Persian ships at Salamis.   Friend, wear
> A crest proud as desert, while I declare
> Had I a flawless ruby fit to wring
> Tears of its colour from that painted king
> Who lost it, I would, for that smile which went
> To my heart, fling it in the sea, content,
> Wearing your verse in place, an amulet
> Sovereign against all passion, wear and fret.
> My English Eyebright, if you are not glad
> That, as I stopped my task awhile, the sad
> Dishevelled form, wherein I put mankind
> To come at times and keep my pact in mind,
> Renewed me—hear no crickets in the hedge,
> Nor let a glowworm spot the river's edge
> At home, and may the summer showers gush
> Without a warning from the missel-thrush !

'Thus then, if only for the sake of one or two true friends, I am glad to have thus put forth my deep ideal of the use of life for men's happiness and the poet's work to that end.'

So the poet resumes his narrative, first entreating his audience not to misconceive his portrait of Sordello, and take him for a devil, who may all the time be a saint, lest they should by such condemnation perchance be damning themselves, as fellow-beings with Sordello.

Now what has this examination of men's and poets' duty in this life to do with the work of the poem of Sordello, and is there any connection in the thoughts here evolved with the thoughts intended to be evolved in the poem itself?

In the first place it is plain that, as already stated, the undertaking to unravel Sordello's soul is an attempt to perform that highest of the poet's duties, the making other men see what he sees in its deepest nature. And is there not an obvious link between Sordello's ideal and that of his narrator?

Sordello saw human nature and tried to display in himself all its attributes without exercising any; that is, he tried the impossible task not merely of showing to men all their deepest attributes in speech, but of actually acting and being all men in all their deepest attributes. The idea was the same, warped by the egoism of youth. When Sordello failed in this, finding his means insufficient to his will, he found a prospective opportunity of influencing men by his actual acquired position as prince and Palma's husband, and of making them happy in acting out all their noblest attributes by virtue of that power of his, wedded to his imagination. That is, he would now show to men all their deepest and highest attributes, not only by his own poetic force, but by inducing them through his power to exercise those attributes for themselves. But still all this time he failed to see not only in all other men, but in his own self, the stern existence of the common attributes of the fleshly nature, or despised those common attributes as clogs to his purpose. He failed to see what his biographer sees clearly, that whatever exists must be used according to its own innate laws and cannot be disregarded. Thus his ideal was plainly the same with the poet's, only it was not so far developed. How it did develop, and in what direction, has been seen in the ensuing books of the poem.

# EPILOGUE

IN bringing to a close the various thoughts evoked by a few grand utterances, some concluding words will not be out of place.

If at a first backward glance over the whole series of essays, it should appear to the reader that the speculative or religious views in each are inconsistent one with another, it should be remembered that each poem has been treated as a separate effort, as forming by itself, in a quasi-dramatic guise, a distinct train of thought. The train of thought, which was the basis of each poem, must necessarily be treated, in the development of it which has been attempted, as consistent only with itself; and the first duty of the essayist was to preserve, as far as possible, in all his ramifications, the same *principle* of intellectual research as supported the actual poem in hand.

And yet, as will appear more plainly in the following words, there runs through the seeming inconsistency of each theme a thread of unity which supports the whole.

Let us shortly review, and bind together into one, the subject to which our attention has been directed.

We have been taught then, how to aspire in our love passion ; we have learned the consequences of thwarting intellect, and the sin of checking human love or charity ; we have learned too the terrible retributions which over-take little evil doings, and the necessity of using failure as a positive force. We have seen the duty of man to man in checking or avenging evil-doing ; we have seen how sexual love, human love, failure and duty, were all united in the grand ideal of Sordello ; we have found in the striving of David the manifestation of an attribute, the spirit of prayer, without which neither passion, nor intellect, nor love, are of any avail.

Is there not a strong bond of unity between all these ideas ? We see first that a man, as man, may, indeed ought to, develop his natural faculties, as typified by the highest natural faculty of all, the power of a man's love for woman, of a woman's love for man. We learn next that he should extend that power of sexual love, in the wider sense of love for all humanity as such. Then we find that love must not stop here, but must elevate itself to sympathy with and help of intellectual power, whether hidden or revealed.

So much for our broad duties as human beings towards our fellows. We now learn that such being our duties towards the attributes which according to the scheme of our nature must be called good, we have on the other hand to combat and resist evil attributes or impulses wherever we find them : we see not only that there will be divers consequences to undergo, if we fail or sin, but also what those consequences involve both to ourselves and the world. And then we have in 'Sordello' the full fraught history of a life which occupied itself on all the duties we have learned from the other poems, and which gives ample evidences of all possible consequences of failure and wrong-doing. We learn from the thoughts in 'Saul' what is the real mainspring of all effort in this life, whether for duty, love, good, or (relatively to the world) evil. Lastly, we have seen what was the motive which has caused the poet to write all these thoughts, and having seen what are men's duties to each other as men, we learn from him a high scheme of life to be followed by that class which in another life should be supreme rulers, the class of poets, in their capacity as poets.

And in all these struggles of men and women, poets and others, we see incompleteness, and little joy ; desire and little fruition. In each we admire not what they did, but what they tried to do ; in each the failure of the achievement, and not the nature of the thing striven for, moves our pity and wakes our sympathy.

But let us not make the fatal mistake of supposing (what many men without knowing it are apt to suppose) that it is rather than otherwise a grand thing to be unsuccessful, and that success is synonymous with coarseness and charlatanry. If sorrow is greater than joy, and failure more than success, can we not live ? Is it nothing that we have beating hearts, and strong health, if we fail in our passion ; or is it nothing that we have love and passion if we fail in intellectual aims ? Surely each man is too often a vexation to himself by reason of his desires ; but of all things the most hateful is that falsest of all false guides, the idealisation of grief or ill success. It so often happens that when a man has plenty and comfort, and wide powers of doing actual good, he thwarts that power by brooding over possible enjoyments, and in seeming honesty of purpose idealising *them* to the utmost. He has, perhaps, failed in love, or in some intellectual scheme : and he straightway erects an idol of his failure, and falls down and worships it, leaving the poor world which has so much really stern sorrow in it to go past wailing or entreating, without moving a finger to help it. He, forsooth, is to be engaged all his best years in lying prostrate before his self-created idol ; he, forsooth, is a man of exceptional aims, and specially fine nerves, and must not let his old useless hopes die out lest he should become even as other men, and all his fine nature be coarsened and deadened by the rubbing of the vulgar ·men and women of the public world. This is the most pernicious form of selfishness; because the subtlety of its insinuations invariably deludes the victim into supposing that he is serving some high end in so abstracting himself from useful work; almost any other form of selfishness has in it some working power, and makes its owner of some actual use.

Then let us take the true lesson, which all these utterances of the poet's have been intended to teach; the lesson which is to be extracted from them and from all others of his works—it is this. Always try to work in the direction of an end which is beyond your power, and get other men to sympathise with and fully understand your aspiration. Such an end is sure to be greater than one which is within your own reach; and is sure, if rightly worked, to command the interest of other men. Never be afraid to admit others to a knowledge of what you desire; never let selfish pride induce you to keep the credit of an achievement all to yourself. If the end be really a worthy one, it must necessarily almost be beyond your grasp; and the more unattainable it is, the more men it will require, the longer time must elapse, before it can be completely gained. And then (to take the instances we have been studying) whether the end be the general idealisation of sexual love, human love, the power of intellect, the utilisation of failure, or the searching out and punishing of evil doing, the same means must be used, the same attribute called into exercise; those means namely, and that attribute, which David and his successors used, and which made up the life of Sordello.

And in trying to draw these conclusions, we are but paying a small tribute to the unwearied efforts of the poet whose works have given us such boundless treasures of thought; we are but acknowledging that in some slight

way we have felt the honesty of the purpose of his life
and his writings, as plainly set down in his laws for the
regulation of poetic effort.

And, to draw one more conclusion before we take a
loving farewell of the poet and his works; from all these
instances we gain one more proof of the unity of human
thought and effort; each for himself has striven towards
his own end, and pursued it by a separate path; while the
poet, as judge and contemplator, has put down, for the
behoof of all, the features and the particulars of life of
each striver.

But at the close of the day, all men must find themselves emerging from the great portal of life, and hand in
hand with the poet, whose work is done, must enter a
grey negative land, which to some is failure, to some
absence of hope, to some joy and rest. All are at last
joined together—in suffering, in disappointment, in joy,
peace, success; all now march forward, as brothers in a
future hope, towards the far off light which beams along
the horizon of that gloomy land, and which is the shore
of a new country.

In that new country, let us hope, all aspirations are
one : in that new country, may the poets realise the
dream of Sordello's creator, and reign unchecked in
thought and act; may humanity, its hopes and fears, its
joys and sorrows, be swallowed up in one perfect love, one
perfect power.

# FIFINE AT THE FAIR

THIS essay is divided into four parts. I. Description of the Contents of the Poem. II. An Analysis, section by section ; in short, a translation of the Poem into prose. III. A Statement, dividing the main subjects dealt with into three heads. IV. A Synopsis of the whole Poem.

The poem 'is preceded by a prologue, and succeeded by an epilogue. On the flyleaf preceding the prologue, is a motto, in the form of an extract from the third scene of the first Act of Molière's *Don Juan*, in which Donna Elvira puts her husband to the blush, and treats him with ironical contempt. The body of the poem consists of a monologue by a husband, speaking to his wife whom he names Elvire, in which the husband introduces in quotation marks, and afterwards discusses or answers, certain objections and observations made by his wife on what he has previously said.

## I. DESCRIPTION OF THE CONTENTS OF THE POEM.

1. §§ 1-14. A talk about the charm Bohemianism has for its votaries, the troupe of strolling actors.

2. §§ 15-34. The character and charm of Fifine, the dancer and beauty of the troupe, as contrasted with or forming one in a line of beauties, including Elvire.

3. §§ 35-42 The character and charm of Elvire the

wife, as contrasted with Fifine and the other beauties, and the nature of her hold on her husband, and his love for her.

4. §§ 43-53.    Hence, how every man, by the necessity of his soul's nature, must strive to seek and find the right wife to love.

5. §§ 54-59.    How every man must develop his soul for fitness for such a search, by learning the world he lives in, and divining the truth under falseness, the whole from the part seen ; and how sooner or later that learning the world will be done, not for the sake of the soul itself, but for love of another soul, and desire to give that soul the result of that learning.

6. §§ 60-63.    A justification of the husband's admiration of Fifine, on the ground laid clear in 3-5 inclusive ; the husband taking the scene around him and his wife as he speaks, and using it as illustrating the necessity of learning the whole from the part seen.

7. §§ 64-69.    A new illustration of the learning of truth through falseness, by the image of a swimmer in the sea, typifying a man in the world ; the things he touches in the sea, typifying the Fifines in the world. What he touches in the sea helps to upbear his body, and enables him to breathe and use his eyes ; the Fifines in the world help his soul to learn truth.

8. §§ 70-88.    How women help in this direction of learning truth, and not men ; how other women than the wife are best for that purpose, and most of all women such a one as Fifine, because she professes to play a part, and gives you a chance to study her underneath her part, while the rest of the world profess truth, but really play a part ; and how this learning to find truth under falsehood in men and women is the soul's prime aim.

9. §§ 89-126.    How the speaker uses the conclusions arrived at, and works out of them the meaning of a

day-dream he had that morning after playing Schumann's Carnival. How he saw in his dream the masque of the world, all men and women disguised in their flesh ; how his business was to learn their reality under their disguise, the true nature of man and his institutions, religious, scientific, or artistic ; how all such institutions must eventually fuse into one belief of all mankind in one God.

10 §§ 127-131. How all the speaker's theories and conclusions crumble to nothing before the face of approaching death.

11. § 132. How his highest strain after the perfect life causes his deepest fall at the end.

## II. AN ANALYSIS OF THE POEM.

### PROLOGUE.

Lines 1-4. As I swam in the bay this morning, a butterfly came floating above me. 5, The sea was mine, the sky was its own, we were alone there. 6. I cannot join it in the air, and did it touch the sea, it would die. 7-8. Does it feel the better for seeing me swim, as I rejoice in watching it floating in the air, it being a creature that had the choice of earth once instead of air ? 6-12. And as the butterfly floats over and sees me in the sea, suppose my love, whose soul left earth early, watches me in this life of thought here, me who, left behind her on earth, live in the world and like its way, though some times warm weather and waves (the joy of passionate life and thought), tempt me to leave earth (the common life of the world), and swim in the sea (live in a life of passion and thought), since I cannot fly in the air (cannot reach heaven during my life on earth). 13-15. We use the sea to swim in, but the spirits of the air need not scorn us altogether—our passion and thought (the sea) upbear us, we have sea for sky, making poems for heaven ; and our sea of passion and thought gives us, in the noontide of life at least, such joy as heaven gives the Spirits.   16-19. They are, we seem : they do, we only dream of doing : but for us, in this life, there is always the earth (the common life of the world) as a refuge from the sea (of passion and thought) to gladly swim back to, return to, when one is tired.   Does my love look at me, and pity, and wonder ?

## THE POEM.

(The letter S prefixed to a passage in brackets means that the passage is sophistical, dealing with the semblance of truth and not its reality. The letters T and S similarly prefixed means that the passage contains a mixture of truth and sophism.   See further explanation in III. A STATEMENT, &c.)

At Pornic in Brittany it is Fair-time, and a gentleman living there, says to his wife Elvire :

§ 1. Come and let us see the tumbling troupe, and strolling actors.   (§ 2) See what transformation the night has effected !   The rough scaffolding of last night is bright with colour to-day, and presently the dancers will dance. (§ 3, 4) They came by night, this strolling company, so that the glories of their show, their ape, their monsters and their beauties in tights, might take us duly by surprise this morning.   (§ 5) Early in the morning an airy structure between the trees, on the terrace beneath the tower, showed dome-like, surmounted by its red pennon, stretching out to the wind, ' frenetic to be free.'   [S (§ 6) And that very fever of the flag, and the life I know is led by this company of strolling actors, actresses, and dancers, makes my heart leap in sudden sympathy with their lawlessness, though I myself obey Society's calls quite faithfully.]   (§ 7) I feel urged to ask, why do these Bohemians, who have cast off allegiance to Society, relish life so much ?   (§ 8) Certainly, as you see, they still come back

to us time and again, for they need a little of our goods,
(§ 9) even as a bird can't build a nest without putting into
it some bit of human manufacture. (§ 10) But why do
birds do that, and why should these Bohemians want anything from us, want to market with us, when all we hold
dear they hold cheap? (§ 11) We, for instance, hold our
good name dear, but this or that dancer displays her
charms to who will pay: if you tell them their monsters,
two-headed babies, &c., are impostors, they don't care;
you have paid your price and may have your joke. (§ 12)
But ask her husband or any of her people to become re-
spectable, and even for any reward you may offer, they
won't do it. (§ 13) Now I want to know plainly what
makes their lawlessness law to them, their poverty wealth,
their vice virtue, their disease health? (§ 14) You shake
your head, and look pale and sad; why are you troubled?
(§ 15) Let us call Fifine the beauty of the show, she will
make my thoughts plainer to you and me. [S (§ 16) She
is to me a sexless and bloodless sprite, with loveliness for
law, and self-sustainment for morality, and yet I own that
her charm arrests me, as the lawlessness of her companions
has done. (§ 17) Do you account it a fault in the gold-
coloured lily of the East, that just as its golden glow takes
the place of the snow-white of our lily, its drugged scent
takes the place of the chaste perfume of our lily, and instead of nourishing insects as our lily does with its perfume, kills the insects who, hoping to feed on it, are
poisoned by its scent and feed it? (§ 18) No more can you
blame Fifine, call it a fault in her, knowing her to have
qualities analogous to the lily, that she uses her charms
(as the lily uses its scent) to wheedle men's money from
them (as the lily takes the life of the insects to feed on).
Still, lily or Fifine, a wise man looks and praises, does not
taste: admires, not loves. It is the wife we love.] (§ 19)
But, you ask, 'How does Fifine make these thoughts

plain?' In answer to that, let me ask you to imagine
such a procession of beauties as Louis XI, when near his
death, loved to see. A procession of famous women, lawless or not. (§ 20) Helen comes first : Helen who made
men acquiesce in the ravage of the war she caused, and
bless, not curse her beauty ; next comes Cleopatra, whose
beauty was dominated by her soul, but who made victims
of her lovers, from sheer lust of conquest ; then the Saint
on Pornic church, who at midnight, peasants say, often
leaves her pedestal to save shipwrecked sailors, and for
years has endured wind, rain, and snow, and may seem to
wonder at Cleopatra in her sublime nudity, wonder whether
she ever prays or not, and yet thinks, charitably, I suppose
she stripped herself to feed the poor. [T & S (§ 21) Fifine
must take a place in the mask, and shall speak for herself
presently. (§ 22) What does the masque mean, you ask ?
(§ 23) Suppose you, Elvire, separate from yourself and
join in the procession ; then you will judge yourself apart,
as you do the other women, and so I may answer your
question by showing how you beat the whole procession
including Fifine. (§ 24) But let us study her first.—See,
I put a whole franc in her outstretched tambourine.] See
how glad she is that we pity her necessity to show herself, pose, and dance, for hire. She, born perchance
as pure as you ; she, from whose contact you nevertheless
draw back your skirts ; she braves your scorn, because,
after all, she is doing her business in life, solely to
earn money to keep her old parents, and preserve her
sister's purity. (§ 25) Nay, she earns money even for her
brute of a husband. [T & S (§ 26) Well, the phantom
procession of women, ending with Fifine and yourself,
Elvire, stands there to be judged by you and me without
favour. (§ 27) But, you ask, why do I want to make
yourself judge you ? Perhaps I do so because of a myth
I mused over years ago, how Helen really never left

Greece, never saw Troy, but the Helen who went with
Paris to Troy was only a phantom of the real Helen,
made by Jove and set by him among mortals for sport, to
experiment on men, and see who would yield to, or scorn,
the beauties of a mere phantom ; whilst, all the while, the
real Helen sat at home, and could estimate what her
phantom was worth.  For some such fancy, I make you
judge yourself, standing apart among the other women,
phantom-like as they.  (§ 28) I have shown you all these
women, I see the good there is in each of their beauties ;
and now you are glad that, notwithstanding or because
of my so seeing, I hold you the best.  You understand,
then, that the fleshly beauty does not unduly attract me,
but that I look at bodies in order only to learn minds ;
that it has been the inward grace, not the outward beauty
which allured me, and that the coarsest earth covering
may be transpierced by a spark from heaven.  All this
has come of demonstrating the value of Fifine.  (§ 29)
And indeed, even her virtues, such as they are, illustrate
the world somewhile and have their triumph.]   Because
it is my belief that every creature has once in its existence
the supreme moment when God's sun shines on it, and
lets its truth be seen and valued, as any one grain of sand
may for once take the sun's light on its most prominent
facette.  (§ 30) Fifine is no adamant shield like Helen,—
Asian mirror like Cleopatra,—Oriel pane like the Pornic
Saint.  Still, may she not be like a bit of glass on a dung-
hill ?  For, the moment the sun strikes it the piece of
glass shines as bright as your diamond.  (§ 31) Let her
be defiled as much as you choose to imagine, she does not
seek to hide her defilement ; she even calls attention to it
to rouse your pity.  You say, a girl of my breeding would
have died under the treatment she has had ; she must be
made of other flesh and blood than mine, with a power
in her to live through degradation, a power that can only

be possessed by the naturally vile. Surely she was not
wronged too much ; she would not have felt as we should
feel. [S (§ 32) Be it so ; but can you wonder that the
one appeal, the only claim she makes, should find my
heart sympathetic ? Her absolute truthfulness about
herself is what gains her my goodwill. For her silent
pose and prayer, as she held out her tambourine, said
plainly, ' I am true to myself and my fellows ; I don't
pretend to give anything but the sight of me to a Philis-
tine ; nor do I claim the charm, virtues, or idiosyncrasy
of your love, your wife, Helen, Cleopatra, the Pornic
Saint, or Elvire.] [T & S (§ 33) I do not say, like Elvire,
" Why do you not love me now as once ? The soul's
treasures remain, nay, multiply ; though the morning of
love is dead, the noon of love has matured and strengthened it against chance and change ; but the root it so
struck is struck in vain if the fruit tenderness bears is
only praised, not tasted by you. Why is it not tasted ?
Because that fruit is yours now (though once it was not,
and then you were eager for it) ; now, you have it safe.
You can afford to escape my tenderness, if too eager a
manifestation of it bores or alarms you ; any shining
light rather than the sun, which is yours you say." ' (§ 34)
Now these words of yours, that I put into Fifine's mouth,
are just what any woman would say to her husband ; and
all women mistake men in this way ; if women could but
understand mental analysis, much domestic torture, self-
applied by the wife, would be spared to her and her husband.] [T & S. As I said before, bodies show me minds ;
to me the outward sign shows the inward grace. By
demonstrating the value of Fifine, I prove that your
worth surpasses not only hers, but that of all other
women, for me. (§ 35) You and your love I prize, as I
do that rare picture of Raphael's gained by great expense
of time, trouble, tact, and money, from an Italian Prince

who first wouldn't sell because his father had made him promise rather to boast, 'I have a Raphael' than 'I am a Prince'; who then was nearly persuaded to sell it to an American, because at least, as his heart must go with the picture, it would go to a free land. At last I managed to cut out the American and buy it. While the matter was in doubt, I was in a fever of fears and hopes as I was while I was wooing you, and before you had given me your word; now I pass it by, scarcely giving it a glance; nay, turn my back on it perhaps, to loll at ease and look at Doré's last picture-book. (§ 36) Suppose the Raphael were to reproach me with my fickleness, as you Elvire do with regard to Fifine, I should say, 'Of course I hoped and feared while ultimate possession was uncertain; but once my possession is sure, there is no further need for that hope or fear. Not that I expect to hold you free from new hopes and fears of another sort,—far from it. But you are mine; I know you are there : and naturally I look at and enjoy any scrap, sketch, or caricature meant to give momentary and passing pleasure. Suppose though, there was an alarm of fire; even though I were elbow-deep in Doré, I'd sacrifice every portfolio and brave the worst of the flames to save my Raphael or die with it.' You, Elvire, are to me as the Raphael; Fifine as the sketch or caricature. (§ 37) Ah! you are pleased now.] (§ 38) But play out your part in the phantom pageant of women. Let me show you your own beauty, so do I see it predominating over the rest.

> How ravishingly pure you stand in pale constraint !
> My new created shape, without or touch or taint,
> Inviolate of life and worldliness and sin—
> Fettered, I hold my flower, her own cup's weight would win
> From off the tall slight stalk atop of which she turns
> And trembles, makes appeal to one who roughly earns
> Her thanks instead of blame, (did lily only know),

By thus constraining length of lily, letting snow
Of cup-crown, that's her face, look from its guardian stake,
Superb on all that crawls beneath, and mutely make
Defiance, with the mouth's white movement of disdain,
To all that stoops, retires and hovers round again !
How windingly the limbs delay to lead up, reach
Where, crowned, the head waits calm : as if reluctant, each,
That eye should traverse quick such lengths of loveliness,
From feet, which just are found imbedded in the dress
Deep swathed about with folds and flowings virginal,
Up to the pleated breasts, rebellious 'neath their pall,
As if the vesture's snow were moulding sleep not death,
Must melt and must release ; whereat, from the fine sheath,
The flower-cup-crown starts free, the face is unconcealed,
And what shall now divert, once the sweet face revealed,
From all I loved so long, so lingeringly left ?

### (§ 39)

Because indeed your face fits just into the cleft
O' the heart of me, Elvire, makes right and whole once more
All that was half itself without you !   As before,
My truant in its place !   Because e'en seashells yearn,
Plundered by any chance : would have their pearl return,
Let negligently slip away into the wave !
Never may they desist, those eyes so grey and grave,
From their slow sure supply of the efflueut soul within !
And, would you humour me ?   I dare to ask, unpin
The web of that brown hair !   O'erwash o' the sudden, but
As promptly, too, disclose, on either side, the jut
Of alabaster brow !   So part, those rillets dyed
Deep by the woodland leaf, when down they pour, each side
O' the rock top, pushed by Spring !

[T & S (§ 40) And where, you ask, is all this beauty and
wonder I so trippingly describe ?   (§ 41) Where, indeed,
but in my soul and sense, in my capacity as judge of Art?
(§ 42) *Why* I know it, I cannot tell, any more than I can
analyse the moving power of picture or symphony.] (§ 43)
And yet I may in some sort give you an answer : Your

question really leads to the wider question : Why do people choose each other as man and wife ? I suppose they do so something in this way. Each soul I hold to be complete and best of its kind, and no two are similar ; each one has bodily or other hindrances to its true expression. (§ 44) Each soul, therefore, tries to find its complement—what shall help it to full expression—in another soul. Plato's theory of course ; corroborated by the fact that art, which is the love of loving,—the rage to know, see, and feel absolute truth for its own sake alone,—art, I say, once seeing and fixing on a part, instinctively searches for and finds the whole. (§ 45) Let me illustrate this by drawing three profiles : (§ 46, 47) one representing horror; (§ 48) one laughing or smiling joy; (§ 49) one your own portrait, Elvire. (§ 50) If even I, with so feeble power of execution, can, though but imperfectly, so express the three different kinds of emotion required in these three profiles, that you, the critic, can see with your soul's eye, the whole idea I meant to show : how much more shall the *proficient* soul (as distinguished from my unpractised skill in drawing) be able, exercised on *nature* (as distinguished from art) to find out and set free from its bodily and other hindrances the true character of another soul, of which only an imperfect image meets the eye at first sight ? (§ 51) Let each soul, then, amend its love, set free from trammels of ugliness or blunder its comrade soul, as I corrected the ugliness and blunders in my three profiles, and all couples will understand each other. Let them have the result of their mutual soul's work, [T & S. and give me my Elvire, for me more beautiful than beauty completely visible to the eye of sense : for to me, from having been like the perfect Raphael picture, you become as is my unfinished marble statue by Michel-agnolo. (§ 52) That statue is to me as a diamond to a pearl, in comparison to the Raphael.]

In that rough marble hewn by Michelagnolo himself, looking at it with my soul, I found the idea but roughly hinted in the unfinished statue ; for me it meant Eidotheé. My fleshly eye, unaided by my soul, would see little but a shapeless mass. But to my soul's eye she is plainly seen, moving toward me ravishingly, living as a triumph of the master. If I try to see with my fleshly eye what is in that marble block, though it bears plain evidence on it of the master's own hand, I see no more than the fool saw, who, happening to pass when I bargained for and bought it for 10 dollars, said, 'It's worth five pauls to make lime of.' [T & S (§ 53) Will you, who seen by my soul, put all other beauty to shame for me (as my soul's idea of Eidotheé puts to shame the beauty of so many finished statues), look scornfully at yourself, as that fool looked at the marble block, and ask, 'Where is the beauty in me ? ' No ; see yourself as in my soul I see you !

You know now, that as I could discern by my soul's eye the inner beauty of the master's conception, piercing through the hindrances of the rough-hewn marble, so by my soul's eye I see you as you are, were, and will be, really, through the veil of flesh now dimmed by years.

(§ 54) And as each soul can thus find the beauty and completeness in another soul, so each soul gathers, from the outer world, materials to make its own world; whether such gathered materials form an aura, or atmosphere (like our earth's) in which the soul floats and moves (as the earth in its atmosphere), or whether these gathered materials not so much surround as become incorporated with the soul, and so add their worth to the soul's, nourishing it as wine enriches blood, and giving it vigour to conquer through an eternity of battle. (§ 55) And this acquiring from the outer world and adding to its own, and thus making its life richer, must surely be the purpose for which the soul lives and strives, so that the fruit of such acquisition and conquest remains its own for ever, so stored and guaranteed that the actual gain of the soul can be made known at the death of the body. This process, that is, goes on through all the soul's life in the body, and only at the body's death does the amount thus conquered or acquired appear clearly. Nay, I assert that all real worth exists only in the soul that can see, and use what it sees. There is no real worth in the outer world ; that world's worth exists only in the soul's power to see and use it : save for the soul's seeing and using and touching it, that world would remain inert matter. Or again, the outer world is mere material to be transmuted, of no use or effect unless the soul of man, breathing on it, calls out of it elemental flame, that is, fire that lights and warms the soul, and is beauty, life-giving power, for that soul. If, on the soul's so breathing on or touching that mere material of the world, each particle yields such elemental flame, it is no matter whether the particles so breathed on or touched be gum and spice (*i.e.*, apparently precious), or straw and rottenness (*i.e.*, apparently value-less). (Fifine is the latter—Elvire the former.) The outer world then, the soul touches, whether good or bad, if it yields to her touch flame, warmth, light, gives her life : and what so responds to her touch, she finds to be beauty. But supposing it does not so respond to her touch ? Then it becomes repugnant to her, ugly, death-giving : she cannot live with it or near it, and she recoils, for what is repugnant to her is as fatal as death : but, recoiling, and thus put to her own resources, and finding, for the moment, no life-giving, only death-giving, material, she finds in herself the power to create for the nonce a new beauty, giving her life : and that ugliness becomes, thereupon, not merely harmless, but the soul makes it serve its purpose as a contrast or foil to the new beauty she has thus found force to create.*

(§ 56) I gather heart and hope, through or because of these conquests of the soul: (1) her calling out (from roughness, ungainliness, incompleteness) beauty and truth of purpose ; (2) her power to transfer all actual achievement in the visible world to a resting-place in her imagination, secure from being construed wrongly there : (3) her ardour to help where completion is near, but not quite reached : (4) and last, not least, through or because of her conquest even of stark deformity, fighting with which by using her creative power as shown above, she wrings from it symmetry. By analogy, I praise a sculptor's pupil, who, when his master's crude but mighty thought, only roughly-hewn out in marble, is called by fools abortive, puts himself and his finished statue in clay by the side of that roughly-hewn marble, saying, I am his, he made me, and my ideas : by the fact of this my finished work, I and my work vindicate him. (§ 57) So I worked out the idea I found in the rough Michelagnolo block, by making a finished statue in clay from it, which statue, once made and placed by the side of the master's unfinished marble (so as to rivet my conception of the meaning), I destroyed at once. If I made the conception plain to my outward eye, the master was to thank for it : but may he not have smiled for joy, that one man at least was left to recognise the perfection hid in the unfinished work, and able to work out the idea therein, by making a finished statue palpable and visible ? (§ 58)

---

* Take a simple illustration,—Suppose a soul of a loving nature, and incapable of hating, cast among people who do nothing but hate each other ; Hate is so repugnant to that soul that without loving, it must die ; that is, it cannot feed on hate, it can only feed on love. How can it contrive to live without food ? By imagining what love might be, with another loving soul, or taking some animal or flower to bestow its love on.

Now as my gain in learning, and keeping in my soul the statue Eidotheé is my own for ever, so such gains as I have described the soul achieving, from the material of the outer world, are surely its own for ever, not to be given to those who, working with the same material, could not find and see the beauty hid beneath roughness.

(§ 59) But how intense will love grow when hereafter love means the desire in each soul to share with another soul (who has worked in a like but new and changed manner) the treasures each has so gained. The material of the world your soul touches (see § 55) may yield to the touch of your soul roseflame, to the touch of mine, red, blue, green or yellow : need we doubt a time will come, when we each learn the secret of the other's soul's touch,— I, how you developed the power of self-sacrifice from materials which only gave me food for self-indulgence : you, how I developed force from material which gave you pity ? What joy will it be when a further step is taken, and instead of desiring to share, each soul achieves the power to share, one with the other, its gains, so that blended, their gains may make a complete unity, as the fused prism colours make white : when, in short, all souls can so interchange and learn each the other's secret of gaining from the outer world. I say that the foregoing exemplifies a law even now apparent in the eternal progress, viz., Love's law, which I formulate thus : Each soul works, lives, and longs for itself, by itself, *because* of the existence of a soul other than itself, attracting it as towards a lodestar, and, whether an idea, a man or a woman, whether god, man, or both mixed, this other soul, so attracting, is guessed as through the veil of flesh, by parts, seen darkly, which prove a whole, to be one day seen clearly. My soul so found you, Elvire.

(§ 60) But you say, ' With all this boast about the soul and its empire over the world, you accept the rule of sense

when Fifine appears. You talk of soul ; you say that, in search of souls you may, indeed you must, examine and prove the worth of all women ; and that your report of such examination will be, that no face or form is so vile but a certain worth is evolved therefrom. Have you not then to get through some flesh besides ? Of course, like the bee which tries all flowers, you only choose the honied ones, but you must taste all. Is this fair ? ' you say,—
' Are you deceiving yourself, me, or God ? '

[T & S (§ 61) I will explain. You have asked a question that demands a wide answer. I could answer you by music : for while words struggle feebly with the weight of the false (the thick element between our soul and truth) music can electrically *win a passage* through the lid of our earthly sepulchre (our body), which our words can only *push against.* Music *eludes* the mass which words try to *heave away.* But music, dumb for you, withdraws her help from me : and I must answer you in words, but my answer will spread over a wide space. Need you care, if my answer exceeds bounds, and embraces other questions arising from yours ? Let my thought range wide then.

(§ 62) For this is the moment of sunset, this the place, and this the mood, in you and me, when all things we see, hear, and perceive, soothe us by their harmony (as the musician's ear is soothed by the harmony of the common chord). And as, listening to the common chord, one hears the same chord repeated in an ascending scale, till the complete compass of the instrument struck is heard in fancy, so from the harmony struck out of the scene around us just now, for you and me, we can construct and complete the entire scale, compass, or scheme of life. How can you fail to find, or rather lose your question, in the ample and universal reply that nature gives you in the scene around us ? Here, outside the village, at sunset, we can only *see* the spire of the church, but from it I *divine*

the church, the graveyard, and all its graves, and four-
footed and feathered tenants.*   (§ 63) And here, as we go
down the steep descent, we have to pick our steps and use
our eyes: here, we have reached the beach and the bay, and
opposite is the Isle Noirmoutier.   The waters of the bay
run (where they are touched by the night wind) towards it.
But within the cliffs of the bay, the blue water remains
quiet: let us keep our calm also, and take our fill of sights
and sounds: the hum of insects, the scuttle of rabbits, and
the flight of the owl.   Each insect, rabbit, and bird, is intent
on its business, and on doing that best.   So I take the
lesson of this evening and its sights and sounds : learn to
divine the whole from the part, as I divined the church,
the graveyard, and its furred and feathered tenants from
the church-spire : learn to live my life truly, and the best
I can, as the animals live theirs : learn, I to know you,
you to know me, as I know your thoughts at this moment
(though you don't speak) from your beating heart, see
your eyes (though they are downcast) because their lashes
touch my cheek : learn to keep our calm in the life on
this earth, as the water is calm in its life between the
cliffs : learn from the harmony of all this scene around us,
and from all animal nature doing its best, to obey that
impulse in our own nature, which prompts us to try again
for success, even where we failed before, in the effort to
understand each other, and life.   The sum of all the
lesson thus inculcated, the way to learn it, is—that we
should try to rise into the true out of the false.]   (§ 64)
You ask what I mean by that phrase, ' rise into the true
out of the false ' ?   Here is an example : This morning, as
I bathed in the sea, I let my body drop perpendicularly,
and hung erect in the water.   When a swimmer does this,

* That is, just as, from what my bodily eye can just now discern of
the scene around, I can divine what the darkness hides, so the soul
works as I have described, and divines the whole from a part.  By the
same process, I know from Fifine's outside all her soul.

if he keeps quite still, holds his head well back, and raises his chin, he is sure of keeping his nostrils above water, and so he can breathe. But if he tries to rise and look round him, he sinks under, and cannot breathe. The swimmer has only learned this fact by many times trying to rise, and so each time sinking into the water, and getting it into his mouth and eyes. Once he has learned his lesson, through bitter experience of the taste and smart of sea water, he knows, once for all, that he can only breathe and feel the outer air, by obeying the laws of the water's nature. (§ 65) Just so, my soul is apt to try and escape from the falseness of the world and my flesh, which falseness, and my flesh, upbear my soul in this life here, though my soul beats against, tries to escape from them, as too gross to live in. Still they do upbear her, they are the medium that sustains her, though she cannot live wholly in them without breathing truth: and if she tries to escape from them, they leave supporting her (as the sea water yields to the swimmer trying to rise too high in the water), and she plunges deeper into falsehood in the too sudden effort after truth. Still, each spring upward, thus made, causing her, as it does, to sink deeper in the brine of the false, makes her more and more dislike the taste of the false. As, however, she is so upborne by the false, its necessity must be patiently endured, and she must not spring too suddenly upward, but use the false (as the swimmer's hands and body use the sea water, and whatever in it will help him) while she, the soul, reaches and breathes truth, the air. [S (§ 66) Now I pretend to know how to keep my body balanced in the false: that is how to let my body and its functions have full play in the world as it exists, and yet let my soul breathe the truth. And the more I gain skill in the direction of knowing and conquering the false, the more

easily I submit for the time to it, because the greater my
skill, the easier my escape from the world, if I wish to
escape. Though I know my soul's ultimate business is
not with this world (the sea), but with the air (the truth),
and that the falseness of the world eludes me as the sea
water eludes the swimmer, even while it sustains him,
still each time I try to grasp the false, my soul rises
higher, even as the swimmer's head rises higher when he
makes the least motion of his hand towards grasping the
sea water, or what is in it. (§ 67) So, when we are deepest
plunged (through too hasty eagerness to rise) back into
the world's falseness, if we grasp at something seeming
like reality, which may be another soul, we are helped to
rise thereby. It is washed away from us by the wave of
life, but touching or grasping at it has helped us, and we
continue to aspire towards the true, the pure air.]

Even though a man so sent, tossed upward, be lashed
with the spray of the world, he still ascends, and gains
knowledge of the mightier forces above humankind,—
God or demon,—each and all inviting the aspiring soul
to approach, and thus urged upward, find at those heights
the good in evil, the right in wrong, the clearing of
obscurity. To howl at the spray is childish. And (to
bring in another simile) the howl any man raises at being
lashed by the world, if it rouse the whole pack of dogs
and puppies howling in concert with him, merely brings
Huntsman Common Sense to the rescue, who silences the
pack with his thong. (That is, each man's common sense
shows him it is futile, nay, mischievous, to howl.) And
to return to the old image, common sense teaches that
while ocean is blue and rolling, and beautiful (that is, the
world is worth enjoying), it can be dried up, consumed
(the world can be made nought), by the fire of the soul.
[S (§ 68) I then, living in the world, but not of it, seek
the sky, prefer its denizens, not the sea's, and never dive

so deep but I can get a glimpse at the air above. I seize you my wife by catching at Fifine, the melted beryl, the 'tawny wavelet.' Did not you and I come out just to see her and her troop?—and was it not the sight of her, and our talk about her, that led us to change our ground of thought? Has she not given us this chance of thinking out problems of life : and been to me that other soul which helped me to rise from the sea into the air? Let us then not sneer at her, but admit her use in the world (already proved, but now more proved still).]

(§ 69, 70) But you object again, why will I only accept a woman's help, not a man's? (§ 71) Because one woman for that purpose is worth all the men. Say you can rule men : you do so only so long as they find it worth their while to follow you. Each man is content that you should play sun and he satellite, so he can steal your light, heat, and virtue, and while following in your course, turn all the while on his own axis (be self-centred). And then, only complete men are fit even to follow so, as satellites; whereas any sort of woman, complete or not, will rush into and absorb herself in the man she chooses to make more complete by so doing. Women in short, grow into the man. Men depend on him only, at best. And what kind of dependence is it? Say you have even, by your influence, made a man all he is outwardly worth—what of yourself do you find, in his true inner self, at the end? (§ 72) A bubble-fish floats, swelled out by the sea, giving out lovely hues : the real creature is a mere rudiment, head, body, and stomach in one : drain it of water, the beauty and nine-tenths of the bulk are gone : the tenth remaining is the creature's real self, no more akin to the sea than the sea is to yonder setting sun.

(§ 73) But look at the rill, yonder, that empties itself and its joy into the sea; imagine you can disengage it from the sea, and ask for the result, the beauty of its course from inland ; all that result and beauty are given to the sea, to make the sea by a few drops the bigger. (§ 74) Well, the bubble-fish that takes all, and gives nothing to the sea, is man ; the rill that gives all, and takes nothing from the sea, is woman, from Fifine to Elvire. (§ 75) To rule men, you must first stoop to their level, hide your true meaning by vulgarising your words, and so teach by accident perhaps. Just as an Indian entices stags in winter to an enclosure where they may have hay, when grass is frozen, by putting on the hide and horns of a stag, and looking like one: so to benefit men, give them good in lieu of worthless mental food, you must make yourself like them ; for, if you show you are better, higher-natured than they, they leave you. (§ 76-78) You rule women, not by the *stratagem* of concealing your best self, but by the *strategy* of showing them your best self. The Indian leads the stags by pretending to be a stag : the man rules men by pretending he is like them. Arion charmed the dolphins by singing his noblest song ; man rules women by showing himself at his noblest in their sight.

(§ 79) It is no use trying to prove what fruit a man will yield by enriching his mental nature, as a tree's soil is enriched by manure : try quite another plan, and if you want to get his true product, find out his power of action, set him to hate somebody or something. Don't cherish his root, but lop off his over-luxuriant mental growths ; and you will find that as the goat gained favour from Bacchus by cropping the vine's shoots and flowers, because a vine so treated concentrates its juices into the grape, and wine is the result, so a man thwarted in his purposeless or foolish impulses will concentrate his energies in the direction of hate. Take the puniest man-animalcule, starved body, stunted mind, and you will see with wonder that neither heaven nor earth can soothe his spite, or make him content, or by any effort make him propagate love, or produce one virile thought, word, or deed.  For nature, while she lets her failures live out their life, will not give them power to propagate their kind.  But let such a starveling man be touched with hate of some real man, whose existence thwarts his ; and, as a piece of chalk cliff is surprised into effervescence, if by chance acid comes in contact with it, so the creature so touched with hate, 'blows out to thrice his bulk and cuckoospits some rose' ; that is, the touch of hate makes such a spiteful man do his best to poison the life of a real true man, as the aphis, according to *his* nature, tries to kill the rose by surrounding it with the poisonous foam called cuckoospit.  (§ 80) Women give you all, and make you believe yourself worth something.  From Elvire to Fifine, they convince me, at least, that I am a truth though all else be seeming: that, if I dream, at least I know I dream.  Besides the seeming, the falseness, is transitory, fleeting.  *I* can stand still, and let truth come to me.  The woman's touch— yours—steadies me, assists me to remain self-centred, fixed, while all around me moves away, disappears.  You, the woman, by believing in me, at once make me believe that since one soul has disengaged my soul from the shows of things, my soul is a fact, and make me hope that my work will be repaid.  [S. I expect to learn, where, when, and how I shall see truth return, because even the lowest of women, Fifine, knows me.  How much more if my wife does !  (§ 81) But, say you, why is not one woman, the wife, enough ?  Let me answer by an illustration.  When last night we two saw a boatman steering, rowing, and punting his boat, along and round by shoal and sand-bank, instead of waiting till the tide turned and a ship could take his cargo straight across, I commented approvingly on his courage in using his skill and craft in steering. On the same principle, I suppose, I take Fifine for the moment as guide, on such occasions as do not make it worth while to use my wife's help, the ship's resources. Well, take this illustration and apply it.

(§ 82, 83)* Our life is ours, on condition of proving ourselves true. I wish, indeed, one voyage were enough, and that we needed only the steady ship Elvire, the wife, and not the little boat Fifine too, to test our skill in seamanship (our power to know and use the world). But you see, Fifine, the boat, does require mental exercise, and therefore, increase of skill in steering, which skill is not called into exercise by the wife, the ship, What danger do I run with the wife, the ship, on the sea of life? None. But with Fifine, I am forced to use tact, courage, and nerve, and thereby increase my readiness of resource, clearness of judgment, and knowledge of life. I want, in short, to learn Fifine in order to make myself more worthy of my wife's love. So if I chance to see, talk with, learn, and finally dominate Fifine, it is that I may come back to you a better and more knowing man, and above all, come back having proved my truth and love to you.] [T & S (§ 84) See, it is nearly night, and the landscape becomes dim, sea-like, mysterious : does it not seem too as if the sea retired even, and became small, as if it retired to enable some other force to play its part ? You see the night again tells us, by this change in the show of earth and sea, that all is false, fleeting : and yet still we strain after permanence, and the truth that at least ourselves are true. (§ 85) And now, to conclude and gather up this series of ideas, all leading from one to another, and

* End of § 82, 'See Horace to the boat, &c.' That is, Compare Horace's Ode addressed to Vergil (on the latter's embarking for Athens) and to the vessel Vergil sailed in. The Ode is 3rd of the 1st book of Horace's Odes (Sir Theodore Martin's translation, or Conington's). The lines at end of § 82 (p. 103 of the Poem) beginning 'And try if trusting'—ending 'should not touch—the deep,' contain a paraphrase of part of the Ode. The allusions on p. 104 of the Poem continue the idea of Vergil's voyage to Athens : the speaker compares himself to Vergil, Fifine to the boat that takes him to Athens and back.

begun by the sight of Fifine at the Fair. Is it not our recoil from falsehood, fleetingness, which makes us feel the charm of Fifine and her tribe? For she and hers profess falseness, acting, while the rest of the world profess truth, yet lie. You approve an actor in proportion as he imposes on you : the falser to himself and liker to his part he is, the more he wins your praise, the greater his success, and the more vivid the truth his part was meant to teach. (§ 86) On the same principle, in life, each of us has a false outside, our flesh, as the actor has his part ; what each of us has to find out is the truth of each other man's or woman's nature, separated from the falseness of their acted part, their flesh. This truth, however, is discovered only by the exceptionally gifted eye, now and then at a happy moment. Our life in fact means, learning to abhor falsehood and love truth, but to discern under all falsehood (what is acting in the actor), and snatch from it, the truth and beauty that lie beneath. And when these *snatched waifs* of truth are gathered and displayed, and we find them match with *strays* of truth that we have not *snatched*, but which are yet in the world, when I say waifs and strays are gathered alike at the end of life, and the beautiful has been extracted from beneath the foul and shines forth, and truth, first seen only as a point, flashes forth everywhere on the circle of life, manifest to the soul, though hid from sense, and at last unobstructed by sense,—then is the end of life achieved. But we must wait (for this achievement) our appointed threescore years and ten.] [S (§ 87) So I come back to where we started from ; the impulse to sympathise with the lawlessness of these strolling actors, to see what it meant, and to learn some such lessons of life as I have tried to express. And if some of these lessons of life were abstruse, it was a dream that impelled me to teach them. (§ 88) For I am but a dreamer and no poet : poets are not troubled with such

fancies as mine, such as seek other vent than poetry, and
often exceed reasonable bounds.]

(§ 89) I sat dreaming in the house this morning, with
the windows wide, and sights and sounds pleasant enough
were given to me; but fancies too came thronging in,
which by no means could be reduced to visible or articulate shape by any skill of mine. (§ 90) So as my fancies
began to overtask my feeling, and its power of expression
finds best help in music, I bethought me of music to
express and fix these my fancies. (§ 91) I played
Schumann's Carnival, choosing it, you see, as harmonising with the mood wrought on me by the fair here, and
its strolling company. I knew that in that company was
some one, reserved by fate, to give me the electric spark
of sympathy, which proves that, do but each of us link
hands, we can find in the dark of the world the fire of
Truth, until the whole human race, high and low, is
united in one chain : the fair expands to the Carnival,
the Carnival to the world.

(§ 92) As I played, and remarked how each musical theme
in the piece was, so to say, new dressed, I saw thence how
truth is served to us in successive generations as at a
banquet, the viand the same, the seasoning changed
according to the era at which the truth is being discussed
as food. For the essential food, the facts of life, truth, in
short, never vary; their expression (seasoning of the
meat), whether in art or life, is always changing, and
though such newness, change of expression, is repugnant
at first, (as is a new sauce to the palate), it soon becomes a
necessity to the souls of men (as does the new sauce to the
gradually accustomed palate). Most of all is this apparent
in music as a form of expressing truth. For in music
change of method is its law, and what is precious or rare
in music is, not the Absolute, fundamental good, but
freshness of presentation of that absolute or good—surprise

in short.  (§ 93) After playing the piece I dozed (§ 94), and seemed to see the Carnival at Venice.

(§ 95) I looked on it as from the height of a pinnacle. I saw an immense concourse of men and women, all masked. The masks were of all sorts—beasts, birds, fishes; old men, and young; (§ 96) nay, masks such as showed what the man had become through some one passion, love, or hate.  (§ 97) And I asked, why must some such one love or hate task each soul, and draw it its own way, and shape it so?  This thought made me observe closer.  I discovered that the crowd was dumb; no sound arose from them.  (§ 98) But as in dreams one always knows the why and wherefore of everything, I seemed in my dream to know the reason of the crowd's silence. They did speak, but in my dream I knew that I was not to know their speech, but to learn by sight of their masks, not by hearing their speech, what they really were.  A blind man (said I) must get truth by hearing; I seeing, can know, and so dispense with speech.  Then let me come closer among them.  (§ 99) As I descended amidst them, their masks showed less than had at first seemed apparent of divergence from humanity, less of change by reason of slavery to some ruling passion.  (§ 100) Still, though I saw them talk, saw their mouths move, saw their eyes strive to look what the voice was saying, their words and my understanding were not *en rapport* with each other.  I could not understand their speech; but my observation by sight, not by hearing, helped me to see the truth by what men looked like, not by what they said. (§ 101) And I found that each quality thus learned assumed its proper use, and seemed good for something.  What at first seemed ugly withered off, and my repugnance to the seeming wrongness or ugliness perished with it.  I found myself able to choose what, among the different qualities, to observe, and what to ignore or escape from.  Nay, by changing my point of view, I could see how grotesqueness and divergence from beauty assumed another shape, were corrected, added to, subtracted from, and each brute-beast tendency became of use as safeguards to mankind. I found that force and guile are active agents in preservation of life, that peace is only good because strife preceded it, that love is the more precious the more we know of hate, and knowledge the more precious the more we abhor ignorance. (§ 102) I found that I must lessen my scorn of the flesh, the soul's case, for it is distinct from the soul. The soul is, as it were, a drop of dew encased in a crystal globe; *i.e.* the flesh and its attributes—purse-pride, desire to be what one cannot be, lust for praise, and all outwardly-seen qualities—are the crystal round the dew-drop, the case round the soul. (§ 103) And my delight in watching this crowd was such as a chemist experiences who, unbinding composites, tying simples together, and tracing back each effect to a cause, constructs in fancy from the fewest primitives the complex and complete, all the diverse life of beast, bird, reptile, insect, plant, earth, and ore. So I, observing and learning through these various manifestations of men the truth underneath them, separating the composite qualities in each nature into simple ones, tracing the effect (each nature as I saw it in its development) back to the cause (the reason why that nature had become such a development), learned what each man really was from what he appeared to be, and thus gained my object, satisfied my desire of knowing what I myself am, of living my life truly, and knowing why I live it. So I arrived through the fleshly manifestation of falseness, at the true soul beneath, and learned how the naked soul obtained its chequered robe of flesh. (§ 104) I am glad to get all that knowledge and experience, thought I in my dream; but why at Venice rather than elsewhere? (§ 105) And I

became aware that a change ensued. (§ 106) And even
as while watching a sunset we see the cloud-buildings
gradually crumble, fuse, and blend into each other (§ 107),
so as I looked in my dream on the amphitheatre which
held the Carnival, I saw that while the stir of men continued, a subtle change was going on in one and all of
the buildings that formed the amphitheatre, from Mark's
Church downwards. Each building became not new,
but older,—familiar like houses anywhere one sees any
day. (§ 108) I became convinced that what I took for
Venice was the world, the Carnival, the masque of mankind, lifelong. I saw the reason of my disgust at the
apparent grotesquerie and ugliness, idle hate, and impotent
love. It arose from my looking at these manifestations
from my lofty station of pride. I saw, too, why that
disgust gave way when I descended into the crowd,
namely, because wisdom's proper place is the ground, not
the sky,—to be among men, not above them ; and I saw,
that once looked at thus from the proper standpoint, all
qualities, good and bad, are nicely adjusted, the one to
help or set off the other. (§ 109) And so I learned that
we must give up fuming after an impossible ideal, and
welcome what we find actually is (§ 110)—*Is*, that is, for
the hour; for something in my mind suggested next that
not only then, at the moment of my dream, but always
and ceaselessly, change was at work on the buildings that
seemed so eternal. In my dream, temples of religion
towered and sank to make way for other fanes, that
seemed to grow up from within the old, and though
different from the prime aim of God, whose houses they
were, satisfied the generation for whose need they arose.
The buildings so changing all around, at any rate serve
the purpose of making men look up at, through, or over
them, and not down at the pavement. (§ 111) But were
they only temples that so rose and fell ?   Seats of science

surely also rose and fell, nay, were lost twice in a lifetime
of threescore years and ten. (§ 112) But though they were
always disappearing, and new ones appearing, religion
had always her temple. (§ 113) And the one voice which
spoke lastingly, said, ' Truth, though stationed herself on
a rock, builds on sand, and so her work decays, and so
she builds afresh. Nothing is permanent except truth.
*She is*, and will have men know she must exist, thrusting
herself on them by each such attempt (of building) to
live with them.' What truth does, is work, lasting or
not. In the end there will be truth, absolute,—changing
no more in manifestation, no more needing to work.
(§ 114) Meantime, her building goes on, one sort of
building or another bides its time, and has its use.
(§ 115) But, said I in my dream, let us leave watching
the change ceaselessly at work on the greater buildings,
and look at the fabrics built in between them—fabrics
less costly, less rare, but essential to this fair of the world,
which they help to keep in bounds, instruct, and regulate.
Booths, stalls, and shops, were there (§ 116); History,
Morality, Art of all kinds, bade for customers. (§ 117)
(But art, with its capricious changes of mood, made the
larger changes seem like stability.)

(§ 118) And now again the same voice said, ' All is
change, but all is really permanence.' (§ 119) And as one
sees in a sunset the varied shapes of cloud and mountain
become simple and definite, from being manifold and
multiform,—as the contrasting lives and strifes in the
cloud shapes cease their battle quelled by one cloud, and
blend in the blank severity of death and peace into a
shape befitting the close of day,—heaven's repose over
earth's strife—(§ 120) so in my dream the change seemed
to be arrested. Each building melted into each; and
gradually the whole seemed to blend into a common
shape, and become unity in the place of multiformity.

And what shape, think you, did they seem to blend into?
(§ 121) Here is an apt illustration in Nature,—this Druid
monument I have brought you to see. (§ 122) Explore
its passages : the further you go the less you will like it,
for at the end of them you meet with the dread shape of
a cross, to explain whose existence here learning spends
labour, only to leave the question obscure. Whence
came it ? We do not know. (§ 123) Learning will help
to answer this question as much as, and no more than,
ignorance. The cross raised here before Christianity existed, makes an ignorant man recoil : for what could the
symbol mean in those old days ? The peasant's tradition
is, ' People built this building, cross and all, soon after
earth was made, to keep them in mind—(1) that earth was
made (built) by somebody, did not make itself; (2) that
that somebody stays, while we and earth change; (3) that
we must therefore make the most of this life since we live
it in His presence. As to that great stone pillar lying in
the grass, there were stories about it, which, with the
tradition I have named, the Church tried to destroy by
saying : "That stone is no more now than Jacob's stone
is on which he dreamed his dream; it was a means,—it
is not an end." But the more the Church preached, the
more the peasantry clung to their tradition, thinking that
what once a thing had a right to mean, it still must mean.
They prefer the rude character of the ancient story,
uneffaced by the pen-flourishes of the modern scribes, and
their comment. As, that is, the tradition about the
whole Druidical monument had, as shown above, gained
hold of people's minds, so the stories about this stone-
pillar (a part of the monument) held their ground also,
having the same tendency as the tradition, viz., to teach
simple obedience to simple laws. Therefore the stories
about the pillar held their ground against the Church's
words : for there was the stone, immovable (able to give

real doctrine if it pleased), amid the fleeting beauties of spring and summer. So as long as that great stone pillar stood upright, the peasants continued to observe and enjoy the tradition left about it, as being more heartening than the frothier utterances of the Church. At last the Church ordered it to be levelled flat, and even said that it was only the primitive form of the church-spire.'

(§ 124) To the shape of this primeval Druid monument it was that, in my dream, I saw all buildings resolved. Grander far was the simple Druid temple in my dream than the temples which lately had looked so solid :—it seemed that after all strife of sects in religion, mankind would return to one simple faith,—the belief in God, and our duty to Him, as formulated in the peasant's tale. And yet, the simplicity of that Druid monument said no more to me, than (as those many-shaped temples and buildings had said), 'all is change but permanence too' : change, *i.e.* falsehood, and truth, *i.e.* permanance. Each soul works through the shows of sense,—which continually change, are false (though they seem the truth),—up to its complementary soul : through these fleeting changes it lives, and gradually learning wherein they are false, sees through them the true soul it seeks, which at length it reaches, and finds to be 'God, man, or both together mixed.' Let only the soul look up, not down ; love, not hate ; it will see in each change, or falseness, in which truth successively shows itself, the latest presentment of truth : this continually new presentment of truth under successive shapes, tempts the soul upwards, still making it think it has found the actual truth, and keeps on so tempting, until, learning by its successive failures, that for the sake of the soul's development, truth is forced to manifest itself in falsehood, the soul at the happy moment finds skill to discover the truth under its enwrapping false-hood : and learns to abhor the false, which hid the true ; and

as all veils of falsehood fall at last from the truth, change
comes to an end : all types become needless,—instead of
the singer, we have the song ; instead of the historic per-
sonage, the impulse of his age which produced him. [T &
S (§ 125) What did Æschylus mean when he used that
phrase 'God, man, or both mixed'? In the opening
chorus of Æschylus's 'Prometheus Bound,' Sea Nymphs
(creatures more than human, but not goddesses, God,
' mortal,' or mixture of both) came to console Prometheus.
He knew the ultimate, the Truth, and said that the Three
formed Fates only knew it besides : had he learned the
ultimate, the Truth, through lifting the veil from, *i.e.*
learning the nature of, such beings as these Nymphs, as I
can learn it, through lifting the veil that hides Fifine's
soul ? ]   (§ 126) And yet all this has been a dream, even
commonplace by everyday light.   What seemed awhile
fresh and strange becomes tame and trite, and the higher
our pride has lifted us in our dream, the further we have
to descend to earth and fact.   Have we not seen that even
this Druid monument told its story long ago to waking
folk, and never promised to help us dreamers ?   How
then should the buildings of my dream help me when I
come to real fact !   (§ 127) Let us, my wife, go home
together peaceably, complete our circuit of a league, and
end where we began.   Even so with life, wherever we
were nursed to life, death is our last mother,—we find the
last truth first, and final too.   (§ 128) But, you say, ' Why
is that truth final now, more than before, when it was a
truth proved false ? '   Because here a new point arises :
hitherto in my dream of the soul's progress, all falsehoods
discovered were so many triumphs to man's nature, and
implied no submission to another nature quite as real as
his which chose to have its way with man's (namely, nature
which demands death of the body).   But now, facing the
fact of death, man's pride is quelled by necessary acquiesc-

ence with the law of death. Learning the truth of death does not, as the learning of other truth, through successive shapes and grades of its presentment, promote man's soul a stage : to learn the truth of death is to learn defeat, because on the body's death the soul can no longer in this life, in this world, exercise its power. Therefore there is no triumph for the soul now as there was in its progress through its earthly life, in learning the truths of that life. Sense, or the body, can register *its* triumphs, because whatever the body needs in the way of development always comes to it soon or late. When need was to walk or run, legs and feet were developed : when need was to take up and hold things, hands and fingers were developed, and so on through the history of evolution. In short, the body, or sense, gets what it wants by gradual development of the right organs to carry out its wants. Such promotion of the body from point to point, analogous to the growth of the soul by learning the truths of life, is a cause for pride in man : if the soul's prompting to rule and be ultimate master here from first to last, could develop it as the body's prompting to grow because of its needs develops the body, the soul too might be proud. But since the approach of the body's death is the ultimate truth learned by the soul here, there is no cause for pride, for this truth merely warns the soul its right of rule will go, and that another soul, succeeding it, must be master in future. Mere wanting to believe will not of itself develop the soul's power of learning truth, as mere wanting a limb will make the body develop that limb. (§ 129) And to con-clude, as life ends where it began, so does love, in the soul which runs its round (that is, develops itself for its complementary soul, until they are mutually complete). Such a soul has constancy, faith, ripeness. [T & S. Though a man range through women as I have supposed myself to do, and find all the truth that is in them, I so much the more readily come back to Elvire, my wife : the other women represented the change I saw in my dream,—my wife means permanence. Love, as I said, ends where love began. And, as the natural man feels lordlier free than bound, such ending looks like law. There is small chance for pride here, and so far from realising that one has gained anything, each step aside to search after the nature of other women, proves to be mere vain wandering. I, the wanderer, bring home no profit from my quest, but the feeling that I had best keep house altogether, could I begin my life again. Had I stated my problem right, it would have been—From a given point (that is, your wife's nature, and your home life with her), evolve the infinite (that is all nature, men, women, and organic life), not, as I did state it, go out from your wife and home, and find what composes the infinite (all nature, men, women, and organic life), and piece them together into one Elvire. Fifine is the foam-flake, as I have shown, Elvire is the sea, which contains many such foam-flakes, and yet you and I left her, our home, and ourselves to catch at the one foam-flake, and got blistered by it for our pains perhaps (because she raised discussion between us for a moment). We are wise now, and want no more of the fickle sea-foam : enough of it and of the roar of the sea (enough, that is, of learning people's natures, and going out into the world to learn it) : we will live and die henceforth quietly land-locked ; here is our house-door. (That is, I come back from my experiences of men and women in the world, to my true life, with the love of my soul.) (§ 130) How pale you look in the night ! Real flesh and blood should not look so pale, even under the night. Touch me to show you are alive, and do not vanish from your re-pentant husband ! Give me your hand. (That is at a life's end, the night of life,—even his inmost beliefs are apt to become at moments shadowy and unreal to a man.) (§ 131) Now that we agree at last, let me cast our double horoscope. Let me discard that simile of the sea : you, my wife, are the land, firm and safe. All these word-bubbles come from that unlucky bath in the sea (that is, even a man's most cherished experiences become worth-less to him, or seem so, as his physical and mental powers approach death) : with your hand on my heart, I promise never to go bathe in the sea again (that is, taste the varied life of the world), nor bask therein, beneath the blue sky (that is, dream after an ideal development of souls). I will live and die a quiet married man, living in the town, and not in this tower apart, where one may mount to its parapet, and get a sight of that tempting sea (that is, I will bring my thoughts into ordinary practical life, and not let them go off to dreamy heights, nor occupy themselves with the knotty problems of life, among men's and women's souls). Let our house be sober and prosaic, ornamented only by some shell picked up where the angry water cast it once, or seaweed that gets damp and soft at threatening of sea storm or wind (that is, let me have nothing to do with the life of souls in the world, only a memory or two, and now and then news of those who still are in the fight of thought and passion) : soon I shall grow to be astonished how I could ever have gone out, in the sunshine and springtide of my life, to swim in the sea of thought and passion—the more astonished as time goes on, and brings me warning that I grow too old for such enterprise. Come, be but flesh and blood, and no ghost ; smile at me to show you are real, and enter our house for good and all ; let fate bolt the door fast, and shut you and me inside, never to wander again. (§ 132) Only, you are not accustomed to have my constancy tried by my being run after by one like Fifine. See here, some one has just slipped a letter between my palm and my glove. It must be from her. Did I unconsciously put two Napoleons between the two half-francs I put in her tambourine? Now don't threaten to leave me; I must go and clear the matter up. I'll be back in five minutes: if I'm not, I give you leave to 'slip from flesh and blood, and play the ghost again' (that is, after all he has said, Fifine's attraction is stronger than his philosophy).]

## EPILOGUE.

As I was sitting in my house, late, alone, weary, my wife came back to me. I said to her, Let us leave this old house, every brick of which is stained with sin and shame. She said, Well, leave it; but let our leaving be done decently in order. Yes, I said; but time has dragged so. The neighbours have been such gossiping fools; such fancies came to plague me: if you only knew what a bad time I have had down here. She said, Do you think I was much better off up there?

I said, Help me to get away: what epitaph shall we write, by way of notice to the parish of our removal? Here lies M. or N. departed from this life, such a day, month, and year? What shall we put for final flourish, —prose or verse?

> 'Affliction sore long time he bore
>   Till God did please to grant him ease:'

or what? Do end it. She said, I end with 'Love is all, and Death is nought.'

In this Epilogue the poet imagines himself alone at the end of his life, and weary with the world, symbolised by his house; he imagines his wife comes to him from heaven at his death, and they leave the world together for good and all to live in a fairer world, where their love is all and their death nothing.

## III. A STATEMENT DIVIDING THE MAIN SUBJECTS OF THE POEM INTO THREE HEADS.

The poem is put into the form of a monologue, spoken by a man ; throughout he introduces observations and objections made by his wife, each of which he discusses and answers. The whole Poem is dramatic : the speaker is any man you like, of high attainments, lofty aspirations, strong emotions, and capricious will. Being such a man, he deals partly with Truth, somewhat with Sophism. His reasoning is good so far as his intellect and aspiration direct it ; but the last section of the poem proves the truth of his own philosophy (embodied in the swimmer symbol), namely, that a man reaching after too high an ideal is likely to fall the lower, the higher he has striven to reach. The clearest way of shewing where he uses (1) Truth, (2) Sophism, (3) a mixture of both—is to say that where-ever he speaks of Fifine (whether as type or not) in rela-tion to himself and his own desire for truth, or right living with his wife, he is sophistical ; wherever he speaks directly of his wife's value to him (expect in the quotation from §§ 38-39 of the poem,) he speaks truth with an alloy of sophism ; and whenever he speaks impersonally he speaks the truth.* The man and his wife are cultivated people of independent means living at Pornic in Brittany. It is Pornic fair, and the fair has tempted thither a com-pany of strolling actors, rope-dancers, and athletes. The husband takes the beauty of the strolling company, Fifine, as a type, *first*, of womanhood, to point the moral of man's relations with woman ; *second*, as a symbol of any influence good or bad which a wise man is bound to make

---

* In the preceding Analysis the letters T and S, or S, marking bracketed passages, mean that the passage so marked is either a mixture of truth and sophism, or sophism pure.

use of for his soul's development during its life in this world only.  Using her for a text, he moralises on certain facts and ideas connected with the life of any individual man, as a gregarious and progressive being, among collect-tive men and women.  He says in substance :—

I. I take Fifine as an instance of woman in relation to man, and show you her character as a woman.  I show you that although her idiosyncrasy apparently defies social laws, she virtually observes them as strictly and with as high a sense of honour, so far as they concern her relations with her own people, as any delicatest lady.  That is, she is, physically and morally, true now to her husband and her family, and let her antecedents have been what they may, whenever now she frankly displays her charms for money, it is for the sake of her husband and people alone.  To such a man as me, at any rate, she gives nothing but the sight of her.  Therefore she has her real value in the scale of human beings.  And by proving to you thus that I know her worst and best qualities, and take her at her value, I prove also that through my learning to know thus much, I am so much the wiser, and have besides increased my power of valuing your far higher qualities, and being true to you as a high-minded and cultured wife. This simple example of how learning a single fact about some one else enhances the value of my life, and through mine, yours and mine together,—leads me to the wider question of how and why people choose each other as man and wife.  In discussing this question, I begin by using Plato's theory of each soul seeking its complementary soul ; and to illustrate and enforce it, try to solve the question thus :—As the artist is always seeking to make a complete whole from a part,—and as Art is the love of loving, the rage to know, see, and feel absolute truth for its own sake alone,—so the seeking soul is, by the necessity of its being, compelled to find out and set free from its bodily and other hindrances the true character of its complementary soul. But, in order that two such souls may come together, they must each gain their right to do so by learning the world, each in its own way. What each soul thus acquires is its own, to be given only to such other soul whose acquirements complement those. By such a process I claim to have found and to hold you.

*a.* You object ; the process is good as regards soul, but why do I choose Fifine as an example of the world which is to be learned ? Is not her physical beauty apt to dazzle and seduce me ? I answer, No, it is not : my learning Fifine is, in small, merely a type of my learning the world in large. So in answering your objection I will use the type and the antitype interchangeably. The world, then, is to man's soul what the sea is to a swimmer who is, not treading, but standing or hanging in water : as long as he keeps still, with his head well back, the swimmer can always breathe the air and see the sky. If he, unmindful of the law that his body is heavier than the water, tries to rise out of it, the water yields round him, and his heavier body sinks, and he is immersed, with punishment of tasting brine and choking. So, if a man, living in the world, is so unmindful of *its* laws that he tries while there to lift his bodily part out of it, and soar to an ideal life fit only for his soul when it has left his body, the laws of the world assert themselves on his body, and his soul becomes more deeply and disagreeably immersed in the world, than if, using his body in conformity with the laws of the world in which alone it can live, he had left his soul free to see and feel the eternity which will some day be its native element. Now, as the swimmer learns by the disagreeable experiment of one or two tries to rise up out of the water, that the laws of gravitation are against him, so the man who tries to raise his body into the region his soul only can live in, learns by the collapse of his effort, and its ill effect on his soul, that the laws of the world are against him : that the world must be used patiently and skilfully while the body lives in it, in order to give the soul power of living and developing at all.  This being so, just as the greater the patience and skill of the swimmer, the more easily and frequently can he see and breathe sky and air, so the greater the patience and skill acquired by the man in using the world, the easier at any time becomes his temporary escape from it, and power to give his soul breathing and seeing space.

To complete the analogy, and take up Fifine as a type or instance again ; I in the world, as the swimmer in the sea, find and touch Fifine, as the swimmer might find and touch some sea-denizen : it gives the swimmer a momentary support of his hands to keep his head above water ; my learning her, so touched in passing through my world's life, has helped me to find your soul, above the world.  Thus, having already proved the use of Fifine in the world independently of me, I prove her use to me in learning life, and above all, being worthier of you.

*b.*  You object again :  Why will I only accept a woman's help, not a man's ?

Because men's souls do not work towards each other in the way described in my development of Plato's theory. That is only done between man and woman, by reason of their relative natures,—man claiming and receiving, woman offering and giving, all.  Women only expect you to show them *your* best self, and they give you in return all of *their* best.  Women alone show me, from yourself to Fifine, that since I have worked to learn this world for the sake of one other soul, my soul is a fact.  Even if the lowest of women, Fifine, knows me so, I shall expect to learn truth at last : how much more if my wife does !

*c.*  You object again :  Why is not one woman, the wife, enough ?

Because, in life as it stands, a man must come across many women whose natures can help him, nowise guiltily, and take his soul on many a harmless excursion in which he simply learns something new to enrich his and his wife's life. Even Fifine can do, has done, thus much for me already, by my merely seeing her to-day and talking about her to you ; and, using her as a type once more, the fact of my so seeing and talking about her proves (by my not being further allured hy her) my truth to you, as it could not otherwise have been proved. Now, taking Fifine still as a type only, let us see why she does attract at all. Is it not her very avowal that, for such as you and me, she *professes* to lie, to act, to be not her true self, while the rest of the world professes truth, yet lies ? You praise an actor in proportion as he disguises himself and makes his part telling ; the more unlike he makes his part to his real self, the greater his success. In life, each of us really acts a part ; our flesh does, and conceals our soul : each one's business then, is to find the other soul, in spite of the fleshly obstruction ; and to learn how to do this unerringly is the lesson of a life of seventy years. My bringing forward Fifine and her tribe and showing you what they really are, is just an instance, a single specimen of such lessons.

II. Now, take what I have said,—of the way the soul learns, the way souls come together, and the way each soul in learning gains experience in reading other souls, —as the outcome, the impulse, of a day-dream. And let me go on to tell you,—not in further illustration merely, but with reference also to the necessity man is under to study his kind, not only in relation to woman generally, but also in relation to his ultimate development towards fitness for his complementary woman's soul,—an actual dream I had this morning. After bathing in the sea, I sat down and played Schumann's Carnival, and dozing afterwards seemed to see the Carnival at Venice. I looked at it as from a height. I saw an immense concourse of masked men and women, each mask showing in some grotesque or brutalised way what the man had become through passion, love or hate. If they spoke, I could not understand them. I had to learn their real motives from their masks. And I found that I could only really learn their natures right by coming down among them. Then their masks showed less divergence from humanity, and the more closely I examined them, the more each quality thus learned assumed its proper use, and seemed good for something. And from my study of each and all of these qualities, good and bad, I gained what seemed in my dream to be my object, namely, the desire to know the reason of my own life and live it truly. Then in my dream I became aware that this was not Venice Carnival, but the world, and all men and women, moving among temples, and halls of science and art. These buildings I now turned to watch, having in my dream learned the men and women who frequented them ; and I saw change at work in every building. Each seemed to fade, and grow into new shapes, always for the time satisfying the needs of the crowd. But while halls of science and art were always changing, religious buildings always kept some temple-shape. And I heard one Voice which said that Truth, the permanent, was thus continually manifesting itself under changing and false shapes, to keep men looking for her, and wanting her ; and that 'all is change with permanence beneath.' And as the Voice spoke, the building-shapes in my dream gradually fused into one primeval type, a Druid monument.

The meaning of my dream I take to be that change means falsehood ; truth, permanence. You see the lesson is really the same as that shown by my lesson from Fifine;

namely, that as in my dream I had to go down among men, see them on their own ground, not from a lofty standpoint of soul pride, and thus find out men's nature beneath their masks, and the meaning of the change in institutions ; so in actual life each soul must go into the world and live in it as it is, humbly, and so learn, by searching through the shows of sense, what other souls mean, always for the purpose of fitting its ultimate sum of experience into that of its complementary soul, and this for love's sake and truth's sake alone : that truth can only be found at last by gradually learning the meaning of its successive false manifestations, and that in the end truth absolute and unveiled is the reward of such seeking souls. And that the way in which absolute truth will at last be learned will be through all races of men uniting in a simple belief in one God, and living our life as in His presence, seems to be the lesson taught to me by the fusing of all temples and buildings of art and science into the primal shape of the Druid monument.

III. So I have put before you, (1) as fancies evoked by the company of strolling actors, and Fifine their representative ; (2) and in my dream of the Carnival, certain ideas about the best development of my soul, or any competent man's in the direction of learning the truths of life in order to achieve the highest form of love,—that of husband and wife. Let me go on to imagine that my whole life has been so passed, and just as we two turn homeward now, after our stroll, at the end of day, so I turn to the end of my life. What has been the result of my life after all ? Whatever experience my soul gained through my body's union with the world, it can have no triumph on this earth, because it finds itself face to face with death, which takes it away from the body, and renders it powerless to work further in the way it has worked all through his life. So the result of all is only, that at least the soul so working towards its complementary soul has been steadfast to that end, and that all its constancy, as all its efforts after experience, can only end in the supreme love of a man for his wife. But the flesh is weak : and love you as I may, I cannot resist the temptation of going to see Fifine, and justifying my going by the most transparent of excuses.

---

A word as to the connection of the Prologue and Epilogue with the main body of the poem, and with each other. In the Prologue, the poet, by the image of a swimmer floating in the sea, over whose head a butterfly sails past, suggests that his life of passion and thought in this world may be watched, by the soul of his love, from a purer region of heaven where she waits for him to join her. In the body of the poem,—the imaginary husband and wife being both alive on this earth, and living together,—the husband uses the like image of a swimmer in the sea, and highly elaborates it to show his wife how he too can and should use the world as it is, to gain experience, and develop his soul's powers, for his and his wife's sake. This idea is further developed by other similes, ending with the dream of Venice Carnival, and is finally dismissed with the avowal that a time comes in man's life when such enterprise of passion and thought must be laid aside, and he must wait quietly in his house, —his life in the world—for Death. From which conclusion we come naturally to the Epilogue, where, as 'the Householder,' the poet, at the end of his life (sitting alone in his house—his life in the world), is visited by his wife's soul or spirit, which has come to meet his : and together they leave the turmoil of this world, for the calm of that heaven of love and truth which is imaged in the Prologue.

## IV. SYNOPSIS

The poem then divides itself into three heads. I. What ought to be a married man's relations to other women. II. What his relations to the world generally. III. The use of these two relations towards achieving the highest form of love between husband and wife.

I. A husband ought to use the influence on him of any woman he comes to know as a means of developing his nature for his wife's and his own sake. II. He should use the world generally with a like object. III. His love for his wife becomes complete and lasting in proportion as he thoroughly learns the nature of other men and women. These three propositions are variously illustrated in the poem; the sum of what is said in support of the general proposition (contained under the three heads), that man must use every chance to develop his soul for love's sake and truth's, is as follows :—

From the lowest to the highest, each created being has its own individual perfection, and a chance of displaying it. To achieve this individual perfection, each human soul works towards finding out the Truth, the Absolute, which lies hid under the false shows of the world. The knowledge thus gained belongs to the soul that gains it ; but as souls develop, each acquires its knowledge, does its work, for the sake of, and to be imparted to, the man or woman found in its search after Truth, and loved best, towards finding and loving whom it is always striving. To try and find Truth under the shows of the world, we must mix with men and not stay apart, nor ignore the laws of the world around us. By watching men and their institutions throughout a life of seventy years, now and then an exceptional man may, even now, achieve complete knowledge of the true nature of all men. And when in the development of souls, all men have learned to *know*, then all knowledge and all religious beliefs will fuse into one simple belief in God, and in living our life as in His sight, and Truth will display unveiled the principle of all things, highest and least.

---

### NOTE.

It is not my purpose here to write an essay on the poem, or discuss its merits. But it may fairly be said, that in the process of exhausting every argument by which he can justify his unfaithfulness to his wife, this Don Juan certainly puts before us, in every word he utters, truths at least as valuable to an honest man who seeks to learn how his life should be lived among men and women, and specially among women, as they are specious when used by himself in excuse for frailty. I think the character Browning has conceived (as sketched at p. 257) is one very apt to be swayed by either emotions or intellectual subtleties, according as one or the other may happen to appeal to his senses, his higher affections, or his mind, at any given moment; and that while he never ceases to love and admire his wife, that love and admiration have at no time such command over the reckless, pleasure-loving part of his nature as to conquer the fascination of any fresh experience in passion or emotion, when presented to him even in such ephemeral and purely physical guise as the dancer Fifine. Even when he gives her money, deceiving his wife as to the sum given (§ 24), and goes on to speak of her vices and virtues alike impartially, (§§ 24-32 inclusive), he has, I think, no immediate idea of an intrigue. The money is given under the sudden impulse of admiration for her beauty; the same impulse prompts the description of her, so far as it deals generously with the necessity of her life, and her past degradation.

As sudden an impulse causes him to run after her at the end. But the thoughts to which he gives expression throughout the poem cause him for the moment a pleasure as acute (though different in kind) as the sight of Fifine, his love for his wife, or his bath in the sea. And perhaps the sting of the satire which runs through the whole lies in the simple fact that the noble vindication of Fifine's life, and the yet nobler truths which, directly or indirectly, the sight of her prompts him to utter, would have remained unspoken had she been ugly instead of beautiful.

# BROWNING'S INTUITION:

## SPECIALLY IN REGARD OF MUSIC AND THE PLASTIC ARTS.

A GREAT deal has been said and written about Browning's philosophy and religion. His poems on Love; the continuity of purpose found in the second volume of *Dramatic Idylls;* an elaborate theory about personality : how far he is or is not a champion of the Protestant faith; Conscience and art as shown or handled by his works ·— all these and other subjects have been ably treated, both in writing and speaking.

I want to say a little about his more purely human side ; to find out what connection there is between his intimate knowledge of and sympathy with music and plastic art and their votaries, and that choice and method of work which has resulted in the sure grasp of character, fidelity in rendering local form and colour, and profound insight into human nature, which distinguish him ; and having established that connection, to find out not whether he is a teacher, philosopher, or helper, but the net result of what he has done for himself and us, and the value for human life of that result.

No man ever works—not even if philanthropy be his trade—from the primary impulse to help or console other people, any more than his body performs its functions for the sake of other people. All the goodwill to men cannot make a man enjoy a beefsteak unless he is in good health himself, nor make his brain work healthily unless he likes his work for its own sake, at least. In an analogous way, the value of Browning's work consists not in his being a teacher, or even wanting to be one, but in his doing exactly the work he liked best and could not help doing. That he is a teacher, consoler, stimulator, what you will that furthers human progress, is not the less true for all that ; nay, it is only true because of all that. It is because of his intuitive sense of what he ought to do, and his spontaneity in doing it, that he becomes a teacher, consoler, and the rest ; and to the end of time the people who will be the most genuinely moved by him will be those whose natures impel them to choose their fittest work. Among these, musicians and plastic artists are, if not pre-eminently, at least conspicuously, remarkable for this kind of nature.

Any one who takes up a musical instrument or the study of inventing melody, or a brush, pencil, or knife, to learn to make music, paint, or carve, wanting really to render the subject in hand, has made an immense leap in life. He has got something he wants to know about, and by consequence to love. For throughout this essay I propose to use the word love as equivalent for the desire to know, and *vice versâ*.

The productions or attempts of the artist may be wizened children indeed, but they are his own. The moment he has produced in the true sense a work of art, his outlook on life is as completely changed as is that of the woman who has borne a child. Love of his art, that is, desire to know about and influence the future of it, are as much a necessity of his life as love of her children and desire to know about and influence their future are of the mother's life. So far the three Arts may be said to go hand in hand ; but when we come to the method of their production and their effect on listener or spectator, another question is raised. Through the ear the musician touches us ; through the eye the plastic artist. But show any savage a picture of his wife or his sister, painted dark against a light background, and he will recognise it. Paint a white cat against a dark background, or a black cat against a light background, and a dog will 'go for' that cat, if you put the picture in such a place that his eye is not distracted by surrounding objects. But play to a savage or a dog the opening movement of the ' Sonata Appasionata,' and it will affect him only as his aural nerves may happen to be affected by the vibration of piano strings ; the savage may become uneasy or excited— the dog will certainly howl.

Whatever then may have been the past history of music and plastic art, it is evident that to-day music in its highest development appeals only to a civilisation as understood in European and English-speaking nations ; painting or sculpture to any human beings and to many animals. To anyone like myself, technically unacquainted with music, except so far as being able to follow any single part of a score during the performance of an instrumental piece, the influence of music on the brain through the ear presents a strange problem ; and what little I have to say on music as connected with Browning's intuition, will therefore, I trust, be received with indulgence, as being tentative only.

The undoubted difference between the influence of music and plastic art, which I have merely noted as curious, co-exists with the fact, equally undoubted, that the feeling for music is at least as strong and real now-a-days in civilised people of all ranks, down to the poorest Whitechapeller, as the feeling for painting and sculpture.

The poor of Whitechapel, the men at any rate, are, I believe, deeply moved by instrumental music when the

Rev. Samuel Barnett gives them a chance to hear some; and they crowd to see pictures when he gives them an exhibition at St Jude's schools.

Taking the influence of music as well as painting, then, as admittedly existing over every class in Europe, let us see what it is that Browning has found of value in music, painting, and sculpture.

He is of course the first poet who has written about them in any way but what may be called an allusive or secondary way;—for Shelley's lines on Leonardo's 'Medusa,' and Rossetti's sonnet, 'The Monochord,' are the solitary instances I can recall of poetry whose avowed or primary object was a subjective description of the effect produced on the poet by a melody or a picture. To Browning belongs the honour among poets of having discovered, or at any rate told us in verse, that in their method of working and of achieving results, the art which attacks the brain through the ear, and the arts which attack the brain through the eye, have at least one thing in common—the wish to interpret some secret of nature for the benefit of the artist and his fellow-men. An unconscious desire of course: the first makers of hiero-glyphics had probably no other thought than of a method of communication which would pay them with their fellowmen in social consideration at least, if not pecuniary profit; the first makers of music possibly merely sounded rude notes of love or war. In any case, the well-established fact remains for what it is worth: music appeals to civilised beings alone, and to them only as human beings with a mind 'looking before and after'; the plastic art appeals to man and animal alike, through their sense of sight and the power of associating visible images.

Browning then has from his own mind evolved the idea—probably latent in many other minds—that music and plastic art have, as developed in the last 400 or 500

years, gradually sought, and gradually found, a common
standpoint of sympathy. Artists in both lines, according
to him, want to know, because they love, love because
they want to know, their subject. To both he attributes
in their highest development the consequent or antecedent
desire to know, nay, eventual power to know, human life,
and for its sake all organic life. But in dealing poetically
with painting or sculpture Browning has to appeal to a
sense, which exists in a Bornean tree-dweller as much as
in Mr Ruskin, that is, to a sense existent in millions ;
with music he appeals to a faculty which exists only
in a small minority of the human race, though reckoned
by tens of thousands. That he brings the workers in
these three arts together as uniting on the common
ground of loving their race is at least one of the triumphant efforts of his genius.

Any student or master in any of the three, in the
process of learning, finds that to succeed in inventing the
simplest melody, or in rendering approximately some
appearance, however apparently trifling in nature, which
has hitherto baffled all his efforts, takes rank in his mind
as a discovery. Just as Pippa's song tells us 'with God
there is no last or first,' so the right invention, or rendering on a musical instrument even of a single phrase—the
expressing the bloom of a fruit, the look of a wet day on
a moor, the iridescence of glass or jewels, some hitherto
unnoticed quality in the luminosity of flesh, nay even
the secret that lies hid in the texture of a beast's hide—
should be to the musician or painter as important as the
rendering of a great tragic or joyous emotion, the composition or conducting of a fugue or a symphony. I am
not asserting that no proportion is kept in a work of
music, a picture, or statue, between the main subject and
the accessories, because of course the contrary is an
axiom ; but that the artist cannot help wanting to know

as keenly about the least important part of his work, *while it is yet to learn*, as he is about the supreme effort of his life. It is through this quality of impartiality, of being able to care as much for the small things as the great, if there is anything to be learned from them, that sculpture has risen from the simple forms of Egyptian art to the heights where the Theseus was evolved, and where he still sits supreme.

Here then is one link between the melodic and plastic artist, and Browning; the incurable desire to know and render, each in his own way, those secrets which nature yields sparsely or abundantly, in proportion to the width of perceptive power, and the skill or strength used in seizing results and rendering them; and the need to learn the most trifling fact that can help in perfecting the work.

Another and cognate idea makes yet a stronger link between them; the idea that soul and sense are interdependent. The very process by which a painter or sculptor gets his effects, and the composer or virtuoso his technical knowledge and skill, tends to make each of them consciously or unconsciously, accept that idea as a necessary principle of all artistic development.

Throughout Browning's work, his intuition seems to demand our belief that all organic life however manifested is continuous and interdependent. He does not, as other writers before him have done, assume the existence of a hopelessly ideal soul, apart from all natural phenomena; he makes us see the soul working in the most trifling action of the meanest being, in the smallest effort in the direction of his art of the veriest student; each action and effort is as much a step in the soul's development—and a step only—as the greatest action, the greatest work of art, are each such a step, and no more.

With this introduction let us now glance at Browning's poems dealing directly with music and plastic art, or indirectly suggesting those arts. *Master Hugues, A Toc-cata of Galuppi's, Abt Vogler*, are his three avowed poems about music. In each, there is the poetic presentment of the soul, man's essence, at the back of, and more or less plainly moving with the inarticulate harmonies or discords; and however astonished any such composer as, Master Hugues might be at having any meaning apart from that of technical construction applied to his fugue, Galuppi would surely have said, You divine the world I lived in and played for; Abt Vogler or any great inventive composer would admit the value of even simple musical intervals (the 'commiserating sevenths' of Galuppi, the 'blunting into a ninth' of the Abbé) as modes of soul expression; nay the latter is distinctly formulated in the poem :

'I stand on alien ground,
Surveying awhile the heights I rolled from into the deep.'

I stand apart, see myself as I was, exalted too high and brought too low; the C major key brings me back, not to the height of fantasy or aspiration, but the firm middle ground of this life.

A similar and much more elaborate blending of soul's action with the construction of a composition of Schumann's, the Carnival which is worked out in *Fifine at the Fair* (see the preceding essay), is Browning's only other direct and complete use of music as an interpreter of the soul. True, all the poet's allusions to music are those of a man to whom music speaks in a plain tongue; and speaking in a less direct way, *One Word More, In a Gondola*, the songs in *Paracelsus*, the songs in *Pippa Passes*, the description of Arion in *Fifine at the Fair*, seem as if written to a rhythmic chant or harmony audible only to the brain-sense of their maker. Not merely vocal melody: strings, reeds, pipes, silver or brass instru ments, wail or triumph as only wordless music can, above the rhythm of the words.

But the great apparent difference between Browning's intuition as directed towards melodic art on the one hand and plastic art on the other, lies in the difference of those arts' history; for in speaking through or for a painter or sculptor he must needs go back to a period which is in the history of those arts what prehistoric civilisation is to that of to-day ; speaking through or for a musician he can at best give sympathy to great aspirations only, not great achievements, in the past :—for painting and sculpture centuries back reached heights which those arts to-day are only climbing : while music up to the present time has had but one upward impulse. Hence, while Browning speaks like a painter in *Andrea del Sarto*, he does not, to me at least, speak so much like a musician in *Abt Vogler* as like himself searching for the soul secret of a great musical aspirant's motive.

The poems avowedly about painting or sculpture are *Old Pictures in Florence*, *Fra Lippo Lippi*, *Andrea del Sarto*, *Pictor Ignotus*, and the scene between Jules and Phené in *Pippa Passes*. This scene, like the previous one in that work, is a poem in itself, epical of a sculptor's soul.

In each of these, and in burning words, Browning shews so plainly his sense of the passion of work for love's sake, which is the life of the plastic artist's soul, that I had best quote his own words.

From Fra Lippo Lippi :

> 'Suppose I've made her eyes all right and blue,
> Can't I take breath and try to add life's flash,
> And then add soul and heighten them threefold ?
> Or say there's beauty with no soul at all—
> (I never saw it—put the case the same—
> If you get simple beauty and nought else,

> You get about the best thing God invents ;
> That's somewhat : and you'll find the soul you've missed,
> Within yourself, when you return Him thanks.'

Of course this does not describe for us an actual mental
process, but it does embody for us in words, as no writer
that I know of has ever done before or since, the aspiration of any true painter or sculptor.

From Andrea del Sarto : he, the artist, perfect in
technique, speaks thus of men who strive higher than he,
and fail of achievement ;

> ' I do what many dream of all their lives,
> Dream ? strive to do, and agonise to do,
> And fail in doing.
>
> .        .        .        .        .
>
> There burns a truer light of God in them,
> In their vexed beating stuffed and stopped-up brain,
> Heart, or whate'er else, than goes on to prompt
> This low-pulsed forthright craftsman's hand of mine.
> Their works drop groundward, but themselves, I know,
> Reach many a time a heaven that's shut to me,
> Enter and take their place there, sure enough,
> Though they come back and cannot tell the world.
> My works are nearer heaven, but I sit here.
> The sudden blood of these men ! At a word—
> Praise them, it boils, or blame them, it boils too.
> I, painting from myself and to myself,
> Know what I do, am unmoved by men's blame
> Or their praise either.'

From Pictor Ignotus :

> And, like that youth ye praise so, all I saw,
> Over the canvas could my hand have flung,
> Each face obedient to its passion's law,
> Each passion clear proclaimed without a tongue ;
> Whether Hope rose at once in all the blood,
> A tiptoe for the blessing of embrace,
> Or rapture drooped the eyes, as when her brood
> Pull down the nesting dove's heart to its place ;

Or Confidence lit swift the forehead up,
And locked the mouth fast, like a castle braved,—
O human faces, hath it spilt, my cup?
What did ye give me that I have not saved?

The scene between Jules and Phené might for its lucid story be quoted entire; its length alone prevents me from doing more than select some of the beauties:

    . . . I inured myself
To see, throughout all nature, varied stuff
For better nature's birth by means of Art;
With me each substance tended to one form
Of beauty—to the human archetype.
On every side occurred suggestive germs
Of that—the tree, the flower—or take the fruit—
Some rosy shape, continuing the peach,
Curved beewise o'er its bough; as rosy limbs
Depending, nestled in the leaves; and just
From a cleft rose-peach the whole Dryad sprang.
But of the stuffs one can be master of,
How I divined their capabilities!
From the soft-rinded smoothening facile chalk
That yields your outline to the air's embrace,
' Half softened by a halo's pearly gloom:
Down to the crisp imperious steel, so sure
To cut its one confided thought clean out
Of all the world.   But marble! 'neath my tools
More pliable than jelly—as it were
Some clear primordial creature dug from depths
In the earth's heart, where itself breeds itself,
And whence all baser substance may be worked;
Refine it off to air, you may,—condense it
Down to the diamond;—is not metal there,
When o'er the sudden speck my chisel trips?
—Not flesh, as flake off flake I scale, approach,
Lay bare those bluish veins of blood asleep?'

Next, let us notice a few poems where Browning proves in actual poetic construction his sympathy with, and power of using in words, the primary law of plastic art, which demands a right presenting of an image.  .

It has been well said in a note on *Childe Roland* which I have been privileged to read that Browning has shown in that work his skill as a painter.  Probably no poem in the language forms by its mere collocation of words so vivid a series of actual pictures.  But this and some other examples (such as the description of the lion in *The Glove*, of the stag in *Donald*, of the sky in *Easter Day*,) differ from other poets' descriptive work, in this way : Browning so chooses words and phrases,—gives so direct a sense of seeing the thing described,—that by very aptness he baffles all attempt at plastically rendering them.  Other men may stimulate a painter or sculptor by suggestiveness ; Browning rather deters such a one by the very force and clearness of his imagery.  The picture or statue is there already.  Take for example his description of the Fighter in *Sordello*.

> Upgathered on himself the Fighter stood
> For his last fight, and wiping treacherous blood
> Out of his eyelids, just held ope beneath
> Those shading fingers in their iron sheath,
> Steadied his strengths amid the shock and stir
> Of the dusk hideous amphitheatre.

It matters very little whether this be a description of an actual statue or an invention ; no picture or statue could *make* the whole thing so well.  And he embraces all forms of plastic art :  See the landscapes in *The Flight of the Duchess*, and *Home Thoughts from Abroad ;* the portrait painting in *A Face*, the rich perceptive and decorative beauty in *The Bishop orders his tomb in St Praxed's Church*.  These are a few instances only.

In *Pauline* there are notes struck in accord with plastic art, such as had never been struck before, and which will not vibrate again for many a year.  Certain passages contain the germ, not of all that Browning dreamed of doing, but of all that in this direction he has achieved. In word-making landscape it is a herald of similar though weaker utterances by other men ; and for a vision of earth's beauty illumined by Greek myth I know nothing in modern poetry outside of Landor to compare with this.

> 'And I myself went with the tale ; a god
>   Wandering after beauty, or a giant
>   Standing vast in the sunset ; an old hunter
>   Talking with gods, or a high crested chief
>   Sailing with troops of friends to Tenedos.

　　*　　　*　　　*　　　*　　　*　　　*

> 'Yet I say, never morn broke clear as those
>   On the dim clustered isles in the blue sea,
>   The deep groves, and white temples, and wet caves ;
>   And nothing ever can surprise me now,
>   Who stood beside the naked Swift footed,
>   Who bound my forehead with Proserpine's hair.'

Sordello is full of the same quality in landscape, painted with human passion.   And unless Michael Angelo and Rembrandt were fused into one being, who shall paint this :

> 'Dante, pacer of the gloom
>   Where glutted hell disgorgeth filthiest spume ;
>   Or where the grieved and obscure waters slope
>   Into a darkness quieted by hope ;
>   Plucker of amaranths grown beneath God's eye,
>   In gracious twilights where His chosen lie . . .'

So much for examples where directly or indirectly Browning has used his intuition in sympathy with musician, sculptor and painter.

But I say further that for me that intuition bears fruit in the wider and more directly human field of his work ;

for it is thanks to that idea of reacting soul and sense, and to the likeness I have tried to establish between Browning's poetic method and the artistic methods employed by sculptor, musician, and painter, that I have seen and know Pompilia, Caponsacchi, Guido, Franceschini, the girl in *Too Late*, Salinguerra, Balaustion, and Aristophanes, Mildred, Ivan Ivanovitch, Mulèykeh and her master, Pippa, Jules, Phené, or Martin Relph. I do not mean their outward semblance only, I mean their whole being. For there is this in common between Browning's way of getting at and putting in evidence such characters as these, and the processes of the musical and plastic artist : Browning has learned to *make* his characters as the musician learns to compose or play, as the artist learns to model or paint a face, a leaf, or a piece of stuff. The musician does not waste time on learning the nature of the vibration of air, he has enough to do in mastering the science of music, or the mechanical difficulties of bowing or fingering ; the sculptor does not dissect the leaf or the face, or pull the stuff to pieces, he has more than enough interest in attaining skill to make their outward semblance as like as he can ; but each does above all *want* to *know* how the musical or visible effect can be rendered so that other people can hear or see it ; and each in his way loves what each has sought how to render. Browning begins by wanting to know too ; but it is not the musical phrase that is his object ; it is how to show men what a great *maestro* means when he uses music as a means of speaking plain words about the deepest secrets of death and life ; it is not drawing a leaf that is his aim, but how to render poetically the moment whose consequences mould a life, as in *Pippa passes* or *The Statue and the Bust ;* not painting a piece of stuff, but how to show men, in verse, the complex tapestry of Leonce Miranda's life : not carving a face, but giving us a clear vision of the evanescent contradictions in the gold-haired girl of Pornic.

All this shows how the melodic and plastic artists' love of their art resembles Browning's poetic love of all human beings and nature as touching them, and how the hold which Browning has on us comes from his choosing his work as those other artists choose,—because he likes it;—and in each case the small things in their place as much as the great in theirs. The music-maker loves equally for the moment a simple melody, a march, or a symphony; the painter a mountain range, a tropical sunset, a flower; the sculptor a king, a beggar, or a child. So Browning loves man as he is, great and small, good and bad.—He may deny that he likes man as a development on a theory of evolution, though *Caliban* and *Tray* prove that he does. But at any rate the puzzle of man's apparently self-thwarting though always really consistent progress or reactive impulse, is what has supreme fascination for him. In short, he loves us all *quand même*. Having an intuitive sense of all things human, like other artists' sense of their subject, he works by that unconscious assimilation which Mr G. H. Lewes attributed to George Eliot.

Hitherto we have only got so far with Browning and the melodic or plastic artist as their common desire to know and render the secrets of their art (which in Browning's case are those of nature and human life), and their common intuition that soul interacts with sense. Let us see how they go together yet another step. 'From the desire to know,' says Browning, 'comes the desire to grow, to continue growing, the desire to go on living. Love, or the desire to know, creates and keeps alive the desires to grow and live, and so develop our knowing or loving power; but we can no more grow and develop without a further faculty, faith, than we can breathe without air.' Love, in short, for Browning and the artist, produces faith.

'Now faith is the substance of things hoped for, the evidence of things not seen.' The artist possesses the substance of what he hopes for, because he believes it will come; the day's work is for him evidence of the future not seen, of what he will achieve.

This faith, as much as his love and thirst to know, is a talisman which not merely puts him *en rapport* with the nature his senses can perceive, but enables him to divine the mysteries which his senses cannot fathom. He works both with sense and with intuition. His intuition is his working faith,—as the desire to know is his working love, —and on this human basis Browning meets and welcomes him.

The artist's faith is strengthened too by his knowledge that he can learn. So long as his health is sound and his brain power increasing he cannot help capitalising his resources; for under these conditions he cannot help working, observing, imagining, and always doing these things interdependently, that is, learning; so that his supply must needs be greater than his demand. But faith in the future of his work is its vital nourishment. This of course is quite a different state of mind from that usually called religious belief; but it is not the less faith in the sense of St Paul's definition. This faith, like the artist's best work, is urged, not by hope or fear of reward or punishment, but by the impulse of his nature  The incitement of reward, the deterrent of punishment are there for him as for all other men; but they are, or ought to be, into the bargain, not part of the bargain which he makes with his generation, and his faith is none if it be not independent of them.

It seems pretty clear then, that the faith which Browning's works poetically formulate as a necessary factor of all such life, and the faith of the plastic or musical artist as I have just described it, are the same thing ; with this difference, that in the former case the faith is exercised in respect of an after life or lives without *necessary* reference to any special work here—in the artist's case is confined, for the purpose of this essay, to the special work of his hand and brain.

And how does Browning the poet meet and welcome the artist on this ground of faith, as we have seen he does on the ground of love ? We shall find the answer in two poems at least, *Pictor Ignotus* and *Abt Vogler*. Not that he declares in either poem his own belief, for both are avowedly dramatic. But compared with other well-known *personal* utterances there need be no hesitation in accepting these two poems as striking the keynote of his own artistic and spiritual, that is immortal existence. In the former a painter speaks ; a painter who retired from the world's life because too fine strung to live amidst its jarring dissonances ; the latter raises to a noble ideal the possible dream of an aspiring and inventive musician.

In *Pictor Ignotus* is gathered up, in a few lines, not only the whole aspiration of any plastic artist, but such a hope as, association and national training allowed for, might have been that of Michael Angelo, Titian or Pheidias. In *Abt Vogler* is resumed, quite as comprehensively, what might be the dream or hope of the mighty dead, and possibly mightier living in the future, among music makers.

But as coming from Browning the poet, the eloquence of these two works bears a deeper meaning. With the poet, it has been not a dream, but a reality, to 'dwell on this earth, earth's every man his friend' ; he has shrunk from nothing : his cup has not spilt, for the human faces crowd his many canvases : through his works he realises what *Pictor Ignotus* aspired to.

That the poet should desire to continue his being in 'more worlds yet,' that he can say with *Abt Vogler*, ' all that we willed or hoped or dreamed of good, shall exist,' is but a further step in his strenuous life.

Love of their art, and faith in it, as now fully explained, are then the common ground of sympathy between Browning and the musician and plastic artist. His intuition has met and joined hands with theirs on the basis of these two principles.

But, human nature being Browning's subject for poetic art, how does his intuition shew itself, outside of the artist's, in his poetic work as regards mankind?

It has been complained that Browning takes his character from people whom nobody ever heard of, and makes them a peg to hang a theory upon. The answer to that is plain enough. Not their value as prominent actors on the world's stage, but their value as actual units in a great scheme ; man's nature as warped by passion or evil, or nourished by love and stress of purpose, man's bewildering nature, as it is in any social status whatever, so only that his soul presents a drama ; that is Browning's study. He works with the searching and unerring power of mind to which the one thing of importance is, ' What is the value of this character or incident in the history of human progress or reaction ? '

His early dream, or rather belief, of being in himself, though not in this life, a great artist in the three kingdoms of music, poetry, and sculpture, is an indication of the tendency in him to want to know thoroughly or not to know at all.

The desire to examine and interpret human nature is of course the property *par excellence* of all dramatists and of all poets ; but as I have hinted already, Browning's forerunners went on the more obvious lines of well-known historical situations or popular traditions, or stories of love, or war, or mystery. Browning seeks his subjects like a true democrat ; he ranges from the highest to the lowest of human conditions; *nihil humanum a me alienum puto* is essentially true of him. He does not search in dark corners because he can find nothing in the daylight, but he will search any corner sooner than miss a chance. His insight into human nature to-day is a consequence of his many years of assimilative learning; and the answer to the question as to the result of his work is contained in the poems themselves.*

But through all the research, all the varied dramatic interest of his poems, and quite apart from though of course in nature similar to his sympathy with art, we can trace the poetic idea of a living and practicable faith—a faith without dogma, without superstition, whose effect even on any one who merely understands without accepting it, must be to make him wish he had it.

The religious faith rests primarily, not, as in the case of the artist, on the conviction, that to make the best of our own best powers is the right thing to do for the world at large, but on laws prescribing a certain course of conduct under definite penalties or rewarded by definite prizes.

But Browning evolves a faith which, to many who know his work, takes in the strongest parts of the artistic faith as well as the deepest human qualities of the religious faith; for we find dramatically presented in his works, faith in the continuity of life after death, in the interchanging and mutually reacting powers of soul and

---

* It is strange that this love and research which is the secret of Browning's intuition of human nature, which is the motive force as well of science and art, should in him coexist with avowed disapproval of one particular form of scientific research. On research generally his mind is wide open ; and his own examination of the motives and actions of human beings is conducted with just as much exactness as that of a chemist trying to find a new force.

sense, and in the oneness of the universe with man, of man with the universe.

Cardinal Newman is possibly the only man now living who has publicly avowed, not in set terms, but virtually, that he believes in the way in which Bishop Blougram said it was impossible to believe. But of such faith as Browning depicts, say in *The Grammarian's Funeral* or *Rabbi Ben Ezra*, it may be said that his own Bishop never even conceived its possible existence in any man. Browning makes his characters say in effect, 'as you work here, so shall you live hereafter; if you are idle or waste-ful of force here, you will but manure the ground with bone dust after your death; if you use your powers to their utmost here, you shall have the chance of using them on a larger or more unhampered scale hereafter, the scale ascending in exact proportion as you continue to use the powers so amplified.' Thousands of men would gladly believe all that if they had the strength ; while thousands make it a creed unconsciously to them-selves.

This faith which Browning's intuition has evolved is so woven into his sympathy with the musical and plastic artist, and the faith of these is so much in keeping, on a limited scale, with the other on the wider scale, that there is strong presumptive evidence of its having on artists throughout the world an abiding, though to them more or less unknown, hold. A kind of proof that they possess it lies in the fact that they do their work at all.

The idea used by Browning, that man's power of development is incalculable and immortal—which might be supposed to have attracted him specially in youth— has, it is noticeable, gone on increasing instead of decreas-ing in the teeth of advancing years; and one s interest in the belief arises not from the feeling that he possesses it for himself as an exceptional man, but from his insisting that all men possess it, or may possess it, if they will only try. He nowhere says, men shall live more lives, the same man only developed or elevated; he only says, man shall live. How, in what personality, under what trans-formation, he dare not say, being too wise; but almost at any point of his writing we can see expressed or implied, a prophetic idea that every man who lives right will con-tinue—in some form more vital than that of printer's ink and paper, or the traditions handed down by friends—to live hereafter. It may be objected that this belief is based solely on that desire to go on living which I have earlier mentioned as a proof of its truth. We need go no further for Browning's answer than the *Death in the Desert*— perhaps the noblest exposition of faith yet put forward— *Fifine* and *La Saisiaz*. ' Man,' he says, ' sees power *outside* him; he sees order and law everywhere ; *in* himself he feels the need of loving and being loved. In his own physical and mental nature he knows that either for good or bad, obedience or disobedience to power, order, and law produce a logical and mathematical result. The one thing inside him that does not tally with the law, order, and power seen outside, is his need for loving and being loved. If then the law, order, and power are analogous in him and in nature so far as he can see it, why not the love ? He does not see the love outside as he does the other forces named ; he sees much to contradict its existence. But, taking himself as a com-plete whole,—and himself alone he can judge by,—he cannot leave out of the calculation the most important factor, the motive power which, known or unknown to himself, but always *felt*, governs his life, that is, love or the wish for it.'

This love, which exists in however germinal a form in every sane human being, is the foundation on which Browning bases the idea of faith in the continuity of life.

He says in effect, 'We all need it here; we are all inter-dependent on it here; we all act and live in other respects in accordance with laws which, however perfectly or imperfectly known, are traceable as the links of a chain; the sequence of links seems to break off or disappear at the point of disease, misery, poverty, crime; but the inherent quality which keeps the metal from rusting or crumbling, and consequently holds the chain together, is the wish to know, to love, to help others to live.

'The fact that we are so interdependent as regards love goes far to prove that if the other laws we know produce permanence through change, this desire, as much a part of our universal human nature as the laws of health, cannot possibly drop out of the fabric without causing the whole to fall.' And if I am confronted with some brutalised type of humanity, and asked, where is love or the desire to know in it? I say that so long as a man can be horror-struck at what he has done to another person, his desire to love and know is there, and end this part of the question in Browning's own words,—

'Is there any reason in nature for these hard hearts? O Lear,
That a reason out of nature must turn them soft, seems clear.'

For Browning the poet, as for the artist, the body is not only a tenement, a clay lodging to be discarded at death, nor the earth only a place of sojourn or pilgrimage; for him the mortal and immortal parts are just as much interfused as we are with the rest of nature, as the earth with fire, air, and water, as our planet with the sun and stars; in short, there is continuity in our nature, physical and spiritual, as there is connection between the earth and the solar system. It is but another way of stating the first problem as to the continuity of life. He chooses to see and depict each man as part of the universe; he chooses just the same to see each faculty, function, or smallest atom of a man as part of that man, and therefore of the universe.

Let me conclude with the poet's single personal utter-ance of a great desire which in him at least is faith;—

> ' I shall never, in the years remaining,
> Paint you pictures, no, nor carve you statues,
> Make you music that should all express me,
> So it seems; I stand on my attainment,
> This, of verse alone, one life allows me;
>
> .    .    .    .
>
> Other heights in other lives, God willing,—
> All the gifts from all the heights, your own, Love.

# THE DEVELOPMENT OF BROWNING'S GENIUS
## IN HIS CAPACITY AS POET OR MAKER

THE object of this essay is to look at Browning as an artist, to whom, for the purpose of his art, morality and immorality, right and wrong, are of equal value.

I leave out *Christmas Eve*, *Easter Day*, *La Saisiaz*, and *Ferishtah*, because none of these works, considered in their entirety, can be said to be works of art in the sense in which that phrase may be applied to the rest of Browning's work. And I assume that the development of his genius as poet or maker may be said to begin with *Pippa passes*, and to culminate in the *Ring and the Book*.

Throughout this essay I confine the meaning of the words 'poet,' 'poetic,' to that of the maker's faculty; the power to present in rhythmic words a living image to the mental eye.

Before we enter on the subject, let me say a word or two as to the form in which his creations are presented to our mind's eye. The still vexed question in many minds, whether Browning writes poetry or not, may be put into the dustbin with much other rubbish of the same kind. Does he or not, when such is his purpose, place a scene, or a character, or a face, before us? Is the method he employs metrical or prosaic? The answer to the first question is, Yes. To the second there is no categorical answer. Browning's style is unique; it is itself as much a creation as is his *Count Guido;* you can apply to it no

test or measure whereby to compare it with other verse,
contemporary or otherwise. When Carlyle began to
write, or indeed, some time after he began, even Sterling
could not quite put up with his 'style'; but Carlyle
adhered to it, and because he did—or because of his
reason for it, which was to get the utmost value in sense
for his word coinage—he lives, and will live. For a very
similar reason Browning seems to have chosen his style,
or evolved it; and although the following passage from
Mrs Orr's *Handbook* is of deep interest, it does not
preclude the possibility that Browning's style was as
much an outcome of his development as poet or maker as
was Carlyle's, in his different manner.

'He values thought, more than expression; matter, more than form;
and judging him from a strictly poetic point of view he has lost his
balance in this direction, as so many have lost it in the opposite one. He
has never ignored beauty, but he has neglected it in the desire for
significance. He has never meant to be rugged, but he has become so,
in the striving after strength. He has never intended to be obscure,
but he has become so from the condensation of style which was the
excess of significance and strength. Habit grows on us by degrees
until its slight invisible links form an iron chain, till it overweighs its
object, and even ends in crushing it out of sight; and Mr Browning has
illustrated this natural law. The self-enslavement was the more inevitable in his case, that he was not only an earnest worker, but a solitary
one. His genius—(and, we are bound to admit, the singular literary
obtuseness of the England of fifty years ago)—removed him from the
sphere of popular sympathy in which the tendency to excess would
have been corrected; and the distance, like the mental habit which
created it, was self-increasing.
'It is thus that Mr Browning explains the eccentricities of his style;
and his friends know that beyond the point of explaining, he does not
defend them.'

The peculiar value of this passage is, that it is a clear,
historical account of what may be called the external
facts about Browning's style as seen by himself. Dr
Holmes has said that every man is three men; John

Smith as he knows himself, John Smith as his friends, enemies, and acquaintances know him, and John Smith as God made him. I venture to think, in regard to Browning's style, that the last description of John Smith will apply. The style as it stands is God-made, not Browning-made ; nor does Mrs Orr's account, so far as it relates to Browning personally, in any way militate against that theory. So much for the question of style.

Now, taking the strict meaning of the title of this essay I find on the face of it a contradiction, and in a manner the title belies itself. For of the genius which produced *Pauline* in 1832, *Paracelsus* in 1835, *Sordello* in 1840, and *Pippa passes* in the following year, who can say that it developed at all ? It seems to have no regular seed, flower, and fruit time, but, to use another metaphor, appears and recedes in flashes of light and periods of dark. Or, once more to vary the image ; if you watch the incoming tide, you will see it, for several laps, recede apparently, until you are deceived into thinking it is going out ; but sit down with that belief, and it will soon be washing about you. Such a fact may be used to illustrate Browning's development. It has taken place by an apparently capricious (but really ordered) flux and reflux. One reason for this is that his twofold nature, the poetic on the one side, and the intellectual and spiritual on the other, have been perpetually at war. Now one of these, now the other, plays moon to his tide of struggle. So that sometimes the poetic or making faculty seems to ebb, only to come on with a mightier rush in the next turn of flood ; sometimes the intellectual and spiritual function draws back the making faculty to its farthest ebb.

When Browning himself says in his dedication to *Sordello* (dated twenty-seven years back), ' my stress lay on the incidents in the development of a soul ; little else is worth study,' we may at first sight take it that he has set himself that vast field to cultivate, and only that ; to be the dramatic artist of men's hopes and loves and hates, and of nothing of meaner consequence. But examined more closely, the phrase is exact enough in its wording ; '*Incidents* in the development of a soul ;' any incident, animate or not, is of importance to him so far as it illustrates or enforces his main theme. But when he adds 'the historical decoration was purposely of no more importance than a background requires,' he does himself either more or less than justice in respect of the poem as a whole. For the wealth of detail and descriptive power in *Sordello*, while excellent in itself, add much to our difficulty in seeing the whole picture ; to use a modern art phrase, the values are not rightly given ; and *Sordello* himself is more difficult to see and understand because of the elaboration—skilful as it is—of his surroundings ; just as many excellent Preraphaelite pictures failed as pictures because of a similar elaboration.

The value of any given making or poetic gift, the presentment in words or otherwise of a picture, can, for the reader or spectator, be appraised only by that picture's clearness to the mind's eye of another ; just as, in painting, any picture is valueless which is intelligible only to its producer. In *Pauline* and *Sordello* there are allusions and long passages which—though excellent and picturesque by themselves—need some key or interpretation if the main purpose of the poem is to be made clear. And the need of such a key weakens and hampers the making quality in these two poems. Here then is an instance of the reflux, the ebb-tide; for the real poetic force had, five years before, produced the songs in *Paracelsus*, which for graphic word painting, for perfect material imagery—and in the spirit-song of the poets a reach beyond that—may, to say nothing of their lilt and melody, frankly challenge any lyric in the English language. Not but what, as I have said, there are dozens of detached passages in *Sordello* full of the poetic faculty. The description of the territory about Goito, the masterly sketch of Salinguerra, or the opening description of Palma, are a few instances. In short, the whole poem displays the struggle between the true making faculty on the one hand, and the intellect and spirit on the other. That Browning conquered the two latter powers, and mastered them to his uses as an artist, is proved by the three supreme studies, Pompilia, Caponsacchi and Guido (the two studies of Guido) in the *Ring and the Book*.

But the whole poem of *Sordello* shows that the severity of the struggle was great ; just as such work as those three parts of the *Ring and the Book*, as *A Forgiveness*, as *Halbert and Hob*, *Clive*, or *Hervè Riel*, show how the making faculty had its own indomitable way through forty years of wrestle between the intellectual, the spiritual, and the creative qualities. As he is man, Browning cannot help speculating, looking before and after ; as he is philosopher he cannot help weighing cause and effect ; as artist he uses his qualities in the two other lines, and those qualities have become his comrades or allies, not his masters.

In saying that his genius culminated in the *Ring and the Book*, I mean that since that work, Browning has, it seems, simply used his powers at ease, showing how dramatic he can always be, whether his subject matter be speculative, sensational, or tender. *Hohenstiel Schwangau* of course is in no ordinary sense dramatic; but it is intensely so in Browning's daring to enter the mind of his subject and showing us what the man himself was (in Browning's own conviction);—how the essence of him worked on the essences he had to deal with. The *Inn Album* gives us four as clear and differing types of essence in human nature as can be found in any of our greatest dramatists; each speaks as the girl or man, guided always by the master's hand it is true, but never losing individuality. So in *Turf and Towers;* Leonce Miranda, his mistress-wife, his mother, tell out distinctly as characters. But in all these three poems I feel that he is using his dramatic power on puppets he has found, and knows how to work the springs of, rather than inventing them. He is using the stored-up power gained by the poetic over the intellectual and spiritual faculties, to show us how certain people who have really existed really acted in the crises of their respective lives, having for his material nothing more than a newspaper report, an *on dit,* or the general sense such a genius as Browning's would gain from the outward life of Louis Napoleon III. But these characters are not poetic inventions such as are the speakers and hearers in *Holy Cross Day, The Spanish Cloister, The Confessional, Rabbi Ben Ezra,* or *Bishop Blougram;* nor have they, though worked out on the same principle, the sense of poetic delight in the creation of them, which marks every line of the *Ring and the Book.* Still, we must not forget Ivan Ivanovitch and the woman whom he slew because she came short of motherhood; nor *A Forgiveness ;* nor *Pan and Luna,* which is as fresh as the fancies of Jules in *Pippa passes,* with the added strength of years.

It is no paradox to say that the struggle which has up to within the last ten years of Browning's career been going on in his twofold nature before suggested was the necessary condition of his producing at all. In this necessity he stands alone among contemporary poets, and by reason of it surpasses them all in wealth and variety of image and situation. It is much to be regretted that he has found no modern English motive for such a drama as the *Blot in the 'Scutcheon.* For he is pre-eminently, though carelessly, so to say, the poet of modern English life—indeed, of modern English-speaking life. Can one have in shorter space three more vivid pictures of different kinds of English life than are given us in the little poem *A Likeness?* Every word tells in making a scene to you. And yet it cannot be called verse if that word includes the idea of flowing melody. Compare this passage with an undeniably beautiful one of Swinburne's, which no one but he could have written. Hear Browning first. I quote from the poem called *A Likeness* in *Dramatis Personæ*, pp. 159, 160 :—

> ' Or else there's no wife in the case,
> But the portrait's queen of the place,
> Alone 'mid the other spoils
> Of youth—masks, gloves and foils,
> And pipesticks, rose, cherry tree, jasmine,
> And the long whip, the tandem lasher,
> And the cast from a fist (' not alas ! mine,
> But my master's, the Tipton slasher ')
> And the cards where pistol-balls mark ace,
> And a satin shoe used for cigar-case,
> And the chamois-horns (' shot in the Chablais ')
> And prints—Rarey drumming on Cruiser,
> And Sayers, our champion, the bruiser,
> And the little edition of Rabelais;
> Where a friend, with both hands in his pockets,
> May saunter up close to examine it,
> And remark a good deal of Jane Lamb in it,
> " But the eyes are half out of their sockets ;
> The hair's not so bad, where the gloss is,
> But they've made the girl's nose a proboscis ;
> Jane Lamb, that we danced with at Vichy :
> What, is she not Jane ? Then, who is she ? " '

Now hear Swinburne :—

> ' There star nor sun shall waken,
> Nor any change of light ;
> Nor sound of waters shaken,
> Nor any sound or sight ;

> Nor wintry leaves nor vernal,
> Nor days, nor things diurnal ;
> Only the sleep eternal,
> In an eternal night.'

Of course there are different kinds of creation, or making ; and Swinburne in his manner is a king among creators. But I have juxtaposed these two very simple examples of these two masters for the sake of shewing how in the second instance a skilful use of negation and a supreme mastery of verbal rhythm and melody will produce an impression but not an image ; how it is a collocation of the words, making music of them, that produces this impression, this idea of void, of nothingness, of annihilation. How on the other hand, in the passage from *A Likeness*, an equally skilful use of positives—an apparently wilful disregard of rhythm, or at least melody—makes on the mental retina a vivid image, produces something far more real than a mere impression ; for these few lines put before us as if we were there, not only the chambers of a young man of fashion of the present time and their tenant himself, but the touch of passion which made a man of him, and if you want to know whether or no Browning is concise, just put the passage in question into prose, and see if you can put it as shortly.

Using as Browning has done so many of the moods and phases of the mind, it is no wonder that he has been called names—dubbed a philosopher and a thinker and the rest.

If a man's genius spurs him into every possible field in which men's minds have ever dwelt or pastured shortly or long, one can hardly wonder that sometimes the occupants of those fields claim fellowship. But I think it must be finally admitted that wherever he enters—into whatever chamber of experience or aspiration or fear—he enters as the art worker, to make a picture of it.

Every artist is great in proportion to the cubic content of his natural sympathy, with organic life first, and in an upward gradation with the infinite range of man's mind and spirit; and while possessing that sympathy in its utmost capacity, he must possess also the power and the patience to gather all facts, from the meanest to the highest, and mould them to his use, whether it be plastic or verbal.

From the humblest plant, through the lowest form of insect and animal life, up to the genius of Luria or Caponsacchi, the perfect flower of womanhood of Mildred or Pompilia, Browning has unrestingly used his powers and insight as maker through his half-century of poetic work from *Pauline* to *Ferishtah*.

*Pauline* is full of natural knowledge of moss, flower, tree, and beast; indeed there are few pages in that poem without some touch of what may be called animalism.

Such widely differing poems as *Ghent to Aix*, *Muleykeh*, *Donald*, *Tray*, *The Glove*, *Karshish*, *Death in the Desert*, and others (I purposely throw them together regardless of date), owe much of the realism of their presentment to Browning's natural knowledge of all inarticulate organisms.

The love or knowledge of plants and animals, and the power to draw or describe them (I may say this as a short digression, but striking back to the point at issue), is the simplest, the earliest, the primary form of the making art. Pass over the cave-man's bone drawings, about the authenticity of which artists are apt to be sceptical; but at this day, in South African Bushmen, nearly the lowest type of humanity, their power of tracking, hunting, and drawing animals, constitutes their main claim to be human beings at all. And if these words come to Browning's knowledge,* I trust he will punish me no

* This essay was written in Browning's lifetime.

more severely than with a pitying smile for suggesting that the rudimentary form of animal love displayed by the Bushmen as hunters and draughtsmen is the germ, in an evolutionary sense, of the creative genius which stooped proudly once, and wrote *Donald.*

The germ, I say—or the basis. We should claim no more for this love, this knowledge, of inarticulate nature, than that it is an essential part of the motive power, of the foundation, which directs, which supports, the highest flight, the noblest structure, of this poet's mind and hand.

But passing on from inarticulate life to the material or purely dramatic presentment of men and women, first in their animal or bodily, and through that in their spiritual nature, it is noticeable that the first clearly *created* idea of a next or spiritual life—an idea vividly pictured I mean— occurs in *Pippa passes.* 'God's in His Heaven' is the key to the scene of Ottima and Sebald; and no faith rings clearer than that of the tyrant-slayer Luigi, when his whole being is put before us, body and soul, in that unequalled passage (his mother has just said, 'You never will escape,' and he replies) :—

> 'Escape? to even wish that, would spoil all.
> The dying's the best part of it.   Too much
> Have I enjoyed these fifteen years of mine,
> To leave myself excuse for longer life.
> Was not life pressed down, running o'er with joy,
> That I might finish with it ere my fellows
> Who, sparelier feasted, make a longer stay?
> I was put at the board-head, helped to all
> At first ; I rise up happy and content.
> God must be glad one loves his world so much.
> I can give news of earth to all the dead
> Who ask me ;—last year's sunsets, and great stars
> That had a right to come first and see ebb
> The crimson wave that drifts the sun away—
> Those crescent moons with notched and burning rims
> That strengthened into sharp fire, and there stood,

> Impatient of the azure—and that day
> In March, a double rainbow stopped the storm—
> May's warm slow yellow moonlit summer nights—
> Gone are they, but I have them in my soul ! '

In the essay on Browning's intuition specially in regard of music and the plastic arts, I stated what appeared from his works to be his personal belief in respect of the after life; and Dr Furnivall remarked on that statement that my theory seemed to be that Browning's intuition—by which I meant practically the same thing as his poetic genius—'depended on his faith in a future life.' But who would dream of saying that Browning was a great artist *because* of his faith in a future life? We might as well say the same of Michael Angelo, or of Shakespeare, of whose personal beliefs we know little or nothing. Browning being by nature and becoming by development a great poet, increasingly found, as his life went on, the immense dramatic value, in his study of men and women, their hopes, and loves, and hates, of the sublime truths and ideas whence have sprung the nobler religions of the world. And I quoted that speech of Luigi's in *Pippa passes* to shew how important a poetic element in Browning's development those ideas are; how they govern his work in an increasing ratio as his other creative power increases. He sees their ennobling effect, and chooses it for his use, just as the Greek sculptor chose noble forms for his study. Indeed, we must say of Browning that these ideas have gradually become so much a necessity of his artistic or poetic existence, that he could hardly work without them; he can in no other way get at the hopes and loves, and hates; but that is a very different thing from saying that his gifts as a poet *depend* on his beliefs.*

---

* I have used ideas similar to the above in the subsequent Essay on Leading Poetic Principles ; but the different reason for their use there sufficiently justifies their retention here.

From *Pauline* to the *Death in the Desert* and *Prospice* and thence to the Pope in the *Ring and the Book*, there is no evading the fact that the need of this central idea becomes, from the poetic or making point of view, more urgently an essential in the process of production. It would take too long to quote many passages; a contrast between the earliest and the later poems will serve our turn better. Hear the speaker in *Pauline* :—

> 'Suntreader, life and light be thine for ever !
> Thou art gone from us : years go by and spring
> Gladdens, and the young earth is beautiful,
> But thy songs come not; other bards arise,
> But none like thee . . . .'

See how completely Shelley, the 'Suntreader,' fills the religious chamber in the speaker's mind. Throughout *Pauline* the idea of God is a desire rather than a belief. Shelley may be almost said to take his place. Now hear *Prospice*, the concluding lines :—

> 'For sudden the worst turns the best to the brave,
> The black minute's at end,
> And the elements' rage, the fiend-voices that rave,
> Shall dwindle, shall blend,
> Shall change, shall become first a peace out of pain,
> Then a light, then thy breast,
> O thou soul of my soul ! I shall clasp thee again,
> And with God be the rest ! '

Or, again, compare that passage just quoted from *Pauline* with an opening passage in vol. iv. of the *Ring and the Book* :—

> 'In God's name ! Once more, on this earth of God's
> While twilight lasts, and time wherein to work,
> I take His staff with my uncertain hand,
> And stay my six and fourscore years, my due
> Labour and sorrow, on His judgment seat,
> And forthwith think, speak, act, in place of Him,
> The Pope for Christ.'

But having said thus much of what continuity there is to be found in Browning's development, I have said almost all I can find to say.

Now that we have come to a sort of conclusion about the only manner in which Browning's development may be said to be continuous or not, I should like to touch on a sentence in Mrs Orr's *Handbook* which affects the subject of this essay. She says, 'his personality may be constructed from his works.'

The essence of the poetic art is being able to get outside one's self, to stand apart, study and draw that other self, the imaged character of another, for the eyes and brain of the outside world of men and women to see and know. Has not Browning done that in Pippa, in Sludge, in a *A Soul's Tragedy*?

And again, what is Browning's personality? Is he chivalrous and prompt like Count Gismond or Caponsacchi, or cruel and carnivorous like Guido, or slack in moral fibre like Andrea del Sarto, or dilatory like the Duke in the *Statue and the Bust*, or too fearsome of physical pain like the wife in Ivanovitch, or a liar, self-deceiver and half-mystic like Sludge? Let us dismiss the idea of personality altogether; grant Browning's beliefs, still these have to do with his work as an artist just as much as, and no more than, the model who sat for Madame Recamier in Orchardson's picture had to do with that painter's career; she was used to express a social drama; Browning's beliefs are used to express a spiritual drama. In so far as Browning expresses his personal creed, as in *La Saisiaz*, he ceases almost to be an artist at all—except in the rhythmical management.

It is because he takes some belief or spiritual idea which is common to humanity or some section of it, and (whether it be sympathetic or no with his own nature) treats it from outside himself as a human attribute more or less grouped or individualised,* that he is so incontestably a poet in the making sense, the artist who really does paint man's soul. In short, it is in the manner alone, and not in the matter, that his personality can be said to tinge his creations.

On p. 14 of the *Handbook* it is said that 'if the first three poems represent the author's intellectual youth, the remainder are one long maturity'; that 'Browning's work is himself; his poetic genius was in advance of his general growth, but has been subject to no other law.' These are the dicta of a high authority; but though I am not going to dispute them, we must remember that *Pippa passes* was published when Browning was about thirty; *A Soul's Tragedy* when he was about thirty-four; *In a Balcony* say in his forty-second year, the volume called *Dramatis Personæ* when he had passed his fiftieth year. (*May and Death* I think was written or published in 1857.) The progress, the development of skill in making, may have had its ebb and flow as before suggested; but the main development from *Pippa passes* to *A Soul's Tragedy* thence to *In a Balcony*, and thence to the supreme spiritual drama of human aspiration contained in the epilogue to *Dramatis Personæ*, has been steadily upward, and not level—while *Echetlos, Pan and Luna, Clive,* and *A Forgiveness*, are in their different modes corroborative of the same law.

It may be worth while now to go into some details of chronological value and even into the material amount, the amount in lines, of the different periods in Browning's poetic career.

Taking dates of publication as being approximately dates of production, we find Browning's two most productive periods in point of bulk lay, 1st (with respect only to the six volumes published in 1868) between *Sordello*

* See the essay on 'A Death in the Desert.'

(1840) and *Luria* (1846), that is to say between the twenty-seventh and the thirty-third years of his life; and 2nd, between 1864-68, at which latter date the *Ring and the Book* saw the light—that is between the fiftieth and fifty-fifth years of his life. *Luria* he marks in the dedication as his last attempt for the present at dramatic poetry. (In 1853, seven years after *Luria*, he publishes *In a Balcony*, which might be called an Act in a drama.)

And here is an approximate summary of his work, in lines, from *Sordello* to *Ferishtah* :—

| | |
|---|---|
| Between 1840-46 the seven dramas and many Dramatic Lyrics and Romances, | 21,000 lines. |
| Between 1850-64, *Christmas Eve* and *Easter Day*, *Men and Women*, many Dramatic Lyrics and Romances, the Shelley Essay, *Karshook*, *May and Death*, and *Dramatis Personæ*, | 12,000 ,, |
| Between 1864-68 the *Ring and the Book*, | 21,000 ,, |
| Between 1871-85 twelve volumes containing 'mostly single Poems, | 33,000 ,, |

I remember how astonished I was when Dr Furnivall told me to count the lines of so many of Browning's poems as I possessed. What could be the use of it? I remember very well counting every line of every book of Browning I possessed, and that means nearly all. But in most cases I counted wrong, and got small credit for what seemed to me quite Herculean exertions. To-day, I am grateful to him; for without that counting, which was correctly done by somebody else, I should not be able to say what I am going to say; viz., that with Browning counting a line is like casting up figures; his word-currency is of uniform value; you cannot say that six words written in 1855 are worth sixty written in 1880, or *vice versâ*. His artistic continuity is in that sense complete

The period then least productive in point of bulk is that between 1850 and 1864, being fourteen years; but in this interval we have some of the strongest, most concentrated, and most fruitful work of his life. All the Men and Women of the edition of '68; many of the lyrics and romances; among all these *Before and After*, the Painter Monologues, the Music Monologues, *Karshish, Blougram, In a Balcony, Holy Cross Day, Heretic's Tragedy, The Grammarian's Funeral*, and, above all, *One Word More*.

To summarise again in a poetic, and not an arithmetical sense, we have, 1st, the three poems of his youth; 2nd, the seven pure Dramas, and some of the Lyrics and Romances of varying interest; 3rd, the poems before named, showing great increase in power of concentration between the thirty-fifth and fifty-second years of his life; 4th, the final triumph of dramatic, psychological, and analytic qualities, between the fifty-second and fifty-sixth years of his life:—a triumph carried on at the same height of power to the present year.

The subject I am maltreating would be incomplete did I not consider the importance of what Browning himself has said, from outside so to speak, on the subject of his own art. We learn from Dr Furnivall's Bibliography that when Browning wrote *Pauline* he thought of being in a manner a universal artist, producing under different names *chefs d'œuvre* in music, drama, and oratorship. Here are his words :—

'*Pauline*—written in pursuance of a foolish plan I forget, or have no wish to remember; involving the assumption of several distinct characters; the world was never to guess that such an opera, such a comedy, such a speech proceeded from the same notable person.'

See again the forewords to *Paracelsus*, which really contain the history of what I am going to insist on, the uniqueness of the dramatic quality of Browning's genius :—

' . . . instead of having recourse to an external machinery of incidents to create and evolve the crisis I desire to produce, I have ventured to display somewhat minutely the mood itself in its rise and progress, and have suffered the agency by which it is influenced and determined to be generally discernible in its effects alone, and sub-ordinated throughout, if not altogether excluded.'

Next, let us recall some expressions which he uses in regard of the objective and subjective poet in the Shelley Essay.

He himself then, Browning for whom I claim so much, says of the objective poet :—

' Doubtless we accept gladly the biography of an objective poet, as the phrase now goes; one whose endeavour has been to reproduce things external, (whether the phenomena of the scenic universe, or the manifested action of the human heart and brain) with an immediate reference, in every case, to the common eye and apprehension of his fellow men, assumed capable of receiving and profiting by this repro-duction. It has been obtained through the poet's double faculty of seeing external objects more clearly, widely, and deeply, than is possible to the average mind, at the same time that he is so acquainted and in sympathy with its narrow comprehension as to be careful to supply it with no other materials than it can combine into an intelligible whole. The auditory of such a poet will include not only the intelligences which save for such assistance would have missed the deeper meaning and enjoyment of the original objects, but also the spirits of a like endowment with his own, who, by means of his abstract, can forthwith pass to the reality it was made from, and either corroborate their impressions of things known already, or supply themselves with new from whatever shows in the inexhaustible variety of existence may have hitherto escaped their knowledge. Such a poet is properly the ποιητής, the fashioner; and the thing fashioned, his poetry, will of necessity be substantive, projected from himself, and distinct.'

That of course is clear and exhaustive ; and he goes on to say—

'Doubtless, with respect to such a poet, we covet his biography. We desire to look back upon the process of gathering together in a lifetime the materials of the work we behold entire; of elaborating, perhaps under difficulty and hindrance, all that is familiar to our admiration in the apparent facility of success.'

And after suggesting the things we should like to know about such a poet, as, for instance,

'The inner impulse of this effort and operation, what induced it? Did a soul's delight in its own extended sphere of vision, set it, for the gratification of an insuppressible power, on labour, as other men are set on rest?'

he concludes, with regard to this objective poet—

'Still, fraught with instruction and interest as such details undoubtedly are, we can, if needs be, dispense with them. The man passes, the work remains. The work speaks for itself, as we say; and the biography of the worker is no more necessary to an understanding or enjoyment of it, than is a model or anatomy of some tropical tree, to the right tasting of the fruit we are familiar with on the market stall,— or a geologist's map and stratification to the prompt recognition of the hilltop, our landmark of every day.'

Of the subjective poet, however, he speaks in more affectionate terms—more reverently also, as of one directly in contact with the highest :—

'We turn with stronger needs to the genius of an opposite tendency, the subjective poet of modern classification. He, gifted like the objective poet with the fuller perception of nature and man, is impelled to embody the thing he perceives, not so much with reference to the many below, as to the One above him, the supreme Intelligence which apprehends all things in their absolute truth, — an ultimate view ever aspired to, if but partially attained, by the poet's own soul. Not what man sees, but what God sees—the *Ideas* of Plato, seeds of creation lying burningly on the Divine Hand—it is towards these that he struggles. Not with the combination of humanity in action, but with the primal elements of humanity he has to do; and he digs where he stands, preferring to seek them in his own soul, as the nearest reflex of that absolute Mind, according to the intuitions of which he desires to perceive and speak. Such a poet does not deal habitually with the picturesque groupings and tempestuous tossings of the forest trees, but with their roots and fibres, naked to the chalk and stone. He does not paint pictures and hang them on the walls, but rather carries them on the retina of his own eyes; we must look deep into his human eyes, to see those pictures on them. He is rather a seer, accordingly, than a fashioner, and what he produces will be less a work than an effluence. That effluence cannot be easily considered in abstraction from his personality, being indeed the very radiance and aroma of his personality, projected from it but not separated. Therefore, in our approach to the poetry, we necessarily approach the personality of the poet; in apprehending it we apprehend him, and certainly we cannot love it without loving him. Both for love's and understanding's sake we desire to know him, and as readers of his poetry must be readers of his biography also.'

Is it not strange how this applies to Browning's individuality, so far as he lets that escape in his work?

Is it not strange, too, how he treats less cordially the very qualities by virtue of which he has become a seer, and shown us these roots and fibres of the forest trees?

I think the explanation of this oddity, if one may so call it, lies in the fact that Browning seems to have always looked on his fashioning or picture-making power as a servant, while he should perhaps have treated it as his comrade. Grant his position that 'incidents in the development of a soul' are almost solely 'worth study'— grant too that the speaker in *Pauline* is really Browning himself when he says—

> ' I am made up of an intensest life,
> Of a most clear idea of consciousness
> Of self, distinct from all its qualities,
> From all affections, passions, feelings, powers;
> And thus far it exists, if tracked in all ;
> But linked, in me, to self-supremacy,
> Existing as a centre to all things,
> Most potent to create and rule and call
> Upon all things to minister to it ;

> And to a principle of restlessness
> Which would be all, have, see, know, taste, feel, all.
> This is myself; and I should thus have been
> Though gifted meaner than the meanest soul.'

Grant the truth of this passage as applied to Browning, first, as man, second, as maker or fashioner, third, as subjective poet or seer, the fact remains that without the power of objective picture-making shown in *Childe Roland*, in *A Likeness*, or in *Porphyria* (I purposely take three poems of different periods), he could never achieve the subjective and supreme picture-making by which he makes us see the essence or soul of such widely-differing people as Luria, Guido or the nameless heroine of the *Inn Album*.

We get to the root of the matter, as it seems to me, when we trace the continual interweaving of soul with sense in his actual upward progress. The mood of Porphyria's lover is determined by the nature of the night, the sense of contrast between it and the warmth and beauty which Porphyria sheds through his cottage; the act of murder done is a direct result of the contrast between the wild dripping night and the blackness of his own soul on the one hand, and the fire she has lighted and Porphyria herself on the other. What would have become of the motive of the poem as a work of art had Browning been unable to lead up to it by the strong opening lines, which personify the wind as a wayward demon, too much akin to his own wayward mood? In passing, it is curious how, to a reader like myself, a title is of service in deciphering the poet's intention. For of course the intention is half, or more than half, of the picture. When I first read *Porphyria* I thought the man did quite right, and that Browning thought so too. In fact, I forgot that Browning is an artist, describing, putting himself in the man's place, and standing aside to

see what he would do under the stress of the situation—
all at once. It only came to me that he was doing all
this when I learned, many years later, that the poem was
really classed with *Johannes Agricola* under the title of
'Madhouse Cells.' Never was a classing more significant,
or more suggestive. And yet to the proper knowledge
of the two poems that classing is quite unnecessary.    It
tells too much.    Look at everything Browning has done
as a picture and no more, (unless he plainly gives you a
reason for his doing it as in *Gold Hair* and the *Statue
and Bust*) and you will find, what is too often forgotten,
that all these utterances are, as he has once for all insisted,
those of so many imaginary individuals, not his own.
He only edits them in fact.

Here by way of parenthesis, let us notice one among
many instances in which Dr Furnivall's invaluable
bibliography has brought back into light forgotten secrets
with regard to Browning's poetic development; the fact,
namely, that the third, fourth, fifth, and sixth poems in
point of date, coming, that is, next after *Paracelsus*, were
the song in *Pippa*, 'A King Lived Long Ago,' *Porphyria*,
*Johannes Agricola*, and the first six stanzas of Section 6 of
*James Lee's Wife*. These four poems were written in
1835-6, in his twenty-third and twenty-fourth years.
But as to the first, the song in *Pippa*, it in itself shews,
by the changes made between the years 1835, '41, and
'63, a whole history of poetic development. To substan-
tiate this there is no time now, but the changes are
carefully noted in the Bibliography, and very valuable
the noting is.

As to *Johannes Agricola*, I know of no poem of Browning's which is more complete a 'fashioning'—to use his
own phrase—a rendering objectively of a mood of mind.
The idea of poetic development becomes a contradiction
in presence of it.   Imagery, wording, idea, all take their

places as in a well-ordered puzzle; the grip and sympathy of the author on and with his subject are here felt to the extreme of pain almost. The same grip and sympathy are felt when one reads *Guido* in the *Ring and the Book*, or the *Inn Album*, where any one of the characters speaks. The man who wrote *Johannes* had in him the germ of *Guido* or the *Inn Album*, but only the germ. In the first case he could present you with one mood in which he sympathised when he wrote it; in the two others he was enabled, through vastly-matured powers, to present with equal *verve* moods and character as unsympathetic as possible to his own nature, otherwise than dramatically.

The first division of Section 6 of *James Lee's Wife*, like *Porphyria* and *Johannes* produced about the same time, is marked by an almost goblin-like power of insight into the darker recesses, the wilder moods, of nature and man. And this quality almost dies out in the later work. There is no longer the love of a subject for the sake of its dramatic queerness merely—there must be a substantial human interest too. The two 'Madhouse Cell' Poems might better be called preter-human, or ultra-human, than human. And the difference between the first and second parts of Section 6 of *James Lee's Wife* is that, while the plaint of the wind was enough to make Browning write in 1836, he must have the plaint of a soul in 1863.—And yet—something is lost.

Having dealt with the physical or natural chronology of Browning's work, and with his own elucidation of his aims, let us attempt a very incomplete artistic chronology of his poetic life. I begin with *Sordello* because although *Pippa passes* is declared as the beginning of his making faculty, the struggle which led to that began in *Sordello*.

I have spoken before of the struggle shewn in *Sordello*, and in subsequent works, between the making faculty, and the intellectual and spiritual faculties; and I have assumed that the first has in the main conquered and used as allies the two others. But another conflict, for my present purpose more important yet, has, through Browning's whole artistic life, (and side by side with that other struggle), been going on between his objective and subjective powers as poet or maker.

In *Sordello* the objective power, of which I have lately been speaking, struggles hard to assert its real mastery, and with much, though unperceived, success. Regarded as a step in the development of Browning's own soul, occupied as a maker or fashioner of another soul (this is, I admit, somewhat a straining of his dicta in the Shelley essay), this poem is the record of a struggle, and nothing more. It is an instance (alas, how many there are) of the vastness of the subject overmastering the powers of execution. All through, the poem abounds with evidence of the continual wrestle between two forces—the one, the almost matured power of 'fashioning' a material word picture, the other the very immature power of fashioning —the same word is applicable—in an intelligible word picture the very result aimed at, the development of a soul.

Browning's development, then, as poet or maker, has been two-fold: his fashioning quality, as used to portray objects of sense, has been born nearly full-grown, and, like Pallas Athene, quite full-armed; the fashioning quality, as applied to the deeper and mightier secrets of mental and spiritual nature, has been of gradual growth.

This young Titan of his, this power of word-picturing a material scene, and even vividly picturing certain moods of mind, stands sturdily at the gate Browning so much wants to win, behind which lies the soul itself—and says, before you go in, you have to reckon with and master me, or own me always your master. He, that Titan, wins a victory in *Sordello*—as I have tried to shew. In *Pippa* the battle is more even; Ottima and Sebald may be reckoned a victory, hard won, in which the Titan, defeated, becomes a powerful, but for the time subject, ally.

The next great battlefield is the *Blot in the 'Scutcheon*. Here I pause for a moment in wonder at the possibility of looking at that play—even at any single word of it— otherwise than as Browning wrote it. It was a piece of full-grown work when it was actually performed; drama then had exigencies in quite different directions from the demands of the present year. But to attempt to 'adapt' the play to the needs of a theatre of to-day, is, it seems to me, the worst kind of profanation. And I should say the same were Browning himself to sanction such alterations.

But looking at the play as it was written, it seems a striking instance of a truth, not so far as I know, hitherto formulated or crystallised. There is the modern play of incident where character is quite subordinated—where what happens to people, and not what the people are, is presented to us by the playwright. There is the modern play of character such as the *Man o' Airlie*, which is an attempt to render the soul of the chief character in that play. There is the sound acting play which attempts to combine both the foregoing qualities, such as *Caste*, and *School*, by Robertson; and *Money* by the late Lord Lytton.

I have cited some indisputably good and high-aiming work, expressly for the purpose of bringing the *Blot in the 'Scutcheon* into correlation with them. It may be, very likely it is, an unactable play now; that is, one which does not fulfil the conditions required by a London audience of to-day. But it has qualities beyond those of what is usually called a play to be read at home—a student's play. Nay, more; if there were living an actress capable, *physically* as well as mentally, of playing Mildred, I am convinced the rest of the play would go with acclaim.

Now all this has to do with Browning's development as poet or maker; because, at the age of thirty-three he produced a play, which, whether in the study or on the stage, gives you, compactly, a crisis in the development of four souls, and as such includes Browning's own development.

Mildred, Tresham, Gwendolen, and Mertoun, each do the right thing at the right time, due allowance made for the fetters of half-civilisation that bind them; but they divide into two groups—Mildred and Mertoun act out their nature, and God, not man, is their just judge; they have no need of pardon, they have disobeyed no dictate of that judge; Tresham stumbles and falls, not through clumsiness or blindness, but through the thwarting of the fetters that cramp and infuriate at the same time his healthy and noble force; Gwendolen *understands*, as all women have understood from the beginning till now, and only fails to bring her soul's powers to bear, because of the veil which convention has dropped between her and the two lovers.

Here then is a play in which the material and the psychical elements—the former constantly changing or reacting, the latter as constantly progressing—meet in conflict. The handling of both by Browning is done with equal force; here his objective and subjective gifts join hands, enemies no longer.

*Colombe* is a curious instance of the reflux in development of which I have spoken; it fails to give the same sense of standing aloof from, judging, and presenting as living human beings, the *dramatis personæ*, which is so evident in the *Blot*. But this necessary reflux or ebb brings its full tide in *Luria*.

That play—it seems to be admitted on all hands—is not, even so much as the *Blot* or as *Colombe*, an actable play. Whether that be so or not, it is a drama, and unique as a drama. Luria, Domizia, and Braccio are to me as real as Othello, Emilia, or Iago (I am, it is needless to say, drawing no parallel between the two plays). But though Browning might possibly have given us these three characters in such a narrative form as the *Inn Album* with equal force, the play must be judged on its actual form; and as such it is one of a class of dramas apart on the one hand from the purely modern acting drama, on the other from the Elizabethan drama. Indeed, Browning's dramatic instinct must be reckoned as a unique thing, like his style. Before him was nothing like him, nor after him shall be.—And in the process of our development, these plays, *Luria*, the *Blot*, the *Soul's Tragedy*, and *In a Balcony*, will see the light of another stage than ours—always granting the birth of an actor and actress who can conceive the characters for scenic representation as vividly as they can be realised by the reader who is in touch with the creative faculty which begot them.

It is useless trying to make anything like a complete chronological survey, from the mental point of view, of the years of Browning's productive life which succeeded *Luria*, until *The Ring and the Book*. But in the period from 1840 to 1846, which saw the birth of the dramas to which I have alluded, how does the idea of development as here imagined justify me by results? We have in this period a vast energy in the lyrical, romantic, and monologue forms. The most prominent poems in all these branches as indicating progress or achievement, are *My Last Duchess, Soliloquy in a Spanish Cloister, Rudel, St Praxed, Pictor Ignotus, Meeting at Night and Parting at Morning*, and *Time's Revenges*. Each of these poems contains, one may say, the elements of a drama, remaining the while absolutely complete. That is, they have this unique quality—that they give us, if we have eyes to see, the

complete history in each case which leads up to and descends from the crisis in the individual life handled in
each poem.

But though I have purposely excluded *Waring* and *The
Flight of the Duchess* because they are both conceived in
a spirit rather fanciful than dramatic, it is also difficult to
deny the superiority of the next period of years in force
of handling such similar poems to those previously
grouped, as *Love among the Ruins*, *A Lover's Quarrel*, *A
Woman's Last Word*, the painting and music poems, *Any
Wife*, *Karshish*, *Instans Tyrannus*, *A Light Woman*,
*Blougram*, *Before and After*, *In Three Days* and *In a
Year*, *In a Balcony*, *Holy Cross Day*, *A Heretic's
Tragedy*, *A Grammarian's Funeral*, and *One Word
More*.

All this latter group was published (for my present
purpose I am forced to take that as synonymous with produced) between 1846 and 1855; that is, they represent the
development, in the sense in which I am using it, which
was acting according to its laws between the thirty-fourth
and the forty-fourth years of the poet's life. It is quite
plain, let the circumstances have been what they may,
that these poems represent a suppressed or abandoned
play-writing faculty. And here Mrs Orr's proposition
that Browning's poetic genius has been subject to no
other law than that of his general growth, must be
accepted as a postulate.

In *Blougram* and in *Instans Tyrannus*, in *A Light
Woman*, and in *Before and After* the dramatic—the
objective—the fashioning quality which paints men's
souls—calls out for recognition. Of course I don't mean
to say that *Blougram* could be other than it is, practically
a dialogue; but I do say it is such a dialogue as also fulfils
the conditions laid down for the poems named in the
earlier period up to 1846—it gives you the rise and de-

cline of the essential life of two remarkable men (Blougram and Gigadibs) with a vividness which was not within Browning's scope up to 1846.

So with *Holy Cross Day* and *A Heretic's Tragedy*, what may have been the personal history leading up to their production I don't know, and would rather not know; but taking them as they are written they make together an instance of almost a springtide of development, if we admit in the former case the dramatic idea that the Jews have ever thought of Christ—in strange dark moments of self doubt—as their Messiah after all. The whole point of the poem, the whole of that contrast we are so often told about by Browning, lies in this idea.

[It is remarkable that during this ten years' period, in 1855 indeed, Browning has given us for once only, not to return to it, a crowning instance of his power in the weird and purely fanciful line—I mean *Childe Roland*. For descriptive power, and, as such, a story, unrivalled. For suggestiveness—right suggestiveness—in thought and conduct—unequalled.]

*A Grammarian's Funeral* and *In a Balcony* are the next monumental poems marking, again, a flow of the tide of development during these years. Both are as widely different in motive as possible, for two poems given from the same hand, the same year. The first deals in a purely dramatic sense, and uniquely, so far as I know, with the vast force evoked by the first stir of man's mind in the direction of getting knowledge for its own sake. The other deals with a crucial point in two young and full lives of to-day or any day, lives both governed by another life, cramped and confined by royalty, but with capabilities beyond the grasp of the other two. Here Browning has surpassed himself, and, until the *Ring and the Book*, has not equalled this achievement. The Queen is the great creation in this *chef d'œuvre*. No dramatist before or since has even attempted to shew us a royalty, with vast but undeclared powers, and yet tied by etiquette, by state observances—breaking bounds at a touch of human love, without for a moment losing her queenliness. The character is there, struck out at one blow.

*One Word More* is a shrine, to be approached with reverence. It is almost alone among Browning's purely personal utterances ; it stands quite alone, in the thrill of its beauty, amongst the contemporary verse of this century.

Our next starting point is *The Ring and the Book*.

Is it not worth while to bring ourselves to the point of achievement arrived at in *The Ring and the Book*, upwards through the other struggles I have alluded to ? From the sketch of Palma we reach, (through Michal,) Ottima and Phene ; from these two last, to Mildred, from Mildred, through Colombe, we reach Domizia and Constance ; from Constance, the supreme creation Pompilia. (So, in another manner, through *Any Wife* we reach Fifine, or perhaps Elvire and Fifine rather— and for all its wilful intellectual puzzlement and sophistical truth, this will always remain a poem, shewing with dramatic force only to be understood by those who will take the trouble to read it, the mental situation of most able men in regard of women).

So, from *Johannes Agricola* through the sketch of Salinguerra and the study of Sebald (who only exists because of Ottima), Luigi, Jules, Tresham, *Luria*, *The Spanish Cloister*, the *Grammarian*, St Praxed's Bishop, *Karshish*, *Blougram*, we reach Caponsacchi, Guido, and the Pope. The net result is that while in the earlier poems we have men and women drawn firmly and truly indeed, but only in some simple or complex incident of their lives, in the men and women of the *Ring and the Book* we have those men and women as they were, in their growth, development, or degeneration, throughout their whole lives. Tresham it is true lives for us; but we hardly see what he had been or might become outside of the few days of tragedy that the play comprises. Mildred, I grant, lives as Pompilia lives; she is simply an instance of premature development on the poet's part. The Grammarian, too, gives us a life in its kind, complete. So do St Praxed's Bishop and Blougram in their differing and converging lines of portraiture. (A study of the two poems side by side would be fruitful).

Guido is a greater creation, from the point of view of completeness, than Iago, Macbeth, or Wolsey; Caponsacchi is greater, too, than Coriolanus, Antony, Henry the wild prince, or Edgar. These three presentments—Pompilia, Caponsacchi, and Guido—are, it must be remembered, evolved from a somewhat obscure Italian story; the actual woman, and the actual two men, might, but for the great event uniting their lives, have died, one a misused wife, one a poor noble of dubious character, one a high-bred but self-indulgent priest. But the wand of genius has touched them, and they live for us as Antony lives, as Henry V. lives, as Wolsey lives. Not for what in the world's eye they achieved—rather for their failures. They have none of them shaken the world for a woman's sake, played with the fortune of a great kingdom for mere wantonness, or been cast into nothingness by the fiat of a king; and yet, even in this railroad age, we shall not forget either the heroism, the womanliness, or the hopeless villany of these three.

In conclusion, what has the development of Browning's genius as poet or maker given to the future world of English-speaking people? Let us take only a few representative instances.

We have the seeker after all knowledge in *Paracelsus;* the subjective poet in *Sordello;* the girl who lives through and amidst the crises of other lives, in *Pippa :* Mildred is herself, and can only be known, not characterised ; we have the influence and growth of a mighty faith, sinking through savage bigotry to art dilettantism and its inevitable sensuous environment, linked with superstition, in *Holy Cross Day*, *A Heretic's Tragedy*, and *St Praxed's Bishop* ; the same mighty faith, rising in the course of history to that curious mixture of cynical intellectualism with a faith which would aspire, but fears itself, in *Blougram ;* the heroic but hopeless giving away of a kingly nature in *Luria ;* an epic drama of human nature, in all gradations from its basest to its noblest qualities, in *The Ring and the Book.*

# CLASSIFICATION OF BROWNING'S WORKS

BROWNING has implied or avowed (in his Essay on Shelley, in the dedication to *Sordello*, in the Epilogue to *Pacchiarotto* and elsewhere) his belief that study of the soul of man,—his true essence which is to live or die, develop or dwindle, according as opportunities are used or wasted,—is the poet's highest aim. The Dramas apart, I have therefore thought this leading idea should be first dealt with in classifying. So I have begun by grouping together under three heads, all poems whose avowed or obvious primary subject is either the whole life or some ruling incident in the life of a man or men, as tending directly to the development or degradation of souls, through this life and succeeding lives. From these main groups the transition seems easy to a group of poems dealing primarily with some form of emotion, where feeling at particular moments or periods, though not necessarily a ruling incident in the life, has its influence for good or ill—thence we come to Art, where the perceptive qualities come in aid of character and feeling to elevate man's nature; and thence to national and political feeling, which give a like aid, but by the more localised motive of race and historical tradition. The few poems classed as stories and myths, hero poems and Greek Poems, are so separated because such seems their primary character.

In this classification the word 'soul' must be taken to

mean a man's physical, mental, and spiritual attributes, developing interdependently throughout life on earth, and culminating or sinking into an identity which may or may not be immortal.

The subject under each heading is to be understood as the *primary* subject or purpose of each poem.

I. Dramas.

| | | | | |
|---|---|---|---|---|
| Strafford (1837) ... ... | Vol. 1 | Ed. 1868 | p. 207 |
| Victor and Charles (1842) ... | ,, 3 | ,, | 1 |
| Return of Druses (1843) ... | ,, 3 | ,, | 229 |
| Blot in the 'Scutcheon (1843) | ,, 4 | ,, | 1 |
| Colombe (1844) ... ... | ,, 4 | ,, | 61 |
| Soul's Tragedy (1845) ... | ,, 5 | ,, | 1 |
| Luria (1845) ... ... | ,, 5 | ,, | 43 |
| In a Balcony (1855) ... | ,, 6 | ,, | 1 |

II. A. Poems not strictly dramatic in form, but which deal with the history, or some incident in the history, of the souls of two or more individuals, mutually acting on each other towards (1) progress, or (2) arrest, in development.

1. Progress in development, from right action at a critical moment, and right disregard of social or religious surroundings.

*Pippa Passes* (1841), Vol. 2. Ed. '68.

Ivan Ivanovitch (1879).

Halbert and Hob (1879)

Ned Bratts (1879)

2. Arrest in development, from failure or mistake in action, and wrong regard for social or religious surroundings.

Statue and Bust (1855)     Le Byron de nos Jours (1864)

Youth and Art (1864)

3. Progress and arrest in two or more souls, from their influence on each other, and as governed by social, domestic or religious surroundings.

The Glove (1845)
James Lee (1864)
The Worst of it (1864)

*Ring and Book* (1868-9)
*Red Cotton Nightcap Country* (1873)
*Inn Album* (1875)

II. B. The like history or incident as regards (1) progress, (2) arrest, in development of the soul of one individual.

1. Progress in development caused by (*a*) the individual acting on or using circumstances; (*b*) his or her being acted on by them.

| *a.* | Clive (1880) |
|---|---|
| *Pauline* (1833) | *b.* |
| *Paracelsus* (1835) | *Sordello* (1840) |
| Waring (1842) | Flight of the Duchess (1845). |
| A Grammarian's Funeral (1855) | (? IV 5) |
| At the Mermaid (1876) | *Hohenstiel-Schwangau* (1871) |

2. Arrest in development caused by (*a*) like action on, or (*b*) being acted on by circumstances.

| *a.* | *b.* |
|---|---|
| Lost Leader (1845) | Protus (1855) |
| | Sludge (1864) |
| Gold Hair (1864) | Martin Relph (1879) |

III. The spiritual element in man, and the attributes of his soul; these subjects being treated (1) historically, or in narrative; (2) philosophically, or by way of speculation; (3) in connection with the idea of, or faith in, God as a radical element in man's nature; (4) in reference to that quality in man's nature which demands and believes in a continuity of life before and after physical death.

| 1. *Historically, or in narrative.* | 2. *Philosophically, or by way of speculation.* |
|---|---|
| Ben Karshook (1856) | Cleon (1855) |
| Pacchiarotto (1876) | *Fifine at the Fair* (1872) |
| House (1876) | Pisgah-Sights I & II (1876) |
| Shop (1876) | Bifurcation (1876) |
| Filippo Baldinucci on the Privilege of Burial (1876) | Lines preluding 2nd Series of Dramatic Idylls (1880) |
| Pietro of Abano (1880) | |

3. *In connection with the idea of, or faith in, God.*

| | |
|---|---|
| Saul (1845-55) | Karshish (1855) |
| The Patriot (1855) (? VI) | Johannes Agricola (1836) |
| Boy and Angel (1844) | Blougram (1855) |
| The Twins (1854) | Death in the Desert (1864) |
| Heretic's Tragedy (1855) (? IV 5) | Caliban (1864) |
| Holy-Cross-Day (1855 (? IV 5) | Epilogue to Dramatis Personæ (1864) |
| *Christmas Eve* (1850) | Fears and Scruples (1876 ) |
| *Easter Day* (1850) | |

4. *In reference to that quality in man's nature which demands and believes in a continuity of life before and after physical death.*

| | | | |
|---|---|---|---|
| Evelyn Hope (1855) . . | Vol. 3, *Works* Ed. 1868, p 110 | | |
| Rabbi Ben Ezra (1864) . | „  6 | „ | 99 |
| Prospice (1864) . . . | „  6 | „ | 153 |
| La Saisiaz, and lines preceding it (1878) | | | |

## IV. Poems dealing with some play of human emotion, caused by,—1. Love; 2. Hate; 3. Love and Hate; 4. Love of Animals; 5. Humour.

### 1. *Love.*

#### *a.* Husband and Wife.

By the Fireside (1855)
Any Wife to Any Husband (1855)
Count Gismond (1842)
One Word More (1855)

#### *b.* Mutual Love.

Meeting at Night (1845)
Parting at Morning (1845)
A Woman's Last Word (1855)
Love among the Ruins (1855)
A Lover's Quarrel (1855)
Respectability (1855)
In Three Days (1855)
Mesmerism (1855)
In a Gondola (1842)
Confessions (1864)
May and Death (1867)

#### *c.* Self-Renunciation.

The Lost Mistress (1845)
One Way of Love (1855)
The Last Ride Together (1855)

#### *d.* Worship or endeavour—ennobling influence of Love.

Garden fancies. (1) The Flower's Name (1844)
Song (1845)
My Star (1855)
Misconceptions (1855)
Love in a Life (1855)
Life in a Love (1855)
Women and Roses (1855)
Rudèl to the Lady of Tripoli (1842)
Prologue to Pacchiarotto (1876)
Natural Magic (1876)
Magical Nature (1876)

Poem following two Poets of Croisic

#### *e.* One sided or incomplete love.

Cristina (1842)
Two in the Campagna (1855)
A Serenade at the Villa (1855)
Another way of Love (1855)
In a Year (1845)
Time's Revenges (1845)
A Light Woman (1855)
Porphyria's Lover (1836)
Too Late (1864)
A Face (1864)
A Likeness (1864)
Numpholeptos (1876)
Appearances (1876)
St Martin's Summer (1876)

#### *f* Ephemeral love.

Earth's Immortalities. (1) Love (1846)
A Pretty Woman (5 ?) (1855)

### 2. *Hate.*

Soliloquy of Spanish Cloister (5 ?) (1842)
Instans Tyrannus (1855)

### 3. *Love and Hate acting on each other,* (*a*) *From man to woman.* (*b*) *From woman to man.* (*c*) *Between men.*

#### *a.*

My Last Duchess (1842)
A Forgiveness (1876)

#### *b.*

The Laboratory (1844)
The Confessional (1845)

*c.*

Before (1855)
After (1855)

    4. *Love for or in animals.*

How they brought the Good News from Ghent to Aix (1845)
Tray (1879)

Muléykeh (1880)

    5. *Humour or Satire.*

Sibrandus Schafnaburgensis (1844)
Up at a Villa—Down in the City (1855)
Doctor——(1880)

V. Art, Plastic and otherwise. 1. Poetry ; 2. Music ; 3. Painting ; 4. Sculpture, and Architecture.

    1. *Poetry and Poets.*

Popularity (1855)
Memorabilia (1855)
Transcendentalism (1855)
How it strikes a Contemporary (1855)
Two Poets of Croisic (1878)
Epilogue to Pacchiarotto (1876)
' Touch him ne'er so lightly,' 2nd Dram. Idylls (1880)

    2. *Music and Musicians.*

A Toccata of Galuppi's (1855)
Master Hugues of Saxe-Gotha (1855)

Abt Vogler (1864)

    3. *Painting and Painters.*

Old Pictures in Florence (1855)
Pictor Ignotus (1845)
Fra Lippo Lippi (1855)
Guardian Angel (1855)
Andrea del Sarto (1855)
Eurydice (1864)

    4. *Sculpture, and Architecture.*

The Bishop orders his Tomb at St Praxed's (1845)
Deaf and Dumb (1868)

VI. The expression of some (1) national or (2) political feeling.

    1.

Cavalier Tunes (1842)
Nationality in Drinks (1844-45)
De Gustibus (1855)
Home Thoughts from Abroad (1845)
Home Thoughts from the Sea (1845)

Through the Metidja to Abd-el-Kadr (1842)
Incident of the French Camp (1842)

    2.

Italian in England (1845)
Englishman in Italy (1845)

VII. Hero Poems.

    Hervé Riel (1871)    Pheidippides (1879)    Echetlos (1880)

VIII. 1. Stories, or 2. Myths.

    1.

Pied Piper of Hamelin (IV 5 ?) (1842)
Childe Roland (1855)

Cenciaja (1876)

    2.

Artemis Prologizes (1842)
Pan and Luna (1880)

IX. Greek Poems.

    Balaustion's Adventure (1871)    Aristophanes' Apology (1875)
                Agamemnon (1877)

# ON ERRONEOUS STUDY OF BROWNING

IF the Browning Societies had done nothing else,—and much sterling work has been done by them—we should be grateful to them for having evoked Mrs Orr's Handbook. That is real work. It is clear, exhaustive within its limits, and authentic throughout, and has abundantly justified the often questioned necessity for such an undertaking. So long as it is in print Browning's poetic reputation may be safely left to stand the shock of the most well meant adulation.

Although the poet's imperious personality makes an ethical basis for his most dramatic work, I maintain that his ethics are governed when he will by his creative genius; and that one of the most important methods of looking at his work consists in regarding him as pre-eminently an artist or maker in the vast majority of his productions.

The subtlest and most intricate dramas of human life are to be found, not in the events which make history, but in the clash of lives to all appearance commonplace, in the development or urging upwards or downwards of characters seemingly trivial. A painter or sculptor with the gift of portraiture in its highest sense might spend a lifetime in interpreting only a few of the struggles that gradually evolve themselves in the slow change, purifying or degrading, of the lines of the face and form, from youth to age. Some such analogy is needed for rightly judging Browning's work at this difficult time of transition, when his personal influence is close about us yet, while many of his most thrilling productions are historical. He like my hypothetical painter is above all a great portraitist; he too searches the obscurer paths of human life for his materials. And even outside of his dramas proper he will be found almost always, certainly in his strongest and most vivid moods, (as in the Ring and the Book, the Inn Album and Red Cotton Nightcap Country) using a framework not imaginary at all, but based on actual lives. About the two first named poems this fact is generally known; but the turn given to the story in Red Cotton Nightcap Country is a singular instance of divination. Everything *happened* as described in the poem; only Browning divined that the death of Miranda was no suicide, but the result of a wild attempt at proving the genuineness of the miracle-working power of the Virgin. Indeed, 'Angels will take me,' (p. 240) his last known words uttered in soliloquy, were overheard by a gardener the day before his death, as described in the poem. The idea in Porphyria's Lover (originally published fifty years ago under the title of Madhouse Cells) even at that date was not singular. It is only the perversion of a very commonly felt desire to fix and end a life at its best moment, its culminating point. Who has not said in sober earnest of some friend 'He should have died *then?*'

Not to multiply instances, Ivan Ivanovitch and Clive are both founded on actual story, and the crisis each presents is not of the poet's making; although in the latter as in Red Cotton Nightcap Country Browning has used the divining rod. The mental situation is his, and I had best quote Mrs Orr to explain how that is given: 'It was not the almost certainty of death which for one awful minute made a coward of him; it was the bare possibility of a reprieve which would have left no appeal from its dishonour.' These and plenty of other cases shew—are good types to prove—the leading fact which it is just now my business to establish ; the fact that weary yourself as you may in tracking the labyrinth of Browning's personality, you can only find your way to its heart by holding fast the truth that Browning's is the artist's mind, that its first sign-marks are receptiveness and creativeness hand in hand. Let him delight in abstract theory, be moved by the heroism or pathos of a story ; endow him with what qualities you will ; but you must come, and the sooner the better, to this conclusion ; the *raison d'être* of his brain is that its keenest nerve pleasure lies in portraiture ; in telling you impartially but vividly and rightly the story of what So-and-So did under such and such circumstances. So-and-So may be, and his story may be the story, of either a seraph or a sweep ; the delight of telling it and not its moral value is Browning's impulse. Of course with all the world to choose from, personal bias must come in ; but it comes, at the utmost, only as a selecting power, not as colouring, distorting, or modifying the particular traits to be depicted. Once for all, if Browning's ' personality' is shewn in his work, it is shewn mainly in the impartiality with which he chooses, and delights in treating, themes as wide asunder as the poles : in his *lust* (the German word) for the revel of invention in song or speech ; in his boundless delight in production. Whoever modelled the Theseus and Ilyssus had the same hunger for form in its minutest detail.

Pleasure in production is the one incentive, the ' procreant urge of the world,' for which men make creeds, and for lack of which they will die like Roderick Hudson. A great phrase said, a line well laid, it is in these that the master's touch is shewn. This artist's pleasure in creating has put Browning where he is, and makes our nerves thrill in reading him; not only those ideas expressed dramatically and subjectively concerning the fear or hope of death, his reach beyond the span of a single life—not even the abstruser thought whose farthest strain comes only to 'I believe because all analogy tells me I must.' And thus much had doubtless been clear about Browning, it has probably been often better said—in the minds of most leading men of the last fifty years, always excepting Mr Besant.

Speaking of the essay on Shelley, Dr Furnivall says:—

'The interest lay in the fact that Browning's utterances here are *his*, and not those of any one of the "so many imaginary persons" behind whom he insists on so often hiding himself, and whose necks I for one should continually like to wring, whose bodies I would fain kick out of the way, in order to get face to face with the poet himself, and hear his own voice speaking his own thoughts, man to man and soul to soul. Straight speaking, straight hitting, suit me best.'

That was Dr Furnivall's view rather more than eight years ago, and it is unlikely that he has essentially changed it. He is exceedingly sincere in his research, and has done yeoman's service for Browning's poetic reputation, and for the assistance of his readers; and so one can but feel sorry that his only reward for placing so severe a limit on his personal study of the poet, must, so far as its dramatic interest extends, be the proverbial recompense of virtue.

It is perfectly true that one powerful *raison d'être* of Browning's work lies in the fact that it is Browning. Men admire it, like it, know it, dislike it, feel its force; but it will live through its lovers, the people who assimilate it. To these, and they are many, the first discovery of Browning has been like nothing else but what is called falling in love or making a friend,—functions whose only durable basis, founded on surprise, rests afterwards on something they can no more explain than Heine could his friend's guttural way of saying ' what.'

But there are various ways of loving Browning's poems; and if one may symbolise the force, sometimes latent, often triumphantly used, the swift movement and rich and varied colouring which characterise them, by the image of a beautiful tropical beast, untameable, of splendid vitality, and resistless when there is need—we can also conceive his genius as for a time caged to meet the necessities of that particular mode of study, where the personality of the student confines his research to the limits of his unaided vision.

The dual nature of the poet's genius, the fact that it is at once objective and subjective, has been ably treated by Professor Johnson.  He says:

' The objective poet tries ' [to shew us truth] ' by presenting to us in poetical dress nature and life as they immediately seem to be.  The subjective poet by transcendent acts of insight apprehends transcendent truth, he rises to heights which many indeed of his hearers borne along with him may catch sight of for a moment, but when they sink again and are bereft of his assistance they are liable to apprehensions that the vision may have been an illusive dream.'

A little further on in the same essay we are told that 'especially does Browning believe in the immortality of the individual'; Professor Johnson quotes Caponsacchi and Evelyn Hope as proving this.  True; there are also *Pompilia*, and the poems called *Prospice, the Statue and the Bust*, and *Rabbi Ben Ezra*.  But the value of these poems as works of art does not depend even primarily on their being an expression of Browning's own belief; nor would he himself thank us much for trying to make only that out of them, let his beliefs be what they may. Indeed in one of the few instances in which he may be said to be speaking for himself he says (it is in the last volume of the Ring and the Book,) that

> '. . . . Art, wherein man no-wise speaks to men,
> Only to mankind,—Art may tell a truth
> Obliquely, *do the thing shall breed the thought,*
>
> . . . . . .
>
> 'So you may paint your picture, twice shew truth,
> Beyond mere imagery on the wall,—
> So, note by note, bring music from your mind
> Deeper than ever the Andante dived,—
> So write a book shall mean beyond the facts,
> Suffice the eye and save the soul beside.'

Surely; and when Browning in *Evelyn Hope* makes a man of fifty in love with a girl of sixteen, and makes the man say he will wait, not for the next life but for many lives, before he can win her, the poet is not (*primarily*) telling us of his own belief that each one who lives right here has a succession of lives hereafter; he is only putting in an exquisite art form an idea, dormant but brooded over in the minds of most men of energy and purpose. The *poetic* value of the great poem 'Prospice' is that it gives a voice to every strong man's passionate sense that death is but a fight upwards towards the next life; and it is spoken to and for mankind; while the pleasure derived from reading 'the Statue and the Bust' springs from the masterly fashion in which the moral 'There is no work nor knowledge nor device nor wisdom in the grave whither thou goest' is woven, half sadly, half cynically, into the form of a beautiful poem of two fruitlessly wasted passions.*

Even Rabbi Ben Ezra cannot be enjoyed to the full if

---

* In indicating here or elsewhere in this essay the motive of any poem as I conceive it, I do not pretend to give its full scope, only to insist on its value as a piece of *making*, as opposed to the prevalent mania for second or interpolated meanings.

it be read only as a didactic expression of Browning's philosophy.

'The idea of Personality as a quickening power.' . . . 'The idea of art as an intermediate agent of Personality' are undoubtedly, as Professor Corson need hardly persuade us, interesting in connection with the study not only of Browning's but of any great poet's genius.

But after quoting the passage from the Ring and the Book cited above, he says—'What is the inference the poet would have us draw from this passage? It is that the life and efficacy of art depends on the personality of the artist.' And he adds that 'this fusion of the artist's soul with his work kindles, quickens, informs those who contemplate, respond to, reproduce sympathetically within themselves the greater spirit that attracts and absorbs their own.'

He proceeds—and here, at least, his meaning is very plain—

'The work of art is apocalyptic of the artist's own personality. . . . Titus Andronicus could not have been written by Shakespeare. Even if he had written it as a burlesque of such a play as Marlowe's Jew of Malta, he could not have avoided some revelation of that sense of moral proportion which is omnipresent in all his plays.'

But even supposing there is lack of moral proportion in 'Titus Andronicus' how does that prove it was not Shakespeare's? If moral proportion means just reward and punishment for good and evil doing, Antonio and his friends deserved some severer punishment than a needless fright, for their previous ill-treatment of Shylock; Timon was too severely punished for his profuse generosity; Iago is quite as wicked as Tamora or Aaron. The play of Titus Andronicus is below the level of Shakespeare's genius; is not that reason enough for saying it was not his?

'Literature and all forms of art,' says Professor Corson,

' are but the intermediate agencies of personalities.' That sentence contains a truth, but its wording perverts the truth as I would use it. If I see or read a picture or poem, I want, it is true, to know who did it, but not in order to find out what the personality of the producer was; only to learn what else he has done which shall touch me even nearer. And looking at the phrase another way, who can tell from the construction of the plays of *Othello* and *Julius Cæsar* whether Shakespeare's personality was more or less intimately concerned in his creation of Iago than in that of Brutus? What of Browning's personality is there in his creation *Pompilia?* She is a woman made for us by a man; but could the creative genius of George Sand or George Eliot at their best have made for us a woman more subtly real?

'The highest worth of all great works of genius is that they are apocalyptic of great personalities.'

Against this dictum I protest. It is good to know that a personality *is* great; a great personality, a good personality is fruitful to men as compared with a small or bad one, just as sun in August is fruitful for harvest as compared with grey wet weather : but the greatness or smallness of a work of art is fruitful only within its own bounds and in proportion to those qualities; it is in no way affected by the character of the maker. If you say a bad character cannot produce a good art that is another matter, and not the subject in hand.*

Once more; is Caponsacchi's magnificent apology an apocalypse of Browning's personality, any more or less than are his creations of *Luria, Sebald, Clive, Martin Relph,* or *Mildred Tresham?* You destroy all the delight in the making of these things if you will drag Browning's personality into them.

* Shelley, Balzac, Milton, Keats, Thackeray ; were the personalities of all these men great ?

It is an axiom that the nature of any real artist must be simple and true; his moral and physical health must be sound; his mental sight clear and direct; before he can produce the smallest work of real art. But these qualities are only his tools; or they are the mould in which the work is fashioned. The more perfect the work the less sign of the tool, the less impress of the hand which fashioned the work. That is one reason why the Ring and the Book is so much finer than Sordello. If we must have the word 'Personality,' let us at least give it its true significance when applied to Browning; range of subject, choice of subject, high theme, low theme, touch of pathos, humour, or terror—all these he gives us, and in the giving them let him prove as personal as he will; but whatever he presents to us is presented not by a man who wants to teach, or is possessed of this virtue and the other, but by a man who must needs make—produce—the ποιητής; having found his subject he calls imperiously on his making power solely, and enslaves it for the time, until the thing great or small is made as well as possible, whether the result be beautiful or hateful. There can be no doubt in the world that Browning's pleasure—the creative pleasure—in conceiving and presenting to us the character of *Count Guido* was as great as his pleasure of the same kind in making *Caponsacchi*, or (to look back) *Luigi* in *Pippa passes.*

Professor Corson's essay also speaks, and ably from his point of view, about *Cleon.* The monologue of *Cleon* is one of the pure Greek poems of Browning's earlier method, whose first note was struck in certain passages in Pauline.

*Cleon* tells the King Protos of his own work; of the result of achievement; of the subsequent sense of incompleteness; and of his 'joy hunger,' his longing for a new life to carry on the old. In short, he sketches as an impossibility the hope of a hereafter which marks the life of a modern Christian. It is a very beautiful poem, and breathes the transmitted genius of the mightier Greeks of old. And the outreach towards the new life then already felt and expressed by the older men is perfectly touched off even in the slighting allusion to St Paul. But alas! the demon of second meanings cannot leave the poem alone:

'By the slave women that are among the gifts sent to *Cleon* seems to be indicated the degradation of the spiritual by its subjection to earthly ideals, as were the ideals of Greek art. This is more particularly indicated by the one white slave, the lyric woman. . . . '

'He ascribes to the King in the building of his tower, (and by this must be understood the building up his own self-hood) a higher motive than work for mere work's sake ; that higher motive being the luring hope of some eventual rest atop of it (the tower),

'Whence, all the tumult of the building hushed,
The first of men may look out to the East.'

As Lord Melbourne said when one of his colleagues was more than usually urgent 'Why can't you let it alone!'

Writing of Karshish, the Arab physician, an essayist says, that for Karshish 'the soul's life perishes with the body.' In the poem, Karshish says, his business is to keep the soul in the body to stop

. . . . 'flaws in the flesh
'Whereby the wily vapour' (the soul) 'fain would slip
Back and *rejoin its source* before the term.'

Is this the soul's life perishing with the body?

The fourth gospel says 'Lazarus is dead; and I am glad for your sakes that I was not there, to the intent ye may believe.' Raising the dead to life was to be a wonder, but a boon also.   The poem shows how the mind of Karshish was affected by the new phenomenon of Lazarus's recovery; how, failing to reconcile, with any of his acquired rules in medicine, the obvious contradictions which the newly awakened mind of Lazarus presented, he was forced to invent new theories to account for those contradictions. The poem is simple enough ; it starts no conclusive theory of life here or hereafter, but contains the puzzled specu- lation of a clever doctor about a patient whose madness, so- called, while it takes the form of a delusion that he has died and lives again, makes the speculator wish to be mad like him.   But the essayist says—

' We have in Lazarus the study of a soul that has seen things as they are, whose life has therefore passed out of the sphere of the phenomenal into that of the real.' ' *Therefore is the moral discipline of life over for him ; he can will only God's will.*' ' *Virtue can only take root in the darkness; we live in a world opaque for us.*' ' *Lazarus has lost his characteristics as a man, because for him the work of this life is over.* . . . *This life too has lost with its educative power, its interest.* . . . *He is no longer able to help others.* . . . In conclusion *the poet leads us to feel* that we must learn by degrees to use the heavenly treasure ; not demand our inheritance ere we have attained our majority.'

I venture to say that not one of the italicised passages has the smallest didactic foundation in the poem ; and that deliberately to twist into Browning's work meanings he never placed there, is dangerous and unprincipled in pro- portion as it is well undertaken.

Even professor Westcott, keen and beautiful as is much of his criticism on Browning, falls into the error of thinking that Browning writes because he wants to teach.

Nay he actually describes that instant of Count Guido's self revealment, when the executioner being at the door he screams ' Pompilia, will you let them murder me ? ' in these words .

'The ministers of death claim him. In his agony he summons every helper he has known or heard of ; . . . . and . . . . then the light breaks through the blackest gloom . . . . in this supreme moment he has known what love is, and knowing it has begun to feel it. The cry, like the intercession of the rich man in Hades for his five brethren, is a promise of a far off deliverance.'

It is regrettable that a cultured and poetic scholar can have so overlooked the essence of Guido's character as to be led by the very refinement of his own mind into so misleading an interpretation as this.

I repeat that Browning is an exponent from their art side, and not an inventor or teacher, of creeds and modes of life. He does not say 'I tell you this is the right and that the wrong ; ' but 'I make you pictures, stories, or plays of what I have seen of the right and the wrong as found acting on human lives from the beginning of time.' The growth of a tree, an effect of moonlight, a phrase in music, teach us something ; but not because these things are right or wrong ; they only give our physical and mental senses something to do.

Browning's *teaching* is in a similarly unconscious fashion ; only his energy is inexhaustible, and his research bounded only by the limits of farthest human experience and insight. As a poet-worker he is among the last of a race, and nature's productive power needs to lie fallow for a time before such another rich yield can be given as his life has proved. Meantime if it can be made doubly productive by its right use in other minds well and good, but there is no harm in remembering that it is possible to make vinegar out of grape juice. Many true things have been said, many useful facts found and stated, about Browning's work and history ; but it is the fatal leaven of egoistic wrongness that destroys the nutritive value of such criticism as I have been discussing. All such attempts by conscientious students of Browning to read the writer's own theological or other views into poems dealing with portrait drama pure, should be gibbeted as high as Haman; they are poisoning the wells.

## NOTE

THROUGHOUT, while writing the succeeding pages, I have studied the first edition of Mrs Orr's Handbook in its full scope: the study has been one of exceeding profit, and any 'annexing' from the work is either involuntary or acknowledged.

My own purpose in writing was a selfish one, namely, to make a picture in my own mind of the leading ideas used by Browning as a base in his construction of soul drama. I assume the credit of understanding that the greater contains the less, that any trunk line of idea throws out many branches, and that the light of Browning's genius contains more colour rays than can be refracted or recombined by any merely intellectual prism or lens.

# LEADING POETIC PRINCIPLES OF BROWNING'S ART

THERE can be little doubt that certain interdependent psychic principles, as well as some 'hell-deep instincts,' however little apparent in an appreciable minority of his works, do form a *foundation* for the various edifices, stately, graceful, or homelike, which Browning's genius has builded. But any attempt to shew, by complete comment on each single work, even *how* these principles form such a basis, would defeat its own object by producing hopeless confusion.

Nevertheless, I found at one time a curious pleasure in trying to range all Browning's varied creations in a series of groups or moulds, each labelled with a leading idea; and the process was called ' Classification.' How it was that the very phrase did not frighten me, it would be hard to say;—but the thing was done and printed. And just as Lord Tennyson's reformed cobbler placed a bottle of gin on his window-sill as at once a warning and a visible memory of a vice forsaken, so I gibbet in this volume that attempt at ' classification,' as an awful example of yielding to the seduction of such a phrase (it is not my own) as ' Let us get a line through Browning.' Imagine a sane person trying to harness between the traces of an ethical code, the play of *Luria*, or the characters of Caponsacchi, Guido or Blougram; or *Sibrandus*, the lady in *The Glove*, the legate at Faenza, the heroine of the *Inn Album*, Leonce Miranda, or the subtle portrait study of *Prince Hohenstiel Schwangau;*—you can as soon bind Leviathan for your maidens, command the eagle, or stall the unicorn by your crib.

It is the charm of accident, of life chance, the shock of surprise, that unforeseen of human life and character which is the one certainty, it is these that arrest us in Browning's verse, always supposing that we are born sympathetic with it. And it should never be forgotten (as alas ! it is sometimes, even to-day) that he is a poet in *all* senses; that to huddle up winsome grace, humour, fancy, and pathos, under one grey cloak of philosophic idea, would be as unpardonable as to robe the Apollo Belvedere in a cassock.

Just as criminal it would be to conscientiously ticket with those or similar qualities (humour, pathos, etc.) a whole series of the more transiently emotional poems; but for the purpose I have in view there will be good rather than harm done in selecting a few instances of pure light fancy and rich passion as a sort of prelude.

The beauty and girl-womanliness which fascinate us in Mildred and Pompilia, the light touch and grace of the lyrics *A Pretty Woman; A Toccata of Galuppi's;* the passion of *In a Gondola;* the perfect human charm of *Pan and Luna;* the splendour of earth and sky in *Gerard de Lairesse;* the grimly satiric humour of *Doctor* ——; the tragic force of weakness and ill-luck in *Too Late* and *The Worst of It;* the poignant pathos of *May and Death;* the love-charm of *Rudel, A Lovers' Quarrel,* and *Meeting at Night;* the joyous swiftness of *Love among the Ruins;* the unique beauty of all poems where animals are portrayed —in these and in very many other cases what delights or moves us is some such poetic quality as I have mentioned, vivifying each poem quite independently of any serious principles, however true it may be—nay undoubtedly is

—that these very poems owe their throb and impulse, even when most lightly touched, to a 'sterner stress' of soul beneath them.

Any one who 'takes to' Browning's style can find at will, scattered broadcast in his work, the thrill of love, the beauty of girl, youth, and man, the grandeur of age, the terror of hate, the force of tyranny, the ruthlessness of crime, the splendour of heroism, or the pathos and bitterness of effort unrewarded; but the origin and principle of soul-life which sets these many souls working for good or ill, the *why* of them all—that seems worth enjoying too.

Still, can you make any moral and sermon of Galuppi's Toccata, or put Ottima into a pinafore; and *Love among the Ruins*, *My Star*, the lyrics at pp. 8, 92, 104 of *Ferishtah's Fancies;* the lyric preluding *Jocoseria;* the exquisite song which ends *Gerard de Lairesse;* are not these and many others pure song, and shall we strike them dumb with prose ? Can you discern any rule of life in *Adam, Lilith, and Eve*—just a glimpse as it is—and what a glimpse !—of the inexplicable *être ondoyant et divers ?*

But though such genius must of force defy by its many fronts any pressure from outside in the direction of ordering or ranging its domains into provinces; from within, a certain functional obedience to self-created laws of poetic life is observable. Certain master principles do underlie all the deeper searching and spiritually passionate work, that is to say a very large proportion both in bulk and importance of Browning's poems, though of course to say that those principles are all the poems contain of beauty or attraction, would be like saying that the nerve system of a great actress or contralto singer was her only fascination. And indeed that last image is coincident; for what I shall seek to do, working from within, is to shew some master lines of truth which by the help of the poems to be treated can be easily discerned woven through the many stranded fabric of Browning's art, and like nerves, vitalising it.

From my point of view then, Browning, neither inventing, nor preaching to men that they should acquire, certain principles of faith, hope, love and progress, found those forces, in embryo or in development, the most important motors of the soul's life, and imperatively demanding use by a poet aiming at the portrayal of humanity in its widest aspects, in its most complex and varied actions or moods.

In mankind as poetically interpreted by Browning, the mainspring, the nerve-force, which moves the mechanism or vitalises the function of man's soul is and must be, not natural perversity which is a resistant force, but the active and propelling force of faith and love.

After God, the initial spasm of life, the *first* force that moves the soul and keeps it living, is man's necessary upward strain, the faith and love whose 'reach exceeds their grasp,' the progress which is the necessity of the soul's principle of movement.

For instance, it is clear that the poem of Paracelsus, the earliest work in order of date, is naturally the herald of these truths; and whoever has read the poem and assimilated it as thoroughly as, to judge from her lucid synopsis of it, Mrs Orr has done, will see at once that Paracelsus as imagined by Browning is a crucial instance of the consequence of setting aside or diverting that principle of the law of progress which determines its purely relative character in this life. Paracelsus, with his dream of perfectibility,

> Make no more giants, God,
> But elevate the race at once,

starting with the noble vision of absolute truth, scorning

love, but recklessly spending the faith and love he professes to ignore (hoping for man's *sudden* mastery of the
world)—ends prophesying for man

> Thou shalt *painfully* attain to joy
> *While hope and fear and love shall keep thee man!*

(The italics are mine).

In Strafford, the firm based faith and love of the Earl,
in and for Charles, undermined by the punic faith and
weakness of the latter,—the human love of Lady Carlisle
and Pym for Strafford, the one striving to save his life
here, the other deliberately destroying it in the faith of
patriotism, for the higher faith in the life hereafter, these
act on the same principles intensified by the thwarting
and stress of ever present earthly passion and selfishness,
without spoiling or even touching the numberless and
complex charms of scene, dialogue and character.

In *Pippa passes*, one easily finds the idea of faith, love
and progress visibly illumining the work.  For Pippa
herself is throughout an impersonation of them, influencing in a definite and practical way the souls of those
her soul touches by song, and awaking in each in turn
the faith, love and upward effort for progress which has
lain dormant or asphyxiated by egoistic passion, sudden
treachery and humiliation, the bewitchment of a pure
earthly love, or the priestly ambition and personal greed
which would have winked at murder to procure its end.

So, in *A Blot in the 'Scutcheon*, underlying not only
the immediate fascination of the insight with which each
character is created, but also all that makes it a thrilling
drama of passion at push with pride, we find vitalising
these beauties the principle of love at last overthrowing
hereditary *morgue*, the faith which accepts and so conquers death; nay, the very remorse which proves faith

and love, and which is progress baffled by evil environ-
ments.

In *Popularity*, the idea of the poet cherished by God,
embodies the same faith (in the teeth of hindrance and
neglect) in the divine purpose which keeps the poet's love
and song hidden till the appointed time.

*Instans Tyrannus* shews how in the blindest despot's
heart dwells that fear of the unseen Power, which *is*
faith and love, thrust by passion into the dark recesses of
which pride keeps the key.

The creation of Count Guido Franceschini in *The
Ring and the Book* is a conception apparently of pure
unadulterated evil; nor do I seek to disturb that conception. But looking a little deeper, we find his very
existence calling into life the chivalrous heroism of
Caponsacchi, the exquisite genius for love in Pompilia; he
is the incarnate obstruction, the personified barrier, which
is needed to make the faith of the priest and the pure
ideal love of the girl wife grow and progress towards the
Divine. But for him Pompilia might have remained a
soulless beauty, and Caponsacchi would probably have
become a dilettante cardinal.

Lastly, like Guido, the Duke of *My Last Duchess*
though at first sight the very opposite of any lofty idea,
is, if rightly looked at, another image of the obstruction
to love and faith which seems to kill them ; he is an
example of that existence of evil unmitigated without the
battle with which good would cease to develop. But
neither in the character of Guido nor in the present case
are we at all touching the dramatic interest of self-revealment, the outward picture of subtle motive and passion
which the poet's hand has worked for us in so masterly a
fashion.

These are a few instances taken at random; and without
closely examining the many more, it is easy to see how

neither the beautiful fanaticism of *Through the Metidja to Abd-el-Kadr* with its onomatopœic resonance and realistic imaging, the introspective cynicism of *Bishop Blougram's Apology;* the tortured passion of *The Confessional;* the humorous pathos of *Old Pictures in Florence;* or any of the serious love poems, could cohere, as poetic renderings of their various human moods, unless shot through by the nerve force of faith, hope, love and effort.

If, in fine, it has been the poet's business to present men and the phenomena of universal life, in all their varied forms of action, passion, thought, colour, beauty, repulsiveness, and endless conflict and contrast; it is surely no fruitless enjoyment to search below the phenomena to the causes, to discover the darkness of despair, by means of the light of faith, in *Paracelsus* and *Luria*, the ultimate triumph of effort for progress through the blank failure of Sordello, or the dead Grammarian ; and under the lurid light shed by the demon of hate to discern in Pompilia the ideal of human love.

But throughout all the more important works, these truths are for the first time in the history of the poetic art, used so essentially and avowedly, (in pursuance or what I may call the poetic ' declaration of faith ' which precedes Sordello) that an examination of their nature and essence, so far as Browning enables us to divine it, will be a distinct step, not towards impossible classification, but towards a comprehensive study of his work at large.

This examination of leading principles and the manner of their poetic use seems to come fitly after the introduction made by the last few pages ; and it will be followed by criticism and treatment of a few poems which seem fairly representative types of Browning's psychological drama.

Faith, hope, love, and progress of the soul through uncertainty and effort ; the life of the soul sustained and its progress achieved only by means of the perpetual conflict of faith, hope and love, with their opposites, and with all hindrance, massed under the name of evil—these are the master motives of Browning's soul drama, that is to say, of the greater part of his work, including the plays.

Faith in God, His infinite power, wisdom, and love; faith between men and women as friends or lovers; faith in any great principle of Science or Art, in any high aim or far-off ideal; this comprehensive idea of faith, twinned with hope, as used by Browning, may be expressed by the formula 'I do not know, but I am sure.' Faith, not only living in spite of, but actually depending for existence on the hindrance and resistance offered by wrong and evil.

Browning, therefore, in poetically employing this principle so inherent in man, is forced to take into account, and continually present in contrast, faith's opposites, as well as hate, pride, tyranny, and all forms of obstructing evil. But faith is shown as primary to, and underlying all these latter, capable of, though not always successful in, rising beneath and overthrowing them.

I have said enough elsewhere to make it quite clear that this selection of a human principle, as selection, owes nothing whatever to the poet's idiosyncrasy; if he chooses to say in so many words as in his few avowed utterances in published work, 'I think this myself,' well and good; but that is not my subject just now. The importance of Browning's choice of a foundation for his ' Theatre d'Ame,' as M. Sarrazin aptly calls it, rests on a deeper base than even a great poet's predilection.

The human link which unites all great art with science, philosophy, religion and ethics is so close that any principle of human life, whether its cause can be proved or not, is mutually accepted in any one of these fields as a proper working material for any other of them. Browning could be no more justified in ignoring, or called to account for not trying to prove, the principle of faith, than a biologist would be justified in ignoring or accountable for not trying to prove that the blood circulates. The one is as much a fact to be dramatically used by the Poet as the other to be scientifically used by the physicist. In short, Browning whether as an idiosyncratic artist and subjectively, or when creating objectively, sees in faith and progress, and is right in seeing, something functional, and hereditary or transmitted; functional in the sense that such faith demands from him its poetic expression as imperatively as the physical action of the heart demands the research of the physicist; hereditary or transmitted in the sense of being derived, by some spiritual process no more occult than the action of the brain, in direct succession through all great thinkers and idealists of the distant or recent past, and existing throughout humanity, down to its lowest types, in a more or less warped or incomplete form.

This idea struck me in a quite accidental way on re-reading the 'Parleying' with Bubb Dodington, where through the satire which lashes the politician's short-sighted egotism pierces the poet's profound conviction that the craving for the unknown, the something outside and beyond our daily visible life and appreciable conscience is an essential factor in man's nature, to ignore which is a fatal blunder in any would-be ruler of men. That craving, the germ of faith and progress through evil, is evidenced in the quasi-historical idea of the *Napoleon du peuple* (in Balzac's *Medecin de Campagne*), that weird preter-human monster, immortal, pursued and guided by his star and by *l'Homme Rouge*, working out for good or evil his fate as a demi-god, and yet lighted by a dim Messianic halo; in the great atheist surgeon Desplein, founding, and four times a year attending a mass for the soul of the poor porter who in his youth had saved him from starvation; in Samson, the executioner of Louis XVI, secretly performing the same rite for his royal victim's soul, and giving to the officiating priest the king's bloody handkerchief as a sacred relic; in the truculent and fanatic force which moved Cromwell's army like a demoniac possession, and survived through the Covenanter Burley to the Puritan David Deans; or, to look back, in the spirit which nerved the followers of Mohammed, and the grim conviction that inspired the immitigable fanaticism of Philip II.

Its fuller development produced the genius that burned in the souls of Socrates and Plato; the spiritual insight of St John, St Paul, and the founder of Buddhism; the scientific research of Galileo, Columbus, Cuvier, Newton, Faraday, and all great inventors; the creative splendour of Euripides, Michael Angelo, Palissy, Beethoven or Wagner; the patriotism and prophetic statesmanship of William the Silent; the chivalry of Sir Philip Sidney. It is as much a part of a human being as his nourishment or nerve system.

In short, we must take as a *basis* for Browning's art the axiom that all religions however founded, however sullied by human selfishness or ambition; all progress in science, art or philosophy, however baffled or hampered by bigotry, ignorance, or pride; are not the creation or result of human ambition or enterprise working on human credulity or weakness, but the resumed expression in successive spiritual and intellectual leaders of the universal human need to believe in an ideal source of justice, an ideal goal of progress.

The idea of love, another great cornerstone of Browning's art, needs no apology, since from its grossest material form, through its manifestation between lovers, married folk, parents and children, to the sublimest conception of the greatest religions, its principle is universally accepted.

Men quarrel with the idea of faith because its formula above stated is supposed (wrongly) to exclude the idea of reason or logic ; but who expects logic in love?

And so it will be obvious that the substance of the following pages is applicable as much to the stories of human love contained in the plays, and in the lyric and romantic poems, both in the first six volumes and in subsequently published works, as it is to poems dealing with spiritual life or high endeavour, or any of the complex human problems which abound throughout.

Concerning these principles of human faith, human and divine love, and continuous progress, all in perpetual struggle with evil, which are the basis of Browning's psychological drama, we find two noteworthy facts :— First, that faith in God or between men, and human progress, are each as specially, as uniquely, an attribute of man among created things as is his moral sense according to the argument in the parleying with Francis Furini. They are qualities clearly by no means God-like, for God is complete and unchanging, man is incomplete and progressive. Faith and progress as Browning presents them are the priceless triumph of man's weakness, the noble prerogative which owes its vitality to his utter ignorance not only of God's purpose in making evil, but of what is going to happen in the next second of time. Second, that love, the one attribute by which God and man come into contact, is not a specially human attribute ; it is, according to the widely felt conception of it used dramatically by Browning, a divine thing, ultra-human and infinite in its highest expression, but, as a vitalising conception, necessary to the highest life of man's soul. The love of God and the love of man are the same thing, pure, illimitable and free in God, clouded, limited and obstructed in man. *The same thing*, only differing in degree. The simple limited form of love, as displayed in human beings, *is* the love of God, manifesting itself in human guise; consciously or unconsciously it is joined with and intertwined by man's love to God, and God's to man. Two lovers, two friends, a mother and child, cannot love each other without receiving the love of God and giving love to Him in the very act of loving each other.

It is obvious that this interwoven human and divine love is for its *active* use equally dependent on, and depended on by, faith. For human love *quand même* is only an incomplete bargain that cannot be worked—a *passive* quality; while man's love for God cannot exist without faith in Him, any more than faith in Him can exist without the desire to receive love from Him and give it in return.

Now as I have indicated before in the essay on development, to maintain merely that Browning took stories of faith and love, their hindrance, betrayal or triumph, and made works of art of them, would be saying too little: just as it would be absurd to say on the one hand that he discovered their existence, or on the other that he used them *merely* because he believed in them, merely out of his own inner consciousness. What I do repeat is that Browning uses these qualities as his *primum mobile* of actual fact, from which to interpret the vicissitudes of the soul, exactly as a surgeon or physician uses the qualities of normal health and soundness to diagnose and cure disease or wounds and fractures. As M. Sarrazin lucidly puts it: 'Mr Browning . . . *tient chaque âme humaine pour une représentation nouvelle et différente des vicissitudes de l'Idée du Bien.*'

But the tenacity and conviction with which Browning dramatically enforces the idea of faith and love induces a further step in the study of them: has induced in me, at least, a fancy which is tangible as fact.

I have elsewhere in this book tried to shew how the spirit of prayer may be a transmitted spirit; the vivid fancy I have just mentioned is almost identical. It is, that to-day, as in the first half of the third century before Christ, in the time of Christ as in the time of Cromwell or Comte, the need to love, wonder, believe and advance, is without intermission handed down ; λαμπάδια ἔχοντες διαδώσουσιν ἀλλήλοις

And this brings me to what I feel to be of the essence of Browning's power as an artist ; that he is the nineteenth century *poetic exponent* of the same principle of faith, love, and progress through evil, which animated the great spiritual leaders, the great princes of science, art, philosophy, statesmanship, and chivalry before named.

In *Paracelsus, A Grammarian's Funeral, Holy Cross Day, Karshish, Abt Vogler, A Death in the Desert*, and the Pope in *The Ring and the Book*, the singular vividness and realism of each scene or manner of thought, awoke in me this idea of continuity, the sense that the maker of those poems, speaking so many hundred years later, enriched but not burdened by his nineteenth century knowledge, stretched hands across Time to the physicist, scholar, Jew martyr, Arab doctor, composer, apostle and pontiff.

And although the word subjective is commonly used as to Browning's poetic insight in spiritual or intellectual themes, I know that that word does not contain all the truth. If Browning speaks out these truths which we now know were all life to him, he speaks, it is true, not only as an objective artist, but however cryptogrammically as one of the few men who from time to time are born, foreordained to shew men themselves, whether by means of philosophy, science or art.

Browning's mode of shewing is his poetic art, and its richness, however modern, is no product of a particular year or epoch, but a resuming of the spiritual life of the world.

---

To create a synthesis of Browning's poetic use, in spiritual drama, that is, throughout the great bulk of his work, of the ideas of faith, hope, love, and progress through hindrance, I propose by exegesis and comment or criticism to treat *Christmas Eve*, *Easter Day*, *A Death in the Desert*, and *Ixion*. These four poems contain types of the leading ideas which have prompted Browning from the beginning to the end of his poetic career; I am far from saying (as indicated at sufficient length in the previous pages) that they are to be found as the *primary* subject of every one, or even an overwhelming majority of his poems ; I do say that the whole of his poetic organism having been instinct with them from the first, they may be discovered latently influencing the thought or action of scenes or moods, whose original poetic impulse was due to fancies quite collateral or circumstances seemingly alien from them.

As I have indicated by one or two instances, Browning is continually compelled, as he avers through the mouth of Francis Furini, to know evil thoroughly, in order to know good thoroughly, and the step from the portrayal of noble emotion to the poetic necessity for portraying all forms of evil in man's nature, as a foil or hindrance to his nobler qualities, is an easy one.

Subsequently, the work *Parleyings with certain people of importance in their day* is handled by a treatment similar to that of the four poems already cited, but for a different reason, namely, that this, his latest published work at the date of this writing, is important as being throughout the first complete avowal of *his personal conviction regarding mankind* as to those reciprocally interacting principles, hitherto used as a poetic basis only.

In dealing with 'Christmas Eve and Easter Day,' 'A Death in the Desert,' 'Ixion' and 'Pàrleyings' the importance of a close exegesis as the only way of really getting to the bedrock of Browning's intent when depicting the actual soul's life, seemed so paramount that I preferred to treat these five works in a fashion complete enough to leave no loophole of excuse for any misunderstanding or obscurity in my own mind. The result of this treatment has been for my own self fruitful beyond words ; and I venture to hope that the exegeses may be found of use to other students of Browning, because of their very closeness. They are not taken section by section, as in the case of *Fifine*, because that form of treatment is clumsy when dealing with a poem as a whole ; in the case of *Fifine* it was only done in that way by desire. The difficulty of some of the works now chosen, as compared with the difficulty of *Sordello* even, is great ; for *Sordello* wants mainly the patience of a grammarian who should take the poem phrase by phrase and translate it into simple prose ; it is obscurity of diction rather than depth of thought which is the stumbling block. But in *Ixion* the difficulty arises from reasons in its mental construction and from the onomatopœic rhythm which in a certain sense ties the poet's mind and demands concision ; in 'Parleyings,' it arises from the abstruseness of idea, and the wealth of image as illustrating or enforcing idea, which pervades the volume.

One should hardly complain of *embarras de richesse*, and in Browning's case least of all ; but no doubt the rapidity of his actual mental process, and the brilliancy of the many images that flash upon his mind and seem to electrically increase its nerve force, produce on the ordinary observer a dazzling effect ; for frequently he passes from one image to another in order to enlighten an idea ; the two or more images have no connecting link, or only a collateral one somewhat difficult to perceive, not because of its obscurity, but because the idea becomes by this means 'dark with excess of light.' An instance of this occurs in Bernard de Mandeville, where using first the image of a surveyor's plan of an estate, Browning proceeds with the image of a constellation, both being used to prove the value of symbols in helping man's perception. So far all is clear enough; but he pursues the image of the constellation in a side way; he has said in effect, the stars that mark out Orion are not the man, only marks indicating the salient points of his form; he goes on to say the stars themselves that compose the constellation are spheres, and the light we see is only projected from that side of the sphere which is turned towards us; that light therefore is only the symbol of the sphere.

Seeing that by exegeses only could I get to the root of the matter, I publish them in the hope that others may be induced to make them for themselves with the other poems; for I find there are only two ways of reading a really difficult poem of Browning; (1) simply to read it over and over again, and so master the sense by repetition, until a concisely expressed phrase in the poem becomes a clear unspoken sentence in the mind, a clear idea; (2) to deliberately do as I have done, write down the prose meaning of each phrase in its natural sequence in the poem. The first way is very fascinating, for every one knows the charm of an unspoken idea, one which indeed would lose by rendering in speech, just as all those words which in any language are the most picturesque, fruity, and racy of the soil are really untranslatable in any other language: and with Browning specially this is true, that he is untranslatable in a sense; that is, when after long wrestling you are quite sure you have his breathless soul face to face with yours, and that the possession is yours, you will be quite unable to give the brilliancy and transparency of his thought to anyone else in impromptu words, or indeed in any words which shall be more than a filmy shadow of his. You yourself possess him ; but that is all that can be said for the first way ; its drawback is that it is self-centred and not progressive. The second way has its drawback too, but I am going to show why I think it the better. Mrs Orr's Handbook owing to the necessary limitation of space, has been compressed into so concise a form of synopsis that however clear the insight, and steady the grasp—and both are undoubted—she can frequently do little more than vividly present a diminished picture, the clearer for its minuteness, but still not complete. Nay the very demand for brevity forces her often to transpose a thought or an image so as to fit in all the essentials of the poem treated. My attempts at exegeses are of necessity much clumsier than hers, but they are rigidly kept to following the order in which each idea occurs in the poem itself, always keeping in view as an absolute necessity the utmost plainness and even homeliness of speech. I think that a person reading any poem so treated here, side by side with my dim monochrome of exegeses, will be able to grasp the meaning of any obscure passage, *as well as* the general scope, once for all.

# CHRISTMAS EVE AND EASTER DAY:

## THOUGHTS ABOUT THE TWO POEMS.

In Christmas Eve and Easter Day the quality which magnetises the reader is the power of vision, the seer's gift, alluded to hereafter, which is so eminently a personal attribute of the poet. Whenever he employs it —and it continually appears from the beginning to the end of his work till now—the art, though present, is swallowed up in the splendour of the thought or soul-stress, precisely as it is in the work of the greater Hebrew prophets. Indeed these two poems, in the method of their inspiration, more resemble the Book of Job than any poetic work that I know outside of Browning's own domain. The leading thought in Christmas Eve is the ever present sympathy of the Divine love with all forms of human love reaching up to God in the form of worship, however soiled, or dimmed, or thwarted by human passion, intellectual pride, ignorance, or weakness; and from this thought the transition is easy to the idea that commingled faith and love, as applied between human beings, is the same principle as the complete faith and love for God, towards which all men consciously or unconsciously tend, and can only exist by means of this latter.

In Easter Day the idea of faith and love is brought more closely home to the present life; for the Vision of

Christ becomes a terrible and instant judge, burning into the soul of the man who has faltered in his choice between present pleasure and future joy, shewing him, not the transience, but the incompleteness of any possible pleasure or knowledge on this earth, unless it be used as an apprenticeship only for the vaster experience of the after life. Here in form and diction, though not in psychological situation, the likeness to the Book of Job is remarkable. In both poems, the man doubts, is peevish, knows not what he would, but the Hebrew is overwhelmed by evil and his despondency is natural; the so-called Christian has none but self-made mental troubles to disturb his judgment. In both cases, the man has exhausted his intellect in trying and failing to choose between God and Baal, and in both the Almighty, in visible or audible manifestation (in Browning's poem in the appearance of Christ), shows in words of magnificent eloquence the futility of man's power to judge without faith, to enjoy without love. Only in Browning's poem the Christ is love as well as power, in Job God is a being to be feared and worshipped only.

But although both Christmas Eve and Easter Day are, according to the modern phrase, poems of fancy, dramatic as describing what according to most modern men's experience would be called hallucination, the intensity of the vision in each case is such as lifts it out of the category of ordinary phenomena, because of the seer-quality about it; the words and sentences are so made as to induce a sense that when conceived they were realities to the poet quite in a possessing fashion, realities much deeplier impressed with the grip of supernatural revelation than could be the case with the most poignant dramatic conception of earthly tragedy or passion. This, at any rate to me, is the value of the poems; that no drama or poem I know of except in the Hebrew prophets takes me so completely outside of human life in its widest expression of hope, fear or passion.

The intensity is very much heightened in both poems by the modern commonplace of the accessories and *mise en scene;* the suddenness of the manifestation in dull surroundings of England of to-day; while in reading any Hebrew poem from the Bible one is placed at once amid surroundings where the supernatural forms, or seems to form, a part of the daily life of the actors.

The difference in the spiritual drama as played in these two poems from that of the 'Death in the Desert' is this; in these two poems problems two thousand years old are suddenly and visibly brought to an issue in this century for an ordinary thinking man of to-day by a miraculous rending of the veil which twenty centuries have cast between God and man; the 'Death in the Desert' speaks in a far off voice of one himself used to the awe and wonder of the visible God, inaudible to the outer sense, however silver clear to the inner hearing of the soul.

I have added prose translations of the two poems, not mere explanations, because having found this method the only one that gives the full sense of the original, I think it may help others.

### CHRISTMAS EVE.

In youth I found God's power proved to me : I felt that his love was there too.    God having created man, stands apart to see him act, having given him free will ; so man is not an unconscious machine to do God's will.    Man stands on his own share of love and power given by God, as on a rock-point separated from the mainland, which is God.    Man sees that God's power is the infinite whole of which his own power is a part.    He deduces this fact from the enormous increase of his own power by mechanical contrivance. On the other hand man's stock of love, (drawn from the fountain of God's love) cannot be increased, reduced or caused to cease, as man's stock of power can ; the source of love remains the same, how its stream is directed depends on whether man opens or shuts his heart to it (the simile is of a waterhead directed in a channel, large or small).

I, says the speaker, satisfied of the infinite power of God, analogically believe in His infinite love. God would never need my telling what I, his creature, want ;—(life he has given already—) that is, love growing through strife, made perfect through death.

These had been my thoughts, when one evening, having listened for a time to an ill-constructed methodist sermon, I left the chapel. Suddenly I saw Christ in bodily shape before me. He took me with Him to see His birth celebrated at St Peter's, Rome. I saw the pomp of the mass, the crowd of worshippers; I knew how the love given by God to men in the early days of Christendom deposed intellect, poetry, art, except as serving the Church. Still the love which displayed itself then uncouthly and narrow-mindedly, was love all the same, and I will not quarrel with Catholics who, even to-day, take love from Art, since they gave it to God. After all, the strain after an ideal is as if a sculptor should take a block of marble and strive to make a perfect face only, instead of the whole form, leaving it to future men to complete the statue. So I have seen a partial manifestation of love, the Catholic; I may live to see the complete manifestation. Christ next showed me a professor in Göttingen tracing the source of Christianity back to the myth of Christ, evolved through centuries from the life of a man, whose teaching was so much in advance of his time, that his disciples were justified then in believing him to be God, although we, with our light of to-day, know better. But if the professor rejects Christ's godhead,

what is there to worship ? His intellect ? In that he is
no better than other philosophers; worse indeed, for they
were innocent of any such claim as his to Godhead. His
goodness ? That is his due to man and to God ; it does
not empower him to rule as God, for he certainly did not
invent a quality possessed by all men. To worship a man
for merely shewing and naming goodness, would be as
absurd as to praise Harvey for shewing us, instead of
nature for giving us, the blood-circulation. I might praise
Christ as a saint, as I praise a poet for his insight, in spite
of the objection that if we only knew the secret of that insight we should no more praise it than wonder at the bat's
power of steering in the dark. But saintship and poet-
hood are gifts from God, they do not make man God.
Man is a dim image of God ; he can only tell heaven's
light from hell's darkness by his soul's sight ; but for that,
any demon might proclaim wrong to be right and we
should not know. It is not the expounding of moral law
that is worshipped ; for the wickedest man *knows* the
right better than the best man's acts can *prove* it : God's
function is to give us a *reason* for doing right. God in
Christ does that : but it is not Christ's supreme goodness
that makes him God ; Christ does not tell us He makes
a new justice, a new truth : He only says 'Believe me to
be Lord of Life.' But that involves believing in His infinite love, and that belief gives man a new truth. And
when the professor ends his lecture saying

> 'Go home and venerate the myth
> I thus have experimented with—
> This man, continue to adore him
> Rather than all who went before him,
> And all who ever followed after !'

we can at least respect his learning, however loveless, even
though it be misled from classical Greek to commenting

Paul's Epistles; it is at least better than the ignorance which hates God.

But indifferentism will not do, either : I must find out the best way of worship, and if I can, impart it to other men. If I cannot I can at least testify God's care for me, which I can only know as shown to myself ; and my soul has power to judge my own life, its warnings and providences. I cannot make other men see ; but I can tell them as I have now told, how God called *me*. And coming back to the chapel I learn that that coarse earthen vessel, the preacher, contains as good *measure* of God's truth (however he muddies it) as if he were a golden vase.

## EASTER DAY.

*1st Speaker*. How hard it is to believe in Christ!

*2nd Speaker*. I could endure torture for faith's sake, if God's command were clearly *proved*, and eternal joy were my reward.

1. Yes; if you could fix yourself safely in the infinite life, you would naturally spurn this life ; but when as time goes on your reason shows the impossibility of this, your faith's sight becomes clouded.

2. True ; I know faith is a touchstone, to try and test men's conception of God's purposes ; that is, He gives us faith to use against such doubt—I cannot expect reward or punishment for accepting (believing) what is obvious, or rejecting what I don't need to reject, any more than a man could claim a victor's wreath for merely living, or seeing the sun when it shone. So the only vitality of faith lies in its uncertainty, that is in its conquering doubt. The mutual life of men and women rests on this principle; a human being loves or hates another, according as that other believes or doubts him or her. But should not God act on more exact laws than this ?

1. You want, you say, to live and grow on this earth,

unchecked, in perfect certainty, but you know you cannot, you are hindered at every step. But you who leave simple belief and go through life asking questions which get either no answer or such an answer as you carp at, are no better off at the end than we who believed.

2. I own a scientific or certain faith frustrates its own purpose of developing man's soul. I only ask for probability; the chances must be on the side of faith. For that even I would readily renounce the world. But I see men doing that much for a mere hobby. I should have to do no more than they to go to heaven.

1. True; and if you really desire to be a Christian, you will find evidence enough, if not in history, in the human heart; whatever creed meets its needs will give your faith food enough; you will believe in short, because you want to believe, and renouncing the world will come easy then.

2. Yes; and that renouncing is man's usual gratitude to God for exacting not renunciation, only such temperance and discernment of love in His gifts as enhances their joy; only such discernment as makes even sorrow bearable for that love's sake. In short, the more merciful God's law, the more pettishly man invents pain or discomfort for himself, *i.e.* asceticism, where God meant him to enjoy.

1. But do you really think Christ's sacrifice, the supreme proof of God's love, was made

> Only to give our joys a zest
> And prove our sorrows for the best?

For my part, I should think blotting out of all my joy a small tax to pay in return. Or as a mere matter of fancy I can conceive Christ's sacrifice made to enable the pure to become pure, and yet use pleasure rightly. But the Bible says this world's gain (pleasure) is loss, and that we must forsake it. I cannot be deaf to that! What do you say?

2. I say, if that be true, if I were in your place and believed those words of the Bible, I would obey, renounce the world absolutely.

1. That brings you back to where you began; but how if that be not true, and our sacrifice is rewarded only by death and annihilation? The men with hobbies get a reward for their sacrifices; we may despise them, and say our aims are higher, if they be only hopes with no certain reward; we thus ward off the doubt that shakes but does not overthrow our faith; but such doubt brings *me* too back to *my* first proposition, How hard it is to believe in Christ.

2. I don't thank you for merely trying to make it hard for *me*. I want to live in trusting ease; you try to make me lose the very faith you would grieve so much to lose yourself.

1. But your trusting ease is not St Paul's faith; it is no better than the blind hopes Prometheus gave to man to spice his life banquet; I allege that faith is no such blind hope; it is a nourisher of life, not a mere spice to make it palatable. I say this in no flippant mood: and in proof that I am in earnest I will tell you a vision I had three years ago. I sat watching for the dawn of Easter Day, having gone through the same mental process as ours to-night: but I went a step further and asked myself, What is the real worth of my faith? If I fell dead this minute should I die believing or faithless? Common sense said, 'You believe; your faith has stood the test of obstacles from passion and fancy, and from knowledge which though meant to steady faith becomes a burden like to sink it: your ship of life, guided by your faith, has weathered many storms of doubt such as could never attack that of a peasant.' I answered, 'But I see no port

to end my voyage : I wish indeed for God's kingdom, for the day when I shall see His will clear from doubt ; but in the end His Judgment will be sudden : when it comes, my past life—what now I call my waking life—will shew as a dream.   And as from a dream we always wake too soon, saying, in another moment I should have achieved the climax, so we shall wake to Judgment futilely wondering why we grudged the toil that was to win heaven.'
     As I thus complacently mused,

I found
Suddenly all the midnight round
One fire.   The dome of heaven had stood
As made up of a multitude
Of handbreadth cloudlets, one vast rack
Of ripples, infinite and black
From sky to sky.   Sudden there went
Like horror and astonishment,
A quick vindictive scribble of red
Quick flame across, as if one said
(The angry scribe of Judgment), 'There—
Burn it !'   And straight I was aware
That the whole ribwork round, minute
Cloud touching cloud beyond compute,
Was tinted, each with its own spot
Of burning at the core, till clot
Jammed against clot, and spilt its fire
All over heaven, which 'gan suspire
As fanned to measure equable ;—
Just so great conflagrations kill
Night overhead, and rise and sink
Reflected.   Now the fire would shrink
And wither off the blasted face
Of heaven, and I distinct might trace
The sharp black ridgy outlines left
Unburned like network—then each cleft
The fire had been sucked back into,
Regorged, and out it surging flew
Furiously, and night writhed enflamed,
Till, tolerating to be tamed

No longer, certain rays world wide
Shot downwardly.   On every side
Caught past escape, the earth was lit;
As if a dragon's nostril split,
And all his famished ire o'erflowed;
Then, as he winced at his lord's goad,
Back he inhaled; whereat I found
The clouds into vast pillars bound,
Based on the corners of the earth,
Propping the skies at top; a dearth
Of fire i' the violet intervals,
Leaving exposed the utmost walls
Of time, about to tumble in
And end the world.

                  I felt begin
The Judgment-Day; to retrocede
Was too late now.   'In very deed,'
(I uttered to myself) 'that Day!'
The intuition burned away
All darkness from my spirit too;
There stood I, found and fixed, I knew,
Choosing the world.

In self-defence I cried to God.
'I used a part of the world's pleasure as Thou createdst
me to use it; I did not ignore heaven; Thy command to
renounce the world was not plain enough to obey strictly;
but thou, who knowest all, knowest that I meant to do so
later; is this a mood for which hell is the punishment?'

A final belch of fire like blood,
O'erbroke all heaven in one flood
Of doom.   Then fire was sky, and sky
Fire, and both, one brief ecstasy,
Then ashes.   But I heard no noise
(Whatever was), because a voice
Beside me spoke thus, 'Life is done,
Time ends, Eternity's begun,
And thou art judged for evermore!'

The blaze had left the sky; my terror was gone, and I knew I should presently breathe freely, when I heard the voice again, close by;

> I saw . . . Oh brother, 'mid far sands
> The palm-tree-cinctured city stands,
> Bright-white beneath, as heaven, bright blue
> Leans o'er it, while the years pursue
> Their course, unable to abate
> Its paradisal laugh at Fate !  '
> One morn—the Arab staggers blind
> O'er a new tract of death, calcined
> To ashes, silence, nothingness,
> And strives, with giddy wits, to guess
> Whence fell the blow.   What if, 'twixt skies
> And prostrate earth, he should surprise
> The imaged vapour, head to foot,
> Surveying motionless and mute,
> Its work, ere, in a whirlwind wrapt,
> It vanish up again ?   So hapt
> My chance,   HE stood there.   Like the smoke
> Pillared o'er Sodom, when day broke,—
> I saw Him.   One magnific pall
> Mantled in massive fold and fall
> His dread, and coiled in snaky swathes
> About His feet.   Night's black, that bathes
> All else, broke, grizzled with despair,
> Against the soul of blackness there

He said, 'I who judge the whole race, judge you as if you were the only man.   You have chosen the world in disbelief of My word.   In your probation of life, I gave your soul the choice of earthly joys or heavenly.   You chose the earthly, you chose that spirit should serve your flesh, rather than that your flesh should refine beneath the spirit's play.   Claim then no fellowship with those who chose to live by the spirit's gleams, however fugitive, desiring that those gleams might become fixed as stars, true worlds, the soul's home.   You said, " Let spirit be a

star to light the soul to earthly joy; I wish no more of it."
Have your will.'

I said, 'Is the world, all earth's delight, really my
own?'

God said, 'Yes; take your self-ordained heaven, you
shall have the earth and its joys for ever; your faculty to
enjoy shall remain, but My spirit, that makes an end of
the natural human life, shall not visit you.

> 'So, once more, take thy world!  Expend
> Eternity upon its shows,
> Flung thee as freely as one rose
> Out of a summer's opulence,
> Over the Eden-barrier, whence
> Thou art excluded.  Knock in vain!

I said, 'Then shall I have all knowledge of the earth's
beauty?'

God said 'Yes; but the earth is only an ante-chamber
to heaven; all earth's rich beauty was meant for you and
all men, of whom not one in a million could see any
wonder in it—not one in many millions could, if seeing
the wonder, find out its meaning; you yourself were
baffled by the least fern leaf, and scared by the northern
lights; earth's finite beauty was but a pledge of heaven's
infinite beauty; since the pledge was enough for you, take
it.'

I said, 'Though I should lose care for the Earth's
natural beauty, I will at least know all Art's beauty.'

God said, 'You shall; but all true artists' work on
earth is but a hint of all they conceived; they think
shame to be judged by such mere tentative effort.  And
if Buonarroti did such vast work on earth, what must the
glory be in heaven which lights his brow'—

> If such his soul's capacities,
> Even while he trod the earth,—think now

What pomp in Buonarroti's brow,
With its new palace-brain where dwells
Superb the soul, unvexed by cells
That crumbled with the transient clay !
What visions will his right hand's sway
Still turn to form, as still they burst
Upon him ?   How shall he quench thirst,
Titanically infantine,
Laid at the breast of the Divine ?

'Earth's work is but the title page emblazoning heaven's inheritance.   The earthly shows both of art and nature, needed for man's earthly life, are useless, when that life is done, for heaven.

'As the lizard's niche on the rock which a man shatters, letting in the day, so was the earthly life of My saints, which I abolished, letting in the heavenly light their soul hungered for, but which you have scorned.'

Then, seeing the futility of all natural and art beauty on the earth for its own sake alone,

I cried in anguish, ' Mind, the mind,
So miserably cast behind,
To gain what had been wisely lost !
Oh, let me strive to make the most
Of the poor stinted soul, I nipped
Of budding wings, else now equipped
For voyage from summer isle to isle !
And though she needs must reconcile
Ambition to the life on ground,
Still, I can profit by late found
But precious knowledge.   Mind is best—
I will seize mind, forego the rest,
And try how far my tethered strength
May crawl in this poor breadth and length.

'And when science, philosophy and history fail me, I will steep my soul in the fire-dew of poetry, till at least earth's bond is broken.   But no, all still is Earth's ; when I reach the goal of all such knowledge, I shall still be forced to ask, what is its use? and that goal will become a ruin like the other joys of earth.'

God said 'Yes; and this quest of mind's knowledge is so much worse than the other of natural and art knowledge, that whenever even a poet has tried to fit Infinity into his finite intuition, he has found himself only a craftsman, a mouthpiece; he knows which is his knowledge, which Mine; he knows that the world of My spirit has been made plain to him by glimpses only; that I would not give him heaven on earth permanently; that the glimpses of heaven I allowed were meant to sting his hunger for full light; that he can only shew men glimpses of that light through veiling weakness '—

> 'Truth by means
> Of fable, showing while it screens,—
> Since highest truth, man e'er supplied,
> Was ever fable on outside.'

'But those gleams of truth lighted the world for a time; and now he sees the full light. You have chosen the cloud of earthly knowledge.'

I said, 'Then I renounce all; natural beauty, art beauty, mind's knowledge; let me have love, even though those I love be mere masks and shows of men and women; I will join my love to some fragments of the love of those who are dead, take what poor love I may find left on earth, and make its barrenness fruitful.'

God said, 'But love was every where for you on the earth, My love. You refused it. Now, take the show of human love, and content yourself with that. But remember Who it was, that, creating you for love, and love for you, was said to become man, and die, to prove to you My love. How could you disbelieve the tale? On the ground that such love was inconceivable, too much? You know God's love was the basis of His creation of the earth for man's sake; yet you said that only man, the descendant of the fratricide Cain, man who could plainly hate, could have invented such a scheme of perfect love as involved the murder committed by the sacrifice of Christ.'

I cried, 'Thou love of God, let me have back my old life; with its darkness and sorrow, hoping for heaven at last.'

# A DEATH IN THE DESERT

THE master charm this poem has for me, leaving aside the question of what is its historical value, local colour and rightness of detail, lies in its spiritual reality. It is alight with the idea of transmission before alluded to. The poetic value of the work is enhanced rather than disparaged by the fancy that in some mystic fashion the spirit of the Apostle John inspired the words, lived again in the soul of the nineteenth century poet. A similar fancy, as regards the idea of transmission generally, no less gives value to the visions in *Christmas Eve* and *Easter Day*, to the whole of *Saul*, to the dedication ‘O Lyric Love’ in the beginning of the *Ring and the Book*; to *Pisgah Sights*, *Prospice*, and the *Epilogue* to *Dramatis Personæ*. That faculty of vision, the seer’s gift so rightly attributed to William Blake, the faculty of the Hebrew prophets—the power to move men’s souls rather than convince their minds—cannot be denied in any of these poems, and Browning’s work has many instances of the same kind. But the vision, it is needless to say, is splendid with the cultured light of to-day. There is a feeling of accountableness, of direct responsibility, a message to men.

The idea is the more vivid because of the specially nineteenth century life led by Browning both physically and mentally. There is nothing about his personality, his surroundings, or his mode of phrase or thought in conversation, which is in the least out of tune with his time; on the contrary, no man, whether in many poems, or in actual life, ever threw himself more joyously and whole heartedly into the movement of his era.

This element of *all timeness* in Browning's poetic personality, gives his work the greater mental value because one feels that never once does he slacken his hold on the idea that the man of to-day is the man of ten thousand years back, worked on, impeded, and helped by time, circumstance, climate, or the growth or reaction which comes from mere contact with nature.

And here is the place to record my conviction that neither in this poem of the Death in the Desert, nor elsewhere, is there a conscious moralising or sermonising or telling us like a pedagogue what is right and what is wrong in thought or action; Browning shows us men as they are, and leaves us to draw the moral.

The spiritual life of to-day, as much a fact as it was in Christ's time, is one point of contact which quite apart from any idea usually called religious, gives Browning his poetic sympathy with men and women, although, if not because, that life is continually repressed, dwarfed or twisted into uncouth shape by worldly interest, bigotry, the fighting element, or the strain of the pace at which life is lived now.—Anglicanism, the *odium theologicum*, Puritanism, Roman Catholicism, are to-day so many witnesses for that life, however much or little they direct it ; and all battles in its behalf, from the earliest, are fought for something else besides chafed pride or the mere love of fighting.—The man who fights to-day for the particulars of outward observance and ceremony, has as real a cause as existed when Christ shook the world with his denunciation of the desecrators of the temple. The fact that worship of God holds its ground throughout the world against the creeping palsy of egoism, makes as much for faith, love and progress as Edison's discoveries in light and sound, as the latest theory in evolution, as Michael Angelo's Pieta:— as much as the pure, self-sacrificing life of Father Damien, or of many an English clergyman unknown outside his neighbourhood and connections.

So that Browning in dealing with the last thoughts of John the Apostle, as when dealing with the shameful dishonour and noble abnegation which go to make harrowing the poem of *The Inn Album*, has no obsolete story to tell, nor has he a sermon to preach, or a truth to declaim from a pulpit; in the one case as in the other he gives us a human phase of that faith, love and progress which is a force of nature, dimly seen, but moving men's lives and conduct most powerfully when it moves them in spite of themselves.

Let it be clearly understood that *A Death in the Desert* goes no single step in the direction of proving Christ's divinity as a dogma, any more than do the poems *Christmas Eve* and *Easter Day* already dealt with, nor indeed does it deal with any of those mysteries which are now usually spoken of as the dogmas of the Christian Faith. The spiritual reality of which I spoke is evidenced by the fact simply that this poem represents a man permeated with pure faith in the love of God as once manifested in human shape. It is a monologue-drama of 'incidents in the life of a soul,' prophetically projecting itself into the future, charged with a new message of love. And it is physically dramatic in the sense that the images or ideas show no anachronism; the whole habit of mind and body is reproduced, while every truth prophetically spoken by John is equally a truth to-day.

Into this soul-drama the 'morality' that M. Sarrazin so strongly insists on does not enter at all; the poem merely represents the last spiritual life's scene on earth of the man last left alive who had seen and touched the Being whom he believed to be the Christ Man, the visible God made flesh for love of mankind.

John as drawn here is what we should call to-day a poetic and intellectual genius presented to our regard through his idea rather than through any marked physical personality. A far subtler and more complex type than Lazarus in the monologue-drama of *Karshish;* Lazarus is a plain craftsman, so absorbed in God that the bodily existence to which he has been called back seems a mere incident, a mechanical process of which he is scarcely conscious. John's ardour for faith and love may be compared to Paracelsus's overwhelming thirst for knowledge, to Aprile's passion for beauty, or to the Grammarian's comsuming strain toward scholarship; it is as human as they, as disinterested, and the faith and love in him is, just the same as the faith and love in them, directed towards the unknowable which is ever reached up to; for him as for them progress in faith and love is a condition of soul's life; but for him, unlike them, his soul is infused with the ever present spirit of Christ; and perhaps he resembles them as much as anything else in this, that he too is not so much a reasoner as a diviner of the truth.

The spiritual action of the drama, starting from the fact or belief that John was the last living person who saw and touched Christ, represents the passion of his soul's faith prophetically confronting the doubts that will sway men's souls in the future, and marshalling the incidents and wonders of his life, under the command of his intellect, to conquer the doubt and win the doubters to the side of faith.

And throughout the poem the spiritual action is dictated by absorbing love not only of the Christ God, 'The Word made flesh who dwelt among us and we beheld his glory,' but of all humanity. A passion as real as (say) the love between Orestes and Pylades, David and Jonathan; as absorbing as any possible passion between man and woman.

The passion in this poem is therefore an intellectual and emotional study, as keen in its reality for Browning as were in their different moods the play of *Alkestis* for Euripides, the *Eroica* symphony for Beethoven, or *King Lear* for Shakespeare ; as real and as thrillingly present as the passion of *Wuthering Heights* could have been for its author.

The poem takes the form of a narrative by a disciple, one of four who were eye-witnesses of John's death, and ear-witnesses of his last words. The scene is a cave in some desert of Syria or Asia Minor ; John lies there in an unconscious trance ;

> I at the head, and Xanthus at the feet,
> With Valens and the Boy, had lifted him,
> And brought him from the chamber in the depths,
> And laid him in the light where we might see ;
> For certain smiles began about his mouth,
> And his lips moved, presageful of the end.
>
> Beyond, and half-way up the mouth o' the cave,
> The Bactrian convert, having his desire,
> Kept watch, and made pretence to graze a goat
> That gave us milk, on rags of various herb,
> Plantain and quitch, the rocks' shade keeps alive ;
> So that if any thief or soldier passed,
> (Because the persecution was aware)
> Yielding the goat up promptly with his life,
> Such man might pass on, joyful at a prize,
> Nor care to pry into the cool o' the cave.
> Outside was all noon and the burning blue.

Seeing that the trance continued, they tried to dispel it with wine and restoratives ; and one of them prayed. But all was without effect.

Then the Boy sprang up from his knees, and ran
Stung by the splendour of a sudden thought,
And fetched the seventh plate of graven lead
Out of the secret chamber, found a place,
Pressing with finger on the deeper dints,
And spoke, as 'twere his mouth proclaiming first,
'I am the Resurrection and the Life.'

Whereat he opened his eyes wide at once,
And sat up of himself, and looked at us :
And thenceforth nobody pronounced a word :
Only, outside, the Bactrian cried his cry
Like the lone desert bird that wears the ruff,
As signal we were safe, from time to time.

And John begins to speak ; first in words shewing he
has scarce returned to consciousness of the world and
time ; but after a pause he speaks on uninterruptedly,
thus :

I, once all fire, am now ashes save a spark ; but that
spark, my soul, lives ; and I rekindle it for a little while ;

                                     I urge
'What ashes of my brain have kept their shape,
And these make effort on the last o' the flesh,
Trying to taste again the truth of things'—
(He smiled) 'their very superficial truth ;
As that ye are my sons, that it is long
Since James and Peter had release by death,
And I am only he, your brother John,
Who saw and heard, and could remember all.
Remember all !  It is not much to say.
What if the truth broke on me from above
As once and oft-times ?  Such might hap again :
Doubtlessly He might stand in presence here,
With head wool-white, eyes flame, and feet like brass,
The sword and the seven stars, as I have seen—
I who now shudder only, and surmise
How did your brother bear that sight and live ?

> If I live yet, it is for good, more love
> From me to men ; be nought but ashes here
> That keep awhile my semblance, who was John,—
> Still, when they scatter, there is left on earth
> No one alive who knew (consider this !)
> —Saw with his eyes and handled with his hands
> That which was from the first, the Word of Life.
> How will it be when none more saith, "I saw?"'

After eloquently describing how he had upheld the truth of Christ and His Love in speaking and writing against doubts already afoot, and as eloquently presaging the doubts to come, he resumes :

How shall I, whose aged flesh is worn to a shred, so that my soul lies almost bare to the light, share my knowledge with those whose youthful flesh veils their soul from truth ?

To me, Christ's life and death *is*, here and now : *I see* God's love at issue with sin, *I see* the need of sin and death, their transiency, the good they consummate ; *I see* Christ's love, that was weak because of its fleshly chain, take again the power of his godhead. But what *I see*, you, the young ones of to-day and the future, in order to understand that Life and Death in their true relation to past and future men, must *apprehend* mediately as historic fact, at a distance, as through an optic glass.*

Now, what *I see*, and would shew you how to apprehend, is that life, for man, means the chance of learning Love,— how it has been and is,—and holding that truth as a prize against the world. But the soul learns differently from the flesh. For while the body's principle of life was learnt and known by men a thousand years ago as well as we know it to-day, the soul has gone on learning, still goes on, and will go on ; and sages to-day learn, by observing it, more of God's power than they knew yesterday. And

* I think Mrs Orr is wrong in interpreting this, 'He (John) *must needs be* as an optic glass.' (Handbook p. 196, 1st. Ed.)

by as much as they see more of that power, by so much they see more of His love, just as the more of earth you see, the more of sky you see.   Then, as during our earthly life our souls daily learn more, break down more barriers between us and God's truth, God gives us daily new barriers to break down, new provisions for keeping the soul at work and on the stretch to find out and assure itself of God's power and love.

To prove the worth of fire, to warm or burn our bodies, one trial is enough ; fire is as precious to the wise man of to-day as it was to the primeval man who first by touch or feeling, learned that it did burn or warm.   If the virtue of this truth of God's love were realised by the soul at once, and as completely as the virtue of fire by the body, man's probation would be at an end.   For his nature is to reason, before deciding on the value to him of anything ; therefore, to test the strength of his desire to know, to practice and develop it, God shifts, alters the form of, the proofs, so that man shall only find the value of the truth by repeated effort and therefore development.

See how my story, and that of later believers, proves this ; you know what things I saw, what strong reason I had to believe ; yet I failed at the first simple test of my belief.   I forsook Christ, in panic at the soldiers and fear of the Jews.   In a few years, so had belief grown,

> Another year or two,—what little child,
> What tender woman that had seen no least
> Of all my sights, but barely heard them told,
> Who did not clasp the cross with a light laugh,
> Or wrap the burning robe round, thanking God?

But truth was not safely gained yet.   The next test was that men whispered doubts, or garbled Christ's life. These men I confuted by restating that life, as I had seen and known it.

And I am dying now ; I foresee that men will say of me too—

> 'Was John at all, and did he say he saw?
> Assure us, ere we ask what he might see !'

Through the rest of the poem, John becomes a prophet, and speaks to the born and unborn men of the future. He says to them—

Let me use my dying weakness to help your living strength. Suppose a babe, born in this cave, grew to be a boy here, never having seen more light than yonder glimmer. I should be glad that my sight too had been weakened by the cave's gloom, because I should the better know how his sight was defective. And could I not easily explain to him what full light, the sunlight, really was ? Would he, in order to believe in the sun's light, need my assurance that I had seen it ?

So, you bear the burden of only having a gleam of the truth whose full light I saw ; can I not help *you ?*

> It is a heavy burden you shall bear
> In latter days, new lands, or old grown strange,
> Left without me, which must be very soon.
> What is the doubt, my brothers ? Quick with it !
> I see you stand conversing, each new face,
> Either in fields, of yellow summer eves,
> On islets yet unnamed amid the sea ;
> Or pace for shelter 'neath a portico
> Out of the crowd in some enormous town
> Where now the larks sing in a solitude ;
> —Or muse upon blank heaps of stone and sand
> Idly conjectured to be Ephesus :
> And no one asks his fellow any more
> 'Where is the promise of His coming,' but
> 'Was he revealed in any of his lives,
> As Power, as Love, as Influencing Soul ?'

And one, reading my written words, will say, 'this tale

of miracles done ages ago proves no truth for *us;* we must have similar proof to-day, if we are to be convinced. The only part of the tale which we can accept, is its injunction to love; that is true for us; man must love, and he loves best power and love combined. The idea of Christ realises that combination; did *he* therefore exist ? did not men make him, the idea of him ? Say, we acknowledge Christ's ideal love; that only proves we comprehend it, from having such love as his in ourselves; otherwise we should not recognise it. We embody our need of this perfect love in the idea of Christ; it is a mere projection from man's mind. Next, say we acknowledge Christ's, that is God's power, and that He made and rules the world. What does that acknowledgment amount to, judging from the past history of the ideal God? Our world exists, it is ruled. We must either *assume* that God made it and that He now rules it, or that it has always been as now. There is no proof either way. Man has constructed an ideal power of God from the earliest time, out of his own qualities; our forefathers thought the sun was moved from east to west by a being with will and hands like themselves, only mightier. But now we say, why needs all power be like human power? Men have *will* as well as power; we know the sun is moved, we name whatever moves it, power and law, but we do not know what the power is, while we do know what our will and love are. True, our fathers told us, as a proof of God's will and love, that the sun stood still, or rose and set unduly, to reward or punish men; but it does not do so now, so we say they were mistaken in attributing will and love to the force which controls the sun. Further back still, we find men idealising their own will, love and intelligence in the persons of many deities; then they ceased to believe in the persons, but continued to believe in their quasi-human pride or wrath; next, they idealised an abstract will, power, and love, instead of personal human qualities ; now, we put the word law in place of those three. The idea of God, now embodied in the word law, like the idea of Christ, is and always has been merely a projection of man's mind.'

In answer to the claim to be convinced by fresh miracles, I say, replies John, that those miracles you refuse to accept were employed when man needed them, and ceased when his need for them ceased. For man is a progressive being ; he is created to climb, not stand still or go back ; having climbed, he needs the ladder no more ; the miracle-proof which was once his ladder may drop when it has served its purpose ; or, to change the image, as in a garden twigs are put to shew where the seeds are, and removed when the seeds are grown up, so when the seed of truth was sown first, miracles were needed to shew men the truth was there ; but when the truth had grown to be visible, the miracles were no longer needed.

Again ; as the body with nourishment, so the mind with truth, must be fed according to its growth and maturing ; the miracle I wrought to feed young minds with truth, whether they would or no, as one feeds a babe, is useless for the adolescent mind of to-day or of the future, which claims another more advanced nourishment, and must choose its own food. The result has been that as men's minds grew in faith, they found the babe-nourishment of miracles superfluous, void :

> I say, the acknowledgment of God in Christ
> Accepted by thy reason, solves for thee
> All questions in the earth and out of it,
> And has so far advanced thee to be wise.
> Wouldst thou unprove this to reprove the proved?
> In life's mere minute, with power to use that proof,
> Leave knowledge and revert to how it sprung?
> Thou hast it ; use it and forthwith, or die !

If you, having the miracle-proof thus given, ask for the same or similar proof again, instead of using, assimilating, the proof you have complete, you are defying the law of your soul's life, progress, and your soul must die; you reject the gain you have, and it becomes your loss; you thrust away the light of Christ, and your soul is dark; you refuse His knowledge and become ignorant; you spurn His love and become loveless.

Just as a lamp burns bright with its due amount of oil, or a stomach nourishes the body with its due amount of food,—and either lamp or stomach, overcharged with oil or food, ceases to give light or to nourish;—so with a man's soul; a repetition of a truth already proved is too much nourishment, which his soul cannot assimilate; and thus over-fed it ceases to burn or to nourish, that is, dies.

In answer to your argument that the ideal power of God and love of Christ was mere projection from man's mind, I say this:

1. Man has always had, on a limited scale, might, and will the one source of that might. At first, appalled at Nature, man asked, what if there be a Might, illimitable as man's is limited, that moves this might of Nature?— God shewed him by miracles,—you have God's word for it —that His Might was the mover. If, seeing God's Might, man yet asks, since God's Might exists, where is the use of His will? he denies the will he knows himself to possess—

> That man has turned round on himself, and stands,
> Which in the course of Nature, is to die.

2. Man has always had, on a limited scale, the quality of love in him. That quality implies the need to be loved again. Feeling this need, and seeking therefore for a perfect Love, he asked, what if there be Infinite Love

too, behind the Will and Power? God showed him by miracles,—you have God's word for it—that there was that Infinite Love, and that it was His. If, accepting God's love, so proved once, man says since love is every-where, we ourselves have made it, God's love does not exist except as made by us,

> How shall ye help this man who knows himself,
> That he must love and would be loved again,
> Yet owning his own love that proveth Christ,
> Rejecteth Christ for very need of Him ?
> The lamp o'erswims with oil, the stomach flags
> Loaded with nurture, and that man's soul dies.*

If a man thus confuted rejoins, but you told the story of Christ's life, death and love inaccurately at first; your truth therefore became no truth, and doubt and per-plexity follow; how am I to distinguish what is true and what is inaccurate? Why not tell us the whole plain truth once for all? Are you only dealing with us as Œschylus did with his hearers in his myth of the

---

* As an illustration of the truth that proof repeated is superfluous, the idea of over-nurture is in strict analogy with the idea of over-know-ledge. But, reading this passage as written, one at first sight comments thus : A man who rejects God's love just because he needs it, and be-cause the proof of it has been given him, rather resembles an *imperfect* lamp, rejecting *needful* oil, a stomach which cannot digest *needful* food, than either of these *over*-charged with *needless* nourishment.

We must presumably understand an ellipse between the line ending 'need of Him ' and the line beginning 'the lamp o'erswims.' The fal-lacy might then be stated in prose thus : 'The proof of God's love, by miracle, has been given to man, he has seen that love everywhere; he thereupon turns round and says, But I assert I made that love myself ; [ellipse : and I will accept no miracle which I did not *personally* see ; to confute my assertion, you must show me another miracle.] But, says John [ellipse : I have shewn you that demanding a miracle twice is a sin against the law of your soul's life ; that] giving you the same proof twice would be an over-nurture, ensuring your soul's death, precisely as over-filling a lamp with oil puts out its flame.'

I think, however, that in the passage as it stands, clearness is in some degree sacrificed to concision.

Promethean fire, making a fable and forcing us to find out
for ourselves the fact in it?

I answer, man, which includes you and me, is not God,
complete; we were created incomplete, to serve God's
ends, to live our course, and, as I said before, to develop
through life. Man therefore must pass from mistake to
fact, from the seeming good of the past to the proved best
of the present; else how could he progress and develop?
I say further, that if man now, recognising power, will
and love in himself, believes that God, or, as he now says,
Nature's Law, can have power without either will or love,
he makes himself the first, last and best of things, that is
makes himself God; for if he only of organisms in the
universe possesses these three qualities, he is as much
higher in the scale of being than any power existing
without love or will, as a living midge is more marvellous
than a dead mountain; that is, he is God, unchangeable,
which by the hypothesis he can not be, and live. But if
he admits that he is only man, created conscious of his
power to know *i.e.* learn and therefore progress, he must
then fall into his place as man, below God, whose knowledge and power are perfect, above the beasts which know
to the limit of their nature, but are unconscious of their
knowledge. Man knows partly, is conscious that he
knows, by his nature strives to know more, and finds
progress so, which is the quality distinguishing him from
God and from beast. His soul could no more have this
progress if it found at once what it is always striving for,
than his body could move if instead of space solid earth
surrounded it. Thus conditioned, man finds that what
he thinks he knows to-day, he will find not rightly known
to-morrow; the condition of his soul's life is learning,
instructing himself by his past self. As a sculptor takes
a mass of clay, roughly sketches his figure, corrects mistakes, says ever, Now this is right, that is my idea, but still

changes and corrects,—so man moulds his life and uses his mistakes to improve his knowledge and develop his life. Only God makes the complete thing at a jet. If you demur to this, if you renounce this pact of creature-ship, you will never reach the highest place of all, the angels,' where law, life, joy, impulse are one thing.

> Such is the burden of the latest time.
> I have survived to hear it with my ears,
> Answer it with my lips : does this suffice ?
> For if there be a further woe than such,
> Wherein my brothers struggling need a hand,
> So long as any pulse is left in mine,
> May I be absent even longer yet,
> Plucking the blind ones back from the abyss,
> Though I should tarry a new hundred years.

The final words of the disciple who reports the fore-going utterances of his master are too pathetically real to be omitted ; and they moreover help to make a picture of the whole visible scene which enshrines the beauty of the thought ;—

> But he was dead : 'twas about noon, the day
> Somewhat declining ; we five buried him
> That eve, and then, dividing, went five ways,
> And I, disguised, return to Ephesus.

> By this, the cave's mouth must be filled with sand :
> Valens is lost, I know not of his trace ;
> The Bactrian was but a wild childish man,
> And could not write nor speak, but only loved :
> So, lest the memory of this go quite,
> Seeing that I to-morrow fight the beasts,
> I tell the same to Phœbas, whom believe !
> For many look again to find that face,
> Beloved John's to whom I ministered,
> Somewhere in life about the world ; they err ;
> Either mistaking what was darkly spoke

At ending of his book, as he relates,
Or misconceiving somewhat of this speech
Scattered from mouth to mouth, as I suppose.
Believe ye will not see him any more
About the world with his divine regard !
For all is as I say, and now the man
Lies as he lay once, breast to breast with God.

# IXION : AN EXEGESIS OF THE POEM

IXION says : my mortal flesh, made immortal by Zeus, suffers the torment of the wheel for ever, to satisfy Jove's revenge. But above is a rainbow [of hope] made from the vapour of my tears, sweat and blood, which, cast off by the whirling wheel, are shone through by the light above. My flesh, bestowed by Zeus for high and varied ends, has become vapour through pain. Zeus has re-fashioned my body for this eternal torment ; this is his final employment of the sense once pledged to give my soul pleasure. And even now my soul would know no pain could she destroy my body, or escape from it into the light of absolute truth. I erred, it is true ; I was a man, I was foiled by my senses, I dreamed. I awake and find that what I took for God's light, was darkness. I have learned that much ; will torture teach me to know it any better ? My sin was to believe Zeus when he said he was my friend, to believe Hera when she said she was my love : my sense was wrong in the way I used that belief ; but Zeus could have cured my sense's blindness with a touch, so that my soul would have seen the truth. But instead of curing it he condemns me to be punished for it, by eternal pain.

When I was a King of men on earth I made laws, and punished those who broke the laws. Any such criminal, though weak and ignorant, was punished ; for I being only a man, could not know and take account of all the circumstances that warped his life and made him disobedient.

Had I been like Zeus, a God, I might have saved him
from disobedience by watching him from birth, hindering
the distortion of his mind ; nay even as a *human* King, I
would have reprieved him and given him another chance,
could I have seen through the outward mask of his face to
his heart, and read real repentance there.

How much more then should Zeus, the King of Gods,
whom I believed to be my creator, have seen into my
human heart, his own creation as I thought then. Say
his charge was true ; say I was arrogant. I made an even
stranger mistake than that. I, a man, actually believed
Zeus and his fellows to possess our human grace, our
human nature, and on a higher and more generous scale.
But when I, possessed by that idea, believed Zeus when he
said he was my friend, believed Hera when she said she
was my love, and acted on that belief, Zeus and Hera
turned on me and cast me from Heaven to Hell, from
rapture to torment, from fellowship with Gods to a man's
mateship with misery.

Yes, I became a man henceforth and for ever. But
my eyes are opened now. I see that Zeus never created
man, it was man who lent warmth to Zeus's coldness,
colour to the sheer black and white of Godhead. That is
the way a man conceived passion, feeling, and love in
Zeus and his fellows ; he believed that they had man's
good qualities in greater degree, and so trusted and loved
them. I see now that it is man who is the truth, the
gods who are the lie—nay more ; they have no right
even to aspire to be man ; it was man who created them,
they only try, and in vain, to ape man. They are merely
a hollowness, a shadow which man has filled and illumined
with his nature.

And the proof of the reality of my human nature is
shewn by an emblem : for from my agony, and the
capacity of my manhood to suffer, from my tears, sweat

and blood that burst into vapour above the whirling of
the wheel, is born the rainbow arching my torment;
that rainbow exists by means of the light above, is the
visible sign of a sympathy between the source of that
light and my human suffering ; it justifies and glorifies
my pain. For, as the sun's light touches, mixes with and
glorifies the cloud, making a rainbow, so the source of
light touches and mingles in sympathy with the vapour
of my pain, glorifying it, justifying, shewing the use of
pain, by the rainbow emblem of that sympathy

Therefore I say to mankind, strive, as I strove by
mounting to heaven and sitting beside Zeus and Hera,
strive, even though the strife should endure through
endless obstruction. Strive still though each rise you
make is marred by as deep and certain a fall as mine
from heaven to hell.

For man, though baffled for ever, is never so baffled but
that, even when his entity, his ego, is checked (by the weakness of the flesh or essence, clothing it), in the strife towards
the Not Thou, the eternal disembodied Love,—even when
on the verge of the new life, his struggles only bring him to
the old weakness of flesh, the bad qualities it strove to escape
from, and ever finds fresh-formed,—even when, paying
the price of his endeavour, he (like me) is thrust down
to Hell and despair,—even then he may look up through
the tears, sweat and blood of his torment, and rejoice.

For what is the influence high above, beyond all baffling
obstruction that turns pain to rapture ? must I fall back
to ruin, into the weakness I ever try to flee from ? No,
for above the obstruction, the weakness, is the Eternal Purity unobstructed. Zeus was weak, his weakness
wrecked me ; I rise out of it,—past Zeus to the potency
o'er him, the infinite Pure ;

Pallid birth of my pain,—where light, where light is, aspiring
Thither I rise, whilst thou—Zeus, keep the godship and sink !

## I. A TENTATIVE INTERPRETATION.

The poem might show us, through its mythical present-ment, the turning on man's self of the consequence of man's imagining that he can create a divine love out of his own human love. The creation is a thing marred by its maker's imperfection ; phantasmal, neither divine nor human ; a faithless ghost. Ixion is the victim of this man-created god of his ancestors ; and expiating the sins of his fathers in this regard, sees prophetically the ultimate downfall of that God, and man's natural need to progress for ever through hindrance and weakness rewarded, if carried out to the end,' by the sympathy and love of the true God, whose light shines above the hell of evil.

## II. A CRITICISM, AND A SUGGESTED INNER MEANING DEVELOPED FROM No. I.

This poem is contained in fourteen pages ; the first ten may be taken as the actual speech of Ixion, King of Thessaly, and as if his ascent to Olympus, his fiasco there, and his subsequent thrusting down to Hell, to expiate his folly by eternal torture on a whirling wheel,—were real facts ; the power of his Gods was made plain to him, and his only protest is against their lack of those attributes which, as their creature, he assumes them to possess, the same in kind with men but greater in degree.—His protest is enforced by a comparison, unfavourable to Zeus, between his own equitable action as a King and judge of men towards criminals, and Zeus's action as the King of Gods and supreme judge in dealing with him, who was no criminal, only a blunderer at worst.

But here the protest must end, for the fact (assumed so far) was that Zeus did exist, was a creator, and had power to do as he willed with man. Ixion's revolt up to this point has no more justification than in the fact that he

did not understand the nature of the Gods. And so far I
suppose he merely echoes the mental process of the poets
of his time.

But at page 66, with the line beginning 'man henceforth
and for ever,' and throughout the remaining three pages
of the poem, the mental attitude becomes quite un-Greek,
and in fact is that of a man of the nineteenth century,
confronted with problems which may be foreshadowed in
the myth before us, but which assuredly could never have
troubled the minds either of the makers or of the believers
of that myth. For by a transition wholly unaccounted
for by the artistic basis of the poem, the King Ixion proceeds to express ideas such as could not possibly enter the
mind of a man believing in the fact, however unjust, of
man's being punished by Gods whose notions of right and
wrong could only be formulated by the word Tyranny.
In fact, Ixion on his wheel, after the protest as stated
above, proceeds to prophesy. He retains the image of the
wheel with its rainbow, and states his case in effect thus ;
'I am now suffering the eternal pains which my God Zeus
has unjustly awarded me for an act of mere folly : and
therefore I say that Zeus is not a real God, only a hollow
phantasm created by man's imagination, and which must
one day fall and vanish.' That, of course, is a *reductio ad
absurdum* as coming from a man who believes himself to
be actually suffering eternal torment of his body (made
immortal for the purpose of torment) as an unjust punishment inflicted on him by a God who he believed was real
enough when actually dooming him.

But it is possible to make a coherent and valuable idea
from the poem, and to see in it without undue strain of
meaning an instance of the truth which affirms faith and
progress as necessary forms of the soul. Taking Ixion as
a type of a soul at strife with evil, he might be supposed
to be symbolising thus : ' My pain is real enough, but it

was brought on me by my own pride, selfish ambition and lust ; by human faithlessness, revenge and cruelty. All these vices I have personified as Gods, and bowed down to for a time. I, and I only, am responsible for my own folly : my past worship of evil passion has caused the ensuing pain. Under the stress of pain my soul's sight is purified ; I am enabled to see those qualities which I deified as Gods with an unclouded eye ; to see them as hindrances to be overcome by the nobler qualities of love, faith, and effort against them. Does this prove that there are no Gods at all ? No ; on the contrary, through the agony of my soul I still see hope : and beyond it, I see the Eternal Light of God, towards whom my soul must ever strive, through seemingly endless obstruction, beaten back by seemingly endless exhaustion, but reaching Him at last.

## III. SOME THOUGHTS ON THE POEM.

At the end of her synopsis of this poem Mrs Orr says ; 'If any doubt were still possible as to Mr Browning's attitude towards the doctrine of eternal punishment, this poem must dispel it.' But how many people to-day, possible readers of Browning, believe in the doctrine of eternal punishment at all, in its dogmatic sense ? If the idea of that doctrine were in the poet's mind when he wrote *Ixion*, that idea must be taken as its primary impulse, for it could not collaterally touch the subject of Ixion and his wheel. But I cannot conceive such a primary impulse ; for was it worth while for a great poet to write a poem which for clang and rhythm, to say nothing of its beauty and majesty of image, equals his highest efforts, merely to slay a dogma which never had real vitality ?—Even should Browning himself avow that he had no other intention in writing it than this, I should fall back on the before quoted words of George Eliot,

'The words of genius bear a wider meaning than the thought which prompted them.'

And because of this dictum, and because,—if the poem is supposed to contain only a personal expression of Browning's conviction on the subject of a stupid, cruel and illogical superstition, its value as a work of high art is absolutely nullified,—I have chosen rather to read in it another soul drama, presented in the form of a terrible myth; a drama whose mental and psychological import-ance ranks it as second to none in the whole of Browning's noble repertory. The clash and whirl of the wheel, the wide hell, become symbols of a real truth indeed; the drama of a self-created theocracy, faithless as lust, sudden in attack as wild beasts, strong as death, cruel as the grave; in short the real and awful force of human pro-pensity unbridled. The high over-arching rainbow typifies to me the reflection of eternal light emanating from that unseen power whose love and wisdom is discerned in nature's urge, felt or desired in the soul of every one of us, lightening our darkness, soothing the pain of our self-inflicted wounds and tortures, making bearable the wrong continually wrought on us by the evil impulses, the false gods, which man lets loose to work with unbridled savagery upon himself and his fellows. Faith is here, fighting against them; love, and thirst for upward progress towards the Divine ever struggle up and out from the whirl of self-constructed torment, and the light shines eternally above our man-created hell. Is it not a supreme picture of faith, hope, love and progress through hindrance?

In the whole range of Browning's vast conceptions I know of none which can surpass if any can equal in pure truth and majesty of analogy, this image of the mystic rainbow, refracted through the dew of the soul's agony; the mythic whirling wheel, its torment symbolis-ing the imperious force wielded by the spirit of evil upon the slave of flesh which enthroned it in power ; the ever agonising spiritual form racked by that force ; the light above, symbolising the eternal power over-brooding the universe and its conflict; the Divine love, visible to the soul in refracted and many coloured light, the divinely healing sympathy touching and soothing it and vitalising it, through the dew of its torment, into ever fresh struggles upwards towards God. But prose is hopeless ; here is the music :

> What is the influence, high o'er Hell, that turns to a rapture
>   Pain, and despair's murk mists blends in a rainbow of hope ?
> What is beyond the obstruction, stage by stage tho' it baffle ?
>   Back must I fall, confess ' Ever the weakness I fled ? '
> No, for beyond, far, far, is a purity all unobstructed !

> .     .     .     .     .     .

> Out of the wreck I rise, past Zeus to the Potency o'er him !

> .     .     .     .     .     .

> Pallid birth of my pain,—where light, where light is, aspiring
>   Thither I rise . . .

# INTRODUCTION TO 'PARLEYINGS'

'I do not mean,' says Mrs Orr in the first edition of her handbook, 'that human experience solves for' Browning 'all the questions that it can be made to state, or that everything he believes can be verified by it,' but 'so much of abstract truth as cannot be given in a picture of human life lies outside his philosophy of it. He accepts this residue as the ultimate mystery of what must be called Divine thought. Thought or spirit is with him the ultimate fact of existence; the one thing about which it is vain to theorise, and which we can never get behind.'

'He is convinced that uncertainty is essential to the spiritual life; . . . that where uncertainty ceases, stagnation must begin; that our light must be wavering and our progress tentative as well as our hopes chequered, and our happiness even devoid of any sense of finality, if the creative intention is not to frustrate itself.'

'The circumstance of life is as much adapted to the guidance of each separate soul as if each were the single object of creative care; . . . while the individual knows nothing of the Divine scheme, he *is* everything in it.'

'Evil remains for him essential to the variety and invested with the dignity of human life.'

I make free with these somewhat wholesale quotations from the first edition of Mrs Orr's Handbook, partly because their diction expresses certain characteristics of

Browning's poetic nature more gracefully and incisively than I could do,—for I should have to say similar things in regard of the book before us, ' Parleyings'; partly because their interest on the present occasion lies in their applicability in the main to this very work, of which, since it was published two years after the first edition of Mrs Orr's book, she may be presumed to have been ignorant.

The manner in which from first to last I have determined on studying Browning's work, as that manner has been previously explained, precludes my taking account of any opinion or aspiration of his as it may have been expressed in conversation or in letters to friends. Any such informal or friendly expression must, as compared with writing he avows by publication, be as a wax sketch would be to a finished bronze.

A further reason, giving these dicta of Mrs Orr's an exceptional value for me to-day, lies in the avowed personalness of 'Parleyings.' It is Browning's first proclaimed declaration of what he believes, he the man. I do not even except ' Ferishtah's Fancies,' or the personal poems in 'Pacchiarotto,' or 'La Saisiaz.' Of course in each parleying he to a certain extent dresses the idea in the personality of the man with whom he is supposed to be talking, but the disguise is hardly more effective than a transparent veil through which the real features of a face can be discerned.

In this work—its full title is ' *Parleyings with certain people of importance in their day* ' Browning then avowedly speaks not as a dramatic poet but in his own person. And this is noteworthy, not only because he does so now for the first time *ex cathedra* so to speak; this his latest published work at the date of the present writing, contains in seven poems, in the form of imaginary conversations, the poet's deliberate personal conviction that faith, hope, love and progress through uncertainty are the law of life ·and of

God. The prologue and epilogue express the same principle, dramatically. In all Browning's *dramatic* creations those qualities *appear as* the mainspring of all noble thought and action, and are the essence of all human life, however repressed or warped in the worst or weakest souls he depicts.

In the prologue, the Eternal First Cause, as Zeus, rebukes Apollo and the Fates, the mediate rulers of men's lives and destinies, for imagining that they can command faith to become fruition, and hope, certainty ; each is bidden back to the function of each, the one of cheering faith and hope, by his gift of light, the other of irresponsibly weaving men's earthly lot in obedience to the unknown cause which created and moves the Fates themselves ; and man is by implication reminded that light and joy are only helps to faith and love; that illusion cannot take the place of faith, nor joy the place of love.

In Bernard de Mandeville the argument points to the advantage of faith and love over pessimism and despair ; and indicates that it is better for man's progress (admitted as a principle by the pessimist) to use the analogies of nature's bounty for heartening faith by the unavoidable inference of an Infinite Love, than it is to complain supinely of the existence of wrong and evil as tending to overthrow faith, and, by insufficient *assumption*, to negative the existence of an all-powerful Love.

The telling, in Daniel Bartoli, of a story of a pair of lovers, one of whom, the man, forsook his love under the pressure of tyranny, is at once a rebuke to the weakness of his faith, and a divination (by the poet) that his love, though weak at the crisis, could not die, but would rise again to full strength and reward in the new life. It shows faith, love and progress thwarted but not destroyed by weakness.

In Christopher Smart the duty of a poet to believe in himself and use his powers to the utmost for his fellowmen, is inculcated by the judgment Browning passes on Smart's lack of faith in his own power of sustained creation, while his unique effort is applauded as one which—beginning by poetising earth instead of attempting to soar before he could walk—is based on the principle of step-by-step progress upwards.

The parleying with George Bubb Dodington, a satire on the virtual nullity of that politician, shows that man's craving for the supernatural, the embryo of faith and love, is the master-chord which a ruler of men must touch, if he would keep his place as a ruler, however selfseeking.

The painter priest Francis Furini is made Browning's mouth-piece for the exposition of the true principle of progress, as developing faith and love ; the principle namely of (1) learning the bodily life in order to learn that of the soul, (2) using faith and love as a help to the insight which *divines* a purpose in God's scheme of conflict, between evil and good (3) acknowledging man's powerlessness in this life to *know* that purpose, or indeed anything beyond the scope of this earthly life.

In Gerard de Lairesse, we have again the poet's conviction that men, and poets above all, must work onwards, progress, and not retrograde, in life and art, and that faith and love see in death only such a temporary loss or check as gives, precisely as do hindrances here, gain and progress and love in the new life. The exquisite lyric at the end, gives too, the poet's conviction that a man's passionate love of earth to its smallest flower, is continued mystically in new life.

The parleying with Charles Avison, apart from its special value as being Browning's personal tribute to music, reasserts, as to music, the law that faith and love in the use of each successive music-worker's effort towards

manifesting the soul is needed by each musician in turn—
faith in the law of progress, which decrees, that however
imperfect a composer may feel his work to be, it is not
lost or useless, but a step towards the completer work of
the future.

The epilogue, showing Fust at the moment his effort is
rewarded by the success of his invention of printing, indicates how each discovery in knowledge, however beneficent,
is still a matter of progress only ; that it contains the
seeds of future abuse of knowledge, abuse to be again conquered by new knowledge.   It is Browning's final example
showing that incompleteness in each life's achievements,
while a necessary condition of the soul's life, is an earnest
and law of future progress, an incentive to faith, hope and
love.

### PROLOGUE : APOLLO AND THE FATES.

The fates represent forces unknown but conceived,
working out the lot of man as it is governed by Zeus's
unseen laws, laws whose scope is wider than any one
man or all men can in this life see; wider, deeper than
even the god of light, Apollo himself, can illuminate or
fathom; not to be shaken by the temporary illusion of joy
and hope, expressed by the symbol of wine, the gift of
Bacchus; and so, when Apollo and the Fates have joined
hands in a dance of joy celebrating man's supposed triumph
over evil, an explosion from the earth's centre, Zeus's
portent, warns them that neither Apollo's life-giving light,
nor Bacchus's life-giving joy or illusion, can either
illumine or divert the working of the cause which moves
the Fates.

Apollo, the god of light, descends to the cavern of the
Fates, to plead with them for the life of Admetus, who
lies in mortal sickness.

The Fate Lachesis has woven Admetus's life up to the

period of his triumph and happy marriage; Atropos is about to cut his life short, when Apollo enters the cavern, and stays her hand.

Equals in power, Apollo and the Fates are at perpetual war; they weave men's lives in darkness and mystery; he makes light and warmth to help men's live...

Apollo asks that Admetus's life may be spared now, and extended to its span of seventy years. The Fates tell him he is asking a doubtful boon; that it would be an act of love to end Admetus now, before he has known sorrow, that Apollo's gift of light is only valuable as giving illusion, brightening the weariness of man's life; that stripped of that illusion man's life is, in childhood, ignorant, idle and mischievous, in manhood, arrogant, foolish, and greedy, in age, impotent, churlish, and rancorous.

Apollo says, Is it so, tnat my gift of light is only illusion? Then why do men desire to live at any cost of misery?

Because your gift of light gives them hope, which is illusion once more, reply the Fates.

Be it so, says Apollo; but suppose man has some compensating power in himself, making him independent of illusion?

The Fates scorn the idea.

Apollo offers them wine, man's invention, prompted by his brother Bacchus,—to prove man's compensating power. They drink, and become dominated themselves by illusion. They see life as it can be, not as it is. They see the relation between evil and good in man's life.

Apollo proceeds to put before them his view of man's life. My brother Bacchus, says he, the youngest of the gods, found that all gifts had been given to men by the other gods, so he judged that some new gift must be invented by him for men to pay him homage for it. The mixed woe and weal, false mingled with true, of man's life, had been settled by Zeus. Bacchus, human of instinct, but divine in reason, sought no destruction of the order established by Zeus ; but since my beams momentarily lighting your cavern, and shewing crystal and gem embedded in the rock, prove that your darkness is only a mask, since the wine god's gift makes even you Fates see the helpful and kindly in life instead of the adverse and thwart, shall we not thank Zeus, the anterior Wisdom, for both gifts ? I do not seek to fill your cavern with the full glory of noon-blaze , that would be against Zeus's law, and confusion would be the result. So, I give man only such light as helps him in his life, to accept the bad with the good, to change despair to acquiescence. Zeus's wisdom has worked this state of things ; Zeus stings Man's mind to go on learning, to press from the part to the whole. You, the Fates, play a poor part in insisting on man's existence as evil from first to last.

The Fates are so warmed with the wine that they, with Apollo, break into a Bacchic dance and song ;—

> Quashed be our quarrel ! sourly and smilingly,
>   Bare and gowned, bleached limbs and browned,
> Drive we a dance, three and one, reconcilingly ;
>   Thanks to the cup where dissension is drowned,
> Defeat proves triumphant and slavery crowned.
>
> Infancy ? what if the rose-streak of morning
>   Pale and depart in a passion of tears ?
> Once to have hoped is no matter for scorning !
>   Love once—e'en love disappointment endears !
> A minute's success pays the failure of years.
>
> Manhood, the actual ? Nay, praise the potential !
>   (Bound upon bound, foot it around !)
> What *is* ? No, what *may* be, sing ? that's Man's essential !
>   (Ramp, tramp, stamp, and confound
> Fancy with fact—the lost secret is found !)

Age ?   Why fear ends there :  the contest concluded,
    Man *did* live his life, *did* escape from the fray :
Not scratchless but unscathed he somehow eluded
    Each blow fortune dealt him, and conquers to-day :
To-morrow—new chance and fresh strength,—might we say ?

Laud then Man's life, no defeat but a triumph !
                            (*Explosion from the Earth's Centre.*)

Both Apollo and the fates are warned by Zeus's portent
not to treat joy, hope and illusion as a permanent solution
of life.   The fates are frightened back to their darkling
implacability ;  they in their turn state the law of life, and
their own inability to do more than spin, weave, and sever
man's life ;  what is ill or good in their web they do not
seek to say :

Known yet ignored, nor divined nor unguessed,
    Such is Man's law of life.   Do we strive to declare
What is ill, what is good, in our spinning ?   Worst, best,
    Change hues of a sudden :  now here and now there
Flies the sign which decides ;  all about yet nowhere.

'Tis willed so,—that Man's life be lived, first to last,
    Up and down, through and through,—not in portions, forsooth
To pick and to choose from.   Our shuttles fly fast,      .
    Weave living, not life sole and whole :  as age—youth,
So death completes living, shews life in its truth.

Man learningly lives :  till death helps him—no lore !
    It is doom and must be :  dost submit ?

Apollo assents ;  but claims the full span of life for
Admetus, to be chequered or not as the Fates will.
    They grant it, on condition that Admetus can find any
one to give their life for him.
    Apollo takes the responsibility, in certainty that
Admetus will refuse.—He ascends amid the jeers of the
Fates, who know better.

## BERNARD DE MANDEVILLE.

### REMARKS ON THE POEM.

Adopting the first quoted of Mrs Orr's dicta, which is perfect in expression of the idea to be conveyed, we find in the Parleying with Bernard de Mandeville a complete instance in point.

In the very first pages the poet disavows—one might almost adopt Mrs Orr's words—any attempt to verify or prove all possible questions which can be stated, or arise, from human experience. Carlyle's pessimism, his wail or Jeremiad against wrong and its triumph, remain; they are very human utterances, and represent the impotent rage, the futile blasphemy, of tens of thousands of men and women. Nay, the idea of keeping man's conception of God, his power and will, within the inconceivable terms of immensity or eternity has a certain grandeur, and leaves an escape from the weak foot-hold of protestation. Perhaps hardly credit enough is given in the poem to the strength gained by a man who takes up the burden of despair and carries it through a long life, doing helpful work the while, the amount of which at the end far overweighs the outcry of revolt. But for working purpose, Browning's standpoint possesses a far more powerful leverage.

If the poem is carefully read through it will be seen that no refutation of Carlyle is either attempted or intended ; it is rather indeed a parleying with Carlyle than with the now forgotten Bernard de Mandeville. And it can not be said that one word of it claims any greater *portée* than lies within the sphere of any thoughtful man's or woman's life experience.

But obviously, when a man like Carlyle is supposed to declare his ability to do without any application of human attribute, in symbolic form or otherwise, to the explaining of what he says is inexplicable, he would hardly admit that the 'truth' contained in Browning's image of a map or a constellation was either new to him, or could have much, if any, working value for him. In short, here are two great men, speaking outside all forms of dogma, who are fully agreed on the main point, as old as any known religion, that God's ways are past finding out. Neither of them denies God, both assert him. But neither can go beyond assertion. Only imagine any human being in distress of mind, either from the natural bent of man's mind to enquire, or from very subjectively special reasons, coming to either Carlyle or Browning, and saying as follows : I know that I can have no proof, but will you help me to a balance of probability, on the side of God's purpose in evil and wrong being ultimately for the good of the universe ? If you can, you will take away from my mind a load of poisonous idea which para- lyses its action and makes me unfit to play my part as a citizen or brother or husband or what you will.

Carlyle would answer, I see no proof, I can shew you even no balance of probability, and I can only beg you to take your load and bear it through life as best you may.

Browning would answer, I can give you no proof, but I can shew you probability. I see purpose everywhere, in man, in all animate nature, in the laws of gravity, in heat, in electricity. Taking the one idea of heat in its simplest form, and using that as an illustration merely, I see that all man has found out up to now, in regard of heat and light, is consistent with the life-giving qualities of sun- light to the earth ; that it creates a thousandfold more than it destroys. You and I admit God. I say the bal- ance of probability of his beneficent purpose in allowing evil to stand and triumph sometimes, overweighs the contrary assumption, by so much as the proved good of light and heat overweighs the harm it does.

Any man so distressed would be more likely to be helped and made effective by Browning than by Carlyle.

## BERNARD DE MANDEVILLE: EXEGESIS OF THE POEM.

> Ay, this same midnight, by this chair of mine,
> Come and review thy counsels : art thou still
> Staunch to their teaching ?—not as fools opine
> Its purport might be, but as subtler skill
> Could through turbidity, the loaded line
> Of logic casting, sound deep, deeper, till
> It touched a quietude and reached a shrine,
> And recognised harmoniously combine
> Evil with good, and hailed truth's triumph—thine,
> Sage dead long since, Bernard de Mandeville !

I ask, says Browning, no knowledge you may have gained since death ; only your approval of my study of your work done on earth. It would be as much against universal law to seek full truth as it would be to expect a babe to become at once a strong man without the transition of childhood and youth.

You taught that the soul strives to good through evil. I hear one complain, 'But God gives no sign of His will that good should conquer evil ; we need an instance of His interposing between evil and its victim to nerve our faith. Why does He not crush evil at its birth ?' You, de Mandeville, would answer, 'You admit a purpose in God's creation, therefore you admit a purpose in the evil part of it   How then can you ask Him to destroy evil once for all ?  If He sows the seed of evil, He means it to grow—perhaps to stimulate the growth of good, for some purpose certainly ; or you make His law futile.'

But he answers 'We are told an enemy, the devil, sows the seeds of evil ; I say that God's purpose is invented by man's fancy, and that the enemy, the devil, means just man's craft and malignity. And · even supposing good ultimately triumphs, why does God permit evil here and now to triumph over good ? These human symbols of sowing and seed are merely man's endeavour to fit God's Infinite into his own finite. And such endeavour must end sooner or later in man's discovering that his rudimentary aspirations will not sustain him side by side with the Infinite. Any human attempt to represent the Infinite by human symbol must end in failure.'

But we use symbols in daily life, says Browning ; a surveyor's map of an estate, or a constellation, are alike symbols. You don't expect to see in the plan the whole details of the estate, or in the constellation Orion the actual shape of the hunter ; in both these cases you are content to take the sign for the thing signified ; or to change the image, each of those luminous points of light which make the constellation, are in themselves only symbols each of a sphere ; they only represent that part of the sphere's surface which takes the light.

He answers, ' What do we want with symbols in dealing with God ? I admit God's power, knowledge, and will ; I admit immensity, eternity ; these are the accepted words for the inconceivable. ' Why,' I repeat, seek to symbolise God by human attributes ? '

I answer, says Browning, God is conceivable to man only by some symbol appealing to his human nature. Before man's mind can believe a truth, he must—if it be beyond his ordinary reasoning power—prove it to himself by a symbol. The myth of Prometheus giving man the gift of fire is a case in point.

Imagine the thing thus :

> Boundingly up through Night's wall dense and dark,
> Embattled crags and clouds, outbroke the sun
> Above the conscious earth, and one by one
> Her heights and depths absorbed to the last spark

His fluid glory, from the far fine ridge
Of mountain-granite, which, transformed to gold
Laughed first the thanks back, to the vale's dusk fold
On fold of vapour-swathing, like a bridge
Shattered beneath some giant's stamp—Night wist
Her work done, and betook herself in mist
To marsh and hollow, there to bide her time
Blindly in acquiescence.   Everywhere
Did earth acknowledge sun's embrace sublime
Thrilling her to the heart of things : since there
No ore ran liquid, no spar branched anew,
No arrowy crystal gleamed, but straightway grew
Glad through the inrush, glad no more nor less
Than, 'neath his gaze, forest and wilderness,
Hill, dale, land, sea, the whole vast stretch and spread,
The universal world of creatures bred
By sun's munificence, alike give praise—
All creatures but one only ; gaze for gaze,
Joyless and thankless, who—all scowling can—
Protest against the innumerous praises ?   Man,
Sullen and silent.

Man complains that though all nature, including himself, is nourished by the Sun's light, his mind demands to
know *how* that light works in nourishing.

            .  .  .  Let the oak increase
His corrugated strength on strength, the palm
Lift joint by joint her fan-fruit, ball and balm—
Let the coiled serpent bask in bloated peace,—
The eagle, like some skyey derelict,
Drift in the blue, suspended, glorying,—
The lion lord it by the desert spring,—
What know or care they of the power which pricked
Nothingness to perfection ?   I, instead,
When all developed still am found a thing
All incomplete : for what though flesh had force
Transcending theirs—hands able to unring
The tightened snake's coil, eyes that could outcourse
The eagle's soaring, voice whereat the king
Of carnage crouched discrowned ?

What of all this? says man.    What I need is to understand the working of the unseen Mind outside of me, *i.e.*,
God, who makes this wonder of light; for I alone of all
creatures recognise His existence.    I do not ask to know
His actual nature.    But I want to take one sunbeam and
use it, as God uses the whole of the Sun's light which
quickens the universe.    If instead of leaving me merely
to surmise, he would enable me to make and use light for
warmth and seeing, that would prove, make palpable to
me, the Sun himself.    Prometheus, says the fable, granted
this desire by his gift to man of the burning glass.

The fire thus obtained is the symbol of the Sun's self;
the Sun's self no man can look at.    But the symbol
obtained by the burning glass, and the spectrum, helped
man's knowledge and belief.

So the human ideas which we use in regard of God and
His purposes are at the utmost but a symbol of Him and
them; His essence, the Mind that directs the universe
no human mind can conceive.    Man cannot know what
God is by means of any symbol; but He can infer Him,
in a way impossible without the symbol.

### DANIEL BARTOLI.

> 'Don, the divinest women that have walked
>    Our world, were scarce those Saints of whom we talked.
>    My Saint, for instance, worship if you will;
>    'Tis pity poets need historians' skill;
>    What legendary's worth a chronicle?'

A certain Duke had given his verbal promise to his King
to grant him the reversion of two great estates at the
Duke's death.    Almost simultaneously, and before he
had ratified his promise by signing the deed of gift, the
Duke had proposed to and been accepted by a beautiful
girl beneath him in station.    The King hearing of this
feared the Duke would refuse to sign the deed.    So the

King's Prime Minister appeared at the banquet preceding the marriage, and calling the bride from the hall said to her, handing a paper, 'If the Duke will sign this paper, ceding his two estates now and at once to the King, His Majesty will sanction the marriage, and you shall be placed high in his favour at court, but if the Duke refuses, the marriage is broken, and you will be placed in strict seclusion.'

The lady and the minister returned to the banqueting hall ; she told the Duke the King's ultimatum. 'You and I,' she said, 'love each other for ourselves alone ; for our loves' sake we could waive power and wealth. But we must answer the King. Bid me tear this paper ! Never dare to give away your Dukedoms, God's gift, for my sake. Can you barter, for the dross of Court favour, the gold of your honour, or stumble in your choice, blinded by my youth and beauty ? If you can, you lose my love besides, slain in the slaying of your honour. Now, choose, are you still worthy of my love ? '

The Duke raged, but refused to tear the paper ; and the lady thereupon left him. They never met again, and she married, obscurely but happily, and died soon.

The lady's sacrifice in those days was great ; for to be the king's favourite was almost like being a queen.

Browning imagines the Duke's after-life ; he has fallen back on a life of light pleasure ; some sleepless night he reviews his memories, and finds that his present hides his past no more than a cloud, moon suffused, hides the moon. He soliloquizes on his mistress as she lies asleep. He admits her right to scorn one who once prided himself on being a tower of strength and constancy. 'It was the novelty of your impudence,' says he, ·that conquered and still holds me. Mere wisdom, virtue and beauty would have been powerless to drive away the memory of my lost love. Only, I am but the ghost of what I was ; it is but the ghost you conquer. My real self is dead, but will rise again some day and soon, when her soul comes to call mine, now prisoned in flesh, into freedom again. And meantime

> Ghosts tired of waiting can play tricks, you know !
> Tread, trample me—such sport we ghosts devise,
> Waiting the moonstar's reappearance—though
> You think we vanish scared by the cock's crow.'

## CHRISTOPHER SMART.

### REMARKS ON THE POEM.

The ideas dealt with in this poem are not in themselves involved ; it is the case of a man who, Browning says, once in his life wrote verse fit to rank with that of Milton and Keats ; the 'fire-flame' appears to have burned in him about his thirtieth year, if the poems referred to later contain the revelation of genius on which Browning dwells : he seems to have written subsequently more lively and satirical pieces, and clever renderings after Horace : Browning suggests as the reason for his only once writing real poetry that, mistakenly or not, he having once had the power given him to make a poem of nature as displayed in earth, air, fire and water, and no subsequent vision inspiring him, made no effort to use his sole experience other than descriptively, no step towards anything more than showing men his vision, without giving its spiritual meaning for their use and teaching. Browning then suggests that in this he failed of his duty as a poet, but was right in his beginning with the earth first, before visioning the stars.

In this as in most other poems of this volume, the meaning is wrapped in images which render the complete unravelling a very interesting but somewhat difficult process. And here what I have said elsewhere comes

true; each image is, by itself, a delight to dwell upon, a
brilliant illustration of the idea, only the fertility of
imagination is such, that the reader is apt to be led aside
or delayed by the bewilderment of its richness, to the
detriment sometimes of the search after the gold of the
meaning beneath.  What can be more complete in poetic
vision than this passage for instance :

> 'All at once the ground
> Gave way beneath his step, a certain smoke
> Curled up and caught him, or perhaps down broke
> A fireball, wrapping flesh and spirit both
> In conflagration.'

or this;

> 'Till heaven's vault
> Pompous with sunset, storm stirred seas' assault
> On the swilled rock-ridge, earth's embosomed brood
> Of tree and flower and weed, with all the life
> That flies or swims or crawls, in peace or strife. . . .

or this :

> 'So indeed
> Wallows the whale's bulk in the waste of brine,
> Not otherwise its feather tufts make fine
> Wild Virgin's bower where stars faint off to seed !'

And yet in each case the attention is drawn off by the
fire of the words from the main meaning they are
intended to illustrate and light up.

Of course I know that the two last quoted passages are
illustrations of the kind of poetic effort Browning for the
nonce chooses to criticise and judge; but amid the studied
reserve with which this parleying is treated, the sudden
blaze of them makes the eyes blink momentarily.  I do
not wish them away; I merely point out, as forewarning
a reader, that these are illustrations, not arguments.

Browning, by the way speaks of the third quoted passage as prose;

> ' My prose—your poetry I dare not give.'

So he says to Smart; but what then is poetry if this is not ?

[NOTE.—Searching through two small volumes of Christopher Smart's poems, published at Reading in 1791, that is to say twenty-one years after his death, to identify, if possible, the original passages of which these two quotations from Browning's poem may be supposed to be renderings, I find five Seaton prize poems on Various Attributes of the Supreme Being.

In one of these, on the immensity of the supreme Being, written when Smart was about twenty-nine, the following lines occur :

> While high above their heads Leviathan
> The terror and the glory of the main
> His pastime takes with transport, proud to see
> The ocean's vast dominion all his own.

In another, on the power of the supreme Being, I find these two lines :

> 'Twere but the echo of the parting breeze
> When Zephyr faints upon the lily's breast.

In both poems there are fine descriptions of nature's terrors and grandeurs, but very little verse above the accepted prize poem level. I find graceful descriptions of flowers too; but nothing which for poetic faculty can compare with the two 'adaptations' by Browning quoted above, p. 413. The poem written during Sharp's lunacy, on which this parleying seems to be founded, contains no passage so closely resembling the two adaptations as do the above quotations from Smart's two earlier poems.]

## CHRISTOPHER SMART.

### EXEGESIS OF THE POEM.

The poem begins by quoting a dream or actual experience of Browning's own ; he was walking through a huge house ; room after room was commonplace and ordered in its architecture and decoration, till he came to the chapel. That was a miracle of plastic art,—old, yet with the glow of youth, young, yet with the crowning thrill of age. Leaving the chapel, he found all the rest of the house at the same dead level of commonplace as were the rooms preceding the chapel. The analogy with Smart's mental history is obvious.

Now, says Browning, could it be that Smart and this unknown architect were not born artists at all? Could it be that they were only two mere mortals, who once only produced art work which brought Smart into touch with Milton and Keats, the architect with the greatest painters and sculptors of the Renaissance and of to-day? A sphere may touch a cube at one point only, but still there is contact. So Smart, alone among songmen between Milton and Keats, once only took rank as a poet.

If so, asks Browning, (speaking henceforth to Smart alone) why did inspiration come only once?

Here Browning abandons the idea that Smart was a poet only once ; he prefers to believe him a poet always, but only declaring himself once. For he says

> . . . Concede the fact
> That here a poet was who always could—
> Never before did—never after would—
> Achieve the feat ; how were such fact explained?

Was this the reason? Once in your life you saw nature, and shewed her unveiled, the absolute truth of her, to us in a poem. The vision faded, the veil fell back—

> . . . 'Straight the world
> Darkened into the old oft catalogued
> Repository of things that sky, wave, land
> Or show or hide, clear late, accretion-clogged
> Now, just as long ago, by tellings and
> Retellings to satiety, which strike
> Muffled upon the ear's drum.'

Did you judge that a poet's only duty was to go on having and giving to men visions of strength and beauty in terrestrial creation—that and that only; and finding that no more such visions came to you, did you judge your poetic work done, give up trying, and purposely become a prose man once more?

Then I say, that though what you gave us was effectual work, it was not enough. You did only a part of your poet's work; you shewed us the strength and beauty, nature's truth, but being men, we want to know *why* this strength and beauty, what is its reason, its use? Man must needs deal so with his smallest piece of knowledge. You might as rationally point out building materials lying loose on the ground for the builder's use, caring nothing whether he uses them or no, as merely shew us nature's truth, and merely tell us to keep on looking at that.

You as a poet ought to instruct too; you must not stop at pleasing when your function is ruling. There is strength and beauty everywhere, but you are not bound to particularise it all; give us types, so much as and no more than is needed to learn life's lesson by.

But your method of beginning with earthly beauty is

better than the prevalent habit to-day of beginning at the end; men begin now with the complete heaven and think to learn that, before learning the earth and her flowers; let them succeed if they can. But those who work right begin at the bottom and climb upwards; for they know very well that to say ' we understand the law that guides the meteor, *therefore* the rose blooms by law also,' is vain boasting; you, Smart, would surely warn such searchers, that sense may be dimmed by fumes rising from unordered brain stress.

It is only on earth that men in this life can *discover* law, that is, God's power, will and love; only from that discovery can they proceed to learn the laws beyond the earthly life. If men pretend to reverse the process, and fancy they can learn and formulate the heavenly law first, and then make heavenly law fit earthly conditions too narrow in scope to contain it, what wonder if things are made worse instead of better? It is useless to accuse the Fates of caprice, whenever you see things happen in discordance with your fancied law ;

Cease from anger at the fates
Which thwart themselves so madly.   Live and learn,
Not first learn and then live, is our concern.

## GEORGE BUBB DODINGTON.

### REMARKS.

George Bubb Dodington, Lord Melcombe, was a politician who lived through the reigns of the two first Georges, and died in the second year of George III's reign. He changed sides several times, and left behind him a diary (since published), which recounts with much frankness the perfectly selfish motives that actuated his political life. Browning in parleying with him shews how much

better he would have succeeded, even from his own point
of view, had he possessed and exercised the statesman's gift
of imposing on men by making them believe him actuated
by moral laws outside or beside the every day morals of
common men.   The poem is, of course, a satire, but it
contains one of Browning's cherished ideas, that, namely,
which insists on belief in the supernatural being an
integral part of the average man's organisation;  see
Sludge, Red Cotton Nightcap Country, Inn Album,
Guido, Porphyria, Instans Tyrannus, and many others.

### EXEGESIS OF THE POEM.

Browning begins  by anticipating Dodington's first objection 'that no one supposes a statesman's professions to
be perfectly fulfilled, that he is supposed, on the contrary,
to be acting a part with more or less sincerity for his own
ends.'   I will admit, says Browning for the purpose of this
parley, that a statesman is permitted, while openly professing to work and endure the hardships and roughness of
public life, solely for the sake of the people he governs, to
take care secretly of his own interests.   Labourers deserve
their hire, and a man who neglects his own household's comfort and advancement, is worse than an infidel ;  you have
bible warrant for that.   The very birds may teach the same
lesson by the way their nests are made.   Outside the nest
is rude and rough like the public life of the statesman
which all men see;  inside it is smooth, soft, and snug like
the same statesman's private care for himself and his
house.   The eagle builds high and cares for nothing but
the necessary, rooks are sociable, crows solitary, bower
birds build for vanity.   But each bird builds to please
himself.   So each man suits his own taste (like each kind
of bird) in the arrangement of his life ;  there are men like
each species of bird in their self care, the very bower bird

is a 'feathered parallel' to the great man who does grand work for mere vanity and display, or to win 'the priceless female simper.'

So, says Browning, you see I take self-interest as a necessary factor in a statesman's life,—while talking to you, Lord Melcombe.

But all the same, supposing your ends permissible, your means were wrong, mistaken.

For to-night, then, we say, you and I, that our aim as statesmen is ourselves, but that we pretend to those we govern that our aim is their good only. Men have succeeded in that way, have even been called Saviours of the State: and so will we manage the rabble, by making them believe their interests are ours, that we go to the height of public life only to give them a helping hand: that we brave its storms, sacrifice our peace, become martyrs, all for them. Only, how are we to get there? For plainly we cannot reach the height of governing, without the help and goodwill of the people who are to be governed. How are we to coax the people to enthrone us?

You, my Lord Melcombe, say 'Lie boldly; persuade the rabble we mean their good only, would use our strength to help the weak, supplement their rudeness by our polish; our powers are meant to be used; we love you, the people, help us to use our love for your good!'

And will they at once believe you, and put their neck beneath your foot? Not they! why, they themselves tell lies every day in just the same way for their own purposes: they know by themselves that the first law is that of sheer strength; he among them who can push the hardest gets the most. They know that no man obeys his fellowman who is just like him, he only obeys the man who is stronger than he. That is the primitive state of things; next, men discriminate, and will not be ruled by mere brute force, they demand intelligence in their ruler, to direct the brute force for their benefit. But that demand comes from their own growth of intelligence ; and if you, George Dodington, come with your stale lie about ruling for the people's sake only, they say, what can you bring, in yourself, to prove to us that you have more intelligence than we ? Your boasted love for us, your passion to serve us, which only wants our help to be made effective in action ? We don't believe in your love and passion ; for we ourselves are used to taking care of No. 1, and to do that nowadays, we ourselves, not individually very strong or wise, must use flattery like yours to get what we want. We know your trick too well by our own use of it. Try some other trick before we will believe you and give you the ruler's chair. There are plenty of men among the crowd as gifted as you, only their gifts are stifled or wasted by circumstances.

Well, says Browning, here is a suggestion for you, George Dodington. Force has been replaced, as we have seen ; now wit, intelligence must be replaced. That can only be done by making men believe you have a special gift not theirs. You must in short, if you would use men for your pleasure, prove to them by your skill of behaviour that you possess the supernatural element that awes men. You cannot do it now by miracles, by mystery : these have served their turn ; your wizard of to-day has no paraphernalia ; outwardly he appears a simple man like any of his audience. But there is something—shall we call it uncanny—in his look or gesture 'half smug, half sinister.' He knows with half an eye who believes, who waits to expose him as a trickster, he will even pretend to be a cheat. Men wonder, in short ; has he, say they, an occult, confederate power—is he, after all, *not* the cheat he pretends to be ?

That is what you should have done, to rule successfully.

You should have made men believe you had some mysterious power answering to the supernatural in miracle-working days; because man's nature can only be governed by the supernatural in fact as well as in phrase. For although all men know right from wrong, truth from falsehood, own, roughly speaking, a common conscience, —though they might have been puzzled what to call you, —it would not have been 'quack'; even though you should belie yourself, upholding to-day what you denounced a year back, your very imperturbability in so doing, which might be innocence as likely as impudence, was so much beyond the ordinary lying power of man, that men must needs believe your conscience to be subject to deeper laws than common consciences obey. You do not work by imposture or guile, men say; for the game of an impostor is to keep men's zeal always at red-heat; guile must always make a show of earnestness, or it would expose itself. But this man, your audience will say, smiles and jests over every act of his; they are tickled with the idea that he may despise when most adulatory, saying, 'though I deal with fools in the mass, there are a few in the crowd who understand, whom I cannot dupe;' and each man in the crowd, before inclined to be hostile, turns friendly under the flattery of thinking himself to be one of the few wise men.

If you try to prove your only motive in ruling is their service, they see through the trick and guess you half despise them; disparage yourself, seem to scorn the end you still push towards, and, they, finding in this careless scorn something above their understanding, take you for certainly a stronger and perhaps a wiser man than they; and therefore they wish to win you to rule, that is, serve them. They would disbelieve a naked avowal of unselfishness; they would believe but reject you if you avowed the opposite. But when they see that though you owe your high place solely to them, you can yet afford to laugh at them, they are puzzled, awed. What, say they, are we to ascribe such rashness to ? Our acceptance of him cannot be the force enabling him to ignore that conscience which is to all of us a power as strong as the command 'Lie not.' He must have some other power, own some other influence which we are strangers to.

That power (says Browning) is man's despot the supernatural. You, Dodington, rejected the commonplace disavowal of greed; hearth and home, the church, the honour of England, soon became worn-out pretexts; nothing was left you but the last resource of persuading them that your real face was a mask, that the truths you tell are lies, that your frankness is duplicity; of saying that you despise not them so much as yourself; that you use men as puppets. That terrifies them, for they think that a man who can dare to be so openly cynical must have some law to guide him above the common man's law, above even God's law. And so they became your puppets indeed.

But this secret you missed, could not conceive of, could not use if you had conceived it; and

> Hence the scoff
> That greets your very name ; men see but one
> Fool more as well as knave, in Dodington.

## FRANCIS FURINI.

### A CRITICISM OF THE POEM, AND STATEMENT OF THE MAIN ARGUMENT.

This poem, if it were remarkable for nothing else, is unique in one respect; it contains a splendid attack on the prurient modesty which finds lust to be the chief motive power in the production of all great statues or pictures from the nude. But its main purpose, with which indeed the bulk of the poem is occupied, lies in a closely reasoned argument, designed to prove the absolute necessity for understanding the bodily life of man before you can penetrate to his soul, and thence to deduce by reasonable inference the existence, *outside*, but *not within* man, though ever in touch with him, of an infinitely wise, strong, and loving First Cause, or God.

Although the form of a parleying with Furini is kept up throughout the work, he becomes, after the victorious issue of the attack above mentioned, little more than a pretext in the thick of the argument ; for no ingenuity or poetic genius can assign, I will not say to Furini, but to the greatest painter or sculptor who ever lived, any more philosophical or even ethical intention in painting or modelling from the nude than is consistent with the highest aim in the idealising *visible* human beauty, grandeur or strength.

For although Browning's magnificent verses on Michael Angelo in Easter Day stand—in *poetic* art—as a supreme interpretation of a great artist's *soul*, just as The Theseus, the Fragment called Michael Angelo's Torso in the Vatican, the Faun of Praxiteles, the unnamed Nereids in the British Museum, Watt's picture of Daphne or his bust of Clytie, stand supreme in *plastic* art as interpretations of the most cosmic types of *visible* human beauty,— the starting-point of the plastic artist is never that of the poetic artist or logoplast.

I am sure not only that the sculptors and painters of the great Greek era, and Michael Angelo a poet as well, were, while working, completely devoid of that philosophic consciousness of self so much insisted on in the poem before us, as the one stand-point to learn life from, but that any such mental state would have destroyed their handcraft.

The respective attributes of hand and brain are so closely and reciprocally blended, so mutually dominant in the process of producing any work that demands hand, that any separation of effort in either the one or the other, would produce a standstill similar to that resulting in the case of equally divergent forces.

Browning himself deals with a truth not unlike this at the beginning of the poem, in his summary condemnation of the kind of artist, who does not keep his imagining power subservient to the conditions of his art ;

> .　.　.　All in vain
> Strives poet's power for outlet when the push
> Is lost upon a barred and bolted gate
> Of painter's impotency.　Angelo—
> Thine were alike the head and hand, by fate
> Doubly endowed !　Who boasts head only—woe
> To hand's presumption should brush emulate
> Fancy's free passage by the pen, and shew
> Thought wrecked and ruined where the inexpert
> Fool-hardy fingers half-grasped, half let go
> Film-wings the poet's pen arrests unhurt !

Even as regards Michael Angelo,—apart from the undoubted poetic genius which was his lever—apart from the intensity of his sympathy not only with the poetic art but with human nature in its essence—I feel that once launched on any great *plastic* conception he knew too well the conditions of the hand's art to mingle or confuse the absorbing process of *plastic* making through the brain with any process, parallel but never linked with it, equally exacting for the presentment of an idea in words. I think that this process, either in the Statue of the Night or in that of the Day, for instance, was simply cerebro-mechanical.　Doubtless his mind and soul, whether in the earliest concept of either figure, or in developing it, or in regarding the completed marble, apprehended it as a visible type and symbol of the whole principle of light or darkness, both sensible and spiritual, as acting on earth and on man : but the conception remained, so far as he and his mental organism were concerned, locked in that wordless silence which is most eloquent.

And though this poem is completely valuable as a poetic presentment of the soul-life, and its urge on the body and on the universe, it is so quite independently of the subject which is used as its *charpente*. In fact, the leading idea of the poem, so completely Browning's own in its logical intensity, would have gained a force and clarity which the introduction of Furini and the question of nude art somewhat hampers and clouds. The continuity of intellectual process which is so necessary to a purely abstract *poetic* conception of human life in its most comprehensive reach,—is disturbed as it never is in the Death in the Desert, La Saisiaz, or Rabbi Ben Ezra.

Modesty, diffidence as to the quality and amount of work achieved or achievable, is the continuous motive power of any true painter or sculptor. But equally so is the concentration and simultaneous working of brain and hand upon the thing to be done; and I think that that modesty and twin-concentration, however it may urge towards completeness of technique and consequent diffidence of its achievement, is directed solely to the perfection of the hand. For the brain conceives at a jet, the idea stands imaged once and forever therein ; no true artist can feel his joy in achieved handwork eclipse his reverent delight in the sudden gift from God's spirit, of the idea itself.

Still, as a powerful rendering of the purity of motive which, within human conditions, is the initial force guiding all plastic genius, this poem will always stand a vindication of all true work in Art, and sculptors and painters should respectfully acknowledge it with gratitude.

The main argument of the poem is conducted in this way ; first, Browning examines the position taken by Evolutionists, that is, I suppose, the school founded by Darwin and Wallace. He assumes that they like himself are searching for the absolute truth which leads to God or the First Cause. The latest truth they have reached is that man is the highest form of existence yet known, and that all forms, from the lowest to the highest, owe their being to the same unknown but admitted force, which they name spasm. They then search for the truth about what that spasm is from the height of completed man, from the height of their to-day's knowledge, that man is the highest evolved form of organic existence. Taking them on their own ground therefore, Browning says, You have your truth of man complete as he is to-day. How will that help you to evolve absolute truth ? Man himself has no more creative power than the simplest atom, nor does the atom tell him anything of creative power ; he does not know even what minuteness *is*. His moral sense, his power to name good and evil is the one right he has to supremacy, for he is the only organism that possesses it. Still, this power gives him only a nominal kingship, for he cannot use it to abolish evil. It is only better than blind force, only superior to knowledge *undirected*. So the utmost value of this unique virtue is, on the one hand, to shew man his impotence to alter or improve the ill of the world ; on the other, to make him conscious he knows nothing.

Browning next develops his own method of search into the nature of the admitted First Cause. He starts from the point of completed man, with his moral sense, its impotence, his knowledge that he knows nothing, and says : Each man knows one other thing, himself. He knows that he exists. He has also admittedly, 1st, his intuition, and the power to suffer and enjoy, his consciousness in short, which in their highest development he names soul; 2nd, his mind or reason.

With this equipment, how shall he proceed towards finding out the nature of the First Cause ? Plainly he can gain no *absolute* knowledge of it, for he can no more take a step outside of his consciousness of self (body, mind and soul), than a man on a sea-washed rock can step from it upon the water. But he can gain a relative knowledge, a knowledge of probability, by study of his own soul through the study of the body of man. The result of this study, is that fears and hopes, pain and pleasure, act and react on each other in his own being; that pleasure is known through the absence of pain, that the uncertainty of fear makes the zest of hope, that in short the principle of his life is uncertainty and contrast.

Throwing the light thus gained on the outside universe, he finds that contrast and uncertainty rule that also; contrast, because he learns what good is only by its opposite, evil, and conversely; uncertainty or illusion, because its presence is the only spur to gaining fresh knowledge, its absence would mean complete knowledge, that is no more knowledge to strive for, the condition of earthly knowledge being that it is relative.

So the condition on which the soul's earthly life depends, is that there shall be for it no perfect knowledge or wisdom.

### AN EXEGESIS OF THE POEM.

The poem begins by telling us, as if Browning were talking to Furini, who and what that painter was, with a view of destroying the tradition that he on his death-bed repented of having painted the nude, and ordered his works in that *genre* to be burned. I never would believe that, says Browning; you were a good painter-priest whose munificence and purity in art and life were openly seen by the world. Not that you were gifted with such a brain and hand as Michael Angelo; precision in hand-work was your gift, rather than inspired imagination. And better this than an unskilful hand directed by a brain full of such fancy as belongs to poetry rather than painting; the twofold ineptitude of poetic idea made worthless by bad painting. But to you who painted healthily and well with no misplaced fancy,

> . . .  the ample gift
> Of gracing walls else blank of this our house
> Of life with imagery, one bright drift
> Poured forth by pencil,—man and woman mere,
> Glorified till half owned for gods,—the dear
> Fleshly perfection of the human shape,—
> This was apportioned you whereby to praise
> Heaven, and bless earth.

And therefore I repeat, says Browning, that no one shall persuade me that you—whom I praise as good man, priest and painter—on your death-bed lost your head, and repudiated your work from the nude. Nay, your very words, on your death-bed, to Filippo Baldinucci, shew the contrary. 'No one but a painter,' you say, 'can know what is a painter's passion for imitating nature: a passion so tense and absorbing that only a fool would credit it with either space or leisure for idle fancies.' I say indeed that not only your art-soul was always master of itself, but your man's soul could never have been so blinded even by the mist of death as to grope for cheer beside a bon-fire of the very pictures painted in your full strength, first as tributes of thanks to the Creator, and next to bless man with a semblance of God's supremest handiwork, woman. I believe rather that you in dying did thank God for enabling you to spend your power in shadowing out that beauty of naked female shape which we fancy the stars trace in such a constellation as Andromeda.

Here occurs a digression from the parleying; and now Browning speaks to his contemporaries. The misconception of Baldinucci about nude work was bad enough to make one mildly angry; but when a man calling himself an artist of to-day wilfully misconceives, wrath is at boiling point; such a man is not an artist, but a pretender, who should be warned off the sacred precincts of true art. Our pity only was awakened at the sight of a human satyr masked as a matron, unable to see any other reason for the existence of woman's beauty, than to serve as a hotbed for sensualism to flyblow with its fancies :—but this self-styled artist—must he go further, and like such a bluefly, himself creep into the presence of the priests of art, sit at their feet unspurned, because unnoticed, and then repay their toleration by stealing outside to tell the gaping crowd that art was only a safety screen for skulking vice, that lust inspired Michael Angelo to produce his Night and Morning, that his Eve was lust born ?

Now, true artists,—with brain to conceive and handskill to render the outside beauty of man, so that the uninstructed may see the soul which it envelops,—who sometimes fear that too high a prizing of handskill may tend to blunt the insight, which sees the soul within the flesh,—are saved by that fear from too earthly a flesh worship.

But you the pretender, who are allowed in a too easy tolerance to dub yourself a painter, is it you the dauber who dare to say a true artist's mind is like yours, that his brain breeds such maggots as yours ?

If a man owns that he dares not look at a royal diadem because of an itch for stealing its jewels, he may be roughly answered 'then keep out of the way of gems, or consort with thieves who have a like itch.'

Here the parleying with Furini is resumed.   Browning suggests a prayer, or rather thanksgiving, for an honest painter like Furini.   'To God, the giver of all gifts to the soul through the sense, I give thanks by means of art. Thou measurest earth and heaven, Thy hands mould the human shape as a mask to match the Divine.   Shall man's love of Thee and Thy creation abate his wonder and reverence?   Too true it is that no gift of thine, however perfect, but is maimed or misconstrued by human weakness or wickedness ; still some few artists have strength to see Thy purpose, to keep their hands from soiling Thy work with their imperfect work, to

> bid us love alone
> The type untampered with, the naked star!'

But next, let Furini tell us his ultimate reason for painting the nude.   He might do it by an appeal to such a philosophy of nature as begins at the lowest step and climbs, in this way :

'The evolutionist,' he might say, 'however he may strain his sight upwards from the highest organic development, man, is forced, in order to pursue his research, to use the facts given him by lower organisms, and must therefore descend step by step until he comes sooner or later to enquiring into atoms, protoplasm, and the unknown first cause of all life, called spasm throughout this argument.   From such beginnings he has evolved man as the highest organism known.   But, arrived at man, he finds in man no absolute creative power, and no absolute knowledge except of his daily proved ignorance. Man, however, alone among created things, has a moral sense or righteousness.   But even having that, can he, in creative power, so much as emulate the smallest atom? No; for he has no power over it and knows nothing about it; he is forced to begin by asking what minuteness *is ;* whether it is the specks of stars in the vault of heaven, as compared with larger stars beyond them, or with infinity, or the smallest speck of down on an insect's wing, that helps to make out the glisten or mimic star on that wing, as compared with the actual magnitude of the stars.

'Man, then, with this moral sense which is admittedly his sole prerogative, can create nothing, nor can he know anything *absolutely*. If the spasm had given him that double power, would he not cure the evil he sees everywhere? Still, man with his moral sense is better than mere blind force, undirected knowledge. No one disputes his unique claim ; and before man existed, is there any sign that the spasm, or vital force, had moral sense? No ; and if we strain our mind's eye to look upwards from man, the higher we look the less moral sense we find.

> The higher that we soar,
> The less of moral sense like Man's we find :
> No sign of such before,—what comes behind,
> Who guesses ? But until there crown our sight
> The quite new—not the old mere infinite
> Of changings,—some fresh kind of sun and moon,—
> Then, not before, shall I expect a boon
> Of intuition just as strange, which turns
> Evil to good, and wrong to right, unlearns
> All Man's experience learned since Man was he.
> Accept in Man, advanced to this degree,
> The Prime Mind, therefore ! neither wise nor strong—
> Whose fault ? but were he both, then right not wrong
> As now, throughout the world were paramount
> According to his will,—which I account
> The qualifying faculty. He stands
> Confessed supreme—the monarch whose commands
> Could he enforce, how bettered were the world !

'As it is, man's own knowledge and contempt of his impotence hurls him from the highest pride to the lowest despair. His ignorance of *why* things are, is so hopelessly wrapped round him like a cloud, that even when over head he sees a glimpse of blue (what seems the truth) he is obliged to confess that that very seeming blue, (the truth) may be only produced by a blackness outside it, a darkness of ignorance.

> . . . What assures
> His optics that the very blue which lures,
> Comes not of black outside it, doubly dense?
> Ignorance overwraps his moral sense,
> Winds him about, relaxing, as it wraps,
> So much and no more than lets through perhaps
> The murmured knowledge—'Ignorance exists.'

This is a variant on Browning's favourite theme that the knowledge of to-day becomes useless as knowledge, mere ignorance, by the light of to-morrow's research. See 'A Death in the Desert.'

That is what the effort of the evolutionist comes to.

'I, on the contrary,' says Furini, (or rather Browning) 'should begin at the base of man's nature ; at his simple consciousness of self. That consciousness, which I call soul, is my solid rock or island amid the liquid sea of my ignorance. The cause which made me, existed before me; after that comes that consciousness, and my conception of the rest of nature. What light of knowledge is shed for me on the Cause that was before me, or on the rest of nature around and after me? Of the Cause, all the light shews me is that I and the universe had our beginning from It, from Its laws, of which I know nothing, but which blend me and all the universe in one effect. Of the universe, all that the light shows me is, that to pierce the cloud of ignorance I must begin, not from above but from beneath ; one step at a time. The first step is that my soul should begin to learn its own nature, by becoming

versed in the body's nature.   This, I, Furini, strove to do
by painting the human form as created.   I tried in so
painting to shew how the soul acts through the body,
makes the body reveal it.

' These paintings, fixing fugitive truth in permanence,
were achieved by unremitting work ; was the work in
vain ?   That can only be answered by the secret men
call nature, which underlies the surface perfection of
flesh.   That secret, not to be traced to its essence, tells
us only that God, the Cause, is *outside of, not inmost
in* man.   There is my first step achieved.   My next step
should have been towards knowing men, and the good and
evil that actuates them.   But on trying this step I found
only that deep sea of ignorance which surges round my
rock-island of self-knowledge.   All outside that rock
remains confusion.

> .  .  .  Well and ill,
> Evil and good irreconcileable
> Above, beneath, about my every side,—
> How did this wild confusion far and wide
> Tally with my experience when my stamp—
> So far from stirring—struck out, each a lamp,
> Spark after spark of truth from where I stood—
> Pedestalled triumph ?

How, that is, did that confusion tally with the truth struck
out of my self-consciousness, as sparks are struck from a
rock by a footstamp ?

With my actual knowledge it tallied nowise ; but my
actual knowledge enabled me to *divine* this amid the confusion ; that evil would become good, that want or void
was but a promise of future plenty and fulness, that defect
insured completion ; but where and when and how the
Cause must be left to decide.

For what but that Cause makes the body obey in every
particle the duty of developing itself imposed on it by the

soul, however obscure the reason for that duty? What but the Cause gives the soul the rapture which all men know, and call Heaven? What but the Cause gives body and soul alike the solace of enjoying the beauty of the earth, their friend?—But is the Cause, which inferentially thus gifts the soul, and yet permits the strife between hope and fear—the Cause whose wonder working we have seen in soul and body—is it after all a mere blind force, a protoplast or first moulder, making all things once for all perfect?

> . . . No, I have no doubt at all!
> There's my amount of knowledge,—great or small,
> Sufficient for my needs : for see! advance
> Its light now on that depth of ignorance
> I shrunk before from—yonder where the world
> Lies wreckstrewn,—evil towering, prone good—hurled
> From pride of place on every side. For me
> (Patience, beseech you!) knowledge can but be
> Of good by knowledge of good's opposite—
> Evil,—since, to distinguish wrong from right,
> Both must be known in each extreme, beside—
> (Or what means knowledge—to aspire or bide
> Content with half attaining? Hardly so!)
> Made to know on, know ever, I must know
> All to be known at any halting stage
> Of my soul's progress, such as earth, where wage
> War, just for soul's instruction, pain with joy,
> Folly with wisdom, all that works annoy
> With all that quiets and contents,—in brief
> Good strives with evil.

Not that I imagine that evil is made for me to gain wisdom by. So far my utmost learning is that first step —my self-consciousness, and my sense that for me the Cause is good, wise and strong. I know nothing of how the Cause will work with you, another man.

And suppose, instead of learning step by step, I knew absolutely that all was illusion ; that evil was but good disguised ; then all knowledge or learning of this earth *as it is now*, would go from me.

> . . . Type needs antitype ;
> As night needs day, as shine needs shade, so good
> Needs evil ; how were pity understood
> Unless by pain ?  Make evident that pain
> Permissibly masks pleasure—you abstain
> From outstretch of the finger-tip that saves
> A drowning fly.

Or take an example from the picture of Andromeda which I, Furini, painted.  If it were so well painted, so true, that it made you believe in her peril, made you believe that she was a real girl in danger of being devoured by a real sea-monster, would you not do your best to save her ?

But even then, it would only be illusion after all, imperfect knowledge, that made you want to act instead of merely looking.  Just in the same way, the very imperfection of men's knowledge of wrong, makes them wish to do service to right ; if they had perfect knowledge of the use of wrong they would cease altogether to try, to act, to choose between good and evil.  That is, they would cease to be men.

But you say that kind of illusion is impossible.  That is only saying that you doubt where I trust.  I on my rock bid back all doubt as to *how* the body and soul act on each other, *how* whether by fact or illusion we learn what is good, and what is evil.  Inside myself, that is on my standpoint of self-consciousness, all seems ordered wisely, for I *do* stand ; outside of that, my knowledge, and your knowledge too, amounts to nothing.  Nor does any man need to be told that his standpoint does not include all the best of will or the best of power to use that will  He can but keep within his allotted space ; perfect will and power exists only in the infinite.

And so you the evolutionists and I, Furini, come back
to a common point, viz., man's ignorance.   Only, to cure
that ignorance, I say, begin by learning the body as I did
for the soul's sake.   This very Andromeda that I have
painted is but a symbol first of the whole bodily organism,
next of a house in which the soul, its master, dwells.

> ' Was such the symbol's meaning,—old, uncouth—
> That circle of the serpent, tail in mouth ?
> Only by looking low, ere looking high,
> Comes penetration of the mystery.'

And now Furini, you have prayed and preached ; give
at last a poem, a psalm, in painting.

People accuse you of too much inclination to richness of
colour, and too little sympathy with asceticism ; paint
me a subject combining the richness of natural life with
the self-control and purity of the maiden patriot's faith.

> .   .   .   Let my spark
> Quicken your tinder !   Burn with—Joan of Arc !
> Not at the end, nor midway, when there grew
> The brave delusions, when rare fancies flew
> Before the eyes, and in the ears of her
> Strange voices woke imperiously astir ;
> No, paint the peasant girl all peasant-like,
> Spirit and flesh—the hour about to strike
> When this should be transfigured, that inflamed,
> By heart's admonishing ' Thy country shamed,
> Thy king shut out of all his realm except
> One sorry corner ! ' and to life forth leapt
> The indubitable lightning ' Can there be
> Country and king's salvation—all through me ?
> Memorise that burst's moment, Francis !   Tush—
> None of the nonsense-writing !   Fitlier brush
> Shall clear off fancy's filmwork, and let show
> Not what the foolish feign but the wise know—
> Ask Saint-Beuve else !  or better, Quicherat,
> The downright digger into truth that's—Bah,
> Bettered by fiction ?   Well, of fact thus much

Concerns you, that 'of prudishness no touch
From first to last defaced the maid ; anon,
Camp use compelling' what says D'Alencon
Her fast friend ?—'though I saw while she undressed
How fair she was—especially her breast—
Never had I a wild thought !' as indeed
I nowise doubt : Much less would she take heed—
When eve came, and the lake, the hills around
Were all one solitude and silence,—found
Barriered impenetrably safe about,—
Take heed of interloping eyes shut out,
But quietly permit the air imbibe
Her naked beauty, till . . . but hear the scribe !
*Now, as she fain would bathe, one eventide,*
*God's maid, this Joan, from the pool's edge she spied*
*The fair blue bird clowns call the Fisher-king :*
*And ''Las,' sighed she, 'my liege is such a thing*
*As thou, lord but of one poor lonely place*
*Out of his whole wide France : were mine the grace*
*To set my Dauphin free as thou, blue bird !'*
Properly Martin-fisher—that's the word,
Not yours nor mine : folks said the rustic oath
In common use with her was—' By my troth ?'
No,—' By my Martin !' Paint this ! only, turn
Her face away—that face about to burn
Into an angel's when the time is ripe !

## GERARD DE LAIRESSE.

A Dutch painter of this name was struck blind
early in his career; he left but a score of paintings
which still exist, and represent mythological and fantastic
subjects, treated with a rich fancy. After and during his
blindness he published a large volume on the art of painting,* a part of which called 'The Walk' contains the
theory that true art finds subjects for poetic treatment
in the commonest surroundings.

* The Art of Painting, &c., by Gerard de Lairesse, translated by J.
S. Fritsch, 1778.

                                    So commenced
That 'Walk' amid true wonders—none to you,
But huge to us ignobly common sensed,
Purblind, while plain could proper optics view
In that old sepulchre by lightning split,
Whereof the lid bore carven,—any dolt
Imagines why,—Jove's very thunderbolt ;
You who could straight perceive, by glance at it,
This tomb must needs be Phaeton's !   In a trice,
Confirming that conjecture, close on hand,
Behold, half out, half in the ploughed up sand,
A chariot wheel explained its bolt device :
What other than the chariot of the Sun
Ever let drop the like ?

Your blindness, says Browning, leaving your mind free,
moved it to use its fancy and invention upon the beauties
only of common daily life in man and landscape.   It
could ignore the ugliness which the vexed sight must
endure.   Can I, who see, use my fancy as you did when
blind ?   Can I, for instance, evolve the fable of Dryope
from the sight of an English apple tree, and yet lose none
of the beauty of the actual apple tree ?   You could; for
your fancy brought your sense and soul into harmony,
because of the soul's need to find out the reason of that
beauty which the sense loves unreasoningly.

That chain of fancy which used to bind earth to heaven
is broken now for us, but for you it remained firm and
unbroken.   Which link in the chain snapped first for us
then ?   Nowadays, men supply fancy's place by what they
call unseen fact, which the mind forces the sense to accept.
Is this a usurpation by mind, an abdication by sense?   Or
is it too late in the day for us to use our fancy as you
did ?

Our gait is sober now, we walk in prose, so to say.
But can we not have the fanciful brain too, see, for
example, nothing in a rose unless we imagine it fallen

from the wreath of Venus as she bends to kiss the dead
Adonis?

No ; such freaks of fancy are retrogressive ; poets should
advance, and not go back ; the world must end the
moment the Past exceeds the Present in worth. We
could fancy as you did, but if we did it would be sinking
from great things to small. If we do not choose to see
as you did in fancy, it is because we see deeper into truth.
You only saw the body ; we see the soul, the essence of
the body. You and I can walk together for a time and I
can see as you saw. Only, if we loose arms, you will
stop, but I must needs go on. Let us then in spirit walk
together once more ;

> If I to-day as you of yore
> See just like you the blind—then sight shall cry
> The whole long day quite gone through—victory!

Here is an instance of what a seeing poet of to-day can
discern in the earth and sky, in their various aspects from
dawn till night :

> Thunders on thunders, doubling and redoubling
> Doom o'er the mountain, while a sharp white fire
> Now shone, now sheared its rusty herbage, troubling
> Hardly the fir-boles, now discharged its ire
> Full where some pine-tree's solitary spire
> Crashed down, defiant to the last : till lo,
> The motive of the malice !—all aglow,
> Circled with flame there yawned a sudden rift
> I' the rock-face, and I saw a form erect
> Front and defy the outrage, while—as checked,
> Chidden, beside him dauntless in the drift—
> Cowered a heaped creature, wing and wing outspread
> In deprecation o'er the crouching head
> Still hungry for the feast foregone awhile.
> O thou, of scorn's unconquerable smile,
> Was it when this—Jove's feathered fury—slipped
> Gore-glutted from the heart's core whence he ripped—
> This eagle-hound—neither reproach nor prayer—

Baffled in one more fierce attempt to tear
Fate's secret from thy safeguard,—was it then
That all these thunders rent earth, ruined air
To reach thee, pay thy patronage of men?
He thundered, to withdraw, as beast to lair,
Before the triumph on thy pallid brow.
Gather the night again about thee now,
Hate on, love ever! Morn is breaking there—
The granite ridge pricks through the mist—turns gold
As wrong turns right—O laughters manifold
Of ocean's ripple at dull earth's despair!

That is daybreak amid the strife of storm, imaging the
fable of Prometheus, Zeus's rage against him, his hate
flung back, his love for men, his implacable endurance:—

But morning's laugh sets all the crags alight
Above the baffled tempest; tree and tree
Stir themselves from the stupor of the night,
And every strangled branch resumes its right
To breathe, shakes loose dark's clinging dregs, waves free
In dripping glory. Prone the runnels plunge,
While earth, distent with moisture like a sponge,
Smokes up, and leaves each plant its gem to see,
Each grass-blade's glory glitter. Had I known
The torrent now turned river? masterful
Making its rush o'er tumbled ravage—stone
And stub which barred the froths and foams: no bull
Ever broke bounds in formidable sport
More overwhelmingly, till lo, the spasm
Sets him to dare that last mad leap: report
Who may, his fortunes in the deathly chasm
That swallows him in silence; rather turn
Whither, upon the upland, pedestalled
Into the broad day splendour, whom discern
These eyes but thee, supreme one, rightly called
Moon-maid in heaven above, and, here below,
Earth's huntress queen? I note the garb succinct
Saving from smirch that purity of snow
From breast to knee—snow's self with just the tinct
Of the apple blossom's heart-blush. Ah, the bow
Slack-strung her fingers grasp, where, ivory linked

Horn curving blends with horn, a moonlike pair
Which mimic the brow's crescent sparkling so—
As if a star's live restless fragment winked
Proud yet repugnant, captive in such hair !
What hope along the hillside, what far bliss
Lets the crisp hair-plaits fall so low they kiss
Those lucid shoulders ?   Must a morn so blithe
Needs have its sorrow when the twang and hiss
Tell that from out thy sheaf one shaft makes writhe
Its victim, thou unerring Artemis ?
Why did the chamois stand so fair a mark
Arrested by the novel shape he dreamed
Was bred of liquid marble in the dark
Depths of the mountain's womb that ever teemed
With novel births of wonder ?   Not one spark
Of pity in that steel-grey glance which gleamed
At the poor hoof's protesting as it stamped
Idly the granite?   Let me glide unseen
From thy proud presence ; well may'st thou be queen
Of all those strange and sudden deaths which damped
So oft love's torch and Hymen's taper lit
For happy marriage, till the maidens paled
And perished on the temple-step, assailed
By—what except to envy must man's wit
Impute that sure implacable release
Of life from warmth and joy ?   But death means peace.

That is the joy of the morning after storm, its bright
hope imaging Artemis the symbol of purity, but purity
passionless, cruel and ascetic.

Noon is the conquerer ; not a spray, nor leaf,
Nor herb nor blossom but has rendered up
Its morning dew ; the valley seemed one cup
Of cloud-smoke, but the vapour's reign was brief,
Sun-smitten, see, it hangs—the filmy haze—
Grey garmenting the herbless mountain side
To soothe the day's sharp glare ; while far and wide
Above unclouded burns the sky, one blaze
With fierce immitigable blue, no bird
Ventures to spot by passage.   E'en of peaks
Which still presume there, plain each pale point speaks

In wan transparency of waste incurred
By over daring : far from me be such !
Deep in the hollow rather, where combine
Tree, shrub, and briar to roof with shade and cool
The remnant of some lily-strangled pool,
Edged round with mossy fringing soft and fine.
Smooth lie the bottom slabs, and overhead
Watch elder, bramble, rose, and service tree,
And one beneficent rich barberry
Jewelled all over with fruit-pendents red.
What have I seen ?   O Satyr, well I know
How sad thy case, and what a world of woe
Was hid by the brown visage furry-framed
Only for mirth : who otherwise could think—
Marking thy mouth gape still on laughter's brink,
Thine eyes aswim with merriment unnamed
But haply guessed at by their furtive wink ?
And all the while a heart was panting sick
Behind that shaggy bulwark of thy breast—
Passion it was that made those breath-bursts thick
I took for mirth subsiding into rest.
So, it was Lyda—she of all the train
Of forest-thridding nymphs,—'twas only she
Turned from thy rustic homage in disdain,
Saw but that poor uncouth outside of thee,
And, from her circling sisters, mocked a pain
Echo had pitied—whom Pan loved in vain—
For she was wishful to partake thy glee,
Mimic thy mirth—who loved her not again,
Savage for Lyda's sake.   She crouches there—
Thy cruel beauty, slumberously laid
Supine on heaped-up beast-skins, unaware
Thy steps have traced her to the briery glade,
Thy greedy hands disclose the cradling lair,
Thy hot eyes reach and revel on the maid !

That is noon, tyrannous, immitigable ; and seeking the
shade, I see the old story retold of the Satyr's uncouth
pathos, his semi-human wooing and passion,—and the
Nymph's disdain.

Now, what should this be for ? the sun's decline
Seems as he lingered lest he lose some act

Dread and decisive, some prodigious fact
Like thunder from the safe sky's sapphirine ·
About to alter earth's conditions, packed
With fate for nature's self that waits, aware
What mischief unsuspected in the air
Menaces momently a cataract.
Therefore it is that yonder space extends
Untrenched upon by any vagrant tree,
Shrub, weed well nigh ; they keep their bounds, leave free
The platform for what actors ?   Foes or friends,
Here come they trooping silent : Heaven suspends
Purpose the while they range themselves.   I see !
Bent on a battle, two vast powers agree
This present and no after contest ends
One or the other's grasp at rule in reach
Over the race of man—host fronting host,
As statue statue fronts—wrath molten each,
Solidified by hate,—earth halved almost,
To close once more in chaos.   Yet two shapes
Shew prominent, each from the universe
Of minions round about him, that disperse
Like cloud obstruction when a bolt escapes.
Who flames first ?   Macedonian, is it thou ?
Ay, and who fronts thee, King Darius, drapes
His form with purple, fillet-folds his brow.

That is the embattled sunset ; as if the sun and nature
waited in suspense, to see the issue of a great battle
between two powers for the kingdom of the world.

What, then the long day dies at last ?   Abrupt
The sun that seemed, in stooping, sure to melt
Our mountain ridge, is mastered : black the belt
Of westward crags, his gold could not corrupt,
Barriers again the valley, lets the flow
Of lavish glory waste itself away
—Whither ?   For new climes, fresh eyes breaks the day !
Night was not to be baffled.   If the glow
Were all that's gone from us !   Did clouds, afloat
So filmily but now, discard no rose,
Sombre throughout the fleeciness, that grows
A sullen uniformity.   I note

Rather displeasure,—in the overspread
Change from the swim of gold to one pale lead
Oppressive to malevolence,—than late
Those amorous yearnings when the aggregate
Of cloudlets pressed that each and all might sate
Its passion, and partake in relics red
Of day's bequeathment: now, a frown instead
Estranges, and affrights who needs must fare
On and on till his journey ends : but where?
Caucasus? Lost now in the night. Away
And far enough lies that Arcadia.
The human heroes tread the world's dark way
No longer. Yet I dimly see almost—
Yes, for my last adventure! 'Tis a ghost.
So drops away the beauty! There he stands
Voiceless, scarce strives with deprecating hands . . .

That is the fall of night; it images the ending of all
this spiritual striving, earthly passion, battle and conquest; nothing is left but a ghost, helpless, deprecating,
to represent it all.

In this way can a poet of to-day see and use the pomp
and beauty of nature, of fabled God and man, as you either
painted, or being blind, painterwise described them ; show
by the symbol of a day's course, the progress of man from the
myth of Prometheus to the conquest of Darius; show
how good it is that the past should be past. The future,
all including, is what the soul should strain towards.
Life would be nothing without that strain.

Man's life is as a tree's growth; the root is the past, the
flower, the present, the fruit at the top, the future.
Leave the root, the past; climb upwards, not neglecting
the flower, the present, but not delaying to dally with it,
not losing thought of the fruit because of tangled branches,
life's difficulties, but escaping through them up to the
fruit.

The old poets sang otherwise, but wrongly:—

. . . 'Dream afresh old godlike shapes,

> Recapture ancient fable that escapes,
> Push back reality, repeople earth
> With vanished falseness, recognise no worth
> In fact newborn unless 'tis rendered back
> Pallid by fancy, as the western rack
> Of fading cloud bequeaths the lake some gleam
> Of its gone glory !'

I say, act, do not dream: learn the significance of the earth of to-day, do not go back to the dead Greek lore to learn it; what was the best truth for the future life given to men by the Greeks ?   Nothing but a ghost—

> 'A shade, a wretched nothing,—sad, thin, drear,
> Cold, dark, it holds on to the lost loves here,
> If hand have haply sprinkled o'er the dead
> Three charitable dustheaps, made mouth red
> One moment by the sip of sacrifice ;
> Just so much comfort thaws the stubborn ice
> Slow-thickening upward till it choke at length
> The last faint flutter craving—not for strength,
> Not beauty, not the riches and the rule
> O'er men that made life life indeed.'   Sad school
> Was Hades ! Gladly,—might the dead but slink
> To life back,—to the dregs once more would drink
> Each interloper, drain the humblest cup
> Fate mixes for humanity.

But I, says Browning, though death may seem to me, as to Achilles of old, the last and worst calamity—am assured that :—

> . . . Come what come will
> What once lives never dies—what here attains
> To a beginning, has no end, still gains
> And never loses aught ; when, where, and how—
> Lies in Law's lap.   What's death then ?   Even now
> With so much knowledge is it hard to bear
> Brief interposing ignorance ?   Is care
> For a creation found at fault just there—
> There where the heart breaks bound and outruns time,
> To reach, not follow, what shall be ?

Here's rhyme
Such as one makes now,—say, when Spring repeats
That miracle the Greek bard sadly greets:
'Spring for the tree and herb—no Spring for us!'
Let Spring come: why, a man salutes her thus:

Dance, yellows and whites and reds,—
Lead your gay orgy, leaves, stalks, heads
Astir with the wind in the tulip beds!

There's sunshine; scarcely a wind at all
Disturbs starved grass and daisies small
On a certain mound by a churchyard wall.

Daisies and grass be my heart's bedfellows
On the mound wind spares and sunshine mellows:
Dance you, reds and whites and yellows!

## CHARLES AVISON.

This is Browning's great exposition of the power of music, to interpret and present the soul of man in a more complete way than any other Art.   My belief now, whatever it was when I wrote the essay on intuition, is that his sympathy with this melodic sister is keener and more real, than his regard for the other arts.   He strives to do an impossible thing, to make articulate speech translate, in a narrow field, a form of human spiritual expression, whose essence is so implacably separated from the unique gift of mankind, that speech at the best, even united to melody, only serves as an alloy:—and yet a form of expression which, when it stoops to charm, as it well can, the most primitive human being, moves him as words cannot, as pictures and sculpture never will, as even poetry fails to move.

Browning takes a March by this now forgotten composer to shew, by the thoughts he evokes from a 'somewhat thinnish air,' what may be the conceivable power of really great music in evoking the very essence of man's soul.

He begins the poem with a remote but delightful image. I saw, says he, a blackcap in my London garden this cold spring morning, tugging at a piece of flannel nailed in the wall, to carry away and help build his nest with it. This odd fancy of his to come to London for woven wool, when he might have found natural wool in any hedge near his nest, is to me an image of my own memory, which must needs pass over the rich music of to-day, and fly back to the past century to pluck out this forgotten March of Avison's. And that March has run in my head till from cold and thin it became full orchestrated and instinct with fire, Titanic in my day dream. Waking to every-day life, I set to work to harmonise the March. I would at once have put verse to it, made a great poem of it, but being awake in common day light my day-dream-strength had left me, I was forced to step out of the ranks of the dream March, and face the reality, the smallness of the music of that time. But your music, Avison, had become alive in my brain, as it was to the people of your time. The musicians of your time roused men's hearts with suites and fugues ; that their faultlessness was beaten by fresh achievement was no blame to them, their feat was a feat when they performed it. The music of Avison's time was as real to the hearers then as Wagner's to the hearers of to-day. Had their work been perfection where would have been the need of new music? And yet whence comes it that Wagner's Evening Hymn seems perfect to-day ?

The reason at any rate why the music of each period so moves its contemporary hearers, is that music touches the soul more closely than other arts do.

> I state it thus :
> There is no truer truth obtainable
> By man, than comes of music.

Soul is the something which no adept in speech can

express in any one word, but which, however it escapes definition is known by all men as an absolute fact underlying the fact which men call Mind. Here is an illustrative image. An engineer makes a bridge over an expanse of water; he builds it by causing men to dig, to bring materials and machinery, until the arches and the causeway they sustain are complete. The mind works in a similar way. It takes facts, its materials, and with them builds a bridge and causeway of knowledge (firmly based on earth at each end) over an element which it cannot tame, any more than the engineer can control the water. That element is the Soul, which like an unsounded sea surges beneath the solid bridge of mind's knowledge, shows as it were in sea flower and foam its Feeling, raised from deeps which Mind can neither fathom nor master. Now the process of Mind's work towards knowledge is as plainly to be seen and understood as the process of the engineer in making each inch of the bridge. The senses were the Mind's workmen who collected, used and placed the materials; and knowledge was the result produced by a visible, intelligible, consecutive series of Mind's acts. But who can track the founts of the soul to their origin? Who can tell by its ebb and flow beneath the solid bridge of mind's knowledge whence its essence is drawn, how it is fed, whither it moves? Yet why this ceaseless movement, unless it be to emulate or contrast the stability of mind's knowledge? But to make the working of the soul as plain as the working of the mind towards knowledge,—to fix its passions of hate, love, joy, woe, hope and fear, (as if we should pour mercury into a mould as we do lead)—to put Feeling into a clear shape as we can our knowledge—that is the puzzle, and would be the triumph.

Music tries to do this, as all the arts do, but music comes nearest to, without achieving, attainment.

For Art gives no new knowledge, her function is only to recombine or crystallise into form, colour and arrangement facts already known. It does this even with many evanescent moods of the Soul; little if any of such moods is lost or unseized by painting, sculpture or poetry.

Could Music but fulfil the deeper quest, the capture of the very Soul itself! She has worked towards this end for centuries with gradually increasing force; of all the passions of the Soul which lay or moved, ghostlike, imperceptible, she has made forms visible or audible to any keen eye or ear. All the great music makers from Handel to Beethoven can bear witness to this. And as each star in the firmament of music has waned, a new star brightens in its stead.

Meanwhile, I will use my modicum of power to quicken into momentary life this seeming dead music of Avison's. I might indeed so enrich the March that its simple white flame should turn to the many coloured radiance of harmony which delights an audience of to-day, until it became, as before in my day-dream, a very Titanic march towards Olympus. But I will hold my hand from such irreverent innovation, and make him live in a greater if cognate fashion.

To sum up this dissertation; the music of each successive master lives with his life, and dying with his death, gives place to the next more complete creator. The forgotten masters are not really dead; we, with our knowledge of to-day can make each live again, a king in music.

I will do it now with Avison, by taking this very March in a minor key of A, to symbolise the doubt and fear each man has that the knowledge he acquired becomes useless, futile, instead of being, as it is, a bud to bloom in the future. Then having played the minor to express the doubt, I strike into the major key of C, and call on the doubter to lift his brow and see that he has never been fooled with gifts that were no gifts.  Hope, fear, joy, grief, were gifts to men in the dim beginnings of music; so was truth a gift to him from the first, though it has continuously taken new shapes, which seem strange to man when they first arise.  The leafage, the husk, with which time sheaths and protects the growth of truth, keep fading, become insufficient when no longer needed.*  Will the complete truth be not the same fruit in another shape, but a quite new creation ?  We cannot say; we only know that the myths in which past truth was shrouded, as the fruit in its husk, fade and fall as that husk falls; we have seen the summer fruit not yet ripe but complete in form : let us wait for autumn to complete and ripen it.   And so (to bring the metaphor back to musical phrase once more) the simple truth Avison's music told us, its march movement in the simple key of C major, can become developed in a more elaborate key and instrumentation into a fuller, more complex truth of the future, the march, even now big in the distance, of the federation of English speaking people.—Or I can go back in time, can use the march to express even a simpler form of truth than the form Avison saw.  I can make it express a hanging procession from Little Ease to Tyburn ; make it moan in slow time till the big notes whose significance seems nothing in the plain light of day, become meaningful as stars in the night of past history.

But it is no question of night or day ; one purpose moves Avison and me.  I will adopt the mood that prompted him to write ; he wrote for man's cause ; he and I will make his march a patriot march, a forerunner of Cromwell's commonwealth ; I will give it words, and it shall be the English nation's protest against the kingly

* The simile is of truth likened to a growing or ripening fruit protected by its sheath or pod or husk.

tyranny that tried to fetter freedom by the arrest of the five members.—Thus :

Fife, trump, drum, sound ! and singers then
Marching say, 'Pym, the man of men !'
Up, heads, your proudest—out, throats, your loudest—
'Somerset's Pym !'

Strafford from the block, Eliot from the den,
Foes, friends, shout 'Pym, our citizen !'
Wail, the foes he quelled,—hail, the friends he held,
'Tavistock's Pym !'

Hearts prompt heads, hands that ply the pen
Teach babes unborn the where and when
—Tyrants, he braved them,—patriots, he saved them—
'Westminster's Pym !'

*Lustily.*

## EPILOGUE.

### FUST AND HIS FRIENDS.

Fust is discovered by his friends in a state of dejection because the final process to complete his printing press will not work. As they talk, thinking him a man accursed, sold to the devil, he muses, and suddenly thinks out the final process ; he goes into the printing room, and in five minutes he returns with duly printed proofs of a Latin psalm, which he distributes to his friends, to their terror and astonishment.

He then thanks God for the success of his invention, saying ' Printing will help truth and cure lying tradition ; truth will be in every man's reach. Thou, God, only hast full knowledge, Thou hast granted me this spark from it. Each of Thy creatures—down to the very stone—has its fixed knowledge necessary for its life ; outside itself it knows and can know nothing. Man only was made by Thee to ignore knowledge once gained, and pass on to new knowledge ; so he approaches Thee, follows Thee, never on this earth reaches Thee ! '

Then he imagines the immediate good of being able to refute the Reformers in print. But soon the thought comes, printing which helps truth, will as well help lies, impede and neutralise its own gift. His friends see this too, and that the Reformed Clergy will be able to criticise their doctrine in print. (They and Fust are Catholics).

The goosequill is abolished, they say ; goose is an ominous name, that of Huss the first Reformer. As he died at the stake he said—

> ' Ye burn now a goose, there succeeds such a swan
> Ye shall find quench your fire.'

' I foresee such a man ' replies Fust, foretelling Luther, and yet new Truth.

# LAST WORDS

In the life of peoples, as in the life of individuals, the birth, growth, use, and abuse of nerve force has its inevitable result; a great man, in whatever line he may act, or think, or live merely, fruitfully uses, or recklessly exhausts the outer and inner forces which fate always places at his command. As he uses these, or wastes or abuses them, so are his fellow-men the better or worse, while his race is run and after it is finished : but a great creative artist like Browning may, notwithstanding the demands he necessarily makes, by his mere existence as a poet, on the intellectual and poetic resources of his time, yet have used these resources righteously, though they were yielded to him in sheer obedience to the command of his own energy.

Browning has used these resources nobly, generously, self-forgetting always ; but there is, out of his work, a result mightier than any creation we enjoy from his hand, —the result which gives every right reader of his poems that influx of vitality whence spring the strength of faith and of purpose that go to make a single mind, and a great aim.

In this sense Browning's drafts on the life of his time yield not only rich interest, but to after generations a vast mental capital with which to speculate in perfect certainty of increase.

And in the years to come, when perhaps the words atheist and deist, agnostic and believer, are a dim memory, men will know that there was once on the earth an immortal; and his work shall still bear witness how always and instantly he worked side by side with that great Earth-Spirit who sings

'I weave for God the garment thou seest Him by.'

THE END